Corridors of Deceit

T0168241

Corridors of Deceit:
The World of John le Carré

Peter Wolfe

Bowling Green State University Popular Press
Bowling Green, Ohio 43403

To
Richard Kramer,
who's dreamy, plunky, and highly extraordinary
("Fenmore is the root of all evil")

Acknowledgments

The author and publisher join hands in expressing their thanks for permission to quote copyrighted passages to the following: reprinted by permission of the Putnam Publishing Group from *The Spy Who Came in from the Cold* by John le Carré, Copyright © 1963 by Victor Gollancz Ltd; *The Looking-Glass War*, Copyright © 1965 by D.J.M. Cornwell; and *A Small Town in Germany*, Copyright © by Le Carré Productions Ltd; reprinted by permission of Walker and Company from *Call for the Dead* © 1961 and *A Murder of Quality* © 1962; reprinted by permission of Alfred A. Knopf, Inc. from *The Naive and Sentimental Lover*, © 1972; *Tinker, Tailor, Soldier, Spy* © 1974; *The Honourable Schoolboy*, © 1977; *Smiley's People*, © 1980; and *The Little Drummer Girl*, © 1983.

Author and publisher also want to thank Marla Schorr, who both edited and typed the manuscript; Terence S. Martin, who supplied important background information; and the University of Missouri-St. Louis's College of Arts and Sciences, which provided a grant to move forward with the manuscript.

The combined help of the following people amounts to a major contribution: Eugene Trani, Flor Cruz, Scipio Dominguez, Adolph Fisher, Symona Boniface, Marcia Dalbey, Mitsu Arakwa, Nathan Miltenberg, Ted Struckmann, and Jeanne Gail Harris.

Contents

Chapter One
Mirrors That Mock

Along with Graham Greene, John le Carré, David John Moore Cornwell (b. 1931) in real life, is demolishing the stylistic prejudices that once separated the highbrow from the popular and the vernacular. He tells his stories, a series of variations on a recurring pattern, with a new compulsion and authority. Though familiar, his subject matter reveals an exciting new sensibility at work. His knowledge of why spies act as they do has revolutionized the genre. No system builder or academic philosopher, he prefers the first-hand and the immediate to the intellectual. He brought accuracy, impetus, and integrity to his most recent novel, *The Little Drummer Girl* (1983), by having talked with PLO and Israeli security chiefs in Jerusalem, Sidon, and Beirut. His earlier work delivers the same vibrancy for the same good reason. After studying at Berne and Oxford Universities, he taught German at Eton College (1956-58). Then he entered the British Foreign Service, working in Bonn, Hamburg, and Berlin, cities that have furnished some of his best fictional settings, before resigning in 1964 to write full time. Whether his work in military intelligence included spying has been debated. A [London] *Times* interview published in September, 1982, reports his denying that he was ever a spy. Yet another interview, in the *New York Times Book Review* the following March, claims that he *did* spy for British Intelligence in the early 1960s.[1] What can be said with confidence is that his five years in the Service helped him become a keen observer, social historian, and expert in bureaucratic politics. He has supplanted the technological flair marking much of today's spy fiction with moral complexity and psychological depth. People mean more to him than machines. He shows us what spies are like, how they feel about spying, and how spying affects their minds and hearts.

The community of spies merits our attention because of the importance it has attained. Spying has overtaken modern life, quipped Evan Hunter in 1982: "It seems as if one day there will be more spies in the world than ordinary civilians, and that everyone will be using

1

expressions like 'safe houses' and 'mole' and 'control' and 'cover' as frequently as 'Have a nice day.' "[2] Former intelligence agent David Cornwell understands what prompted Hunter's quip. Spying claims more of our tax dollars, draws more heavily upon our energies, and impinges more menacingly upon our personal security than we may ever know. Many of these encroachments cause regret and rancor. Plagued by inadequate resources, poor coordination among its sister branches, and problems of conflicting jurisdiction, security makes few of us richer, wiser, or happier. It also exposes its functionaries to both danger and moral corruption. A wife in *The Looking-Glass War* (1965), complaining that her husband spends so much time away from home that his small son hardly knows him, asks the husband about his job: "What are they like... ? The agents? Why do they do it?" Though often pondered and sometimes asked in le Carré's fiction, her questions always evoke answers both vague and brief. Le Carré's spies don't talk about improving the world—relieving poverty, healing sickness, feeding the hungry. Neglecting the ethical, philosophical, and even the political implications of their work, they focus on technique. Spies have strayed so far from living values that the only member of the British diplomatic circle in Bonn in *A Small Town in Germany* (1968) who tries to serve justice appears only once in the novel—as a corpse on the last page. His moral conviction defied his government's commitment to waste.

Le Carré's response to Leo Harting's death goes beyond moral outrage; the complexities of modern life have ruled out simple reactions. While he condemns those who put down Harting for his belief in the rule of justice, he does defend their right to exist—and to err. We can't afford security the way it's being mismanaged today, he laments. But we can't afford to do without it, either. In his 1979 review of Thomas Powers's *The Man Who Kept the Secrets: Richard Helms and the CIA* he argues, "Sound and accurate intelligence-gathering is a crucial activity of any modern government."[3] Support for his argument comes easily. Any country's safety today depends upon collecting information about rival countries, sometimes secretly; upon analyzing and assessing this information; upon conducting its own hidden operations; and upon protecting its agents and networks. The former KGB officer, Alexander Orlov, explains the growth of intelligence communities and operations in the cold war arena in the opening sentences of his *Handbook of Intelligence and Guerrilla Warfare* (1963): "The importance of intelligence services in the fortune of nations can't be overstated.... The existence or absence of a well-working spy network on the territory of a potential enemy may spell the difference between victory and defeat."[4] An intelligence gap, Orlov shows, can damage a nation as much as a missile gap. No nation can disregard a rival's military capabilities and aims. Nor is it enough to have this information. Nations must also mislead their rivals by concealing their own aims through the dissemination of false reports. Hopefully, this strategy of misdirection will trick the rivals into wasting its resources.

So pervasive is spying that in John le Carré's fiction it becomes a metaphor for the way society both expresses and perpetuates itself. In his introduction to *Philby, The Spy Who Betrayed a Generation* (1968), he called the British secret services "microcosms of the British condition, of our social attitudes and vanities." Spying, he adds, concurs with British laws, customs, and institutions: "Its borders spill over into almost every area of our public life; its viability depends upon our tolerance, upon our money, and to a sizeable extent upon our complicity."[5] No reader should be surprised to see his/her face in a le Carré novel. But if our implication in the waste and destruction engendered by spying has turned us into Smiley's People, this baleful identification rests upon an impressive literary performance. Abraham Rothberg said in 1981 that *Tinker, Tailor, Soldier, Spy* (1974) "deals with the intelligence services as a microcosm of British society and as a metaphor for human life as a whole."[6] Rothberg's comment can be extended. No mere skilled entertainer, le Carré uses spy fiction to reflect on today's politics and morality; these reflections include issues like loyalty and betrayal. Committed to both the essential middle and the existential extreme, le Carré opens up a closed society and then invests it with our private hopes, fears, and frailities.

I

Le Carré uses the term, The Circus, to designate the London office of British Intelligence, a large, older building located near Oxford Street on Cambridge Circus. Le Carré's Circus combines features of MI5, the Security Service, which deals with counter-espionage, mostly in Britain, and MI6, or the Secret Service, which collects intelligence and plants spies and saboteurs, mostly abroad. Control, the director of the Circus till the early 1970s, recalls Graham Greene's C in *Our Man in Havana* (1958); the letter C indicates the chief of MI6, who, Nigel West tells us, has been operating from London's Queen Anne's Gate in his different incarnations since 1923.[7] Le Carré's Circus conducts operations in Germany in both *The Spy Who Came in from* the Cold (1963) and The Looking-Glass War, but it also works on domestic problems in Call for the Dead (1961). Whatever its real-life counterpart, the Circus intrigues le Carré because it forces decisions, creates actions and allies, and, like many other large governmental agencies since 1945, backs stupid, immoral polices. This shoddiness resounds through its corridors. Information is hoarded rather than shared, the different branches of the service denying each other access to sensitive files. Denial becomes contagious. Office politics create whispering galleries and unstable hierarchies. They also promote the internal danger Circus chiefs fear most—the leaking of secrets; violating security is the best revenge for losers and dissenters within the bureaucracy.

But threats may come from outside. The Treasury sometimes starves the Circus of funds, Whitehall withholds materials and personnel, and the Foreign Office denies mandates to conduct key operations. Meanwhile, with the Ministry pressing for results, the sister services of the special branch compete with the Circus for money, staff, and assignments. Le Carré writes about espionage from the gritty inside, handling the everydayness of intelligence work with atmospheric exactness. One branch of the service may want to conduct an operation secretly. An intelligence officer in The Looking-Glass War says of his counterparts in another branch, "They're cheats. Lying's second nature to them. Half of them don't know any longer when they're telling the truth." This malice typifies the treachery-packed novel. Along with The Spy Who Came in from the Cold, Tinker, Tailor, and The Honourable Schoolboy (1977), The Looking-Glass War shows that agents have more to fear from their colleagues than from the enemy. One's colleagues offer no security. For while the Circus is trying to abort a mission conducted by another office, that office has already protected itself; besides lumbering its agent in East Germany with transmitting equipment so obsolete that it couldn't be traced to its British source, it will also cook up information about the agent's past that will discredit both him and his testimony.

The moral devastation compounds. Old Circus hands enjoy recalling the days when the service was a gentleman's club whose well-connected, high-toned members acted on motives of patriotism— to England, not Britain. Their patriotic commitment expressed a collective quest for a full involvement with English culture. This devotion to a past that may have been invented distorts the nostalgia running through le Carré without blurring its intensity; England is important because the English invest it with importance. Their joint search for a heritage to attach themselves to in an age of rampant individualism fosters Circus comradeship, as well. Le Carré's agents endorse Kipling's definition of spying, from *Kim*, as a "Great Game." The endorsement comes naturally, since many of the agents met on college or university playing fields where they learned the decency, dedication, and fair play they later elevated into a moral and professional code.

This is the public school code that has faded into the glare of bureaucratic rivalry, ambition, and mismanagement, those hard, brittle realities that have been blinding British security from the start of le Carré's writing career. The policy of putting career bureaucrats in charge of Intelligence in le Carré's first novel, *Call for the Dead*, causes such a muddle that the redoutable George Smiley resigns from the service before starting his investigation of East German infiltration of the Foreign Office. *Tinker, Tailor* shows Smiley and several colleagues invading secret files to search out the deep-cover agent, or mole, who has penetrated the Circus's upper echelon. Hobbled by a new organizational policy called lateralism, the Smiley of *Tinker, Tailor* must break the Circus's laws and violate its security in order to save it. In *Smiley's People* (1980), the obstacle to effective spying is detente. Whitehall is looking in opposite directions. While it wants to weaken the Kremlin, it also argues that any turning of a Soviet agent or rolling up of a Soviet network could bring an incipient Moscow-London alliance to grief. But the Circus's freedom has shrunk further still. Classic modes of counterintelligence like double agency have been outlawed by an executive controlled by Washington, D.C. The subsuming of British Intelligence into the CIA has destroyed the devotion distinguishing the wartime Circus. Incorrectly programmed electronic retrieval systems leave out crucial data. A security chief takes a two-hour lunch and then leaves the office immediately to start his long weekend rather than listening to a tape containing a message that, properly responded to, would have saved a field agent's life. One of the chief's colleagues, fearing an investigation and a scandal, secretly erases the message.

His dishonesty symbolizes an encompassing evil. British Intelligence, that notorious government within a government, violates some of the values the British nation has always claimed to support— a concern for justice and a belief in the sanctity of both the individual and human rights in general. Leo Harting, the minor diplomat in *A Small Town in Germany* who tries to stop a neo-Nazi, is killed, not by the Germans, but by his British colleagues. Security chiefs in *The Looking-Glass War* send an agent on a dangerous assignment poorly trained and equipped. A secretary earlier in the novel casually announces the death of another agent while setting down a teacup. Her next words, "The Director's very upset," refer to the impact the death (a particularly nasty one) may have on the bureau, and not upon the dead agent's family. In fact, nobody from the bureau has met the agent's widow, let alone told her of the death. Nor will she be told till the agent's paymasters have assessed the effect of the death upon the hierarchy.

Similar real-life violations of human decency came into public view during the postwar years, and British Intelligence responded to them by mounting several publicity campaigns intended to convey an impression of harmony, order, and unity within the service. Restoring its earlier image of solidness, its chiefs believed, might also create the climate in which Great Britain could advance institutionally, politically, and economically. Unfortunately, the discovery of Soviet agents within British security caused an uproar that no number of publicity campaigns could silence. The recurrence of awkward disclosures threw the special branch into world-wide infamy. So conclusive were proofs of branch incompetence that insiders feared decades would pass before Britain would win back the trust of her allies. Le Carré's Circus reflects a security service whose mistakes have left it numbed and pithed. Le Roy L. Panek speaks home when he says, "Le Carré portrays an enervated Britain reeling from its fall from international power and its own internal problems."[8]

Some of this depletion can be assessed. Dr. Alan Nunn May, a physicist at the University of London, had been using his job in the atomic energy section of the National Research Council to collect information for the Soviet Union before his trial and conviction in 1946. Two senior scientists at Harwell, Klaus Emil Fuchs and Bruno Pontecorvo, were both exposed as underground workers for the Kremlin in 1949-50 (five separate vettings had overlooked the Communist ties of Pontecorvo, who enjoyed top security clearance during his years as a Soviet spy). Again, the ineptness of the British Intelligence Corps was made public knowledge; again, public confidence in the Corps dropped.[9] A variation of this defeat recurred in 1951 with Donald Maclean, Guy Burgess, and Harold "Kim" Philby. Though none of these three men was a scientist, all were Communist agents who had infiltrated the executive branch of the British foreign service. Told by Philby, the mysterious "third man," that they were facing arrest, Burgess and Maclean fled England. Their countrymen were shocked.

Not only were two Communist suspects allowed to leave the country; of particular embarrassment to Whitehall was the publication of Maclean's earlier arrest for drunkenness and streetbrawling and of Burgess's police record of homosexuality, drunken driving, illegal entry, and assault and battery. That these two Kremlin spies had been cleared by security officers before entering the Foreign Service raised universal doubts in Britain's ability to protect its citizens.

The next fifteen years deepened these doubts. Chapman Pincher says that the Soviet bloc penetrated British Intelligence some 200 times between 1956 and 1965. He also notes the 1961 arrest of the KGB officer called Gordon Lonsdale who stole Naval secrets for the Kremlin; the conviction the next year of the Admiralty clerk William Vassall for giving Moscow classified material; the Kim Philby defection to Russia in 1963; the 1963 unmasking of the prestigious art historian and MI5 officer, Sir Anthony Blunt, as a Soviet spy; and the conviction of Frank Brossard, a Kremlin informer serving in the Aviation Ministry, in 1965.[10] Le Carré's metaphor for the devastation caused by these spies is the discovery in *Tinker, Tailor* that the trusted Circus hand and senior officer, Bill Haydon, has been working for Moscow. Haydon's aristocratic family ties, enhanced by his Eton-Oxford academic pedigree, his painting, and the comparisons he has raised with Rupert Brooke and T. E. Lawrence all make his unmasking an indictment of English tradition. One colleague feels like an orphan, Haydon having been "his inspiration, the torch-bearer of a certain kind of antiquated romanticism, a notion of English calling." This idealized devotion had redeemed the unfeatured drabness and the vulgarity infecting England during the post-Philby decade. Because of Haydon's treachery, a world of sentiment and memory could no longer command belief.

Faith shatters often in le Carré. Fresh and startling in his disclosures, he strives for an honesty of subject matter and a coherence of plot almost unknown in intrigue fiction. Smiley's penetration of the mole's stronghold displays a gift for creating scenes whose significance comes out in surprising places and ways. Working with total assurance, le Carré can also write with journalistic accuracy and dry-point sharpness. Sometimes he plays triviality against a coming sense of loss; the gripping finale of *The Little Drummer Girl* finds the novel's distraught heroine conscious of using an expression ("Oh leave it out") for the first time. The humanizing stroke created by this incongruity, all the more arresting for coming on the novel's last page, chimes with le Carré's narrative intent. Suspicious of melodrama, the staple of most spy fiction, le Carré prefers the rhetorical strategies of irony, which he implements through understatement and indirection. Irony helps his novels discredit popular ideas about spying. Decentering them, he blocks the development of both character and plot; he shows loss impinging upon gain and heroism brightening acts of apparent cowardice and treachery. What made Bill Haydon feel so betrayed, we wonder, that he betrayed his homeland in turn for thirty years? The spying profession, as le Carré sees it, ignores traditional moral values and fictional categories. The conservatism conveyed by his Oxbridge tone contrasts admirably with his descriptions of the loss of English tradition and community. He'd not have passed up such a good chance for verbal irony. Perhaps he enjoyed Thomas Powers's *The Man Who Kept the Secrets* (1979) because its subject, master spy and spy runner Richard Helms, "a hero, a victim, a monster ... or a nice American guy," embodies the ambiguity he aims for in his own fiction.[11] He reverses expectations and skews the old continuities in order to tell the truth. Fumbling, apologetic George Smiley, who appears in seven of his novels, stands light years away from Donald Hamilton's Matt Helm or Ian Fleming's James Bond. Unlike these playboy bachelor-spies, the married Smiley has no lovers. In fact, he rarely has sex with his wife, who has left him several times for other men. In the first paragraph of *Call for the Dead*, his debut, Ann describes him to her Mayfair friends as "breathtakingly ordinary." The outset of Chapter 19 of *A Murder of Quality* (1962), his next bow, shows him as "a fat, middle-aged gentleman" being jeered at by typists and office boys as he bounds up some stairs.

Le Carré's redefinition of the spy tale includes narrative form. The classic detective's discovery of the truth restores order and harmony, since the naming of the killer frees all the other suspects of guilt. The spy's discovery of the truth in le Carré usually coincides with his defeat. In *The Spy Who Came in from the Cold*, he learns that his paymasters have misled and cheated him to protect their source in East Berlin. In *A Small Town in Germany*, he learns that London has sent him to Bonn to find and to crush an Embassy worker because the worker threatens a neo-Nazi whom the British are secretly supporting. Truth doesn't set the spy free; it shows him that he has been sacrificed to official policy. Yet he also transcends policies, operations, and networks. Aware of human inconsistency and contradiction, le Carré will intrude a maverick detail into a tense drama to show that his people lead lives beyond the plot they're serving.

Thus the door of a house in The Hague run by Communists is opened by a woman in *The Spy Who Came in from the Cold* who reminds a man "of an old aunt who beat him for wasting string." Like this touch, Smiley's expertise in sailing, voiced to the surprise of a friend in *The Honourable Schoolboy,* displays le Carré's respect for his characters. Smiley isn't talking to impart facts to the reader. Observing probability, le Carré needn't know all or tell all. Nor does he have the arrogance to explore all. Trusting his characters, he enjoys the surprises they spring. Often, he'll either say nothing about their motives or, in the interests of psychological realism, disclose a flock of motives without arranging them in patterns. The truth of the heart is omniform and complex; nobody has clear title to it. Language may be too arbitrary and straightforward to express it, in any case. Le Carré never explains why Jerry Westerby, a Circus agent and the title figure of *Schoolboy,* suddenly decides to help the Kremlin's Hong Kong source after badgering him for 400 pages. Nor does le Carré try to make sense of Smiley's complex, stabbing response to Ann in *Smiley's People* when Smiley visits her in Cornwall; he has come to warn her that the danger of his upcoming mission has put their London home off limits to both of them. Suffice it that she has stirred deep divisions in his heart; he cares too much for her to sort out his feelings while reaching out to protect her:

He loved her, he was indifferent to her, he observed her with the curse of detachment. She was all he wanted, she was nothing, she reminded him of someone he had once known a long time ago; she was remote to him, he knew her entirely.

Such moments make danger vivid without forfeiting the commonness infusing it; husbands will protect and rescue their estranged wives. Smiley is a sensitive man as well as a seasoned pro, and his creator has fine-tuned his mind to the many parallels and convergences between love and work. Such fine-tuning imparts humanity. Le Carré will engross readers who seek the pleasures of watching a superior mind cope with the materials of a hazardous yet also commonplace life. According to Michiko Kakutani, le Carré says more than shows on the surface; perhaps more, too, than any other spy writer has said: "In Mr. le Carré's hands, the spy novel becomes the perfect vehicle for delineating the dangerous, provisional nature of the contemporary world."[12] One needn't look far for evidence to support Ms. Kakutani's judgment. Changes in leadership and policy, bickering and mismanagement, and the paranoia of its staff members make the Circus, the epicenter of Intelligence work in Britain, a splendid image of insecurity in a culture where half the marriages that take place end in divorce.

Some of our leading critics and reviewers have joined Ms. Kakutani in praising le Carré. Writing for *Newsweek* in 1983, Alex Gelber and Edward Behr call him "the greatest fictional spymaster," seconding Stefan Kanfer's verdict in a 1977 *Time* cover article that le Carré is "the premier spy novelist of his time." William F. Buckley, Jr., forsook both his wry, polysyllabic wit and his political conservatism in his review of *Drummer Girl* to praise le Carré quietly as "a writer of great powers." Similar plaudits date from the 1960s. Reviewing *The Looking-Glass War* in 1965, Stephen Marcus called le Carré "both the legitimate heir of Graham Greene" and "the first novelist of the Cold War." Later readers have admired le Carré for different reasons. The Australian Clive James says of George Smiley, "In Britain he has been called the most representative character in modern fiction," and *New York Times* journalist-editor Richard Locke admires le Carré's use of fictional espionage as a vehicle for social criticism. But the commentary hasn't always been admiring, or even friendly. Some critics have scathed le Carré for his supposed ignorance of spying, lack of realism, and sprawling plot structure. *Schoolboy* fails for Robert Lekachman because of its "flabbiness, discursiveness, and self-indulgence"; Timothy Foote complains of *Tinker, Tailor*, "For all its arms and legs, the book remains something of a paper chase"; questioning the authenticity of le Carré's presentation of spying, Hugh Kenner claims that "a former member of German intelligence" gainsays the accuracy of the spying recounted in *The Spy Who Came in from the Cold*.[13]

The severity of le Carré's selection, his refusal to fulfill expectations formed by earlier thriller writers, and a refusal to judge that has been interpreted as a heartless objectivity—these qualities have spurred most of the disagreement about the value of le Carré's work. Let's look at them and some of their more intriguing ramifications.

II

John le Carré has developed an important subject, a consistent attitude toward it, and a style rich and varied enough to lend it force. Few writers today work with his scale and power. Few have refuted more convincingly Bruce Merry's claim, in *Anatomy of the Spy Thriller* (1977), that "the thriller writer is not *mimetic*."[14] Works like *Tinker, Tailor, Schoolboy*, and *Smiley's People* (the so-called "Karla trilogy," published in 1982 as an omnibus volume called *The Quest for Karla*) describe the special branch in historical, dramatic, and institutional terms. Combining astute observation and relentless reporting, these works and most of their counterparts also put forth a deeper sense of judgment. Le Carré spent enough time doing intelligence work to grasp its codes and its rites. A political writer who doesn't write political tracts, he is moved chiefly by the effects of intelligence upon intelligence gatherers and their intimates. He looks at the spy as he really is, describing the inroads made upon him by his work. These inroads run deep. As has been seen, most of the spies recruited before 1945 had public school and university educations which taught them a sense of fair play, helped them look and talk like gentlemen, and encouraged them to respect civilized values. But the growth, increasing impersonality, and bureaucratization of the service corroded these values. No longer run by donnish patriots, the Circus scrapped its liberal-humanist traditions long ago.

A liberal humanist himself, le Carré belongs in the school of fiction-writing that has pledged itself to the individuality of individuals. Writers like D.H. Lawrence, E.M. Forster, and John Fowles value people for themselves and not for the systems or ideologies they serve. In le Carré, too, the responses of characters trapped by absurdity, pathos, or danger can make them lovable. Le Carré will extend compassion to victims, i.e., men, women, and children who lack official approval. No novelist of ideas, he's content to tell a story whose failures exude nobility. But this ambiguity and the compassion that warms it usually seems distant. Le Carré's people end up lonelier than they were at first appearance and perhaps, if they survive, a bit wiser. Their attempts to connect to one another and also to something larger than themselves have failed. They don't move us as much as we might have expected, even though they have fought and bled for their beliefs. We don't feel that we know them any better at the end than we did at the beginning. Our puzzlement has roots in le Carré's selection. His people rarely appear when not working, and their motives, however complex, are usually operational. Rather than immersing us in his characters' lives, le Carré's step-by-step objectivity raises barriers (Bertolt Brecht, our century's champion of literary barrier-raising, or alienation, is mentioned in *Little Drummer Girl*).

Le Carré will focus on lives that touch each other persistently but without generating intimacy. Though his intelligence officers have known each other for years and first-name each other, they rarely socialize. Smiley visits Oliver Lacon's Berkshire home in *Tinker, Tailor*, but for business, not pleasure. And the meals he takes with both Lacon in *Smiley's People* and the Foreign Office chief Roddy Martindale in *Tinker, Tailor* prove boring and embarrassing, if not downright painful. The world of security offers little comfort or joy. Seen in a hard focus, it looks distorted and repellent, freakish and banal. Other disturbances occur on the way. Le Carré's intelligence chiefs are shadowy, as if they've been bled and whittled down by work; Rothberg even finds Smiley "ill defined": "It is difficult to glean any but the most rudimentary idea of the sort of man George Smiley is supposed to be," says Rothberg.[15] His cavil touches a nerve. No authorial blunder or oversight, the vagueness Rothberg notes tallies with le Carré's theme. Cold war spying is no morality play in which courage, skill, and *esprit de corps* conquer evil. Le Carré says more about the patterns of lives than about the lives themselves. And the patterns are dictated by the bureau. They develop less from personal need than from official policies.

Most of these policies ignore human values. Spies have parted company from those they're supposed to represent and protect. Doing their superiors' bidding for money and for thrills, they have also estranged themselves from morality. The steps by which cynicism has replaced faith and hope are clearly marked. Soulcraft has become tradecraft. Control, one-time director of the Circus, admits having adopted scurvy means to promote justice and benevolence:

"You've got to compare method with method, and ideal with ideal. I would say that since the war, our methods—ours and those of the opposition—have become much the same. I mean you can't be less ruthless than the opposition simply because your government's *policy* is benevolent, can you now?" He laughed quietly to himself.

His laughter dies quickly, as his next utterance shows: "I think we ought to try and get rid of Mundt. Oh really. Where is that damned coffee?" His irritability over late coffee seems disproportionate, we might object. And our objection would be valid, as le Carré well knows. Although he hasn't said so, Control is lying to his agent, Alec Leamas. His edginess and impatience refer to himself. He doesn't want to get rid of Hans-Dieter Mundt, a high-ranking officer in East German Intelligence. He has recently turned Mundt, and, to strengthen Mundt's cover as a double agent, he's using Leamas, a battle-weary spy of fifty, to perform one more covert action before coming in from the cold. Leamas has served his chiefs well; he deserves a rest. Spending years in the cold has numbed him. We can see why. Time robs all field agents of their nerve; it wearies them of examining each word for its possibly coded nuance or tell-tale inconsistency; it makes them

careless about security. Furthermore, lowering his guard exposes a
Leamas to enemies not known for their squeamishness. Speaking in
his own voice in *The Looking-Glass War,* le Carré describes the
psychology of the field agent in foreign parts:

> Avery ... walked fast. He was afraid. There is no terror so consistent, so elusive
> to describe, as that which haunts a spy in a strange country. The glance of a taxi
> driver, the density of people in the street, the obscurity of custom and language, and
> the very noises which comprised the world into which Avery had moved contributed
> to a state of constant anxiety, which, like a nervous pain, became virulent now that
> he was alone. In the shortest time his spirit ranged between panic and cringing love,
> responding with unnatural gratitude to a kind glance or word.

Mundt suffers none of this dread. In fact, his iciness induces dread
in others. He has cheated, lied, betrayed, and murdered. Yet he
represents Circus interests in East Berlin, and the innocent must be
sacrificed to protect him. The second chapter of *The Spy Who Came
in from the Cold* voices the moral bankruptcy ruling the spy trade:
"Intelligence work has one moral law—it is justified by results."
Strategies devised by security chiefs may confuse us with their subtlety
and complexity; Karla, says Smiley, will trade ten losses for one big
victory; a mole's paymasters must sometimes wait fifteen years before
the mole produces intelligence; the phrase used twice by a master
spy in *Drummer Girl,* "If you want to catch a lion, you must first
tether the goat," reflects the roundaboutness but also the patience
and the steadiness with which Mossad, Israel's Secret Service, goes
after its quarry. It says nothing about housing the homeless or finding
work for the jobless. As elaborate as spying operations are, they all
serve one master—expediency.

There can be no conflict between the individual and the system
when the system is all powerful and the individual means nothing.
The ruthlessness of the Circus's central executive discourages spies
from evolving a cognitive style, a set of principles, and a sense of
self-worth. The relationship between work, home, and the formation
of character never develops. No spy feels he has created something
of quality; none, in our company, aims at becoming a good provider,
religious example, or head of a stable, loving family. His thoughts
dwell, instead, on the Circus—its factions and cabals, the impression
it always gives of time running out, its promises that are either deferred
or ignored. Whether he's buttering up a superior, smirching the name
of a rival, or shielding a friend, he obeys the basic law of all
bureaucracies: protect yourself. As Rothberg has shown, le Carré has

the perfect pitch of bureaucratic careerism: "Le Carré's delineation of the Establishment is scathing. Almost everyone in it is dedicated to self-aggrandizement and self-protection; almost everyone wants power, prestige, promotion, money."[16] The bureau sidesteps the human factor. Praising and blaming as the needs of the moment dictate, it lacks integrity. A case officer may tell his field men that they should feel honored to be serving England. But he'll teach them to cheat, lie, and kill. And he'll organize the operations in his network so that he'll get credit when they succeed and his agents will be blamed when they fail. His keen sense of self-preservation makes him slow to respond to emergencies. Looking at unimpeachable evidence, security chiefs in *Tinker, Tailor* and *Schoolboy* need to be coaxed, begged, and shamed before taking steps to defuse a clear and present danger to the nation. Even then, they move slowly and grudgingly. In *Call for the Dead, Small Town in Germany,* and *Smiley's People,* they don't move at all.

To protect himself against hard, cynical spymasters, the field man substitutes methods for morals; he shares little of himself with his family and colleagues; tense from being always on guard and on call, he loses his capacity for fun. "The spy," says David Monaghan, "grants no value to feeling, spontaneity, or individuality and instead commits himself entirely to tradecraft."[17] The practice of burying his fears in the details of work, though momentarily pragmatic, will defeat the spy. Neither a hero nor a gentleman-adventurer, he is in flight from himself. Le Carré takes this escapism at its own valuation. Alec Leamas of *The Spy Who Came in from the Cold* never mentions his former wife or children by name. In *Schoolboy,* a novel that stresses the influence of the family, Jerry Westerby communicates with only one of the children (and none of the wives) from his several earlier marriages. As the notorious Karla learns, these men do well to hide their hearts; a spy's commitments dent his armor; he becomes bribable, blackmailable, and ripe for double agency. Thus the novels say little about emotional ties but a great deal about word codes, contingencies, fallbacks, maildrops, and classic formations used by tails and other watchers.

Withal, le Carré says more about spying than his readers thought there was to say. Many of his key meanings lie in elisions and omissions. While being dazzled by the maneuvering of Smiley's circle in *Tinker, Tailor,* we find our admiration blunted by the remark that any nation's security system mirrors its subconscious. The remark both interrupts narrative flow and makes us look for significance beyond the reported action. Le Carré doesn't want to sweep us along by a series of exciting events. His practice of putting meaning either in the gaps or in the offhand remark demands our wide-awake participation. With the margins moving closer to the center, everything merits our attention. Often, the novel we're reading differs from the one that's developing. Like an Alec Leamas, we learn that an exchange will have unexpected byproducts. A word or a phrase at the end of an exchange can refocus issues, forcing a Leamas to rethink both what has been said before and, in view of it, his chances for safety. Skepticism and ambiguity have replaced the old certainties.

One way a fiction writer either bestows importance upon a character or withholds it is by positioning the character on his/her canvas. Controlling his materials skillfully, le Carré evokes the inhumanity of spying. His careful adaptation of his materials reveals him shunning explicitness in favor of developing his themes through complex, discontinuous plots. What happens often stems from the mechanics of plotting, in le Carré often a matter of angulation and rapid cutaways. His most dramatic developments are skewed or summarized, some of them even taking place off stage; introductions and explanations may also be omitted. What Smiley and his fellow spies do seems to lack weight and grace. But their deeds fit inside a growing context of meaning. Le Carré's indeterminate path favors becoming over being, process over completion, and the journey over the arrival. This implied commitment to means-oriented living fends off the accusation that people don't matter to him. Spying does warp and coarsen the spy. But le Carré's ironies and discordancies imply the fragmentation, dislocation, and risk that beset us all. Complicated and varied, life in today's industrial state offers few soothing affirmations. This instability has sent people to literature for consolation; popular fiction is popular because it celebrates cherished common values. No celebrations occur in le Carré. Readers like John R. Coyne, Jr., in his *National Review* account of *Tinker, Tailor,* have been complaining about the failure of his molecular concentration to meet their needs:

The style is complex. Paragraphs are packed with small actions, ceaseless lightly connected internal monologues, constant flash-backs, summaries, and a running description of Smiley's current state of mind. A packed style, at times almost irritatingly dense, illuminating a feverish consciousness.[18]

Without dismissing Coyne's cavils, we should note that le Carré's style *and* his deployment of materials convey the interplay of boredom and terror in a spy's routine. Rather than shaping events to a narrative curve, le Carré's hard-focus technique imparts an intimacy absent from conventional cloak-and-dagger fiction. Yet the intimacy lacks the mediation we're used to. The feverishness Coyne speaks of pertains to the spy as he sifts the atoms of experience bombarding him from both within and without in order to better his chances. The organization the spy serves compels belief. With its wranglers and forgers, lamplighters and cutouts,[19] the Circus is a very conservative agency in which priority, sequence, and precedent rate high. Le Carré shows how this hierarchy affects personal ties within the agency and the tie joining the agency to other branches of government. Hierarchy will beget comedy in a sharp social realist like le Carré. As in one of England's ancient public schools, one's place in the agency can determine which people one can safely ignore, which should be greeted upon entering a conference room, and even which can smoke or risk telling a joke in conference. Some jokes will make us wince rather than laugh, as the participants in high-level policy talks will justify the most heartless pragmatism in well-bred, literate cadences.

Attention to other kinds of realistic details distinguish the novels. As in a police procedural, spying operations rely on informants, a great deal of legwork and research, and the energy of many functionaries, some of whom will sift the same files, comb the same ground, and ask the same questions many times. Electronic technology is included in a sensible, realistic proportion. Secrets going from London to Moscow in *Tinker, Tailor* appear on undeveloped film stowed in cannisters that, opened in any but the prescribed way, will expose the film; tapes containing equally sensitive material can be played only on special machines.

The briefings where such material is discussed may pulsate with subterfuge. Intelligence workers deny each other access to important documents, tell each other less than the whole truth, and use each other as pawns or cats-paws. How can Kurtz, an Israeli security chief in *Drummer Girl*, be squaring with his counterpart in British Intelligence if he's using a false name? Often, the evasion will spring from an agent's distrust of his senior officers. "There's been too much blown. Too much lost, wasted, too many scandals," protests Percy Alleline to Control in *Tinker, Tailor*. A widespread disgust over security leaks, the loss of morale within the Circus, and the Circus's loss of face in the eyes of the West make Alleline's defiance of his chief plausible. In his own view, it's an operational necessity. Because he can't count on the protection of his leaders, he must keep the names of his sources to himself. Yet our approval of his bravery dies quickly. In a typical le Carré irony, Alleline succeeds Control at the Circus's helm and wins a knighthood in the bargain, but, it later comes out, for heading an operation hurtful, not beneficial, to the nation.

Shaping such ironies is a sensibility that owes much to German humor, particularly the gallows humor, or *Galgenhumor,* that directs jokes to our hidden vulnerabilities. As in Joseph Conrad, these jokes unsettle and alienate. While feeling drawn into the lives of le Carré's people, we also find ourselves screened. This paradox is another offshoot of a fictional method devised to separate us from the inner selves of characters who have touched our hearts. Alienation can stem from selection. A character may blurt out a *non sequitur* during a moment of stress. A climactic encounter or the death of a major character may reach us in a subordinate clause. The humor these instances call forth leaves a residue of malaise. The sequence of scenes in le Carré also conveys rue. Fred Leiser undertakes a dangerous assignment in *Looking-Glass War* after being snubbed by his would-be recruiter; "You never wanted to recruit him!" snaps a colleague of the would-be recruiter after hearing Leiser described as "common and singularly unpleasant." With Leiser's agreement to help the service coming by phone moments after this attack, the reason behind Leiser's decision occurs out of view, as well. Le Carré's narrative maneuvering keeps our eyes on the service; official motives have crowded out personal ones. Leiser is threatened. He has put himself under the care of someone who despises him. How can he survive, let alone prevail? Le Carré revives our fears for him periodically. Young John Avery flies to Finland to investigate the death of a British courier who died there on assignment. The investigation goes so badly that the underprepared Avery fears arrest. But no sooner does he panic than le Carré cuts away from him to London. When he restores Avery to center stage a page and several hours later, the tension has already relaxed. We feel bilked of both a big dramatic scene and access to a mind under great stress. This deprivation has thematic import. Denying Avery the right to display his fraught emotions to us, le Carré seems to be discounting those emotions.

But his slight mirrors that of an agency shown elsewhere to be inefficient, self-serving, and cruel. Le Carré discourages identification with the agency. His spies come before us chiefly as drones. Expressing themselves through their jobs, they have little time for rest, relaxation, or soul-searching. The paradigm underlying the way they're presented is the Calvinist one of *Homo faber* governed by discipline and denial; man lives to work. This rejection of impulse and instinct suits the goals of the spymaster. An agent seen to lack humanity won't be missed; he can be exposed to the gravest risks. As someone expected to produce results, he serves a morality as bleak as that of the Calvinism it has absorbed. But the Calvinist doctrine of the elect offers brighter hope than the Circus and its allied branches extend to *their* functionaries. The total obedience exacted by a system pledged to an impoverished ethic invokes a jittery, dark-toned laughter akin to German *Galgenhumor*. It also opens a split between what we read and how we feel. The bureaucratic slovenliness and duplicity passing before us has already killed our faith in the bureau. A corporate self this corrupt can't sink the private self in our eyes.

How does the private self survive other than in the moral imagination? Occupying a central place in the seam between narration and reader response is le Carré's most famous character, George Smiley. "The ways of espionage are not populated by the brash and colorful adventurers of fiction," says le Carré, speaking in his own voice in Chapter 9 of *A Murder of Quality*. Smiley incarnates this formulation, with his avoidance of killing, high tech gadgetry, and sex. As has been seen this lonely man can't keep his wife out of other men's beds. Rather than imposing himself, he finds safety in crowds; assimilation is his highest goal. He has worked hard to cultivate facelessness. He knows that a good spy should be anonymous and inconspicuous; the less that is known about him, the less he has to worry about being blown. Thus he revels in looking ordinary; in *Smiley's People*, he enters a house by day because daytime entries attract less notice than those negotiated after dark. In *Schoolboy*, when he's at least sixty, he shakes his bodyguard on a London street. A colleague in *Tinker, Tailor* says that he has never seen a person vanish in a crowd so quickly.

Smiley also defies the James Bond archetype by combining in his work one part derring-do to ten parts intellectual endeavor and one hour in the field to fifty reading reports and files, checking indexes and serials, and sifting archives. If intelligence work weren't more cerebral than actional, the Circus wouldn't keep interrupting his retirement to press him into service. His skill and patience as a researcher can help the Circus more than any amount of muscle. In *Tinker, Tailor*, he spends nights in a Paddington hotel reading classified materials; his labors help apprehend the mole, whose rolling up of Circus operations and targeting of Circus agents in the field have been crippling British security. Results in espionage, Smiley's lucubrations imply, come from poring over records and reports. The intuitive flash that breaks a case comes only after hours of intellectual slogging have primed the intuition.

Another convention from Ian Fleming and his ilk exploded by le Carré is the belief that the exertions of the spy, a well-trained patriot-athlete, help defend the rule of justice, reason, and love. Weariness, even exhaustion and disgust, pervade le Carré. By serving British Intelligence, Smiley is defending the bad against the worst. Its pettiness and vulgarity make the Intelligence corps betrayable. Yet the evil it traffics in is less foul than that of the Soviet bloc. If le Carré has achieved such a thing as the poetry of treachery, he seats it here— in the moral ambiguity born of causes which repel good people intellectually while claiming their hearts. Enhancing this ambiguity are the spies who run networks and risk their necks in the field. Most of them have advanced well into middle age and/or suffer from poor health. None sport the heroic build and physical stamina of a James Bond. Some, like Smiley and Oliver Lacon, see their marriages crack. The inscrutable Control dies some time before the present-tense action of *Tinker, Tailor;* the death of Steve Mackelvore, the white-haired Yorkshireman who runs the Paris office of the special branch, is discussed in *Schoolboy;* the plot of *Smiley's People* is actuated by the death of a sixty-nine-year-old spy who dies in the line of duty.

Besides jarring our received notions about cold war espionage, the presence of so many weary, aging functionaries adds to the mood of depletion infusing the novels. Balancing Smiley, described unheroically by Merry as "short, podgy, easily depressed, anguished by memories, and uneasy in his retirement,"[20] is his Kremlin foil, Karla. Notorious for his Machiavellian ways, this dragon is small and frail, wrinkled and gray; his first command dates from the Spanish Civil War, some forty years before his defection to the West. Just as harmless looking are Smiley's two main helpers in *Schoolboy,* arthritic, outsized Connie Sachs and the scrofulous old rooster known as the Jesuit, Doc Di Salis. The list of those threatened by time and/or infirmity prolongs itself. Karla's mole in Hong Kong, Drake Ko, Drake's brother Nelson, and the Israeli spy Kurtz are all overweight and middle aged. Mendel, a Somerset police inspector, retires from Scotland Yard during *Call for the Dead.* Like Alec Leamas of *The Spy Who Came in from the Cold,* Captain Hansen, the pilot who flies a reconnaissance mission for the service in *The Looking-Glass War,* comes before us as tired, bitter, and anxious to end his career. Wilf Taylor, the London courier who meets him in a Finnish airport, resembles the small, rumpled heroes of Graham Greene. Like some of them, this "old hand" dies a sad, lonely death.

Characters like Taylor convey a vision darker and more trenchant than most first-time readers of le Carré might expect. Reasoning from what happens to Ian Fleming's Sir Hugo Drax of *Moonraker* (1955), his Emilio Largo of *Thunderball* (1961), and Helen MacInnes's Elissa Lang of *The Salzburg Connection* (1968), Merry sees violence and the triumph of Our Side as staples of literary espionage: "The spy novel revolves essentially on the axis of death and destruction. The enemy's agents must (a) be neutralized, and (b) his machinery must be destroyed."[21] In le Carré, machinery and money count less than motives and manners. Nor does the enemy always lose. Communist spies die in *Call for the Dead, The Spy Who Came in from the Cold,* and *Tinker, Tailor,* and Karla crosses into West Berlin at the end of *Smiley's People.* But in *A Small Town in Germany* the enemy enjoys Whitehall's support. The villains in *The Looking-Glass War* are the British Secret Service officers who send Fred Leiser, poorly equipped and poorly trained, into East Germany and then desert him. Moral ambiguity runs so high in *Schoolboy* that heroes and villains become indistinguishable.

Le Carré holds no artistic brief with the giant squids of Dr. No, the sharks of Largo, or the Amazons of Pussy Galore. Evil in le Carré isn't palpable; we don't feel its breath or smell its stench. On the other hand, it can stop characters from defining their best interests. The enemy always lurks within, where he can't be easily exorcised or vanquished; *Tinker, Tailor* finds him at the Circus's top table. But most of his peers can claim no moral advantage over Bill Haydon. Very few of them would shrink from sacrificing a colleague either to expediency or personal ambition. There are no heroes or real villains in le Carré's later books, just a constant state of jockeying, feinting, and other power plays. This levelling of values was already apparent in *The Spy Who Came in from the Cold* (1963). During his legendary meeting with Alec Leamas at his Kent estate, Control admits that, for him, ends justify means: "We do disagreeable things, but we are *defensive.*" He doesn't let on that one of those disagreeable things is taking shape at that very moment—the betrayal of Leamas. Though the irritation he directs to the late-arriving coffee bespeaks his guilt and self-disgust, it doesn't prompt him to call off the operation and restore Leamas to safety. In fact, to lower Leamas's guard, he even invites him to spend the weekend.

In *A Murder of Quality*, Smiley distinguished between the morality of the West, which rests on the sanctity of the individual, and that of the Soviet bloc, where the individual subserves the system. Yet even this early work (1962) describes the difference as more theoretical than actual. Smiley labels himself "a stringent critic of his own motives" in Chapter 9. But his belief that the bad may lead to the good shows that he's no more self-correcting than Control will be in *The Spy Who Came in from the Cold*. Trying to solve a murder, he interviews the murderee's husband under the pretext of writing an obituary notice. His dark side had already surfaced when he killed a Communist spy in *Call for the Dead*. The spy, a former student and friend, died because his restraint during hand-to-hand combat wasn't reciprocated by his smaller, slower, and older foe. Dieter Frey's humanity shames Smiley, who might otherwise have plumed himself as a defender of democracy. Instead of strutting and swelling, he lives with the guilty knowledge that he has sacrificed a friend to an abstraction. Dieter Frey's death gives Dieter a tragic elevation. But he buys this dignity with his life. Spying perverts the noblest motives. The loving heart that sent him into the Thames and that made Liz Gold the Circus's victim in *The Spy Who Came in from the Cold* helps Smiley win Karla's defection in *Smiley's People*.

"We're all the same, you know, that's the joke," says an East German spy to Leamas while bidding him goodnight. Foreshadowing this remark was Leamas's having noticed earlier an uncanny similarity between the spy, Jens Fiedler, and Control. His intimation forecasts the truth that the real goal of the operation he's working on differs from the stated one. Spying observes a logic that would be hilarious anywhere else. At the end of Chapter 17, Leamas wakes up in a hospital and sees Fiedler standing at the foot of his bed casually smoking a cigarette. Leamas's last recollection of Fiedler had him in jail, awaiting trial for conspiracy and treason. Later, Fiedler *will* be tried and executed for these crimes. His opposite number in the Circus, Control, will get demoted and die a decade or so later. The web of causality has spread. One character says to another in *A Small Town in Germany*, "Go and look for your untamed half." The listener needn't go far. The untamed half often lies nearby in le Carré, a writer fond of identity glides and counter-images; T. J. Binyon speaks rightly of le Carré's "love for constructing parallels in characters and situations."[22] Programs and partisans from opposite sides constantly duplicate each other; in *Drummer Girl*, both the PLO and the Israelis see themselves as patriots serving justice, whereas their enemies are terrorists who must be put down. The mirroring is steady and whole. Charlie, the book's heroine, talks of walking through a looking glass after going from one camp to another. Her mirror metaphor holds, failure remaining the reverse image of success. The shattering of the looking glass shatters her, too. Besides losing her occupation, she finds herself reborn into the nullity of the exile, subsisting among strangers in a strange land.

The endings of *Tinker, Tailor* and *Smiley's People* also mock the difference between winners and losers. Spying has become so ideologically barren that victors can't recognize their victories, let alone enjoy them. Most of the winners disown their successes; they can't reconcile their alleged principles with the sordid means they have used to defend them. No spy, from the dabbler to the cynical veteran, can match his/her ideal vision with the ugly reality. Leaders and followers break faith with one another; larger purposes get lost in bureaucratic bickering; innocents are destroyed. Distrust, disbelief, and terror have become daily realities. Sooner or later, they (whoever *they* are) will come for you and wreck your peace. Le Carré's novels of the mid-1960s show all allegiances in security work to be transitory, disposable, and operational. In these three works, disloyalty triumphs over decency while furthering hypocrisy and moral compromise.

To judge the extent of the moral decay permeating espionage, we can return to the mirroring relationships studding the novels. How much freedom and autonomy does the spy enjoy? these images and counterimages ask. The answers they invite discredit the Great Game itself along with its players. Investigators keep getting shocked by the similarities between themselves and those they investigate. The excitement promised by spying soon dwindles to a half life, as Charlie finds. Jens Fiedler could well remind Leamas of Control. There's no moral difference either between the two men or the systems they serve. At the end of *Schoolboy*, Smiley admits that he has spent the past decades groping in an ethical void:

I chose the secret road because it seemed to lead straightest and furthest toward my country's goal. The enemy in those days was someone we could point at and read about in the papers. Today, all I know is that I have learned to interpret the whole of life in terms of conspiracy. These people terrify me, but I am one of them.

As the passage implies, Smiley and his kind serve conspiracy itself. And conspiracy costs a great deal without returning value in kind. It can also bring out the worst in the conspirator. Cutting across private lives, spying sometimes leaves deep ruts. Just as Karla encouraged Bill Haydon's love affair with Smiley's wife, Ann, so does Smiley visit Karla's daughter in a Swiss mental hospital. The Soviet embassy worker he stands in for the day of his visit, Anton Grigoriev, is a former academic, like Smiley. Bespectacled like Smiley, he also resembles the Englishman in height and body build. Perhaps the most painful resemblance joining the two men is their common plight of being married to women who bring them more sorrow than joy. Seeing in Grigoriev what he despises in himself makes it easier for Smiley to break him down. Any remorse he may feel over browbeating Grigoriev he keeps to himself.

His colleagues would ignore his expressions of remorse, anyway. There's nothing human about spying. In the next-to-last chapter of *The Looking-Glass War*, Smiley tells some fellow spies, "You've made technique a way of life...like a whore...technique replacing love." Overlooking complexity and depth, technique trivializes, blinding the technician to the recesses and shadows constituting adult ambivalence. What remains is the job. Le Carré's summary judgment of the apprehension of the mole at the end of *Schoolboy*, "the case was a victory of technique. Nothing more," erases all moral gains. The good and the true haven't been vindicated; perhaps they can't be ascertained. A character in *Smiley's People* complains about lacking a cause or a clear issue to defend: "It's not a shooting war any more.... It's gray. Half-angels fighting half-devils. No one knows where the lines are. No bang-bangs." In *Drummer Girl*, Kurtz masterminds the killing of the PLO's most potent source in Europe. Yet, rather than celebrating his victory, he feels as drained and wrung as Charlie. His cohort in Mossad, Gadi Becker, feels just as whipped. Lacking purpose or pep, he tries feebly to revive his sinking business prospects; he starts and then abandons a novel; he ignores his estranged wife's attempts to mend fences.

Smiley's People ends on the same bitter note. Yes, Karla, Moscow's top spy, has been turned; the restricted information he has at his fingertips represents a bonanza to the west. But le Carré's treatment of his defection destroys any sense of triumph. Smiley and Karla don't meet as winner and loser (any more than Smiley and Haydon do at the end of *Tinker, Tailor*). Their brief, wordless encounter at the border between the two Berlins lacks moral contour because it's a mirror meeting between members of a shameful brotherhood. Neither man insults the other by pretending otherwise. They're stalemated. In using Karla's love for his daughter as a weapon against him, Smiley has sunk to his base level. Perhaps he has sunk lower. During his visit to Alexandra in the Swiss asylum, she suggested that *he* was her father; she also tried to kiss his hand and leave the asylum with him. The insight behind this desperation joins her father to Smiley more dramatically than Karla could ever imagine.

Chapter Two
Drum Beats Out of the Darkness

The nostalgia that Smiley indulges in *Call for the Dead* refers to a time when patriots of daring, inspiration, and breeding joined hands in a cause they all believed in. The fellowship begotten by the service ruled all transactions. In the days before amateurism gave way to bureaucratic intrigue, a handshake or a gentleman's word carried the force of a written contract. At least people thought or pretended that it did. The corruption infecting the Circus since the 1940s had to come from somewhere, and an effect can't have more reality than its cause. Some fever of wrongdoing had poisoned the Edwardian England of croquet and cricket, grouse moors and the Carlton grill. Perhaps the fever had set in still earlier. Panek traces the spy trials and defections of the early 1950s to alleged shortcomings in British education and government:

For Britons, one of the most disturbing facts of the whole Burgess, Maclean, Philby, Blount Affair was that these men who turned traitor were products of the upper class English system: the Oxbridge route. From a doctrinal point of view, they failed as Britons and they failed the precepts of classical education which should have developed them as British leaders—the playing fields of Eton and all that.[1]

Le Carré translated this failure into a need to reevaluate the conventions and institutions of England's time-honored past. Today's spies are cynics full of talk and technique. They work at a job they know to be immoral and soulless. Much of the corruption that is defeating them comes from without. The remark in *Tinker, Tailor* that any nation's security network mirrors its subconscious means that English morality and civilization were never there to save; the emperor has been naked all along. Monaghan shows stagnation pervading le Carré. Not only have the estates of England's ruling families fallen into ruin; their occupants have also done most of the damage undermining the United Kingdom today. The damage didn't come from the gutters of Cheapside; high-born characters, like Ann Smiley and Bill Haydon, have sabotaged traditional guidelines and controls rather than Cockney radicals. It's fitting that these two aristocrats have sex in the shadow of national security. Symbolizing the wreckage inflicted upon the nation by Haydon is his having been recruited by Moscow some thirty-five years before his capture in the early 1970s. The prestige he enjoyed in English society during his decades as a Soviet spy bathes those decades in an ugly new light. His having escaped detection for so long both as a junior and then a senior officer has hurt both Circus morale and public faith in Britain's leaders everywhere. For it is "the golden boy" Haydon and not the mousy central European Toby Esterhase, the working-class Roy Blount, or the provincial Percy Alleline who commits treachery. If "the best hope of his class" and "the post-Victorian ideal of Englishness" betrays us, whom can we trust? Monaghan asks.[2]

I

Part of the answer to his troubled question lies in le Carré's practice of catching both institutions and people in their decline. The period after Bill Haydon's capture, an event called by insiders "The Fall," both spawns a rash of palace plots and marks the nadir of Britain's place in the international intelligence community; Terence Fielding of Carne School in *A Murder of Quality* is nearing mandatory retirement age, and Peter Guillam, at age forty, is by far the youngest in the circle of spies who bring Haydon to boot. Le Carré's practice of manning espionage networks with tired, creaking agents burdened by years of sour memories creates a mood of melancholy and nostalgia. But not for long; the realpolitik of intelligence excludes sentiment. Le Carré's gray-haired spies recall Agatha Christie's Hercule Poirot and Miss Jane Marple, both of whom were already old when they began their careers as fictional sleuths. The contrast between the kindliness usually associated with age and the ruthlessness displayed by the aging in the canon appeals to le Carré's lively sense of incongruity. But the view of wholesale depravity put forth by the novels recalls American hardboiled fiction; Alan Turner's tough talk, hard drinking, and slapping of a woman in *Small Town* put him much closer to Spillane's scourgelike Mike Hammer than to the genteel, highly informed logician-sleuths of Dorothy L. Sayers and Ngaio Marsh. The betrayals of marriage, friendship, and the service by the high-born in le Carré disclose the decay eroding the foundations of the British nation.

Any spy who has spent a year or two in the field will make enemies who may combine against him. Unfortunately for the spy, the combinations can take many surprising forms. Nigel West reports Field Marshall Sir Edward Ironside, Commander in Chief of the Home Force, saying in June 1940, "We cannot be too sure of anybody."[3] West himself refers to the "caution and secrecy necessary even between colleagues."[4] He means that even a spy's closest intimates within the service shouldn't know the spy's movements or whereabouts; he's supposed to work in private and say nothing about his tasks. The same secrecy applies when the task is finished. The retired spy fears constantly that one of his old enemies will kill him; Smiley's inserting of two small wooden splints into his front door-frame before leaving home demonstrates his well-judged caution. But the caution has a wider focus. In each of the three works comprising *The Quest for Karla* (1982), he faces physical danger from his friends, not his foes. Also, as has been seen, the fight-to-the-death climaxing *Call for the Dead* pits him against a former pupil, colleague, and friend. Danger threatens him as soon as the Circus pulls him out of retirement to lead the mole hunt. Once a spy, always a spy, runs the code of laws governing a career in security. Spies don't retire, keep their private lives private, or grow old peacefully. They know too much and have too many former contacts to enjoy the luxury of safety.

This sad development is recent. British Intelligence changed some of its objectives during the twenty years following Hitler's War. Traditional espionage meant trying to know the enemy in order to anticipate his battle plans. Spies were trained to study the enemy's actions, habits, and thoughts. Nowadays, the loss of community and tradition has changed the spy's purposes. The discovery that institutions set up to safeguard order, decency, and due process have been sabotaging these virtues means that spies now watch and inform on their mates; even high-grade watchdogs can't escape scrutiny. We can see why. The unlikely double agency of Bill Haydon, a man who appears to have all he wants, makes us all suspect. The contagion of suspicion that ensues creates further malaise. First, the escalation a Haydon causes in in-house surveillance defeats its aims. Besides running up the price of an agent's services through prolonged, intensive training, it increases the number of agents to the point where the agency is too overstaffed to work smoothly. Or perhaps work at all; overstaffing creates the disorder and morale problems that the infiltrator secretly loves. The very steps taken to stop him help him.

The pressure caused by the need to constantly guard one's tongue is devastating. It fosters evasions and lies, and it rules out cooperation. It inhibits initiative, too, since it makes the agent worry so much about being watched that he neglects his proper work. His effectiveness wanes. Knowing that he can't trust his colleagues either to let him work in peace or treat his work fairly, he makes self-protection his main goal. Energies he might have directed to more productive channels go into looking out for watchers. Paranoia can infect everybody in this looking-glass war of unmarked battle lines. Karla advises, "Spy on your friends today, they're certain to be your enemies tomorrow," and a Mexican-American flyer in the same novel, *Schoolboy*, follows suit by saying, "Sometimes you got to hide with the enemy to get away from your friends." This counsel recurs in *Smiley's People* when a sixty-nine-year-old Estonian with decades of security experience says, "Enemies I do not fear.... But friends I fear greatly." Well-meaning help from a protective friend can harm more than help, particularly if the friend is hiding guilty knowledge. The reverse also applies. Agents try to know each other's families, work habits, and leisure routines. Such knowledge helps them both learn each other's weaknesses and neutralize each other's strengths. Thus Leamas refers to the Leninist creed, "the expediency of temporary alliances." A closely felt bond like Liz Gold's love for Leamas, Drake Ko's for his brother, or Karla's for his daughter can be turned by the unscrupulous into an instrument of bribery or, better for any spy network, blackmail.

To ward off such threats, the spy covers his commitments. Cover helps any spy. Sir Anthony Blunt's included a knighthood, an honorary fellowship to Trinity College, Cambridge, and membership in the British Academy. Musing on the implementation of cover, Jerry Westerby, the honourable schoolboy, says, "Cover is not a lie.... Cover is what you believe. Cover is who you are." Leamas's cover as an angry dissolute, no arbitrary invention, flows from his background and personality. Rather than falsifying, it extends and deepens traits he is already known to possess. He plays it as a continuation of his psychological profile. Shivering, dirty, and unshaven after quitting his librarian's job, he wrecks his health with tobacco and drink. He goes to jail for assaulting a grocer who denied him credit. Then his surliness angers his fellow prisoners. All along, though, he has kept his own counsel, maintaining a close watch both on himself and the Communist agents who want to reverse his loyalties, or turn him. He's more in charge than anyone suspects. He's not only an actor but also a critic of his own performance; he must evaluate the effect of his acting upon his audience and make the necessary adjustments in both style and script. He'll cooperate but then balk and be insolent whenever his makeshift scenario demands inconsistency. The double remove from which he views himself includes the need for perfect timing and technique. Undercover agents like Leamas and Charlie extend the art of drama. As both a performer and a critic, the spy who has lodged himself or herself successfully in the enemy's camp has triumphed as an imaginative artist. But his/her artistry rests on a delicate balance. Any errors in performance can be fatal. Creator and creation must merge in a seamless unit. Yet how can they? The creator also needs the objectivity to judge his creation. Cover denies the truth of self while deepening it. The spy ignores his responsibility to his uniqueness. His reliance upon the safety provided by cover traps him in so many lies, distortions, and evasions that he can't distinguish between the false and the true.

The paradox that cover both tightens and weakens a spy's hold on life occurs most vividly in the le Carré canon in the person of Charlie. Already an accomplished actress before her recruitment by Israeli intelligence, she brings an array of skills to her role as a PLO partisan. But her mastery in the theater of the real defeats her. Having tasted real tragedy in PLO camps and villages, she will only act in comedies when she returns to the English stage. Then she quits the stage altogether; so fatuous does she find play-acting that even its mildest manifestations offend her. This actress who played the part of Rosalind, perhaps Shakespeare's most polychromatic heroine, in *As You Like It*, can't manage simple comedy. Her cover as a PLO agent has left a residue; the near eastern scenario she acted in keeps playing after the last curtain. Many career spies know her ordeal well. An agent's sensibilities range from the crude to the refined, from the idealistic to the selfish. But this spectrum of response serves loveless expediency. It can be tapped so effectively because in the agent's deepest heart lies a void.

But the agent also creates voids, or traps, that snare others. Drake Ko enjoys great public esteem in Hong Kong. A KBE and the owner of a Rolls Royce, he belongs to an exclusive club, finances local spirit temples, and has helped build a hospital. When Smiley hears of this philanthropist-merchant's proud record as a benefactor, he replies simply, "In my world, we call that good cover." His words extend the mirror metaphor. Spying is a looking-glass phenomenon in that it reverses expectations. Ever vigilant, security officers must read signs and symptoms with an attentiveness unknown to the rest of us; the most benign-looking surfaces can surround a Pandora's box of malignancy. Of Jerry Westerby it is said, "There was a part of him that never ceased to watch." It can't afford not to; a spy's survival depends on an infinite capacity for suspicion. Besides promoting self-preservation, this exaggerated watchfulness both enriches and impoverishes. The sharp eye the spy has cultivated as a way of staying alive heightens his sensitivity in general; a tiny nuance can snap his defenses in place. This superfine attunement to the appearance-reality interplay even endows him with insight resembling that of the religious mystic. In the process, though, life loses its freshness and flavor. All trust between people breaks down, and the world becomes a palimpsest of spying. With everybody a suspected enemy, life rests on a bedrock of distrust. We're back again in the religious sphere; martyr-like, the spy sacrifices himself for the rest of us. His red-eyed wakefulness lets us sleep; his danger serves our safety.

This sacrifice augments our view of spying. If all are suspect, perhaps all merit suspicion, as in an Agatha Christie novel or a Hitchcock movie. Double-agency may be the ultimate transformation, demanding both a leap and standing still. The ultimate betrayal is that of the mole. The immorality of the spying community finds its fullest expression in the mole, a deep-cover agent perfectly placed to foil every operation and field agent sponsored by his presumed chiefs. Unlikely traitors like Bill Haydon and Drake Ko prove that, though demeaning and sordid, espionage has its uses. But these uses summon up the idea, another mirror manifestation, that turnabout is fair play. Just as social abuses in Britain have seeped into and rotted the service, the service has returned the favor by sending the poison back into society. The mechanization and pluralization of modern life can hide most threats to national security. But looking to the computer to order life's multiplicity also puts us under the control of intelligence services. None of us can escape surveillance; all can be called before representatives of a system notorious for its hardness and cynicism.

In *Looking-Glass War, Small Town, Schoolboy,* and *Drummer Girl,* as in Hitchcock and Eric Ambler, an obscure private person agrees to play a dangerous game in which he/she is only a pawn. Merry tells how these innocents are exploited: "le Carré's thrillers are tragic novels precisely because the small fish ... becomes sympathetic to the reader, shows unusual integrity, and is then coldly sacrificed to the power game."[5] Growth precedes downfall. The humanity in the innocent that both attracts the power brokers and accounts for his growth will also doom him. No asset in security work, kindness of heart impairs efficiency. According to Control, a spy ignores morality. He may lie, cheat, steal, break promises, or use blackmail both to gather intelligence and to turn an enemy agent. Out in the cold, he has to do the best he can, regardless of rules and regulations. As has been seen, this best depends on the worst. Spies can forget self-fulfillment. Their work stimulates and rewards qualities of the head, slighting those of the heart. "A man must steel himself against sentiment," says a character in Chapter 6 of *Looking-Glass War*. Such advice is bane touted as therapy. The compassionate, the gentle, and the loving suffer in security work while their more cautious counterparts win promotions and pay hikes. Yet caution, ordinarily a virtue, often slides into deviousness, cunning, and coldness, which are faults. The distance from them to the sins of heartlessness and cruelty is shorter than the spy weaving through a minefield of dangers can stop to assess. Knowing that any false step can destroy him, he thinks clearly but acts desperately.

Spying tries the agent to the utmost. A few weeks of subterfuge and secrecy in the field will gnaw his nerves. To avoid detection, he must plan his most trivial movements together with fallbacks and contingencies. He has to be sure that he isn't being shadowed, that his flat hasn't been searched, and that no compromising material will be found on his person; "in the spy trade we abandon first what we love the most," says Smiley ruefully to himself in *Smiley's People*. To make sure he hasn't fallen under suspicion, he makes periodic security checks. These can never relax. No law can protect an agent caught behind enemy lines. Observing what is called in *The Looking-Glass War* "war rules," he will be treated like an alien enemy if he's caught. This means that he may be tortured into revealing his cohorts' names and purposes; then he may be killed.

Romantic attachments relieve the tension and loneliness of the underground operative, but only at great risk. A character in *The Looking-Glass War* says, "Do you know what love is...? I'll tell you: it is whatever you can still betray." Ann Smiley endorses this proposition in *Smiley's People* with the statement, "There is no loyalty without betrayal." The inextricability of love and betrayal raises the spy's fever level. Imprudently, he may open his heart in spite of the risk. Exacerbation poses as relief in the case of Karl Riemeck. Riemeck tells his woman of his plan to leave East Berlin in *The Spy Who Came in from the Cold*. He is shot near the Wall, and his woman dies soon after. The emotional tie ruling a spy's life needn't be sexual. Fred Leiser's patriotism leads to his exploitation and betrayal by the service in *The Looking-Glass War*. Drake and Nelson Ko risk everything to reunite in *Schoolboy*. But their short-lived reunion devastates both of them. Karla misallocates funds, violates security, and commits murder to help a daughter he has never spoken to. In view of his ruthlessness, his unclutching love, perhaps the noblest in all of le Carré, makes him both the best and worst character in the book. As has been seen, it also compromises this Slavic Gatsby. Karla gave all for love and asked nothing in return. But in serving Alexandra, he also committed crimes so offensive to the Kremlin that their detection would mean death, probably for both him and her. Smiley need only remind him of the Kremlin's attitude toward crimes like his to convince him to defect.

So glamorous on the surface, with its promise of big money, world travel, and intrigue, spying stands for all that is harsh, cramped, and implacable. "He wondered if he'd killed the guard. He hoped so," muses a bruised, aching Leamas after waking up in an East German prison. Neither here nor at any other time does he think of the young guard he assaulted as a person with hopes, a private history, and a family who will miss him. To show how much spying perverts a spy's feelings, le Carré makes the guard an age where he might be Leamas's son. The likeness never registers with Leamas despite his many years in Germany. Inhumanity wheels in the cycle of the family again in *The Looking-Glass War*. Three times Leclerc, a senior officer, stops John Avery from dialing his wife to tell her of his safe return to London. When another senior officer comes in and asks Avery about Sarah, Leclerc changes the subject. Leclerc, a bachelor who lives alone, seems to resent Avery's family enough to undermine it. Perhaps he wants to undermine all families everywhere. He has forgotten that the family is the nucleus of society and that any society draws strength from it. Leclerc is defying a core reality of the civilization he serves.

This defiance of civilized values helps explain the spy's intense, disordered psychology. Rarely will a case officer tell his field agent the reason for what he's doing. Part of this secrecy is routine policy. The fewer the people who know a tactical secret, the less chance there is that the secret will leak. Each agent is assigned a small share of an operation, and he knows no more about the operation than he needs to carry out his tiny but essential job. The less he knows, the better for both him and his friends if he's caught by the enemy. Yet his runner's motives for keeping purposes dark are also selfish. The bureau does jobs which help its government but which the government could never approve in writing. This withholding of official approval puts the agent at risk. The agent who gets caught performing a clandestine mission can only count on his chief's help up to a point, the point where helping the agent will compromise the bureau. Naturally, the agent could help himself by knowing the crucial point beforehand. But he gets no such guidelines or aids. The le Carré novel we're reading isn't the same one that's developing because the bureau withholds vital information. Sometimes, the bureau won't act on the information it has. Smiley's chief in *Call for the Dead* would rather preserve the status quo than investigate the death of a Foreign Office functionary; an investigation might rock the bureaucratic boat and tip the chief into the water. A security officer in Bonn in *A Small Town in Germany* invokes protocol to avoid truth-seeking. When told that one of his staff members has been working in a basement archive to prove the guilt of a local politico, the security officer answers feebly that the archive is off limits to junior personnel. Right and wrong have ceased to matter. Ignoring the evidence incriminating the guilty leader, the Bonn intelligence chief drags in an irrelevancy to hide the true issue; the leader's accuser, he says with manufactured anger, could go to jail for looking at classified material.

His evasiveness solidifies our impression that spying is based on distrust. As Control's betrayal of Leamas has already shown, distrust rays outward from the dubious partnership of the field agent and his chief. This distrust comes forth in the reference in *Smiley's People* to "the stubborn refusal of the born case man to reveal anything to his controller that is not essential to their collaboration." The case man's doggedness takes root in his need to protect himself. The more the controller knows, the more power he has over the case man. But good controllers usually don't question their case men's sources. Nor will they worry case men about breaking rules. People in the field must build their own networks, mostly without help from home, using whatever materials are handy. Only his instinct can tell the field agent whom to trust, which rules to break, and when to duck. Divulging the identity of his contacts both violates his professional pride and compromises his safety. Percy Alleline cites "the failure rate around this place" in *Smiley's People* to justify his silence about an important source. Yet the bureau has to protect itself, too. Agents given total freedom can sell passports, weapons, and classified secrets. How often do they commit these crimes? Leamas's famous description of spies as "a squalid procession of vain fools, traitors ... pansies, sadists, and drunkards" hardly builds confidence in their judgment or moral character. How closely should they be supervised if the system is to survive? At what point does the closeness of the supervision turn cooperation between the agent and his runner into competition? Although these questions come up constantly, they defy answers. There's little good will or freedom of interchange between the two main arms of intelligence. Trained to act instinctively, agents dislike hierarchies and the systems they serve. This same angry individualism produces solid results, and no good runner would pretend otherwise; the male tribalism that sends the agent underground benefits the bureau. Yet it also frustrates the bureau's passion for order and predictability.

II

Like most of the other clashes in le Carré, this conflict of styles and aims suggests an encompassing malaise. Nowhere does his 1968 equation of spying with Britain's laws, customs, and other institutions[6] vibrate more keenly than in the symbolism voicing his disquiet with those bulwarks of the modern Christian state—the family, education, religion, and big business. He seems to be attacking the foundations of society to order his own life. Merry's reference to "the nagging feeling that things are wrong" everywhere in le Carré[7] includes the breakdown of common values and forms. Le Carré's disaffiliation from English modes declares itself, first, in his having gone to the French language for a pen name. His exotic settings and technical sophistication put him in the category of the literary playboy, where very few of today's English novelists (Lawrence Durrell and John Fowles come to mind) belong. Although his ongoing sympathetic portrait of patriotic George Smiley infers an approval of native values like honesty, fidelity, and hard work, his years abroad have also taught him to prize the non-English virtue of brilliance and to search out obscure motives rather than leaning upon English common sense.

This repudiation of the homegrown extends to his fictional practice. His tendency to disrupt and thus disallow narrative flow reflects French, not English, literary practice. In place of coherence and closure, he features plurality and a free play of mind. He finds destabilization a better way to the truth than unity. In his later work, especially, he subverts the rhetorical and moral conventions we automatically look to for support while reading a text. If he chose a French pen name to say indirectly that he would avoid the soothing affirmations found in most intrigue fiction, his subject matter underscores his intention. Recurrent motifs in his books imply that he's using spy fiction to question his moral disquiet; a 1965 article he wrote for *Holiday*, "Wrong Man on Crete," contains the remark, "perhaps depression is just my favorite mood."[8] We've already seen darkness and depletion saturating the fiction. Certain events will enhance this mood of defeat. Leamas abuses his health; Adrian Haldane coughs all through *The Looking-Glass War;* nearly all the books end with the death of a sympathetic figure. The shackles preventing the spy from halting this death drift find expression in Jerry Westerby's comment in Chapter 20 of *Schoolboy*: "Not allowed a past in this game. Can't have a future either."

The forms and norms le Carré has chosen to criticize add sting to his anti-establishmentarianism; to use the foundation stones of society to attack a social practice or institution is to send shock waves through the whole system. Like the prevalence of sacrifice in le Carré's work, the inwardness that makes his books dreamscapes of memory and desire rather than simple action stories turns the mind to religion. A critic who has shown how his work invites a religious reading is Celia Hughes. Writing in *Theology* in 1981, Ms. Hughes said, "Those [of le Carré's characters] who engage in counter-espionage are required in practice to dedicate their lives as if they were entering a religious order—though to what they dedicate their aspirations and ideals is not definable."[9] The quality noted by Ms. Hughes eludes definition because it often lacks substance. Chapter Sixteen of *Call for the Dead* is called "Echoes in the Fog." The house near The Hague where Leamas talks to some Communist spies is called Le Mirage. Granville Hicks quotes le Carré saying of *The Looking-Glass War,* "I think the book touches new ground when it discusses the phenomenon of 'committed' men who are committed to nothing but one another and the dreams they collectively invoke."[10] In *Tinker, Tailor,* a veteran female spy says, "I *hate* the real world.... I like the Circus."

Her preference withal, most spies view the special branch as a denial of reality. She herself, a tipping, arthritic frump, is poorly equipped for the outside world. When seen in *Smiley's People*, she has turned her back on society, her only intimates in her out-of-the-way shack being dogs and her much younger female lover (perhaps her lesbianism is meant to stand for the unreality she has opted for). The statement made in *Drummer Girl* by an Israeli spy, "We are Berkeleyans, you see," describes intelligence work and, by extension, the whole intelligence community as a mental activity. Analogously, someone in *Schoolboy* calls the Circus a "dream factory." This concept isn't new. A dabbler in spying in Greene's *Our Man in Havana* (1958) invents an agent to fly secret reconnaissance missions. The imaginary pilot then turns up dead on an official report. Besides operating in a moral vacuum, spying has razed the difference between seem and be. People are written into life to perpetuate the system. The spy moves in a superfine world of hints, surmises, and whispers, half recording and half inventing what he perceives. Le Carré keeps saying that spies have become the clergy of the cold war era. Liz Gold tells Leamas that he looks like a priest and talks like a fanatic; a security worker in *Small Town* who supposedly looks like a monk whispers "like a crazy priest"; Karla himself is often described in priestly terms; his opposite number, Smiley, reminds Jerry Westerby of a fallen priest. The range of ecclesiastical reference goes beyond people. In *Tinker, Tailor,* a Somerset church serves as a hiding place for a weapon, while another in Hong Kong is used as a mail drop.

The fog belt of subtleties and intimations the spy moves in while searching for clues and leads demands total dedication, as Ms. Hughes says. Though often starved for facts, he must commit himself fully. Religion rests on faith, not on proofs, demonstrations, or tangible evidence. Like a cloistered monk, the spy, too, ignores the substantiality of the secular world. The double agency of a Bill Haydon makes him read and interpret life differently from the rest of us. His inventions can change history. An Israeli spy in *Drummer Girl* imposes fiction on reality in order to reshape the past. Life becomes a gossamer web of conspiracy,some of whose threads can't be traced. But the spy must see them with his mind's eye. Even though he can't distinguish between shadow and substance, his gaze must remain steady. He has truly entered the spirit world; always alert, he hears voices unheard by others and sees dark meanings in bright signs. Keeping faith with his goals means disregarding not only the witness of his senses but also his finer feelings, his instincts, and his moral training. Spying calls for wit, patience, and nerve along with the willingness to abandon these virtues in the interests of policy. Very little in espionage makes sense by ordinary standards, nor can anybody or anything be relied upon. Preferring the elaborate, the farfetched, and the exotic, spies doubt the truth when it's looking at them. The cultivation of total faith in this faithless system is what Leclerc in *Looking-Glass War* calls "the second vow." It entails the suspension of both adult mentality and personal freedom. Unlike American literary heroes from Huck

Finn to Ralph Ellison's Invisible Man, who obey their conscience instead of the law, the spy in le Carré abdicates all. The extent of his abdication can be gauged by the names given to spies in the canon. Evidence suggests a belief in le Carré that names confer reality. The many worknames used by Smiley cloud his sense of self and divide him from the deep truths governing his life. Our never learning Charlie's last name also posits a half life for le Carré's little drummer girl. Her habit of shortening the names of people she knows (Alastair is Al, Joseph, Jo, and Helga, Helg, just as she is called Chas) reflects a tendency to truncate that perhaps helps her adapt so well to espionage. The maimed security chiefs she meets, some of whom are amputees, also portray spying as the enemy of wholeness and stability.

This renunciation of the solid material world for that of the spirit always pushes the spy in the direction of the abstract and the artificial. *Looking-Glass War, Small Town,* and *Schoolboy* all include the statement that it doesn't matter that Christ was born on Christmas rather than a day or two later; what counts is that He was born at all. Yet what le Carré says about spying reverses this plea for redemption. The spy's strict conformism, his elevation of policy to a religious creed, and his rejection of worldly matters and modes all invite a Christian framework. Ironically, this interpreter of signs and rearranger of experience to suit the litanies of his creed answers to a morality which precludes Christian redemption. Nor does it respect the sanctity of persons, as scripture dictates. The spy's spiritual activity observes a discipline that disregards human purpose. It has to; the bureau's pragmatism rests on a morality sterner than Calvinist writ. As in Kafka (where the Calvinist creed of original sin reverberates), the bureau perpetuates itself by sacrificing its disciples. It's fitting that *The Looking-Glass War,* the book of le Carré's featuring the ugliest bureaucratic motives, also contains the most religious language. The revelation burgeoning from Christ's birth finds its parallel in the field agent's discovery that he has been betrayed. Often occurring in November or December, a time when many people's thoughts have turned to Christmas, this unholy revelation parodies the Christian drama by which spirit becomes flesh and then returns to spirit. The betrayed agent's transformation lacks uplift, his epiphany revealing that his meaning lies in his use. And his use consists of serving a morality at odds with the nominal beliefs of the Christian state it's protecting. Although his insight doesn't prepare him to live more fully, since it impinges upon his death, it does glimpse the innermost workings of society. With the service parodying the archetype of the interceder, he has mastered society in order to submit to it.

Education is another hallowed institution whose prominence in le Carré extends his criticism of the spy trade. Like religion, education turns largely on a pattern of dominance and submission. Its fictional treatment also resembles that of religion in that it draws much of its force from the ironic reversals it invites. "The Great Game which never stops day or night" that charmed Kipling's Kim imparts knowledge and wisdom, like any other good educational program. But it prepares few of its apprentices for life. The disappointment felt by the apprentice stems directly from the purity and intensity of his/her commitment. Success and failure are both punished. The Pole Fred Leiser (whose espionage training took place near Oxford) comes to grief because he fails at his job; Charlie, the English actress who performs brilliantly for Israeli intelligence, also loses heart. These two disconsolates share at least one disturbing feature; they show that the spy whose hopes get crushed in the field can be an outsider rather than a career professional.

Most often, the spy is not only home-grown English; he/she will also sport the social and educational credentials that qualify him/her to serve a nation traditionally esteemed as a model of civilization and morality. George Smiley's recruitment as an Oxford undergraduate isn't unusual; several of the personal ties at the Circus began at Oxford and even earlier. The moral darkness the spy commits himself to clashes with the brilliance of these early prospects. English public school education sets out to build character, to teach fair play, and to encourage its charges to act like gentlemen. The gentlemanly offhandedness acquired so perseveringly (and then ignored) survives in many agents. But there's ironic counterpoint between it and the underlying bleakness. Le Carré's spy books attack the ideals of boyhood and youth celebrated in the tradition of the English male romance, which starts with Kipling, includes works like E. Phillips Oppenheim's *Great Impersonation* (1920), and extends in modified form to the generation of Christopher Isherwood (1904-86) and Michael Gilbert (b. 1912). Le Carré disclaims male camaraderie, adolescent extroversion, and the elegance of the old boy network. As has been seen, the public school virtues mean little in the corridors of deceit comprising the special branch other than to make it easier for the agent runner to trick his unsuspecting man in the field.

His trickery will succeed most of the time. Danger often uncoils from the persistence of the English public school as a model for adult thought and action. Though more of an absorbed influence than a palpable presence, the old school tie remains a source of meaning and sentiment. The school metaphor exerts the same thematic drive in le Carré as in Bernard Malamud's *A New Life* (1961) and John Barth's *Giles Goat Boy* (1966). In le Carré, though, the school promotes a different form of mischief than that developed in the two American novels. The difference inheres in the infantilism le Carré sees as a byproduct of the old boy network. If the world is a school, then spies are schoolboys playing at being adults. Morality gets lost in the collective adolescent fantasy. Jerry Westerby, the honourable schoolboy, never grows up enough to give marriage the commitment it deserves; an extension of the school, spying has made him unfit for adult responsibility. Agents first see themselves as bright, irreverent schoolboys. This self-image gives way to that of the benign but stern headmaster ready to disapprove any misconduct that comes under his ever-watchful eye (*Goodbye, Mr. Chips* is mentioned in le Carré's only non-spy novel to date, *The Naive and Sentimental Lover* [1972]). But the transformation falls short. Nearly everyone plays headmaster and boy at the same time, either bending or trying to enforce the rules of the service as his advantage dictates. Control grins "like a schoolboy" while recounting the need to adopt evil means for the sake of good ends. There is also a headmaster in *Tinker, Tailor* who abandons school and family to run off with a woman.

The guilt spies feel for breaking the rules sometimes produces dark consequences. It also calls to mind the masochism few underclassmen have the self-esteem to fend off. Because he has at times made the schoolmaster's values his own, the schoolboy sometimes wants to be caught and punished for rebelling. His knowledge that his chiefs have cheated him by invoking the public school creed of decency and stoicism to gain an edge on him doesn't stop Fred Leiser from signing on with the special branch; he's flattered to take his lowly place in the English hierarchy. His Slavic origins even imply a Kafkaesque sense of guilt that pushes him to his doom. He knows all along that he's being exploited, and never does he believe that his mission will succeed. The same inferiority that makes him the target of his superiors' well-bred verbal sideswipes also brings him to grief. His being is enclosed by that of the system he serves—but only because he wills it. He can walk away from his chiefs at any time. If the system betrays him, he has connived in the treachery.

The mistakes he begins making as soon as he crosses into East Germany count as both a confession of bad faith and a wish to be captured.

The punishment he awaits sharpens the pattern. Physical intimidation helps join the world of spying to that of the public school boy. In 1977, le Carré said that he felt like a prisoner in school, that he was forced to box, and that he was caned till his bottom bled. Perhaps damaging him and his schoolmates still more was the social snobbery fostered by public school tradition; the boys were expected to despise the working class and foreigners.[11] This schooling has left its mark on le Carré. The belief that outmoded, rearguard views are still blocking social equality in England runs through his fiction. It also gives him another chance to study his dark side. Carne School of *A Murder of Quality,* Sherborne School of *The Naive and Sentimental Lover,* and Thursgood School of *Tinker, Tailor* show English public school education opposing frankness, intellectual freedom, and all else that defies upper-class insularity and snobbishness. The motto of Carne, in fact, *Regem defendere diem videre,* i.e., to defend the king is to see the day, celebrates obedience to authority; wisdom comes from conforming to the establishment.

Le Carré builds *A Murder of Quality* around the tension between this conservatism and the chaos erupting in and around the school. A local mad woman, a leading figure in the murder investigation, embodies more of Carne mentality than Carne officialdom wants to admit. But she accounts for only a small part of the chaos. The manners displayed at school functions, the relationships among faculty families, and the traditions governing student behavior all fascinate le Carré. The vanity undergirding this elaborate network of hierarchies, whispering galleries, and pretensions prefigures that of the Circus. The path between the Circus and the public school is also well trodden. The culprit in *A Murder of Quality,* the oldest member of the faculty, is the brother of a former Circus functionary and war hero. This mirroring calls forth another. The Circus and the school are both rotting from the top. The repression of feeling, a tenet of English nurture, speeds the stagnation. Behind the cool charm, donnish composure, and polished speech of both the schoolmaster and the spy chief lurks decay. To worsen matters, the decay constantly denies its existence. The practice of first-naming one's colleagues, the dry humor, and the amiability leavened by well-bred reticence that characterize Circus dynamics all mask a ruthlessness akin to that of a sadistic head prefect.

As Fred Leiser has shown, the victims of this ruthlessness know they've been wronged. Ex-agent Jim Prideaux's reference to "the unpaid bill" when he meets a boy at Thursgood's named Bill sounds more random than it is. Prideaux suspects that he was betrayed by his longtime friend Bill Haydon even though Haydon's identity as the mole is still a secret. Prideaux's many years in the dream factory have ruled out any need for tangible proof. Faint impressions on the middle distance of consciousness suffice him. Before his reason has either formulated or accepted Haydon's guilt, he's thinking about revenge. Haydon's guilt will later haunt the high-born in ways they'd only discuss among themselves. What surrounds these grandees is urban sprawl, pollution, and racial tension. What claims many of their souls is an England that stands for stability and honor, continuity and dedication, in both culture and government.

Haydon belongs to their set. Prideaux, whose French name and Czech-language expertise make him less recognizably English, does not. This difference, combined with that between Prideaux's bravery and Haydon's treachery, poisons the dreams of many aristocrats. Without an ideal to goad them, spies, many of whom boast long family pedigrees, lose purpose. Inheritors of Kipling's creed of the White Man's Burden, Haydon's survivors feel guilty about their kinship to him. The same process of association that allowed them to glow in his splendor now smirches them with his guilt. His treachery, they know, mirrors their own moral depletion. They can't defend themselves when they're blamed for causing England's slump since the early 1950s; in fact, they probably blame themselves. By the late 1970s, the time setting of *Smiley's People,* their cousins in the Circus have all seen their places at the top table taken by younger people of humbler origins. One of them, the Cabinet chief, Oliver Lacon, has also seen his marriage come adrift. And Ann Smiley's marriage to George has only worsened the aristocratic decadence she was trying to purge in herself by reaching into the middle class for a husband.

These defeats sadden le Carré. Though his infusion of class structures into his fiction has made him a cold war social realist, it also discloses deep divisions in him. Intellectually, he rejects the old order; its grand ways were built upon falsehood and inequity; it encouraged obsolete values; it blocked personal growth. The damage it has caused shows vividly in the wreckage strewn about the Circus's corridors. Yet his having found nothing better in England to take its place can make him yearn for Mayfair clubs whose members (all male) wear Bond Street tweeds and sometimes talk like Bertie Wooster.

His "impressive collection of P. G. Wodehouse novels"[12] also concurs with a tendency to condone the blithe posturing and puny malice of the well-born. His dialogue, too, sounds a shade snobbish in its bright elegance. And he will interpret personality as an amalgam of family, taste in clothing and wine, and educational background.

More privilege finds its way into his novels than his satire needs; much of it receives lingering treatment. Drawn to incongruity for its ability to produce humor and irony, he writes mostly about the upper and lower classes. The middle class he usually disregards, except to describe the headway that mandarin effeteness has helped its members make. His groundlings move on a small canvas in predictable ways. He's most comfortable and expansive with characters redolent of English drawing room comedy. Besides voicing his dissaffiliation from the middle class, the bold new uses to which he has put upper-class characters and codes disclose the aristocratic wellsprings of his inventiveness. His gentry, many of whom have known each other from the cradle, share common beliefs in friendship, art, and, perhaps above all, in the importance of succeeding without apparent effort. Of course, they're just showing off, and le Carré knows it. But he withholds blame. Had their failures in public life caused less damage, he might have excused them because of their ability to hold a style.

The pointlessness and inconsequentiality of *The Naive and Sentimental Lover*, a troubled recreation of upper-class chic, merely exaggerates traits found in the spy books. This 1972 work avoids nearly all social and moral concern, psychological insight, and speculation of any import. Its first chapter includes a long, loving description of the dashboard, panelling, and upholstery of its main character's Bentley. Having set most of his earlier work in cold, menacing northern Germany, le Carré steeps himself, in *The Naive and Sentimental Lover*, in English traditions, artifacts, and land forms. The book's first chapter also contains a brochure describing an English manor. The brochure's serious tone, wealth of architectural and historical detail, and family genealogy send the main character, Aldo Cassidy, back to an ancestral womb. Although he will later soil one of his elegant suits by getting on his knees to fix a pram, his real commitment is to a bygone England of his fancy. He kneeled in grease to impress a wholesaler. The wholesaler is more impressed with this show of democratic feeling than we are. Much of Aldo's rapture at being wafted into an ancestral womb comes from the knowledge that he won't have to share it with social inferiors like the wholesaler.

This elitism would be less damning had le Carré distanced his portrait of Aldo. But Aldo's close resemblance to le Carré in age, looks, and body build shows that the objectivity only just maintained in the spy books breaks down in *The Naive and Sentimental Lover*. How much attention this breakdown deserves is hard to say. Perhaps le Carré wrote his 1972 work to relieve the depression built up in him by the spy books. The grimness of the three works preceding *The Naive and Sentimental Lover, Spy Who Came in from the Cold, Looking-Glass War,* and *Small Town,* could have led him to try something more cheerful. On the other hand, he could have written *The Naive and Sentimental Lover* to confront himself. Other writers have chosen literary modes different from those that built their reputations to probe *their* psyches; in *A Briefing for a Descent into Hell* (1971), for instance, Doris Lessing abandoned the realism of her Martha Quest books to address a subject of utmost importance to her. Whether le Carré wrote *Lover* out of the same kind of inner necessity can't be proved. Yet we can't overlook the upper-class subject matter, the similarities between Aldo and his author, and, perhaps most strikingly, the absence of those incongruities and countering motifs that create such tension in his other work. Lacking a principle of intercheck, the book mutters like a big blind mouth. It would be good to know what was on le Carré's mind when he was writing its second half. His five novels of the 1960s showed so much artistic growth that he must have known he was off course.

In any event, Aldo, who, again like le Carré, has a stifled sense of paternity, begins the novel by tapping into roots planted by others. He's poaching on his country's aristocratic past. Yet he goes about his job with a greater sense of mission than moved Smiley to marry above himself socially. Owning Haverdown in Somerset (the county where Thursgood School in *Tinker, Tailor* is located), he believes, will give him access to the splendors of aristocratic England. He has already cultivated some high-toned ways. The name of his dining club, the Nondescripts, reveals his upper-class preference for an exclusiveness both low key and self effacing; wealth and power are assets, but their display is vulgar to the English gentleman, a creature who enjoys taking for granted trappings of taste and quiet elegance. This requirement isn't limited to Aldo. Personal effects that fall short of the Bond Street standard can damn characters in le Carré. Note the following description of a London-bound Fred Leiser: "He left on the mid-day train, carrying one pigskin suitcase and wearing his camel-hair coat; it had a slightly military cut, and leather buttons,

but no person of breeding would have mistaken it for a British warm."
This passage gives distress, coming, as it does, in a book that connects
the foibles of the well-bred to disaster. Not only does the passage
equate appearance and reality, ignoring undertones that produce
elsewhere some of le Carré's best effects. Its yoking of the narrative
self to the perceiving self also joins le Carré to the snobs who are
exploiting Leiser without a pang of remorse. Implying that Leiser
is exploitable because, as a Polish immigrant, he dresses badly, the
passage endorses the worst assumptions of English snobbery. More
grievously, it shows le Carré adopting the values of people he otherwise
condemns.

The gleeful misanthropy that can make le Carré look like Ronald
Firbank or Evelyn Waugh leaves its darkest stain in *A Murder of
Quality*. Like its successor a decade later, *Lover*, this 1962 novel stands
apart from le Carré's spy books. Perhaps more revealingly, it hews
to the curve of that most hidebound of literary forms, the English
country house mystery, accepting the snobbery traditionally connected
with the form. The following passage could have come from Dorothy
L. Sayers; it infers that commoners offend the well-bred at first glance
and thus forfeit their compassion:

As Smiley watched him turn into the center aisle . . . it occurred to him that Rode's
very walk and bearing successfully conveyed something entirely alien to Carne. If it
is vulgar to wear a pen in the breast pocket of your jacket, to favor Fair Isle pullovers
and brown ties, to bob a little and turn your feet out as you walk, then Rode beyond
a shadow of a doubt was vulgar, for though he did not now commit these sins his
manner implied them all.

Smiley's condescension is atypically malicious. Yes, Stanley Rode may
have made a big professional leap by bringing his north-of-England
Grammar School background to the faculty of one of England's ancient
public schools. But he didn't exceed himself. Carne hired him out
of a field of numerous other applicants; many of them had better
social credentials and would have adjusted more smoothly to gown
life in Dorset. Also, postwar England, invigorated by newly adopted
democratic principles, was opening its prizes to all, regardless of social
class. As a man from the middle class with an aristocratic wife, Smiley
should understand this new upward mobility better than his contempt
for Rode indicates.

But he refuses to. Rode doesn't have to blunder socially to earn
his scorn. He need only look as if he might blunder. Smiley is judging
him on the basis of appearances, and imagined ones at that. This

high-handedness causes special regret, coming when Rode is leaving a funeral service en route to a cemetery—to bury his wife. The usually sympathetic Smiley won't be stopped. The next morning he objects to the angle made by Rode's elbow as the bereaved man drinks his coffee. But he has found more to denigrate. "The swift, expert pluck at the knee of [his] trouser leg," undertaken to save the pleat, also discredits Rode; Smiley reads the gesture as an attempt to hide "what he [Rode] was," an arrant social climber.

Smiley's hostility heats up when details about Rode's chapel-going wife come forth. This harpy from Branxome's Gorse Hill is as prickly as a gorse bush. Her father, pointing out that her malice drove away all the family servants, advised Rode not to marry her. Rode should have taken his advice. When he joined the Church of England, admittedly to lower resistance to him at Carne, Stella increased her chapel activities. She humiliated him in public. Her beating and killing of their dog constitutes an attack upon loyalty and devotion. Such virtues she always noted and cultivated, but only to pervert. Rode speaks of her recurring practice of winning people's confidence and then throwing their faults and vulnerabilities up to them. She enjoyed making people cringe ("Every drop of gossip and dirt, she hoarded it away," says Rode). The help she extended to others was motivated, not by generosity, but by a craving for power. Moral blackmail, her husband claims, was her specialty. As in other mainstream English mysteries, like Conan Doyle's "Charles Augustus Milverton" and P. D. James' *Shroud for a Nightingale* (1971), the blackmailer gets no quarter in *A Murder of Quality*, either from the investigator or the writer; both know how easy it is to err and how wretched life can become with someone waiting to profit by our errors.

Yet as murderable as Stella Rode is, she also represents the rising middle classes, coming from both the uncouth industrial north and a religious background that is evangelical, not High Church. Her malevolence even looks trifling when measured against the wrongdoings of Ann Smiley, who sins on a grand scale. Stella's death expresses le Carré's antagonism toward the social changes sweeping England in the twenty years following World War II. The doughty chapel virtues of personal reliability, self-denial, and hard work win little regard in the book. No D. H. Lawrence, John Wain, or John Osborne, le Carré merely pretends, in order to scatter suspicion among her survivors, that Stella embodied these strengths. Her sanctimoniousness infected her with an inverse snobbery more repellent than the drawing-room airs affected by several members of the Carne set. She may have even scared le Carré, who lacks the social precedents to deal with her justly. He kills her before she can defend herself against her accusers. But no defense would have acquitted her; for him, the values she stands for haven't replaced the faded and frayed old school tie.

III

Judging from the wreckage found in his fiction, le Carré seems to have stopped looking for replacements. Amid deceit and corruption, little hope survives. There's no escaping the shadows cast by security. What happens to Smiley in both *Tinker, Tailor* and *Smiley's People* proves that former spies enjoy no rest. The handful of intelligence operations Willem, or William, Craven of *Smiley's People* has performed makes him fair game for security at any time. Not only Smiley but also le Carré himself refers to him by his Estonian name to serve notice that he's permanently on call. But how much domestic peace would he enjoy if the Circus left him alone? Le Carré describes family and home as being as strife ridden as the Circus. Ms. Hughes shows him dwelling on the ugly aspects of family; murder occurs in the home in his first two novels, and children elsewhere become society's victims.[13] The tension in his work between his intellectual rejection of and emotional sympathy for the English elite doesn't limit his field of fire. Spying serves so well as a social microcosm in his work because the images and counterimages it evokes reverberate to the bedrock of society. He may have taken a French pen name to warn the reader indirectly that he favors cosmopolitan innovations not usually identified with English fiction. The English meaning of his pen name, the square, though less apparent, has equal import. D. J. M. Cornwell is not John the Square, defending the yeoman Protestantism underlying the social contract. His criticism of the family, the basic social unit, conveys his unrest with the whole system.

But the system, if shaky to begin with, has been weakened still more by spying. At the least, the bureau distracts the agent from his family obligations. What little family life goes on in le Carré takes place by default, when some piece of business hasn't drawn the agent away from home. Sometimes he stays away deliberately. Far from inspiring idealism or creative energy, families in le Carré sometimes harbor more conspiracies than the Circus. The one-time director of British Intelligence, Control, never reveals his name—to his staff or to us. This secrecy infects his home together with his spy's penchant for betrayal. He never told his wife how he earned his living. Growing no more trusting with the years, he withheld from his longterm live-in lover both his name and the news of his estranged wife's death. Like that of Control, most marriages in le Carré come apart. Jerry Westerby has had several wives, like his father before him. Also in *The Honourable Schoolboy* (1977), the minor figure Humphrey Pelling's incest craving for his daughter has turned his wife into a drunkard and may have caused her stroke. Their daughter, shaken by this domestic strife, has already left her husband and young son before we meet her. But her act of desertion, like Ann's walking out on Smiley several times to live with other men, can mislead the unwary. Men also abandon women. Liz Gold in *The Spy Who Came in from the Cold*, the young mother who lives with Bill Haydon, and the English woman known only as "the orphan" who stays with Jerry Westerby in his Italian farmhouse are all jilted. A similarity these women share with their men, along with Mrs. Oliver Lacon, is a big age difference; each abandoned woman gives away thirty years to her man. Though le Carré avoids Freudian explanations for sexual failure, Humphrey Pelling's incestuous drive implies that intergenerational sex leads to harm.

No age gap is needed in le Carré to doom the family most of the time. Expressive of their troubled homes, the Smileys, like the Fenners in *Call for the Dead* (1961), have no children. Leamas has two children he never sees nor thinks about. Though Westerby alludes to several marriages and children, he has only stayed close to one daughter; the names of his wives and other children are never mentioned. Aldo Cassidy of *The Naive and Sentimental Lover* works more steadily at fathering. But even though he extends himself for his two sons, he ignores both his wife and his father; nor does he mind leaving the boys for long spells. The plaster cast swathing the broken leg of one of them symbolizes the pain Aldo's absences have caused. John Avery of *The Looking-Glass War* (1965), ten years Aldo's junior, spends as little time at home as his fellow Londoner. His prospects for marital happiness are just as bleak. When his pregnant wife complains that he never talks to her, he snaps back, "What is there to talk about?" The pregnant wife neglected by her work-driven, preoccupied husband presents a stunning image of domestic desolation; when Avery isn't quarrelling with Sarah, he's waking her with a phone call to say he won't be coming home.

Le Carré has the art to enhance this image. By calling Avery's wife Sarah, he invokes her Old Testament namesake. Chances are dim that Sarah Avery will achieve the domestic fulfillment attained by the biblical Sarah. Her desolation may touch her son. Her complaint that John neglects Anthony along with her invokes the home of Wilf Taylor, the courier who got killed by a speeding car in the dark and wind of a Finnish snowstorm. The Taylors live in a crowded slum. Though spies are said to be well paid, Taylor's earnings couldn't lift his family out of urban squalor. What is more, his wife has to work to supplement his low salary. When Avery and a colleague knock on his door, they're greeted by "a frail, pallid rag of a girl not above ten years old." This little girl (a rarity in le Carré, the father of four sons) spends most of the day alone. Her unreadiness to look after herself comes forth quickly. Disobeying her mother's instructions, she opens the door of the flat to strangers; she also blurts out the secret that her father took an airplane north "to get money." Little money will be forthcoming. Avery pities her so much that he gives her ten shillings. But he does this without knowing the extent of her and her mother's bereavement. Besides losing Wilf Taylor, mother and daughter may also have to forgo the pension normally given to the survivors of agents who die operationally. For the bureau to grant this pension would be tantamount to their admitting that Taylor was conducting a secret mission. Furthermore, the old boy in charge of securing the pension lacks both the vim and the compassion to fight for the bereft survivors.

Wilf Taylor's death shows that family life, bleak as it may be, worsens with the removal of the husband-father. The removal is often voluntary. Women will compare their men to animals and not ones noted for beauty or courage. A lover asks Aldo Cassidy if he likes being described as a lemur, and, in *Call for the Dead*, Ann keeps calling Smiley a toad; perhaps she's telling him that all her kisses haven't yet changed him into the prince she'll be faithful to. Men can be just as insulting. In front of a stranger, Humphrey Pelling calls his wife an "anthropoid ape." Ironically, Pelling worked for the postal service before retiring. The interchange and openness of communication symbolized by the post office deteriorates into cruelty when brought into the home. Called by his son-in-law "a raving criminal lunatic," Pelling drove his daughter into a hopeless marriage. Charlie of *The Little Drummer Girl* (1983) stays with her parents but rejects them. Her disavowal sends her looking for parent substitutes in dangerous places like Israel's secret service. But it also sent her to the theater, where she has supported herself as an actress. Though lacking star quality, she does have the skill and dedication to work steadily in a crowded, competitive field. Whether she could have earned the money and the self-esteem to forgive her parents their shortcomings can never be known. But she and several other characters in the canon imply that the loss of the family can lead to grief. Bill Roach, whose parents are divorced, is the richest but also the unhappiest boy at Thursgood's in *Tinker, Tailor* (1974). Karla's daughter, Alexandra, clinches the point, her schizophrenia conveying the wreckage caused by the loss of family. Unlike Bill Roach, who can visit either of his parents when school is out, Sasha lacks all family ties. She was taken from her mother as a tot. Her father she never knew at all, even though each has remained obsessively aware of the other. Her living in an asylum outside of her native Russia dramatizes her alienation. But it just grazes the dementia that has institutionalized her. As a split personality, she's divided from herself. Talking sensibly while her hands claw at each other, she has the weird sanity of a mad savant. Adrift in her madness are island of genius. Regrettably, she lacks the control to turn one of them into home port.

Her malaise points to a familiar source. Much of the family unrest in the canon comes from spying. For their own sakes as well as their networks', spies are taught to suppress feeling. The greatest threat to a field worker, alone and at risk in a strange, possibly hostile place, remains the temptation to confide in a woman. Familiar with his anguish and its fallout, intelligence networks use attractive women to lure the badgered field man into giving himself away. The "honey trap" is such a staple of security work that its outlawing by official policy in *Smiley's People* (1980) both shocks and angers Smiley, who knows how mounting psychological pressure cries for outlets in the field. He also knows that the Soviet bloc's security services won't abandon *their* honey traps. Fred Leiser learns quickly that a spy who wants to keep living must renounce intimacy. Called "quite a one for the girls," he appears rarely in *Looking-Glass War* (1965) in female company, and he seems distant, preoccupied, and sullen even then. Yet he makes friends quickly with John Avery, and he accepts most of the other men who prime him for his job. Spies prefer the company of men to that of women. Incomplete and uprooted, they defend a society where they don't fit and whose basic unit, the family, they can't fully share in. The ending of Chapter 4 of *The Spy Who Came in from the Cold* contains the following record of Liz Gold's thoughts after Liz first has sex with Alec Leamas: "She made him stay the night and they became lovers. He left at five in the morning. She couldn't understand it; she was so proud and he seemed ashamed." A fuller acquaintance with him would have explained his letdown.

By giving in to his feelings while on assignment, he has broken a basic rule of his trade. Only from a distance can he love Liz. Le Carré probably made her Jewish (one of the very few Jews in the canon between *Call for the Dead* and *Drummer Girl*) to add credibility to her involvement in leftist causes and, more thematically, to make her the sort of person Leamas might feel he could move close to without compromising his safety.

Leamas will confirm his love by muzzling it, in keeping with the upside-downness of spy ethics. The topic that stirs his most heated verbal exchanges with Liz is the inevitability of their parting. These talks give the impression that the meals the couple have taken and the intimacies they've shared only took place to prepare them to say goodbye. But their moments of closeness occur rarely. Trained to travel light, Leamas is an indifferent lover, extending Liz scant warmth. Most of the time, he treats her rudely or dismissively; out of her company, he thinks of her infrequently and vaguely. Yet he hasn't buried his heart in his cover. The anger he explodes into when he finds out that she has been lured into East Germany for questioning shows that he cares. Distant and casual when alone with her, he protects her fiercely in the company of those who threaten her. The spy hasn't sunk the man. As sour and embittered as he is, Leamas responds vividly to Liz when he finds her in danger. He will try to pad the jolt of this operational mistake. When asked by Liz if he and the sadistic Mundt are enemies, he remains silent. Values like enmity and friendship can't influence a spy. But Leamas can no more deny his heart than Graham Greene's heroes in *Brighton Rock* (1938), *The End of the Affair* (1951), and *The Honorary Consul* (1973). His showing that Liz means more to him than tradecraft prefigures his death. Riddled with bullets at the foot of the Berlin Wall, he never survives the agony of his birth into a world of love.

Other assaults on heterosexual love, the basis of the family, never make it to the Wall. They don't have to. So shaky is the man-woman tie in le Carré[1] that the closest relationships in his books usually exclude women. The process is hinted at darkly in *Call for the Dead*, the main characters of which see a London production of Christopher Marlowe's *Edward II*, a work featuring homosexuality. Le Carré restores this reference from his first novel in *A Small Town in Germany* (1968) by naming an agent Gaviston. Since Gaveston is the courtier Marlowe's Edward loves, the reference recalls the private jokes and in-group jargon infusing W. H. Auden's early verse. How far can the reference be carried? It would be both unfair and dangerous to overwork the facts that Auden was both homosexual and, like le Carre[1], attended Oxford. Yet le Carre[1] feels too strongly about English education to ignore the homosexuality that occupies the fore of Mary Renault's novel, *The Charioteer* (1953), Lindsay Anderson's 1968 film, *If* . . ., and the William Trevor story, "Torridge" (1978). He has also earned artistic capital by drawing upon his schooling. Smiley feels close to Dieter Frey in *Call for the Dead* and to Karla later in his career. John Avery complains to his chiefs that they tricked him into loving Fred Leiser. The bonds of Aldo Cassidy and Shamus in *The Naive and Sentimental Lover* and of Bill Haydon and Jim Prideaux are physical. These bonds, furthermore, dominate the books in which they appear, even though the latter has a rival. This, another male-to-male exchange, makes itself known when Smiley shares his most intimate revelations about Karla with his fellow spy Peter Guillam.

To heighten the excitement bred by the man-to-man relationship, le Carré will bring his male intimates together amid the melodramatic gleams of danger. Supplying an added shimmer is the night-time setting of these meetings—dark, slippery Battersea Bridge in *Call for the Dead,* a disused mansion in *Naive and Sentimental Lover,* the pounding surf of Causeway Bay near Hong Kong in *Schoolboy,* and a Berlin Wall within easy firing range of the sharpshooters manning a sentry tower in *Smiley's People.* Sometimes, though, le Carré's intention can mislead him. If he meant to downgrade the man-woman tie by entitling Chapter 10 of *A Murder of Quality* "Little Women," he was being unfair. The faculty wives and other female guests assembled at a Carne sherry party *are* little in the sense of being mean and petty, and they display this puniness more and more as the sherry flows. But any of them would be hard pressed to rival the senior tutor Felix D'Arcy in snobbery—or bitchiness. In fact, le Carré's calling D'Arcy's sister "a bony, virile woman with . . . an arrogant, hunting mouth" only accentuates failings in D'Arcy usually ascribed to women; virile comes from the Latin, *vir,* meaning man, and hunting is an activity belonging almost exclusively to men in primitive tribes.

A much better way of blurring sexual distinctions occurs in the names le Carré gives some of his people. T. J. Binyon has discussed this technique in his *TLS* review of *Drummer Girl:*

Proust-like, le Carré has given his heroine a masculine name: Charlie (there is also a Frankie, who vies with Charlie for the same man). Is it by intention or accident that this should be the same name as that given, in a feminine form, to the *male* character, Karla?[14]

Binyon might have added to his roster of names that of Danny, the daughter of Ricki Tarr, an Australian-Malaysian agent for the British in *Tinker, Tailor*. And Gadi Becker's questioning Charlie when he meets her, "But I thought Charlie was a boy's name?" reveals that le Carré chose his little drummer girl's name carefully. His fascination with names which might belong to either sex or which suggest the wrong sex shows his readiness to challenge all closed formal patterns. The intrusion of an incomprehensible detail can discredit comprehensibility itself. A Charlie, a Danny, a Frankie, or a Karla calls attention to the ambiguity surrounding us. The distortion of sexuality implied by their names also invokes a threat more dangerous than the one expressed by similarities joining political foes. Regimes change along with national frontiers and ideologies. Life's dependence upon the biological polarity of the sexes stays fixed. Le Carré's small but telling touch addresses life's continuance. In so doing, it shows espionage attacking the basic components of dialectic. The sexual and family discord recounted in le Carré describes the lack of proper relations between intimates today. It also demonstrates le Carré's ability to write about spying in such a way that he's both recounting and criticizing all of human experience. No warning can be more urgent. In its quietness and indirection, none can be more provocatively served.

Chapter Three
The Decoding of
Checkpoint Charlie

His sharpness of eye, sensitivity to language, and empathy for people with different points of view all strengthen le Carré's 1965 claim that he takes his writing seriously. Having just published *The Looking-Glass War,* a work that blurs the sharp plot lines of his last book, the best-selling *Spy Who Came in from the Cold,* le Carré voiced in *Harper's* his wish to be read as an artist. The wish included the following assertion: "A writer makes order out of the anarchy of his heart; he submits himself to a more ruthless discipline than any critic ever dreamed of."[1]

Le Carré fuses instinct, patience, and craft as he prescribes. Combining an acute sensibility, analytical intelligence, and an historical gift, he creates spies who seem to come before us without intervention or manipulation. This naturalness yokes realistic journalism to art, developing character against a solid background while building a suggestive, flowing narrative. From the accumulation of details will rise a concept that unifies the narrative without exhausting or trivializing it. Much of the interest in le Carré comes from the arrangement of details. He knows where to expand his material and where to elide it, when to maintain narrative pace and when to change it, and how to select rather than just add. He also knows the value of indirection. Truths in le Carré are often unstated but subtly understood,anyway. So deftly do hidden persuaders in his fiction reveal hidden dimensions that they make us wonder how much gold we have looked at without seeing.

I

Works like Chaucer's *Troilus and Cressida* and James's *Turn of the Screw* survive because of the place they've won in our imaginations; their best effects uncoil with a quiet, unforced inevitability. Lesser works destroy all illusion. Most fictional characters can't stand close scrutiny, hardly any of them surviving it in the end. If those of le Carré lodge in the imagination, they do so in spite of being seen closely under a bright light. What strengthens their bid for permanence is their author's treatment of them. Practicing a Chekhovian or Pinteresque indirection, le Carré reveals his people through disconnected dialogue and the details of everyday trivia. His books are unemphatic and rounded. The humor they provoke will remind us that the people actuating them live in a world beyond the actions they're caught up in. The reminder can take the form of a well-turned image. While looking in Hampstead Heath for a message an agent may have disposed of before his death, the Smiley of *Smiley's People* weaves about so slowly that passers-by think him "an adherent of the new fad in Chinese martial exercises." Funny in itself, the scene humanizes the investigation. Smiley's being "accounted mad" by passers-by affords a perspective that most adventure writers would neglect in their zeal to build tension. By not moving to climaxes too early, le Carré helps create a smooth texture. He also extends the frame of human reference for the tension that is slowly developing. There's something comical about us all the time, even in moments of heroism; as funny as it looks, Smiley's matching of the dead spy's physical actions to his thoughts (a technique introduced in Poe's "Purloined Letter") proves itself a heroic imaginative feat.

Smiley's odd-looking behavior in the Heath also discloses a Jamesian economy. Le Carré follows James in seating great significance in small matters. In the process, he puts James' later style to new uses. Hewing to a contemporary idiom, his sometimes long sentences use a great deal of subordination; they observe both the vocabulary and cadences of spoken language; as in James, conversation in le Carré can resemble invisible swordplay, with a small hesitation or inflectional tic revealing something the speaker wanted to hide. Jerry Westerby recalls "the thing that stuck in his mind" amid a host of impressions recorded during a long dinner: "It was the expression on Lizzie's face as she first caught sight of him [an approaching acquaintance] for the fraction of a second before the lines of courage drew the gay smile out of her." This tiny facial giveaway discloses volumes of guilty knowledge to the seasoned spy, putting him on his guard for the rest of the dinner.

Later in *Schoolboy*, another indirection opens the world of intrigue to us. The novel attains its climax in the reunion of the Ko brothers. Yet le Carré blunts the joy of the fraternal reunion. Drake Ko hasn't appeared before us for some 300 pages; his brother Nelson hasn't appeared at all. The scene bringing them together takes place in the dark; it's shown from the point of view of an onlooker, who's watching from a distance; it's reported in one sentence; neither brother's face is seen. This flattening has thematic import; the reunion ends quickly, Nelson's being spirited away from Drake by a squad of western security agents within seconds of closing with him.

Le Carré's treatment of the abortive reunion portrays the futility of opposing the intelligence combine. Yes, the capture of the Leningrad-trained Nelson Ko represents a great score for the Circus. But the score violates the sanctity of the blood tie. Love means more to the Kos than the money or status they have won; in fact, Drake has only been working for Karla to move closer to Nelson. But poetic justice has its day; some of the agents who have perverted the Kos' brotherly love for operational reasons find themselves in discredit. This justice sours, though, with our discovery, first, that one of the discredited agents is Smiley and, next, that Jerry Westerby died trying to protect the brothers from the swooping intelligence men. The brokenness, the darkness, and the brevity characterizing the maimed reunion of the Kos create a mood of defeat that tallies with the long-range meaning of the incident.

This meaning descends upon us softly but irrevocably. Le Carré's technique isn't random or imposed. It seems to grow naturally from the subject matter that feeds it. An alert, disciplined writer, le Carré can recover the most fleeting, delicate impressions from the nameless corners of consciousness. His description of the Kos' reunion also reflects his ability to elude the dead hand of overexplicitness. Though carefully adumbrated, his material isn't labored or overcomposed. Nor would it profit from rhetorical imposition. Precise without looking prearranged, his well-built sentences do what he asks of them. And he asks the right things because he knows when to stop. In Chapter 31 of *Tinker, Tailor*, he says of Jim Prideaux, "With a handkerchief ... he wiped away the perspiration and whatever else was glistening on his face." Jim is under a strain because he's telling Smiley about his ambush, capture, and interrogation in Czechoslovakia. In the next chapter he hints at the brutality of the interrogation by saying that "a lot of the muscle [applied to him] was done electrically." Gruesome disclosures like this usually come at the end of paragraphs, where they release the most horror. The hardship of discussing the hideous ordeal that broke his back could well make Jim Prideaux's face exude something more than sweat; he's dredging up pain from a deep source. How deep, we only learn later with his discovery that his former Oxford chum and, most likely, ex-lover, Bill Haydon, betrayed him to the Czechs. Jim's having to carry his heavy physical and psychological burdens on his bent back vindicates le Carré's vagueness about the muck gleaming on his stricken face. The unnamed muck tallies with the scene's mood. A realistic detail in this context would distract us from the trauma Jim's debriefing is causing him.

Le Carré's stylistic and technical brilliance have attracted more attention as signs of his virtuosity than as functional features of his work. One can see why. The dry wit and smart backchat favored by many of his characters help create the crisp, cool charm of the English comedy of manners. Here's a well-bred spy in *Schoolboy* greeting a colleague after a long separation: "Jolly decent of you to come. Foreign Office is in Downing Street these days, isn't it? What did you do? Tube from Charing Cross, I suppose? Come on in, let's have a cuppa." This glitter can veer into darkness, where it's quickly swallowed. "In Lacon's world, direct questions were the height of bad taste but direct answers were the worst," says le Carré in *Smiley's People*, sniping at the high-toned English practice of dodging all serious subjects. But urbanity in le Carré vies with an instinct for the incongruous and the bizarre. His sharp, nerve-jarring images reveal a futuristic fascination for the repellent. Perversity can lead to wisdom in le Carré. His uncanny streak resembles a poet's charged awareness of things being transformed. The originality of the sentence from *Schoolboy*, "The plane was two-thirds empty, and the bullet holes in the wings wept like undressed wounds," with its subtle parallelism in syntax, uncovers a kinship swathing emptiness, tears, and fresh combat wounds that spells out both the horror and the waste of all war.

Earlier, Westerby had passed "an old corpse with no arms. The flies had settled on the face wounds in a black lava." Another horrible portent, the corpse is denied the dignity of so many armless statues of antiquity. Whereas public statues often celebrate a cherished common ideal, the reference to lava degrades the war victims in Cambodia; lava buries the hardest of substances. Amid the metaphorical and literal heat of Cambodia under siege, it's also fitting that Westerby thinks of the dead Hong Kong banker "Frost in the mortuary, and the whiteness of his screaming jaw." This image, invoked by a private war, has been carefully foreshadowed. The clash between the iciness of Frost's name, his white jaw, and the mortuary where Westerby last saw him, on the one hand, and the airless heat of the Cambodian battle zone where Westerby's recollection takes place, on the other, recalls le Carré's description of the corpse in the previous chapter. Violence covers all; pressure is felt everywhere. While introducing the hot-cold contrast he will later build on, le Carré won't specify the outrage performed on Frost's body. His restraint helps him make the most of his contrast. Phrases like "the things they had done to him" and "the thing round his neck" confirm his knowledge that an imagined horror grips us more tightly than a documented one. This knowledge governs his treatment of the sadism inflicted upon Frost by his torturer-questioners:

> He had died twice, Jerry decided. Once to make him talk and once to shut him up. The things they had done to him first were all over his body, in big and small patches, the way fire hits a carpet, eats holes, and then suddenly gives up. Then there was the thing round his neck, a different, faster death altogether. They had done that last, when they didn't want him any more.

Le Carré's restraint fuels his leading subject in the book—the way operational aspects of intelligence work drive out human ones. How can the torture and murder of Frost be justified by any standards? the passage invites us to ask. The answer is that nothing warrants such an outrage. The freakish images and scenes lacing the novels do more than render the dramatic possibilities of danger. Le Carré's management of language promotes a new awareness of the inhumanity of spying. The irony and alienation fostered by his motifs find support in his technique, too. Avoiding straight linear development, he will underplay climactic events by disposing of them in a line or two or by reporting them in a subordinate clause. Sometimes, he'll leave them out entirely. A scene rich in dramatic potential, Smiley's recruiting of Lizzie, or Liese, Worth in *Honourable Schoolboy*, occurs off stage. Practicing a harsh economy of means, le Carré wants to direct our attention elsewhere; Liese's agreement to help the Circus contributes less to his narrative strategy than the effect her agreement has on others taking part in the investigation.

Narrative structure, from the chapter down to the individual sentence, fragments le Carré's novels emotionally. Often the fragmentation is a product of selection, i.e., what le Carré leaves out. He tells very little, for instance, about George Smiley, his most important character. Smiley's 1961 debut, *Call for the Dead*, provides some information about his career—how he started as a spy, where he was posted, what motivated him, and why he has made headway in Britain's spy community. Then there is his long recitation in Chapter 23 of *Tinker, Tailor*, where he tells Peter Guillam about his meeting with Karla in a Delhi jail and the disturbing comparisons between

Karla and Ann the meeting has actuated in his psyche. Such intrusions of background material are rare. Even after conceding that Smiley develops over several novels rather than in just one, nothing like a full-drawn portrait of him exists. Most of the focus is present tense, bearing out Jerry Westerby's belief that a spy has neither a past nor a future. The operation and the materials it calls into play provide the perspective. There can be no catharsis. The inevitably bitter endings of the books don't dispel the building tensions; nor do they help character escape into the open, where our compassion can take hold. Our involvement comes from following the course of events, not from aligning them with fictional conventions. The endings join nothing neatly; right before Westerby dies, he makes us question his loyalties. We wonder what side he's on. But his sudden death bilks us of an answer. Le Carré has fragmented the continuities both of heroism and of straightforward scenic development to foil emotional reaction. The heart can't respond when the mind is puzzled by dispersion and rift. Life goes on in the Circus, which is what it has been doing all along.

Le Carré offers fragments rather than unities in order to avoid arbitrariness and conventionality. His practice of including heretofore repressed materials defies the impulse to consolidate and conform. But his inclusion of the discontinuities and accidents his predecessors have ignored challenges the very order of things. His displacements of the old certainties of stable fact and predictable event give new prominence to the marginal, pushing it closer to the center. This discrediting of traditional narrative continuities allies him with the *nouveau roman* school of French fiction. Like Alain Robbe-Grillet (b. 1922) or Philippe Sollers (b. 1936), he's trying to expand the freedom of both the senses and the mind; his dislocations of narrative elements find new limits. His choosing, excluding, and extending in places where other writers would consolidate creates fresh fields of inquiry, too. Fractured discourse implies that the story being told can neither be squeezed into a single mode nor exhausted by a single point of view. Truth has been served, le Carré having presented it as complex, many sided, and situational .

But what kind of impact does it all make on us? Has le Carré's fracturing of conventional rhetoric and reader expectation robbed his novels of old-fashioned human interest? Has it buried the human factor behind so many fragments that the most it can elicit from us is a detached, intellectual curiosity? Readers of le Carré have asked these questions, particularly while discussing the difficult later novels.

II

Few writers today have been judged as differently as John le Carré. First come the admirers of the best-selling novelist, two of whose works, *Tinker, Tailor* and *Smiley's People,* have won acclaim as TV mini-series with no less of a star than Alec Guinness portraying Smiley. Then there are those who have found these productions as sluggish and as hard to follow as the novels. They'll open a new le Carré novel because they believe that if le Carré wrote it, it has to be good. Some of these readers give up before the end. The ones that do manage to slog through all the way often hide their bafflement by praising le Carré as a technician. Baffling he is if a reader as wise as William F. Buckley, Jr., finds him difficult.[2] One can see why. Avoiding high-speed adventure, his art has grown more severe and individual since *The Spy Who Came in from the Cold* (1963), where he proved he could write a big commercial hit. The involved, obliquely told novels he started writing with *The Looking-Glass War* (1965) don't have strong plot lines, sharply defined moral issues, or heightened action. Instead, they follow an increasing tendency to concentrate on the phenomenology of spying at the expense of melodrama. The later le Carré isn't eager to help the reader who feels confused by the dense, confining trickery of intelligence work. We have to find our own way in. Hidden by shards of fractured discourse, the way in can be hard to find. The control le Carré exerts on his materials implies that pleasing the reader would be cheap or wrong for him; some of his best effects are too subtle to be appreciated by most of us. The job of fitting the pieces together engrosses us so much that we forget about the people.

Yet the people, shadowy as they are, eventually claim our attention. Portrayed in the later work is a clash between individuals, not ideologies. More often than not, the clash resolves itself in a convergence of both interests and identities. By slowing narrative tempo, le Carré forsakes the trite for the human. He'll also remind us that the tempo is being slowed. A paragraph in Chapter 6 of *Smiley's People*, registered from the point of view of a pedestrian about to be hit by a car, begins, "What happened next ... was supposed to happen in a flash." Following through on this implied warning, the next paragraph but one starts, "What happened took place with the slowness of an underwater ballet." Le Carré then takes more than 600 words to describe the steps by which a stranger throws Maria Ostrakova in the path of an oncoming car. Slighting physical movement, he conveys the inwardness—the disbelief, outrage, and numbing terror—of the event. What takes place in the seams between exciting developments counts more to le Carré than the developments themselves. For in these seams, which less thoughtful writers have overlooked for the sake of speed and surface, le Carré inserts fears, hopes, and speculations, lending the suspense story a depth it has perhaps lacked since Joseph Conrad's *The Secret Agent* (1907). Although his recent books move slowly, they're richer, fuller, and subtler than the earlier work. Their unhurried, polyphonic prose imparts a steadiness of conviction and a rightness of tone. Rarely ornamental or indulgent, le Carré's language since *Tinker, Tailor* (1974) is thoughtful, inventive, and secure, giving a strong, credible picture of the one-sided struggle between the individual and the system.

The truth this language tries to establish takes root in le Carré's fine awareness of human complexity. The later novels make up for their lack of forward flow by taking on a new concentration, richness, and wovenness of design. Neither their breaking up of scenic continuity nor their loosening of plot structure damages narrative unity. For all their disjunctures, a recurring harmonic pattern holds the novels together. The pattern, a series of orchestrated motifs, can ground itself in character, setting, or event. Sometimes an idea will develop from the counterpoint created between what is happening and what we expect to happen. This counterpoint has left some readers cold. Richard Condon entitled his review of *Smiley's People* for *New York Magazine* "The Master of Stasis." Carl Ericson uses the parallels he finds in *Tinker, Tailor* with Christ's Maundy Thursday dinner to scathe the novel: "The finale of *Tinker, Tailor, Soldier, Spy* is drab as well as lacking in importance—again, like the revolting end of Judas." Extending Ericson's disapproval to the whole canon, Nick B. Williams, reviewing *Smiley's People* in the *Los Angeles Times Book Review*, cites a "distinguished editor" who has called le Carré "utterly unreadable"; nor does he quarrel with the editor's verdict. Finally, Clive James, in a review pointedly called "Go Back to the Cold!" states his preference for the shorter, more neatly built works le Carré published between 1961-65. James believes that, starting with *A Small Town in Germany* (1968), le Carré's novels suffer from a "stupefying gradualness"; also that the language in these novels, "verbosity run riot," serves a "legend-building tone." He ends his barrage by denying the later le Carré the artistic prominence he accuses his man of coveting: "Outwardly aspiring to the status of literature, le Carré's novels have inwardly declined to the level of pulp romance."[3]

Le Carré's detractors have forgotten that writers with a great deal to say have always made their readers dig hard to find the veins of gold. The patience Clive James might extend to a Conrad or an Eliot he withholds from le Carré; until posterity decrees that a new writer deserves close rereading, he won't get it. Such delaying gives regret, not because le Carré is a major writer but because the reluctance to read him as he deserves is unfair. The proliferation in his work of qualities out of keeping with popular spy fiction makes such reluctance understandable and, to a point, excusable. He will sometimes confuse or bore the impatient. But he has shaped his material to create the psychological, political, and moral realities of spying, and his tiered complex of response by-passes traditional formulas. A novel like *Tinker, Tailor* contains materials usually left out of spy fiction— rejected plans, operations proposed but not mounted, contingencies and fallbacks that are carefully planned but never implemented. Finally, Smiley's smoking out of the mole fails to satisfy the expectations of most readers for decisive action. No networks have been rolled up; no arsenal of advance weaponry has been destroyed; the action doesn't move to the one-on-one clash found at the end of Conan Doyle's "The Final Problem" or a James Bond. Nor is the tightening of the net around the villain described as a triumph. While waiting to snare Bill Haydon, an overcoated Smiley stands in a dark kitchen, "feeling absurd in his stockinged feet." Le Carré moves the narrative into the stream of Smiley's consciousness as the mole enters the occupied building unawares—but not to build suspense. Smiley hears "the latch turn, one turn, two; it's a Banham lock, he remembered—my God, we must keep Banham's in business." The anticipation that his search of many months, perhaps the major effort of his long career, will end in a moment has stirred in Smiley this wayward thought. No waggish indulgence, the effect, like the image of a shoeless Smiley wearing an overcoat, helps derail the heroism of the mole snatch. Withholding *its* approval, the sun won't shine the day after Haydon's arrest.

What looks haphazard in le Carré will surprise us by revealing itself as carefully planned. Without laboring the comparison, he follows James Joyce in leaving a great deal unexplained. Factual background can be sketchy; characters aren't always identified with their worknames; spy jargon may go uncoded: in *Schoolboy*, Oliver Lacon asks Smiley to describe a project he's working on in simple English. Admittedly, Lacon's intrusion does prod Smiley into clarifying his meaning. But it also shows that le Carré is paying more attention to the reader than his detractors have admitted. Elsewhere, the same fidelity to details we have found excessive and disconcerting will lend amplitude and heft, partly for being couched in such rich, assured prose. Le Carré writes suspense stories that discredit suspense because he's hunting bigger fictional game. In *Tinker, Tailor*, he bewilders us temporarily by recounting the tastes and background of an agent who has just been questioned innocently by a colleague. The new information gives the agent's responses a resonance it would have otherwise lacked. Resonance emits meaning in le Carré. The playfulness of the chapter title, "Friends of Charlie Marshall," in *The Honourable Schoolboy*, clashes with the gravity the chapter describes. Though the quest for Charlie Marshall takes Westerby through barking machine guns and exploding rockets, its disjointed, meditative treatment probes underyling realities, too.

Our expectations are realigned again in Chapter 16; instead of divulging "the forbidden secrets" "sobbed out" by gabbling, frantic Charlie in the throes of drug withdrawal, le Carré keeps us waiting a chapter and twenty pages, during which time he touches in the information that makes the secrets so sensitive and crucial. The twenty-page delay keeps us turning pages as avidly as we would in a more conventionally told adventure yarn. What is more important, it clears le Carré of the charge that he's describing the confusion of the world with confused writing. Among other things, disjuncture and discontinuity in le Carré always challenge received notions about closure and solidity. His withholding of steady perspectives on the experiences he describes invites issues beyond the ken of action writing. A series of action scenes racing past us forfeits opportunities to comment on the world's underlying strangeness. On the other hand, the fusing of slowness and speed, casualness and concentration, depicts this strangeness.

Le Carré's practice of suppressing major plot developments looks back to the literary classics whose key movements also resist reader expectation. The main action of Conrad's *The Secret Agent*, the destruction of a retarded youth during an abortive attempt to blow up Greenwich Observatory, isn't described; Henry James's *The Awkward Age* (1899) never mentions the occurrence that propels *its* major characters. Hewing to this decentering tradition, le Carré's villains seldom appear, and what they reveal of themselves often mitigates their villainy; Drake Ko never went back on his word in his life, and Karla contented himself by watching his daughter walking to school with her schoolmates from a parked car. By downgrading the climax, le Carré emphasizes the dragging everydayness of intelligence routine—the legwork, interviewing of witnesses, poring over documents, setting up of stakeouts, and defusing of rivalries among departments and persons. This slogging work symbolizes for le Carré the undifferentiated middle where we spend most of our time, in contrast to the Golden Age, that millennium that structures our lives while remaining out of reach. This middle occupies le Carré; his use of action scenes to stir interior changes in his people stresses process over product. It also teaches the wisdom of means-oriented living. A crescendo that disappoints moves us to look elsewhere for significance. Presented in slow motion, this search discloses dimensions beyond the scope of linear narrative technique.

The ambiguous, emotionally fractured world of the novels implies that significance both lies within ourselves and can be perceived in those random moments between dramatic events. Reordering priorities, le Carré's manner of selection asserts that we're more real when we're alone than when we're with others; a person must *be* something before becoming a part of something else. He has won us a bargain, charging all with potential importance and making the individual both the source and the judge of his actions. This autonomy can celebrate and renew itself over a broad range. The intrusion of the ridiculous, the incongruous, and the uncanny in le Carré creates new meanings and values. What is perhaps more important, it also posits new directions in which to look for meanings and values. The nonlinear structure of the books following *The Spy Who Came in from the Cold,* their disregard of dramatic follow-through, and their shifting of focus all uncover in le Carré a skepticism close to that of Conrad. The world is unknowable. If it's divinely monitored, God has hidden His loving face. Reality is too fleeting, ambiguous, and amorphous to fit the patterns devised by that God surrogate, the omniscient, all-decreeing Victorian novelist. Life can't be comprehended by mental constructs.

But readers have argued that the techniques le Carré uses to capture the tone and character of high-level security rest on a constricting, rather than a liberating, view of life. Strengthening their case is the point that his destabilizing of traditional narrative and moral continuities lowers reader involvement. Yet he isn't challenging convention in the name of anarchy. He organizes his materials to fend off anarchy's dead hand; writing itself is for him a belief in the value of order.[4] Although his intent may not be immediately apparent, it reveals itself gradually; the scenes in his work that don't move the plot enrich it with vibrant images or thoughtful insights.

Le Carré's decentering method keeps faith with both the writer's traditional quest for order and the world's *dis*order. By implication, it also creates a dialectic from which values may be attained. The burden of attainment is ours. Le Carré has freed us in order to test us, placing the responsibility of self-being right where it belongs, on our shoulders. He has adopted many of the techniques of the French *nouveau roman*, while preserving the human commitment of its existentialist forebears. Sending us into ourselves, his work qualifies as adventure fiction in ways threatening to the timid and the unwary.

Chapter Four
A Brief History of George Smiley

George Smiley is the pudgy, worried-looking little man in the baggy clothes who cleans his eyeglasses on the wide end of his necktie. He also researches his cases, does his own legwork, and examines physical evidence with an unerring eye. Aside from what may be gleaned from the bits of information he scatters in movement, we know little about him, although he may be an only child. He has no nephews or nieces, and he never mentions any siblings. Perhaps the absence of blood ties accounts for his magnanimity. Even to enemies, he will act like a man with love to give. In *Tinker, Tailor* he repays a junior agent's verbal and then physical attack by offering the agent's family money, protection, and comfort. His having spent at least part of his childhood in the Black Forest has helped him speak fluent German, a skill he still possesses. It may have also stimulated his interest in German baroque poetry, his area of study at Oxford and his main hobby during his interludes of forced retirement. "Germany was his second nature, even his second soul," le Carré says of him in *Smiley's People*, adding, "He could put on her language like a uniform and speak with its boldness." He gets his chance to display this expertise. *The Spy Who Came in from the Cold* and *The Looking-Glass War* find him in Germany briefly, and *Smiley's People* takes him there for a longer spell, during which he performs brilliantly. This brilliance was shrewdly foreshadowed. Much of the early part of his professional career, following his recruitment in 1928, saw him in Germany. Under cover of a university lectureship, he served as a talent spotter for the Circus. After spending 1939 in neutral Sweden, he returned to Germany using a different cover. Facing the greatest danger imaginable, he ran a spy network for three years (Julian Moynahan mentions his "brilliant record as a spy in Germany during World War II").[1]

Perhaps his ordeal contributed to his having aged at a different rate from the rest of us. In *Call for the Dead*, his debut, le Carré says of him, "He had entered middle age without ever being young."

The book's time setting, somewhere between 1958 and 1960 by internal evidence, finds him no newcomer to middle age as it's commonly understood. His recruitment into the secret service must have taken place close to graduation, when he was about twenty-two. His marriage "toward the end of the war" in 1944 or '45, coming at age thirty-eight or so, is late for a first marriage but not unreasonably so. What boggles the reason is why the marriage has lasted. Ann left him for a Cuban racing car driver two years after marrying him. In Chapter 14 of *Call for the Dead,* which unfolds at least a decade later, she writes him from Zurich under the name of Madame Juan Alvida, asking to be taken back. Why after spending a decade under another man's roof should she want to return to Smiley? Le Carré's time scheme violates sexual psychology. Any passion Ann had for Smiley would have either declared itself or burned itself out long before her request to reunite with him. The same reasoning applies to the many lovers who have lured Ann from Smiley since her return. Common sense dictates that after having had so many affairs over so many years, she would either quit him for good or resign herself to building a future with him in their home at 9 Bywater Street, off the King's Road, in Chelsea, London. Could her slew of lovers have rejuvenated Smiley as well as her? In *Tinker, Tailor,* he's referred to as "at best middle-aged." But in *Smiley's People,* published six years later, this blinking, apologetic man who works for twenty straight hours perceives an agent of sixty-nine as ancient. The book's time setting, probably summer and fall of 1977, makes Smiley the same age, according to the chronology set forth in *Call for the Dead.*

I

If Smiley has aged slowly, he has also matured well. Imaginative, unforgetful, and just, he sees more than his eyes see and is wiser than his mind knows. The expertise in sailing he displays in *Schoolboy* relates him historically to such highly informed (and slow-aging) fictional sleuths as R. Austin Freeman's Dr. John Thorndyke and Ngaio Marsh's Roderick Alleyn. But Smiley's heart knowledge helps him outpace these paragons of recondite knowledge. *A Murder of Quality* recounts how one of his wartime chiefs described him as "possessing the cunning of Satan and the conscience of a virgin." As might be expected, this incongruity has spurred le Carré's imagination. Knowledge leads to power in the Smiley books but not knowledge gained through innocence, as with the archetypal Jamesian heroine; the prevalence of older characters in the spy trade underscores the importance of seasoning in security work. Smiley isn't trying to salvage innocence, which vanished long ago, if it ever existed, but a modicum of integrity. Amid tawdriness, he stands for honor, duty, and decency. He will also defend these virtues with an impressive array of skills. His preoccupied, self-deprecating manner masks the truth that he has mastered the art of close observation, practical psychology, and intimidation (which includes knowing how to manipulate silence during an interrogation). Decidedly unheroic, he's nonetheless capable, game, and quick to seize his chance. He can charm, cajole, wheedle, threaten and compromise.

These strengths make him the person his ex-colleagues call upon for help when the bureau is foundering. He has a quick mind and the ability to make tough decisions. He's also an incredibly hard worker, a diplomat, a negotiator, and a patriot. His staying up all night in a Paddington hotel in *Tinker, Tailor* reading filched files and reports that must be returned by dawn shows him relying on slow, painstaking slog. But he won't creep and crawl if he doesn't have to. Recognizing the benefits of the short cut, he'll also take the calculated risk. *Call for the Dead* shows him saving his life by reacting quickly to danger. Noting that his house has been stolen into, he knocks on the front door and, seeing the intruder, asks for Mr. Smiley. He doesn't enter the house, though, when told that Mr. Smiley is home and invited inside. Instead, he hands the intruder the parcel of laundry he has just picked up, implying that he only stopped to make a delivery. Then he leaves Chelsea—but not before writing in his diary the license plate numbers of the cars parked on his street.

This tradecraft excites envy, just as his independence of mind makes him enemies. Ann's unfaithfulness symbolizing his vulnerability, he's the natural victim of office politics. Except for his appointment as acting director of the Circus after the Bill Haydon scandal, each shift in the power structure sees him diminished. And his more resentful colleagues even refuse to credit him with the Haydon snatch. This pettiness doesn't faze him. His reputation and his effectiveness have both survived the dynamics of change. Nobody in the service can outperform this shy man with pudgy hands and moist, froglike eyes. His skills have already made him a legend in *A Murder of Quality*, where a Dorset policeman says of him, "Looks like a frog, dresses like a bookie, and has a brain I'd give my eyes for. Had a very nasty war. Very nasty indeed." Both his reticence and his practicality keep this nastiness dark. Usually able to shake off setbacks, Smiley defines himself in action. The high success rate of his undertakings is well known. An American CIA chief in *Schoolboy* calls him "one of the true legends of our profession," and Inspector Mendel, the friend who works with him in *Call for the Dead* and *Tinker, Tailor* believes him "simply the best case man ... [he] had ever met." This merit impresses us all the more by declaring itself so unpredictably. Smiley's most brilliant *coups* often follow his having been written off as a has-been or a loser. Someone says of him in *The Looking-Glass War*, "He's a bit past it now." John Avery, the agent to whom this is said, later finds him absent-minded and eccentric. This impression reverses itself quickly. After biting back his impatience over Smiley's doddering ways, Avery is surprised by the clarity and precision of Smiley's mind. In *Schoolboy*, too, Guillam dismisses him twice as "an old spy in a hurry" and then finds his brilliance as a negotiator winning important ground for the Circus. He can't be blamed for long when hopes elsewhere seem to be misfiring.

Yet he tends, if not to blame himself, then to fret and grieve. Rain depresses him, and he keeps confronting the limits set on him by his job and marriage. Sometimes the convergence of the two spheres squeezes him. "It was a cheap trick to play on a man who had suddenly lost his wife," Smiley says in *A Murder of Quality* of the lie he had used to finagle an interview with Stanley Rode. But he condemns his behavior without reforming it. Perhaps Rode has forfeited the basic decencies; perhaps Smiley's hostility to him has overcome both his judgment and his conscience because Smiley sees in him a mirror image of himself. Both men have married above themselves, like John Osborne's Jimmy Porter in *Look Back in Anger* (1956) and John Braine's Joe Lampton in *Room at the Top* (1957). The parallel is instructive. These four men resent their wives for resisting their control. But whereas Susan Lampton and Alison Porter come back home, the murder victim Stella Rode is gone forever.

And so is Ann in Smiley's mind, during Stella's murder investigation. Smiley despises himself because, like Stanley Rode, he won and lost a wife from a higher social station. But rather than accepting the loss, Smiley leans on class differences to shift his scorn from himself to the grammar school-educated Rode. Perhaps, too, he secretly admires Rode, the most likely suspect, for murdering his wife, a wild act he may have contemplated himself but then shrunk from, having found it beyond his powers. Seeing in the mousy, undersized Rode a decisiveness he lacks, Smiley turns the force of his self-contempt on his counterpart from the north. The defensiveness parading as condescension that rules his behavior with Rode recurs with Peter Worthington of *The Honourable Schoolboy*, whose wife, like Smiley's, has left him. Smiley's own prior career in teaching and his having lived in Oxford, that great academic center, when Ann first left him, sharpen his resemblance to Worthington and Rode. This resemblance shows why he reacts so magnetically to the two forlorn academics. They've drawn his attention to a hurt he has been trying to forget. They've also shown him the failure of his attempts. Since the common plight of a departed wife has brought him together with these men, to begin with, he knows that the hurt will both persist and sharpen.

Those he meets on his investigations represent alternate traits and routes for Smiley. Rode and Worthington gauge the limits of his principles, the value and cost of compromise, and the great pressure to concede. An opinion he voices on the subject of goodness in *Tinker, Tailor* shows that he has learned not to expect too much from people: "Each of us has only a quantum of compassion.... If we lavish our concern on every stray cat, we never get to the center of things." His perception of Stanley Rode as a stray cat whose pain mirrors his own reveals his difficulties in squaring practice with precept. He lives in the same tricky, gray world as the rest of us; in *A Murder of Quality* he ponders "the obscurity of motive in human conduct." He also brings to this deceptive, inconstant world a limited fund of kindness and sympathy. His speculation near the end of *Tinker, Tailor*, "whether there was any love between human beings that did not rest on some sort of delusion," refers to his idea about our limited capacity for virtue. Because we can only make small inroads on the darkness, we can never dispel it. Experience has confirmed this belief; the darkness Smiley has seen in both institutions and persons is too deeply embedded to be exorcised by the moral will. Nor does he wonder if his cruelty to Rode rests on delusion; he knows conviction when he tastes it.

Forced in *The Looking-Glass War* and elsewhere to enact policies he disapproves of, Smiley knows the futility of moral crusades. The priorities dictated by lateralism, the Circus's new *modus operandi* in *Tinker,Tailor*, deepen his isolation "You're not family any more," he hears from the ex-colleagues who have pulled him from his Bywater Street snug and then asked him to work long hours under severe operational handicaps. Yet the old pro rises about this slight to take the challenge. In fact, he accepts it on terms shocking to his ex-colleagues. Long acquainted with the moral compromises of his profession, he recommends that Oliver Lacon steal restricted material from a high-ranking minister's safe. Ten chapters later, he asks the minister himself for a look at the secret papers. In *Smiley's People*, he also demonstrates his belief that morality is a luxury no spy can afford. He tells a married couple in Chapter 9 to hold back information from the police, who will be coming as soon as they find out that a murder victim spent time with the couple the day of his murder. "Trust no one," he advises another person, "Not even the police," trying to hide the truth that Vladimir Miller died while operational. Inside Smiley's dumpy, ill-clad body is a core of steel. He will challenge his superiors, discuss atrocities without losing grip, and turn his gaze on corpses, even badly disfigured ones like Vladimir Miller, whose face was blown away by a Russian assassination device.

This shy man's ability to look at ugliness without flinching is part of what he described to Karla when the two men first met in the mid-1950s as "negative vision." "Neither of us has anywhere to go," he said in an attempt to lure Karla to the West, continuing, "Both of us when were were young subscribed to *great* visions.... But not any more." His belief that he and Karla have probably evolved the same ideas about life while serving hostile masters spells out the end of his grand design for progress and reform. The low morale, the internal feuding, and the red tape that ties an agent's hands even while his chiefs are deceiving him have all killed his belief that intelligence work can influence the clash between good and evil.

He also has a softer side, which makes him a victim of the past, of his dreams, and of his spiritual unrest. Along with le Carré, he dislikes the drabness and monotony of post-war England. Also like his author, his focus is always England; Great Britain is only a political concept to him. An old professional acquaintance he meets by chance greets him with the words, "Do you love England still?" The acquaintance's next question refers, advisedly, to "the delicious Ann." Lady Ann Sercombe Smiley's wit, money, and social class recall the glitter of the 1920s, when England's public school men moved in the world framed by bohemian Soho and high-toned Mayfair. Fifty years later, memories of this glitter distract Smiley from his cares: a childless marriage to a faithless wife and the degeneration of a service he once loved. By the time of *Smiley's People* the Circus has been weakened by Soviet bloc infiltration, by scandal, and by its dependence upon American security. The pro-American policies of Smiley's successor as chief of the special branch, Saul Enderby, encouraged no doubt by Enderby's American wife, have made the service a satellite of the CIA. While Smiley might approve of this comedown intellectually as recompense for the Circus's mistakes, his heart rejects it. This sentimentality makes us wince; though confirming his humanity, it can also rule him. This dreamer in the dream factory has chosen the right profession. His hopes that he can find happiness with Ann and that his efforts can help England regain lost honor show him conniving at his own defeat. His staying married to Ann resembles his willingness to return to work whenever asked. His colleagues mistreat him after using him, and Ann leaves sooner or later with a new man. Both at home and at work, he champions lost causes. Bywater Street, the cul-de-sac where he lives, conveys the dead-endedness of his life. His marriage and his career have run in the same grooves, he notes in *Smiley's People*: "I have invested my life in institutions . . . and all I am left with is myself." These institutions have failed him. Kept going by the leanest of hopes, he has little to look forward to.

There's something frail and remote about him. He's so self-effacing at times that the novels seem to develop around him. Shrinking into himself, he'll court self-pity; *Tinker, Tailor* shows him manufacturing a crisis in order to feel like Ann's victim

It had been from the start a day of travail. . . . His bank statement, which had arrived with the morning's post, revealed that his wife had drawn the lion's share of his monthly pension: very well, he decreed, he would sell something. The response was irrational, for he was quite decently off. . . . Wrapping up an early edition of Grimmelhausen, nevertheless, a modest treasure from his Oxford days, he solemnly set off for Heywood Hill's bookshop in Curzon Street.

Spending too much time alone may have damaged both his self-confidence and self-control. On his way to Heywood Hill's he runs into Roddy Martindale, an obnoxious Foreign Service chief whom he rightly scorns. Neither his scorn for nor his being severed from Martindale professionally gives him the courage to reject a dinner offer. His faintheartedness yields predictable results; Martindale's talk at dinner offends him so much that he forgets his package and gets soaked by rain in his hurry to escape. It's not for nothing that a shrewd German cabaret owner in *Smiley's People* tells him, on the basis of one conversation, "Maybe you should have more fun in life."

This advice makes us ask if he hasn't been having fun all along. In *Call for the Dead*, where his leading traits are set forth, he recalls a "deliriously happy dinner with Ann," thrilling over the memory of Ann's wide, adoring eyes. But he has forgotten that her rapturous eyes were at odds with her words. Her longest speech at the dinner extended only two brief sentences, and she followed it with a sarcastic question in which she addressed him as a "toad." In fact, she called him toad *every* time she addressed him in the exchange that made him "deliriously happy." Some inner demon, perhaps roused to life by feeling her social inferior, goads him to self-torment. The very terms of Ann's request to be taken back at the end of the book look calculated to demean him: "I want to make you an offer no gentleman could accept." They also set the tone of any relationship she and he will have if he accepts her offer. She will call the tune. She can afford this brazenness because she has what he wants. Yet what he wants repels him intellectually. Perhaps his knowledge that he's outraging both his moral principles and his self-respect impels him to torture himself with the image of "those black monkey arms" of her Cuban lover. Le Carré's starting the chapter after the one showing Ann's letter with a reference to *Edward II* comments on the letter and its effects. *Call for the Dead* is full of unorthodox passions. The homosexual subject matter of Marlowe's play keeps the unnaturalness of Smiley's love for Ann before us; it may also imply in a waggish vein that homosexuality could compensate Smiley for the hell Ann has put him through.

But what about *her* hell? She leaves him for other men in *Call for the Dead* and *Tinker, Tailor,* and is living with still another in *Smiley's People.* Yet he puts *her* into the street in *Schoolboy.* It's not enough to say that this angry reproof is long overdue. He and Ann share a love of foreign travel, fine restaurants, and beautiful art objects. She carries these mandarin preferences further than he does, though, and she invests them with a desperation that implies escape from a deep personal sadness. Stylish, beautiful Ann descends from the bright young people of the 1920s who buried themselves in fun to forget both the horrors of the Great War and their own survivors' guilt. Her maiden name, Sercombe (cf. Circum), invokes her superficiality without defining it. Ann craves sensation and excitement. Like many other beauties, though, she seeks stimulation and instant gratification because she has never been taught to cultivate her inner strengths. This lack of proper training has cost her dearly. She seems so full of ego that she can't live within normal limits. A wicked sex goddess who keeps Smiley tense and frazzled she is; she knows both the theory and the practice of sexual betrayal. But the sensitivity that led her to choose Smiley as a husband also condemns her for leaving him to be with flashy, lurid lovers.

Her self-division could run as deep as that of her badgered husband. The revelation in *Tinker, Tailor* that she has sold still another piece from their art collection to support a love affair makes him look like one of the most put-upon husbands in modern British fiction. But her need for lovers implicates him in her guilt. His traveling to Cornwall in *Smiley's People* to warn her off Chelsea until he completes his present job lets her know that he wants to protect her and, more vitally, that he has been looking for an excuse to see her again. As touched as she is by his care, she hasn't been won over. He should have known that he'd have stood a better chance of keeping her had he acted with more dash and flourish. Anticipating the words of the Hamburg cabaret owner who reproaches him for his earnestness, she tells him before he leaves Cornwall, "You never knew how free you were, George ... I had to be free for both of us." A little recklessness from him might have turned her thoughts away from expanding *her* freedom. The Smileys dramatize a final effect of the reversal of sexual roles and/or identities in le Carré. Whereas modern man is too cautious, modern woman is too wild.

His caution withal, he once brought her to life in fresh, new ways. In fact, the strong pull he exerts on her frightens her. When she first left him, she claimed "that if she hadn't left him then, she never could have done." Another crucial concession comes three paragraphs later in this first chapter of *Call of the Dead*: "With grudging admiration she admitted to herself that if there were only one man in her life, Smiley would be he." Part of her clings to him. Although rampantly unfaithful, she has been his wife for more than thirty years. Yet the part of her that looks to the wild side panics at being reined in. Intense and conflictive, Ann needs more than physical sensation. Smiley notes in *Tinker, Tailor* that she's "deeply unhappy"; her having lost both weight and "her sense of play" after her affair with Bill Haydon shows more self-questioning and depth than we might have credited. Perhaps even more than Smiley credits? He says that he'd have attributed her doldrums to "a bad bout of the guilts, even of self-disgust" if he hadn't known her better. But how well *does* he know her. And how hard does he work at her happiness? If he knew her as well as he claims, he might have tried to build in her the self-confidence to work at marital stability. But in *Schoolboy* he disrupts the equilibrium he and she had worked so hard to restore by deserting her to spend nights at the Circus. Does the search for the Kremlin's man in Hong Kong demand his 'round-the-clock labors? His not coming home to sleep could be motivated by drives other than patriotism and professional dedication. He does nothing to relieve the "unmistakable discomfort" his moving out of Bywater Street causes Ann. Love to the shy, unassertive George Smiley means emotional combat. He lives by opposition. His many campaigns in the corridors of deceit comprising the special branch have knotted his psyche. Any simple, straightforward impulse he has had in the past twenty-five years he has kept from us. Nothing in his life runs smoothly. He's so accustomed to friction that he can't live without it; when he notices its absence, he'll supply it himself. Normally a source of comfort and nurture, marriage rakes his nerves. It rakes Ann's too. The verve with which he throws away domestic peace in *Schoolboy* shows that he doesn't want to build a harmonious future with her.

II

The frustration and danger facing Smiley both at home and at work channel into le Carré's worries about England and where she's heading. We've already seen how an East German spy tried to lure Smiley into his house to kill him in *Call for the Dead*. Regardless of who is to blame, Ann, too, tries him sorely. Le Carré underscores his criticism of their marriage, and perhaps of marriage itself, by waiting until *Smiley's People* (1980) before showing the pair together in a present-tense action. Underscoring his skepticism is his bringing them together in Cornwall, not Bywater Street. Accordingly, the physical violence directed to Smiley comes from colleagues, a former colleague, or a colleague-to-be. In *Call for the Dead*, he's clubbed by a Communist who later agrees to work for the Circus; the Communist he later sends to his death off Battersea Bridge is a former pupil and friend. Ricki Tarr, a recalcitrant agent with plenty to hide in *Tinker, Tailor*, goes berserk and attacks Smiley when being questioned by him. The pattern of violence takes a dark turn in *Schoolboy*, where East and West collide in the Hong Kong flat of Liese Worth, who is also, revealingly, a faithless wife and absentee mother. Mistakenly believing her late-night visitor to be her lover, Drake Ko, Jerry Westerby jams his pistol into the neck of his "one-time guide and mentor" Smiley as soon as he muscles him into Liese's flat. This double-whammy reversal, besides putting Smiley at risk, gains extra force from le Carré's familiar motif of running together causes, roles, and, here, even races to describe the muddle that spying has made of modern life.

Physical danger threatens Smiley again in a doorway in *Smiley's People*, when Peter Guillam slams into his Paris apartment, knocks Smiley reeling, and swings his arm "into a vicious breaking lock." This scene repeats both the romantic foreign setting and the female sexual symbolism of the doorway from *Schoolboy*. Again, the doorway leads to an apartment occupied by a woman; here, Guillam's heavily pregnant wife, a radiant symbol of femaleness. Again, the doorway scene's occurrence near the end of the book in which it appears puts us in mind of a long-awaited sexual consummation. This reminder flatters nobody, least of all Smiley, who infiltrates women's living spaces for chaste purposes. But besides yoking the dangers of the office to those of the home, the later doorway scene adds a warning more acute than the one in *Schoolboy*. Whereas Westerby is a professional acquaintance, Guillam has been Smiley's close friend for many years. And whereas Guillam is a new husband on the brink of fatherhood, Westerby has been a father for decades but lacks a wife. This breadth of reference blocks Smiley's lines of retreat. Trouble can come at him from any direction; and from anybody.

The lesson conveyed by the two attacks, that insecurity is the norm of life, keeps his guard up. One way he has avoided depression is to use the Jamesian tactic of pushing moral problems into the sphere of aesthetics; he hides behind art. The people who upset him most until the Bill Haydon mole hunt are Dieter Frey and Ann Smiley, both of whom, like Haydon, fuse elements of the beautiful and the monstrous. These two brilliant, spectacular people become Smiley's victims. The point is made skillfully. Dieter comes from Dresden, and, in Chapter 14 of *Call for the Dead*, where Dieter appears, Smiley also compares Ann to a Dresden figurine. She's easier to deal with as an art object than as a person. Perhaps she can *only* be dealt with in this way, having attained an extreme of both beauty and promiscuousness that's inhuman. Smiley has found a way to protect himself. After comparing her to a Dresden shepherdess in *Call for the Dead*, he likens her to a maquette, or dancing figurine, perhaps sculpted by Degas, in *Smiley's People*. He even asks the art dealer who owns the maquette about buying it. His trying to control Ann by appropriating an image of her shows him underrating his powers. Others need protection from *him*. His having been a direct cause of the deaths of Dieter Frey and the painter Bill Haydon, and an indirect cause of that of Jerry Westerby describes him as a dangerous man. The danger persists. Though the practice of relegating his problems to the aesthetic sphere may help him, it hurts his intimates. The coldness with which he views others can produce a sadism that rivals James Bond's or Spillane's Mike Hammer's. A denial of motion and change, his fantasy projection of Ann as a statuette chills her into the image of a corpse. The ruthlessness of his reply to John Avery's distressed plea in *The Looking-Glass War* that nobody is listening to the coded messages being sent by Fred Leiser, "To the contrary ....They'll be listening," shows Smiley and the service at their worst. The listeners Smiley is referring to are the Vopos, the East German border guards, whose capture of Leiser he coolly accepts as imminent.

Yet Rothberg calls this disowner of an agent behind enemy lines, "Le Carré's paragon of English decency" and "the epitome of the best England has to offer."[2] Classical mythology lends credence to his claim. The terror that seizes Smiley in doorways yokes him symbolically to Janus, the spirit of doorways and arches from ancient myth. Besides touching on Smiley's near omiscience, Janus's ability to look in opposite directions at the same time invokes Smiley's moral ambiguity. Smiley's inner devil doesn't rule him. He has intelligent opinions and fine access to his honesty. Regardless of who is to blame, we feel for his wounded heart. He's an elite person in spite of himself. Many of le Carré's characters are witty, shrewd, and imaginative. Only Smiley is gentle and kind. His years in the field have impaired his ability to express his feelings, though. Ann is being unfair in *Smiley's People* for attacking his "apparent composure" after hearing of the death of a friend. In *Schoolboy*, he cried over the death of a field agent, but out of her hearing. At the end of *Smiley's People,* too, his arriving at the East German border two hours before the scheduled arrival of Karla shows him achieving tenderness and compassion without straining. His early arrival insures Karla of his protection and support. This magnanmity had increased his value to the Circus. The Circus burrowers, who use the code names Tinker, Tailor, Soldier, Poorman, and Beggarman to designate the leading suspects in the mole search, label him Beggarman. Deprived of a firm hold on the key realities of his life—love and work—he does sometimes feel like a beggar. But even those who hurt him respect him; Ann calls him her "best lover," and the Circus brass keep begging for his help. He handles people as different as Claus Kretzschmar and Maria Ostrakova in *Smiley's People* because he shows them that he cares about their welfare. His taking off his hat in view of the peep-hole of a frightened, aching Ostrakova's door transcends the niceties of tradecraft. Despite the distortion caused by the peep-hole's fish eye, Ostrakova sees in Smiley a humanity deserving of her trust:

While she watched him, he earnestly removed a straw hat ... and held it at his side as if he had just heard his national anthem being played. And she inferred from this gesture that the small gentleman was telling her that he knew she was afraid, and knew that a shadowed face was what she was afraid of most, and that by baring his head he was in some way revealing his goodwill to her.

But this goodwill serves tainted causes. Smiley's affinities with two-faced Janus and his tempering of a virginal conscience with Satanic cunning both extend to his self-management. In the trilogy, some of his colleagues say that he's obsessed with Karla. They're only right to a point. Foreshadowing the metaphor of the theater that dominates *The Little Drummer Girl*, he has cast Karla in the role of the legendary dragon who threatens and thus strengthens the community. Though this role-casting contradicts his belief that Karla's defection to the West won't matter much, it does rouse his best skills; an old field man likes nothing better than breaking a case or winning a defection. As his "Black Grail," Karla gives Smiley purpose and direction. It doesn't matter that Karla's real name is unknown to him or that he has never heard Karla's voice. A blown-up passport photo of Karla adorns the wall of his Circus office, and he reaches for the seven-volume Karla file handed to him by a co-worker "as if to receive an old friend." But if the file containing information about him is a friend, Karla himself is not. Representing a role in a morality play or the object of a religious quest, he lacks human definition. Smiley only endows him with humanity when he's sure of ensnaring him. Keeping him in an operational, as opposed to a human, context has helped Smiley sustain pressure on his Moscow foil. The double remove from which Smiley looks at his job, at Karla, and at himself confirms his rich humanity. It also alludes to le Carré's wisdom in building five novels around him and giving him small but key roles in two more. A person who can see so much from so many angles and also act on his perceptions will make exciting things happen.

Chapter Five
Skiing Down the Corridors

The materials, treatment, and style of *Call for the Dead* (1961) find le Carré wandering between popular and serious fiction. His first novel fuses the artistic assumptions of the classic English mystery with the political intrigue of the international spy thriller; a murder investigation occurs within the shadow of British security. Le Carré enriches the plot with an infusion of domestic realism, as well. A man dies from bullet wounds inflicted in his home, a development hinting at marital trouble. Heading up the investigation of the man's death is another unhappy husband. Le Carré dovetails political crime with family worries to develop continuities between home and government; the way people act with their spouses both creates and validates the political disorders fretting society. He falls short of his goal. Although his premise is solid, it lacks the plotting needed to give it life. But the book does sustain some of its vital signs. Less of a flop than a bad start, *Call for the Dead* represents a wrong direction for le Carré . Fortunately, it also includes strengths he would later redirect to friendlier, more fertile channels.

I

Neither strengths nor flaws leap from the book's workmanlike opening. An anonymous letter sent to Smiley's department in the Defense Ministry claims that one Samuel Fennan, a member of the Foreign Office, had Communist ties in the past which may be compromising his current job. Smiley has no choice but to investigate. Though he expected no trouble, his interview with Fennan goes even more smoothly than he had hoped. Fennan admits having been a Communist at Oxford twenty-four years ago but adds that he has long since left the party. This information comes out in halves. Having left Fennan's crowded, busy office at the F. O. to talk privately, the two men took advantage of the fine January weather to go to a nearby park, where Fennan was assured that he'd be cleared of suspicion. Now, two days after this friendly exchange, Fennan is dead, apparently a suicide victim. The note found near his corpse mentions his having nothing to live for now that his career in the F. O. has been ruined. His wife confirms this story, insisting that the interview with Smiley two days before had upset her husband. Yet Smiley clearly remembers having left Fennan in good cheer. His recollection of a cheerful Fennan is soon confirmed. When he hears Elsa Fennan's phone ringing at 8:30 a.m., he answers it himself, assuming that the call's for him. He's wrong. It's from the telephone operator, announcing a wakeup call that had been ordered. A police check run later with the local switchboard tells him that the order for the call came from Sam Fennan. Smiley has a lead. Why would a man about to commit suicide place a wake-up call for the next morning? he wonders. But place the call Fennan did, insists the operator, who knew his voice well. The suicide verdict recorded by the local police loses more credibility with the discovery that Fennan had written to ask for a second interview with Smiley. His request shows that he wasn't planning to die. Another confirmation of his intention to live follows shortly. The first letter sent to Smiley's office, impugning Fennan's loyalty, was typed on the same machine as the suicide note; but both the spacing and the pressure on the keys reveal the two notes to have been typed by different people. Somebody wanted to stop Fennan and Smiley from meeting a second time.

Le Carré's troubles start here. The motive for the Fennan murder rests on an improbability—that Smiley and Fennan should be seen talking in the park by someone who knew them both, here, Dieter Frey, whom Smiley recruited in Germany for British security during the war. Serving now as an East German spy, Dieter interprets what he sees in the park as proof of Fennan's betrayal. His suspicions lack force. Yes, Fennan has been passing Dieter information from the F. O. But the past several months have brought major changes. Recently, Fennan has only been giving Dieter low-grade secrets, having held back material from highly classified files. Everything about the Fennan-Frey connection both defies belief and violates narrative aesthetic. Dieter's failure to evaluate intelligence and his chance discovery of Fennan and Smiley together give le Carré more worries. The coincidence in the park makes us ask how someone as flamboyant as Dieter could see Smiley and Fennan and remain unseen himself. Le Carré's treatment of the suicide note also defies belief. In Chapter 13, Smiley explains the note:

Knowing Dieter, I suspect that he had long ago taken the precaution of keeping in London a few sheets of blank writing paper signed with samples, forged or authentic, of Sam Fennan's signature, in case it was ever necessary to compromise or blackmail him. Assuming this to be so, Mundt brought a sheet with him [to the Fennans' Surrey home] in order to type the suicide letter over the signature on Fennan's own typewriter.

Smiley has irresponsibly assumed that Communist agents sign blank sheets of paper at the time of their recruitment to help the agency get rid of them whenever convenient. This assumption defies the instinct of self-preservation; any agent lowers rather than improves his chances for survival by subjecting himself to the whims of official policy. Nor is this implausibility mitigated by Dieter's final, desperate acts.

Smiley has recalled enough of Dieter's "handwriting," i.e. his spying technique, to trick him and Elsa Fennan, Sam's widow, into meeting at London's Sheridan Theater. Suspecting the trickery, Dieter kills Elsa during the last act of Christopher Marlowe's play about a "demented king," *Edward II*. This desperation makes us wonder if Dieter wasn't suffering from dementia himself. His murder of Elsa Fennan, an act of outstanding nerve, meshes with the larger-than-life quality le Carré ascribes to him throughout. Yet Elsa's death doesn't benefit this wild revolutionary, whose misguided moral passion had already steered him to Communism. Not only can't Elsa's death help him flee the theater; it also spoils his chance for freedom once he leaves the Sheridan. Up to now, the only East German agent incriminated in the murder of Sam Fennan has been Hans-Dieter Mundt. Becoming a suspected murderer will make Dieter the object of a nation-wide police hunt. So self-defeating is the Elsa Fennan murder that it undermines one of the novel's basic premises. How could this panicky murderer and misinterpreter of intelligence reports from the Foreign Office have risen so high in GDR spy circles? In view of his blunders, how could he have helped the Allies so much during the war, facing pressure and danger far beyond those of peacetime London?

What happens right after Dieter's bolt from the theater promises to rescue the novel, in part, from the technical blunders that raised these questions. Dieter's long walk from London's theater district to Battersea Bridge traces a maze-like path resembling that in James Joyce's last chapter in *A Portrait*. Like Joyce, le Carré uses a long night journey through damp streets to convey both the mystery and malignancy of today's city. The darkness, the fog, and the echoes created by the alleys and street corners enhance the eeriness by playing tricks with distances and sounds. Dieter's heaving bulk and the contrast between his handsomeness and his severe limp both endow him with the melodrama to unify the pursuit. The fog, the dark, and the bewildering ricochet of sounds caused by his footsteps befriend him. He finds safety among the lonely chattering streets, the ugly, dingy houses, and the vacant riverside mills of mazelike London. Gloom, damp, and squalor are his natural elements.

His safety, though, works better as idea than as performance. Smiley had recalled seeing him walking the edge of a Dresden prison yard, "limping, struggling to keep up with" the other inmates. How could Dieter, some fifteen years older than he was as a stumbling prisoner, walk so far and so quickly without using a crutch that his pursuer can hardly keep up with him? This question points to other trouble spots in the book's closing scenes. A trained intelligence officer like Dieter Frey would have known he was being pursued and soon hastened to kill his pursuer, the just retired Scotland Yard inspector, Mendel, who, at retirement age, would have fallen quickly to the younger, stronger man. Smiley's participation in the chase is also mishandled. Having gone home, Smiley only rejoins Mendel when he learns of Dieter's whereabouts in a phone call. Note that Dieter has helped Mendel by remaining long enough in the houseboat where he had gone to fetch a handgun to give Mendel the time to phone Smiley. Note, too, that the handgun that meant so much to Dieter that he walked across town to fetch it remains unfired. This inconsistency mars the whole chase sequence. Impressive on their own, the sequence's atmospheric effects lack the motivation to create the strong finish the book needs to offset its many flaws. Le Carré hasn't followed through on the interest he builds in Dieter; Dieter is only a collection of exhilarating qualities, colorful and resonant but asserted rather than dramatized. Le Carré's attempt to dramatize them, in fact, only betrays their non-viability.

The Communist value system Dieter stands for slights facts and people. Worshipping cold reason, Communism can't yoke its perfectionist creed to human fallibility; everyday reality is a trifle or aberration alongside Marx's definition of historical truth. Ironically, the brave new world Dieter and Elsa want to create resembles the one that wracked them in Germany fifteen years before. Including all of society in their master plans, Communists and Nazis both rely on censorship, secret police, and forced labor camps. Seeing people as cogs in a dialectical process, these intellectual purists shed more blood than most conventional political thinkers. The mature le Carré won't change his mind about Communist enslavement to a vision. But he will disclaim any superiority he might have once found in the western political ethos.

Anchored in the premise that the most idealistic moralities beget the worst butchery, *Call for the Dead* tries to show how those who aim the highest sink the lowest. The rating of precept over practice dooms the purists in the novel along with their intimates. Because of Hitler's War, Dieter wanted honor, and Elsa, another German Jew, craved peace. But their dreams for a better order made spies and murderers of them before killing them. The feebleness of their holds on life shows in their deaths. Though Dieter's pressure on her thyroid cartilage kills Elsa immediately, it hardly changes her appearance. Several minutes pass before death is ascribed to her sitting, barely slouching form. The difference between a living and a dead Communist proves itself just as marginal with Dieter, who neither shouts nor makes an audible splash falling into the Thames. So enslaved is he to doctrine that he merges silently with both the night and the river below. Concurrent with his abstraction worship is the impression he gives at his death of having forfeited both normal emotions and the solidity of flesh and bone.

But this denouement, persuasive as it sounds, doesn't rise from character. It's given. The pictorial, or imagistic, qualities of *Call for the Dead* fight its underlying ideas. This novel that champions the concrete while deriding the abstract suffers, ironically, from being too distanced. Sam Fennan is called "brilliant, fluent, and attractive," and le Carré includes a great deal of background data to attest to his man's virtues. What he doesn't do is describe these virtues, killing Sam off before bringing him before us. Most of the stylistic flights in *Call for the Dead* refer, in fact, to characters who either don't appear, like Sam Fennan, or who appear briefly, like Dieter Frey; Dieter enters the present-tense action in Chapter 15 and dies about three hours and two chapters later, after saying in our hearing only the words, "*Servus,* George." His thematic import exceeds his dramatic presence so drastically that he looks like a cardboard cutout trying to lift a safe. Le Carré tries to disguise this embarrassment by overwriting. "Erect and handsome, a lock of black hair tumbling over his brow," Dieter looks like "a man apart"; someone in the audience of the Sheridan Theater sees him as "a living component of all our romantic dreams." This verbal dazzle doesn't lift Dieter from the page. Smiley objects to him chiefly because he has forsaken personal for collective values; the dialectical materialism he has allegedly swallowed whole from Marx shirks the individual. Yet nobody in the le Carré canon has a more pronounced personal style, le Carré insisting that Dieter magnetizes all who look at him. Karla, another eastern bloc spy who touches Smiley deeply, will succeed better as a character than Dieter. By being less explicit and more ironic, the Karla portrait offers more imaginative play; by extending over three novels, it provides more opportunities for development.

Some of Dieter's flaws as a character portrait extend to Smiley. Smiley passes out from the ordeal of pushing Dieter to his death off Battersea Bridge. When he wakes up at two o'clock the next afternoon, he learns that in his delirium he was mumbling the lines from John Webster, "I bade thee, when I was distracted of my wife, go kill my dearest friend, and thou hast done it." The reference doesn't apply. Dieter never came close to being Smiley's dearest friend. Once he opted for Communism, he forfeited friendship with westerners, and Smiley should have known as much. Besides, the quotation from *The Duchess of Malfi* infers that the architect of his best friend's death used a go-between. No wonder Smiley changes the subject as soon as he learns what he was murmuring in his sleep. His embarrassment shouldn't surprise us. Both he and le Carré had already miscued in characterizing Dieter's accomplice and victim, Elsa Fennan. Having lived in Germany under the Nazis, she knows the devastation political extremism can cause. Besides losing her good looks (Smiley's estimate of her age is ten years too high), she suffered so badly in the war that she needed three years of medical treatment and bedrest to regain her health. Smiley says of her, noting her commitment to nearest things, "Her instinct was to defend, to hoard the treasures of her life, to build about herself the symbols of normal existence."

Her earlier denunciation of political ideology as "an emptiness, a mind without a body, a game played with clouds in the sky," had convinced him of her will to protect; according to him, she has pledged herself to the truth of the heart. Perhaps his surmise, more fully stated later, that the only difference between Elsa's nerve-raddled intensity and his wife's cool beauty lies in the accident of politics has upset him. But he should have recovered from the upset caused by his surmise before judging Elsa; an experienced agent should know not to mix sentiment and reason while investigating. Credit for misleading him belongs partly to Elsa. Though she knows nothing of Ann, she speaks of her with passionate conviction. Yet she'd have needed both superhuman self-presence to type her husband's suicide note minutes after his death and subhuman emotions to take orders from Sam's murderer. And even if she could have performed this stupendous feat of nerves, she'd have been so drained by it that she'd have no strength to lie so convincingly to Smiley the next morning. And what of her guilt? Nobody, perhaps least of all this ex-invalid and insomniac, could have hidden from Smiley's sharp eye the guilt she had to feel after conspiring in the murder of her husband of eight years.

A medley of implausibilities herself, Elsa accounts for a good deal of implausible plotting. Sam requested a second meeting with Smiley because he wanted to say something important—that his wife was a Communist agent. Why didn't he report this crucial information during their first meeting? Smiley reasons that Sam wrote the letter impugning his own loyalty in order to close with someone from the special branch. Seeing Dieter observe him together with Smiley, a possibility le Carré doesn't mention but which can't be dismissed, would have moved Sam to speak out when he still had a chance. And why did Sam need to write the two letters in the first place? By walking into the Circus and asking to talk to one of the agents, he'd have acted decisively and effectively. This direct approach would have appealed to someone who converted to Marxism in 1930s Oxford, a milieu which promoted the belief that reality is discovered through action, not thought. For somebody trained to value direct action, Sam miscues often. He wastes his chance to confide in Smiley. A loyal Communist for four and a half years, he sours on Marxism. His change of heart fails to boost his efficiency. After giving the East Germans chicken feed for six months, he finally decides to explain himself to British security. It's hard to see how someone who stumbles and crawls as much as Sam could enjoy skiing. None of his undertakings go smoothly. Even the 8:30 a.m. wake-up call he orders the night before his death makes no sense. Here's Smiley's feeble explanation for this call for the dead:

> Fennan wanted to see me at Marlow and he'd taken a day's leave. He can't have told Elsa he was having a day off or she'd have tried to explain it away to me. He staged a phone call to give himself an excuse for going to Marlow.

Everything connected with the phone call shows bad authorial judgment. Le Carré deserves credit for including in the meaning of the novel's title Smiley's anguished unanswered cry to Dieter as his former friend drops into the Thames. But this enlargement of focus doesn't negate the truth that the wake-up call is too small an item to merit the prominence it gets. It isn't central to the murder case. Several times, le Carré will dangle it before us as if it holds the solution to the mystery of Sam Fennan's death, whereas the true answer lies in ballistics and fingerprinting. Le Carré should have known that it's nearly impossible to make a murder look like a suicide. Obviously, his knowledge of intelligence work by passed some major investigative procedures. More blameworthy than this ignorance, though, is his attempt to hide it. Elsa claimed to have ordered the wake-up call herself but then insisted that she forgot why. Preposterous enough on its own, her story rests on shaky logic. Telephone operators always record the names of subscribers ordering wake-up calls; in a town as small as Walliston, where the Fennans live, the operator who took the order would have recognized Sam's voice straightaway, which is exactly what she did. Elsa's testimony is an outrageous fabrication of the kind that le Carré, having once perpetrated, learned how to avoid in his later work.

Perhaps more than any other blemish or flaw, his failure to rise to the imaginative challenge posed by Elsa Fennan did *Call for the Dead* in. Helping him cover his tracks, Smiley, after pronouncing Elsa innocent of her husband's death, ponders the elusiveness of motives and the opaqueness of personality: "What did Hesse write? 'Strange to wander in the mist, each is alone. No tree knows his neighbor....' We know nothing of one another, nothing." Such musings replace both sinewy character development and an ability to convey life's instinctive rhythms. By not confronting its materials directly, *Call for the Dead* slights the issues it raises. Le Carré indicates elsewhere a loose commitment to his materials. In Chapter Two of *The Spy Who Came in from the Cold,* he gives 1959 as the time setting of *Call.* Yet the action opens on Wednesday, 4 January, which fell on a Monday in 1959. The aging of characters also foils any attempt to time-date the book. Smiley says he met Dieter in Germany when Dieter was nineteen. Elsewhere, he makes Dieter's age about thirty-two, a figure which puts him a decade short (the same decade he added to Elsa's age in his miscalculation?). In Chapter 14, he recalls a Watteau sketch given to him and Ann as a wedding gift by Peter Guillam. But if he's correct in giving Guillam's age in *Smiley's People* as fifty, then Guillam must have been about seventeen at the time of the wedding. How many teenagers' tastes run to Watteau? How many have friends twenty years their senior? And why would Guillam call Mendel, who has reached retirement age, "you clever youth," in Chapter 11, whereas Mendel always addresses him as "Mr." Guillam if Guillam is so much younger? Not only does le Carré fail to answer these questions; he also introduces another that skews the novel's time setting still more. In Chapter 12, Elsa says that she and her husband first met Dieter in a ski hut five years ago, i.e., 1956 (without explaining, incidentally, why the appearance there of Dieter, who obviously couldn't ski, didn't rouse Sam's suspicions). Her arithmetic makes 1961, not 1959, the book's true time setting. Supporting it is the truth that *Call* opens on Wednesday, 4 January, which fell on a Wednesday in 1961.

Accepting Elsa's calculation means rejecting that of le Carré in *The Spy Who Came in from the Cold*, a step most readers would resist taking; certainly an author knows the realities ruling his fiction better than his characters do. But if choosing between the two dates is silly and empty, the issue of time-dating the action of *Call* only came up because le Carré's attention strayed from his materials. This inattentiveness hurts the novel in other vital ways, as we have seen. An uninspired author can hardly expect to inspire his readers.

The consistency that saves the novel from falling apart comes in with Smiley. Fortunately, le Carré's ideas about Smiley were clear from the start; he was intended to convey his author's views about both the intelligence profession and modern man. The description of him in the novel's second paragraph sets forth those views as decidedly unheroic; critical rather than flattering, it makes Smiley's physical unattractiveness a function of his badness in both judgment and taste: "Short, fat, and of a quiet disposition, he appeared to spend a lot of money on really bad clothes, which hung about his squat form like skin on a shrunken toad." The scurviness of this description stays before us, le Carré referring to his "chubby wet hands," "pouchy, lined face," and "slack and stupid mouth." Often his behavior will tally with the impression formed by his sluglike looks. He shouts and cracks wise while interviewing Elsa Fennan and feels like "an obscene coarse bully" prying information from her. Yet he survives, whereas the Byronic Dieter dies, after performing acts of outstanding cruelty and kindness in his final hours. Smiley's Beckett-like statement to Elsa in Chapter 12, "I don't know. I just don't know. I think perhaps I do," fits le Carré's portrayal of him as a marginal man, a fusion of mind and heart lacking in both ballast and emotional support systems.

Last seen riding an airplane to Zurich, he's literally suspended in space. The young passenger sitting next to him who sees him as a "tired executive out for a bit of fun" couldn't be more mistaken. If Smiley ever found fun, he'd recoil from it. Besides, the purpose of his flight, to collect Ann, can hardly be called an errand of joy considering the pain she has caused him. Little or no relief appears in sight. He has just rejected an offer of a promotion. Having bolted the service in Chapter 5 to protest his superior's dishonesty in the Fennan case, he lacks both a job and a wife, those confirmations of reality in his middle-class culture. He has only himself. What is more, this unsponsored self must fend off danger from all directions while walking the edge; for a while, even his home is off limits to him. *Call* is organized around his worsening plight. His thoughts about Ann describe the lover's agony of being both apart from and together with his beloved. His conscience and moral purpose can't ease this pain. John Kirk has shown how pain ruins even his finest achievements: "The enemy agent [i.e., Dieter] is Smiley's friend and former pupil. For Smiley, professional success can only mean personal heart-break and yet another sickening and insoluble problem in personal morality."[1]

His fortunes keep tailspinning. Mundt threatens his life twice, first, by invading his home and trying to lure him inside and, next, by bludgeoning him from behind in a used-car garage. So violent is this bludgeoning that Smiley needs a month in the hospital to recover from it. Nor is his recovery smooth. The first three sentences describing his recuperation, beginning "He hated," "He hated," and "And he hated," make us ask if he'd rather die. Even after leaving the hospital, he has nowhere to turn. The assurances of job and home mightn't comfort this self-doubter, anyway. Knowing that his age has lowered his employability away from the Circus, he worries about holding on to his pension. His uneasiness with his superiors aggravates his worries. Rank makes him nervous even if he dislikes or disapproves of the rank holder. Fearing that his report of the Fennan death will anger Maston, his chief, he begins most of his statements with the apologetic "Well." Then he shrinks from confronting Maston with his anger, resigning from the service in writing rather than in person. Dissatisfied with Elsa's explanation for the wake-up call, he also affects aimlessness and drifts out of her house. When he questions her several hours later about the call, he takes Mendel with him. But his shyness hasn't impaired his powers. Acting with skill, instinct, and dedication, he'll apply pressure in the right places. Others will help him, too, because they believe in him. Though he underrates himself, he has won the trust of enough colleagues and friends to count on their support when he needs it. He might not admit it to himself, but his record brings honor to anyone joining forces with him.

II

The form of *Call* owes much to traditional English literary detection. Like a Golden Age mystery, it rouses the reader's intellectual curiosity and invites his/her participation in solving the crime. To pique this curiosity, le Carré keeps bringing up the imponderables surrounding Sam Fennan's death. Why did Sam order a wake-up call at 7:55 p.m. on Tuesday for the next morning if he was planning to die before taking the call? Why should he make himself a cup of cocoa and not drink it? (And why would Mundt, his assassin, leave the brimful cup for the police to discover, particularly with Elsa nearby to remind him to pour the cocoa down the drain?) Trying to answer these questions, Smiley travels between London and Surrey in the manner of a Sherlock Holmes or Hercule Poirot. But the issues raised in *Call* transcend both the closed society and the literate, gentlemanly detection of the English country house crime puzzle. Most of the detection *is* cerebral. The investigation miscarries when Smiley unwisely lets his emotional response to Elsa cloud his judgment. He also speaks of the case as an "academic exercise" whose components must be moved about like "pieces in a puzzle" to fit "the complex framework of established facts." But the framework shatters. More than mind is needed, Smiley sees, to crush the evil that killed Sam Fennan. The crime in *Call* is international, not local; the motives behind it are political, not domestic. Sex and money don't lead to murder; le Carré's sexless people don't complain about being financially squeezed. Twice, in fact, the unemployed and celibate George Smiley spends £5 for information. Nor are he and the other principals of the case upper class: Mendel, Dieter, and the Fennans are all middle-income Jews; the aristocratic Ann never appears in person; the mail awaiting Smiley's homecoming to Bywater Street in Chapter 14 proclaims him as solidly middle class: "circulars ... bills and the usual collection of soap vouchers, frozen pea coupons, football pool forms."

Le Carré indicates elsewhere, too, that the solution to the crime won't restore the bliss that the crime disrupted only temporarily. There wasn't any bliss to disrupt. Crime is more than an aberration. Reading reality as an unsteady fusion of blessings and curses, Smiley looks defensive, not elated, when he reports his first breakthrough to Mendel in Chapter 11. Perhaps he's wondering what new danger his find has unleashed: "'I think we've found the murderer and a lot more besides...' There was no triumph in his eyes. Only anxiety." Perhaps his capacity for gladness has become jaded. Anticipating the inertia that overtakes him when he sees Karla crossing into the western zone at the end of *Smiley's People,* he cries "like a child," "his voice choked with tears," when he sees that he has pushed Dieter Frey into the Thames. Just as his cries get mangled by the fog and dissolve into the night, so does his ordeal reap, at best, dubious gains. Whitehall can't protest to East Germany that two of her operatives, Mundt and Dieter, were spying in Britain; Whitehall didn't recognize East Germany at the time of the novel. The idea of lodging a protest through an intermediary wouldn't work, either; Moscow, the only feasible go-between, would only lose by helping Britain extradite Mundt; finally, security would oblige Moscow to keep silent about any tie it might have had with Dieter, particularly in the country where Dieter was operating illegally.

Cooperation from the Kremlin may not have helped Whitehall in any case. Voicing a distrust of authority more American than English, Smiley says inwardly in Chapter 6, "He knew how intelligent men could be broken by the stupidity of their superiors, how weeks of patient work night and day would be cast aside by such a man." The man Smiley is referring to is Maston. Less stupid than obstructionist, this new chief of the secret service represents the new breed of civil servant. This sleek, polished bureaucrat has cultivated the benefits to be gleaned from diffidence, flexibility, and loyalty. He directs them to the end of self-protection; he wants to solidify his power. He sends Smiley to Surrey to confirm the police verdict that Sam Fennan committed suicide, a verdict that will cause his office the least work and trouble. Preferring the slick and the easy, he scolds Smiley for exposing Elsa's lie about ordering the 8:30 wake-up call. Smiley knows that he'll have to resign in order to investigate honestly, Maston's commitment to smooth surfaces blocking open-mindedness. But neither Maston's slick expertise in pleasing his chiefs nor his studied sartorial elegance improves his office demeanor. His self-seeking is shamelessly transparent. Yet he later sees that the concurrence of Smiley's resignation with his dismantling of an enemy spy ring could discredit the circus's executive. Thus he offers Smiley a promotion to lure him back to the security dovecote, calling him all along "George." But Smiley wouldn't take the offer even if he wanted to. Even more than Maston's "arid paper and his shiny politicians," Smiley loathes his chief's ignorance. Maston's asking high-handedly at the end of the case, "This man Mendel, what's he like? Is he trustworthy?" draws the full force of Smiley's hatred. Maston deserves no better; his selfishness has made him as crass and as morally blind as any of the bagmen in the Bay City Police in Raymond Chandler.

The literate, nonchalant tone of the opening chapters belies le
Carré's angry anti-authoritarianism. In no rush to launch his murder
case, le Carré spends Chapter 1 surveying the career of Smiley. After
reporting the news of Sam Fennan's death in Chapter 2, he relaxes
narrative tempo again. He starts Chapter 3, in which Smiley will
visit Elsa, by touching in local atmosphere, inviting his descriptive
flair, and making some sociological insights about village life in
Surrey. This realistic foreground firms up the ensuing investigation;
the characters move within a believable milieu. Le Carré's
documentation also makes for stylistic counterpoint. His level,
measured syntax controls the surprises later created by the many plot
twists. Despite its faults, *Call* often moves swiftly and involvingly.
At the end of Chapter 6, Smiley spots the old MG he had first seen
on Bywater Street the day Mundt had broken into his home and tried
to kill him. But the uplift caused by his discovery vanishes in a storm
of blood and pain. While looking at the car, he's hammered so violently
that he spends the next month in a hospital bed.

The convalescence that restores Smiley's health also helps the
novel. Mendel takes up the investigation while Smiley is on his back,
keeping *Call* from being a one-man show. He also invites Smiley
to discuss his findings. Le Carré judged wisely to send him to Smiley's
bedside because the novel needs slowing at this point. It also needs
the intellectualizing so central to literary detection in general and
to the scholarly George Smiley in particular. Fittingly, Chapter 8 ends
with Smiley's written inventory of the leading facts of the murder
case as he and Mendel have pieced them out. Knowing that good
detection rules out coincidence, Smiley is searching for the common
element joining the mysterious car, its lessee, the East German firm
the lessee claims to have worked for, Smiley's own blackjacking, and
his earlier escape from death on Bywater Street. Connections do form.
The weeks Smiley has spent in the hospital both allow them to come
forth and give him the chance to ponder their meaning. The following
chapter, Chapter 9, completes the first half of the novel, and le Carré
ends it in a way calculated to launch the reader into the second half—
with a death.

The character chosen to turn up dead adds vigor to le Carré's
solid page-turning device. For if used-car dealer, gambler, extortionist,
and tax evader Adam Scarr isn't the leading suspect of the book's
first murder, his criminal ways nonetheless shift narrative tempo when
he's found dead. The shift occurs because Scarr had served the novel
well during his two brief appearances. His garage occupies a shed

on an old bombsite near a hospital, carrying forward the idea of suffering and malaise (the weather is always bad) haunting the action. That Smiley will be a patient in the same hospital sharpens the idea. Scarr's Dickensian name and Cockney malevolence capture both his nastiness and the nastiness that shadows us all. In his threadbare black suit, dirty shirt, and flowered red tie, this peddler of false bonhomie comes before us directly, without authorial intervention. His evil is utterly believable. But besides being important in his own right, Scarr is also the first of many lower-class characters who invoke le Carré's powers of vocal impersonation. Scarr clears the artistic path for the memorable cameo turns of Harry Praschko in *Small Town* and Charlie Marshall in *Schoolboy*.

Le Carré succeeds less well in keeping us abreast of the main features of the case. In his zeal to play fair, he has Smiley write them down together with his thoughts on them in Chapters 8, 13, and 17. Smiley's memorandum, "The Fennan Case," in Chapter 17 takes the place of the traditional sleuth's long recitation to the witnesses and suspects, who have all gathered to hear him. Like Poirot in the library of Styles in *The Mysterious Affair at Styles* (1920), he reviews the case, sets forth the evidence, and weaves a fabric of proof. His demonstration follows his inventories of Chapters 8 and 13 in rousing our mental activity. Unfortunately, this verbal climax rouses little else. Three addresses to the reader in a short novel are excessive, robbing the book of freshness and drive. Inferring a faith in the power of reason that the book denies, they also mislead us. *Call* hasn't inherited the rational optimism of classic English detective fiction. Any book bristling with so many psychological inconsistencies as le Carré's first novel belongs outside the cool, cerebral tradition of Agatha Christie. The obsessiveness the novel ascribes to human nature belies the idea that the brain can solve any problem and thus right any social or moral wrong.

Smiley's long demonstration, in fact, resolves very little; nor do the survivors have much happiness in store. The rain that falls constantly enforces a pessimism extending from the various personal relationships. All close ties described in the book are dangerous. Ann is beautiful but also, alas, damned; without straining, she can make Smiley wince with pain. Elsa Fennan connives in the murder of *her* husband, traduces him to Smiley, and is then killed by her controller. Mundt ends a four-year association with Adam Scarr by getting him drunk and then drowning him. The only human bond deserving of trust involves professional colleagues. In Chapter 6, aptly called "Tea and Sympathy," one veteran crime stopper eases the duress of another, as Mendel offers Smiley a bed for the night just after Smiley's discovery of the Mundt murder plot. Later, Mendel visits Smiley in a hospital, bringing him a book about bees and a jar of honey to boost his spirits. Still later, Mendel serves Smiley and Peter Guillam a snack of beer, bread, and cheese when the two intelligence officers visit him to discuss Sam Fennan's death.

But his kindness both as a host and a hospital visitor can't offset the negation and squalor dominating the action. Le Carré's first novel ranks with his darkest. To its credit, much of its pessimism is artistically achieved, le Carré using counterpoint rather than agglomeration to depict it. Various motifs interlace and cut across each other to weave a rich web of dark meaning. Starting with the mechanical, he parks the old MG sedan Mundt rents from Scarr where Smiley can see it during both of Mundt's attempts on Smiley's life. Two of the book's three victims die in the Thames, Scarr and Dieter; two are Jewish, Dieter and Sam Fennan. A third jew, Mendel, is nearby when Dieter falls to his death. Theaters also play a role. Mirroring the flow of the action, which moves from London to Surrey and then back to London, Elsa passes government secrets to Mundt at the Weybridge Repertory Theater before her fatal meeting with Dieter at London's Sheridan Theater. The author of the play running at the Sheridan, Christopher Marlowe, invokes Marlow, the London suburb where Sam had asked Smiley to meet him the day of his death. The deathliness evoked by this pattern of repetition and correspondence depicts the characters' lack of freedom. Smiley is as hemmed in as the others, his final appearance in an airplane negating the truth that his wings have been clipped. His hopeless dream of happiness with Ann resembles that of Sam, who believed he could turn his back on the Communists after spying for them. Smiley hasn't seen Ann during the five years that Sam, another beleaguered husband, has been working for the Communists.

This last identification bodes ill for the British nation itself. Three British subjects die in the course of the book, Scarr and the two Fennans. It also comes out that the Foreign Office has been compromised for the past five years. Whatever success Smiley's investigation enjoys has left a sour residue. Smiley investigates without official approval, the head of the secret service, Maston, not even knowing Mendel, Smiley's chief aide. Maston's attempt to squelch the investigation invokes the words of John Vincent in his 1981 review of Chapman Pincher's *Their Trade Is Treachery*: "An Intelligence Service which lacks political judgment is more dangerous than one penetrated by the other side."[2] *Call* raises this argument a notch, portraying British Security as infiltrated, naive, and pernicious. The principles that the Circus is supposed to defend are smudged everywhere by the means used in their defense. Nor can all the blame be heaped on Maston. As has been seen, Smiley browbeats Elsa at a time when he believes her to be helpless and vulnerable—less than twelve hours after Sam's death. Though the browbeating lowers Smiley's own self-esteem, *she* rises above it. He is always making mistakes in her presence; his belief in her innocence, even after he hears the preposterous story about the wake-up call, reflects poor professional judgment and instinct.

If his fallibility is less pronounced in the later works, he also investigates differently. First, le Carré steers him into different investigative channels. Never again will he get the battering inflicted upon him by Mundt at the end of Chapter 6 of *Call*. What this near-fatal pounding does prefigure is the truth that he won't play the detached logician-sleuth. Though death won't stalk him so closely again, pain, fever, and loss always will. This negation will unfold in a slightly different environment from that of *Call*. He'll rely less upon Mendel, the highly likable weasel-faced Scotland Yard inspector. Mendel gives Smiley a roof during the time Mundt is occupying Bywater Street; he interrogates Adam Scarr, follows Elsa Fennan from her Surrey home to London, and trails Dieter Frey from the Sheridan Theater to Battersea Bridge. His discussion of the case with Smiley in Chapter 4, in which the two men talk astutely and seriously without trying to upstage each other, implies that le Carré may have intended the newly retired policeman from Mitcham to become Smiley's investigative partner. Le Carré enforces this impression by turning over the investigation to Mendel during Smiley's hospital stay. But Smiley's fictional career was to develop differently. Though none of the adventures featuring him is a one-man show, Mendel only reappears once, to do a brief watching job in *Tinker, Tailor*.

Peter Guillam will work more steadily with Smiley. But the Guillam who reappears in the Karla trilogy acts more sensibly than the popinjay who helps corner Dieter and drive Mundt out of the country. Belying le Carré's description of him as "a polished and thoughtful man," the Guillam of *Call* affects superior airs. This languid, faintly decadent intelligence officer calls Smiley "dear boy" and "old dear," even though he's Smiley's junior by twenty years. The years between *Call* and *Tinker, Tailor* will improve Guillam. He's less self-consciously witty and more down to earth, and he cares more about people in the Karla books. He also has depths not revealed in *Call*. A womanizer of forty who disapproves of his dalliance but feels compelled to enjoy it as long as he can, he wins our hearts with his losing bouts of conscience. *Smiley's People* finds him reformed. He has married a much younger French woman and is waiting to become a father for the first time at age fifty. His emergence as a likable person with ordinary worries and involvements parallels his author's growing commitment to everyday reality. This commitment, barely in evidence in *Call for the Dead*, will slide from view nearly altogether in *A Murder of Quality*, a book that comes closer to formula writing than any other from le Carré's hand.

Chapter Six
Lenten Rites

A Murder of Quality (1962) finds le Carré a traditionalist in matters of narrative form. More synthetic than exploratory in its inventiveness, the work hews to the curve of the cerebral drawing-room murder. It also resembles *Call for the Dead* in both its strong awareness of social class and assumed ease of storytelling manner. Murder again disrupts a marriage because of a longstanding secret tie, as well. But Stella and Stanley Rode aren't Communists like the Fennans; the politics of *Murder* are small scale and academic. Stella Rode has unearthed a scandal in the past of Terence Fielding, one of her husband's faculty colleagues at venerable Carne School, and has been persecuting him by threatening to divulge it.

Like the Fennans, the Rodes have been married about eight years. They also live outside of London; one of them is slaughtered both near home and in winter (the book's time setting is given in Chapter 2 as February 1960); Stella died, as Sam did, after asking in writing for protection; recalling that of Sam, her murder occurs before Smiley discusses her pleas for help with the magazine editor and former Intelligence colleague she had written to. After hearing of Stella's death, the Londoner Smiley will investigate in Dorset, site of Carne, just as he did in Surrey in *Call*. He will also have help. But because the crime he investigates disregards national security, he won't call on Peter Guillam. Nor does the skilled, likable Mendel reappear, even though he's mentioned (in Chapter 3). The Smiley of *Murder* reinstates le Carré's belief that crime-fighting is a team effort by relying on Miss Ailsa Brimley in London and upon short, thickset Inspector William Rigby of the Carne Constabulary in Dorset; to clinch the point, Rigby, Brim, and Smiley are all present at the culprit's arrest in the last chapter.

Anthony Boucher probably had the mainstream tradition of English mystery fiction in mind when he praised *Murder* as an "admirablywritten study in levels of snobbery and cruelty, rich in subtle explorations of character."[1] The people in the book, most of whom are connected to Carne, with its strong sense of class privilege, prize important social and family ties, a good wardrobe and address, and a public school education. Affecting the nonchalance and civility of the public school man himself, le Carré works within the artistic limits staked out by Conan Doyle, Sayers, and Christie. Standing in for the weekend country house is Carne, a four-hour train ride from London's Waterloo Station and a community so self-enclosed that it has never formed ties with the neighboring village of Pylle. The gory and the demonic come in with the female. There is, first, Jane Lyn, a local eccentric who inhabits a derelict church, which she festoons with dead animals. Next comes Stella Rode, a power-hungry schemer from England's industrial north. Like so many other murderees in English mainstream mysteries, she saddens few or none of her survivors by dying. The way she dies, being bludgeoned fifteen or twenty times by a length of coaxial cable, saves the investigation from being cold and mechanical. "I've seen some nasty things in my time, but this is the worst," says the policeman who finds her corpse; "Blood everywhere. Whoever killed her must have been covered in it."

This savagery stays in our minds as we read on. And what we read is largely analytical and logical. In *Murder*, Smiley investigates private rather than public crime; the way to the felon isn't provided by the safe house but by the microscope. Smiley's career as a spy, which has been temporarily halted, only grazes the action. As has been seen, he and Brim served together in the war; only slightly more thematic is his tie with Carne housemaster, Terence Fielding, whom he met once recently and whose brother Adrian he served with before Adrian died in the war. The challenge of naming the killer before Smiley does offers many enticements. In the chapter following the discovery of Stella Rode's body, a local policeman says, "We've got enough clues to cover a Christmas tree." Some of the clues are dead ends; others form patterns that invite tracing. The crime puzzle format dominates. Skillful and compact most of the way, *Murder* features a crime, several suspects, and clues which the detective finds, analyzes, and interprets in order to name the culprit. Like many other works belonging in the mainstream of literary detection, it's more cerebral than actional, the apprehension of an abortive escape of the culprit taking only a paragraph.

Tallying with the book's academic setting, power and social rank move the characters more than sex and money. Stella Rode raises so many hackles in Carne because the bitchiness and intrigue surrounding her mean nothing to her north country chapel independence. She won't play the Class Game along with the Dorset Anglicans comprising her husband's academic set. But her inverse pride in being middle class among the well-born has also sharpened her destructiveness. Several of her acquaintances, therefore, have reasons to kill her. The murder victim who's either controversial or nasty enriches the hunt because he/she extends the field of suspects. The sleuth must work harder, sifting evidence, deciding the worth of leads and clues, and checking the stories of witnesses as the culprit bounces suspicion off himself to foil the investigation. In *Murder*, the sleuth is both helped and handicapped. The long recitation in the book's next-to-last chapter, setting forth the evidence needed to convict, which traditionally belongs to the sleuth, comes from the most likely suspect. His words supply the psychological background which joins the loose ends. What Smiley hears from him lets him confront the murderer with an accurate and detailed reconstruction the next day.

But the evidence that dooms Terence Fielding comes to Smiley from the police laboratory—analyses of both the handwriting on a student's exam paper and the blood found on the murder weapon. The solution to the mystery hinges on scientific detection. Accustomed to empirical observation himself, Smiley builds much of his case around the close examination of physical evidence. Forensic detection resolves the crime puzzle in the book. Besides analyzing blood and handwriting, police experts dust surfaces for fingerprints, examine footprints in the snow, and search the area around Carne for other tips. Yet this scientific rigor only moves to the fore after murder has been done; though reason regulates life, it can't constitute it. Nothing has a fixed value in *Murder*; no logical system is reliable; priorities may shift without warning; appearances deceive. Two of the physically largest people in the book (one of whom is a woman with a man's name), Shane Hecht and Terence Fielding, are also the most mean spirited. Also, Fielding commits murder, not his colleagues, Charles Hecht and Felix D'Arcy, even though their foreign-sounding names might imply a tendency to flout values usually connected with English public school education.

I

Le Carré's 1968 statement in *Saturday Review*, that the phrase, "gentleman-writer," seems to him "a contradiction in terms,"[2] refers to the social criticism set forth in *Murder*. At times the novel reads like a series of bright remarks. The witty irreverence of faculty wife Shane Hecht recalls Oscar Wilde. The day after Stella Rode's funeral, she quips. "I hate funerals, don't you? Black is so unsanitary." Even Shane's compliments are tipped with poison. Within minutes of delivering her Wildean *non sequitur*, she says, "Stella Rode was such a nice person.... She did such clever things with the same dress." If this witty malice amused le Carré, it didn't limit his attention to the social milieu which gave rise to it. Building a cultural frame for his mystery, he invents for the area surrounding Carne a topography, an architecture, and a history dating back to King Arthur and St. Andrew, patron saint of sailors. Family histories expressive of life styles and value systems also enrich the action. Stella represents a decadent fringe of England's nonconformist mentality, just as her assassin, Fielding, exposes the frayed edge of genteel Anglicanism. Stella's grandfather was a Lancashire pottery king. Both her magistrate father and the Baptist minister who conducts her funeral service display the moral fortitude, seriousness, and tradesman's shrewdness that earned the grandfather a fortune. Stella's inverse pride in descending from trade, her refusal to conform to Carne society, and her obsession with sin portray another side of her northern inheritance. The Calvinism and Wesleyanism of her dissenting forebears betray her into revivalist excursions. Unfortunately, as her husband says, these outings worsen rather than relieve the disorder actuating them. Stella will help people in order to pry secrets from them which she'll later use to make them squirm.

Other outsiders influence Carne School more than insiders would care to admit. The process is symbolized by the local madwoman Jane Lyn becoming both suspect and star witness in the Stella Rode murder case. Stella herself plagues hearts both within and outside Carne, despite being new to Dorset. Her husband's students also glean knowledge outside the classroom that will stay with them longer than what they learn from their academic studies. The first recorded conversation in the book shows two Carne boys enumerating Stanley Rode's shortcomings and agreeing that Rode's not a gentleman. The snobbery infusing this conversation stems from centuries of Carne insularity. Having turned away from their neighbors, Carne's schoolmasters have always wheeled in a tight groove, rarely exceeding the limits defined by the Abbey, the classroom, the playing fields, the sherry party, and High Table. No wonder they're such easy prey for Stella; no wonder, too, that Simon and Anne Snow, a young faculty couple new to Carne, are planning to move on. Carne stands for what is rearguard, narrowminded, and vain. The suspicion that their members lack wit and culture has turned the faculty against itself.

The various receptions, dinners, and teas described in the book convey this animosity. Because they fear that their colleagues may be reciprocating the contempt they exude, Carne's schoolmasters live in a fogbelt of insecurity and barely suppressed self-hatred. Nor will the vapors lift. Having been faced with their worst selves, the academic family of Carne tries to hide behind manner and pretense. Bound by tradition and proximity rather than choice, they delight in sideswiping one another in polished but scathing jests. The posturing of Felix D'Arcy, the senior tutor, is colored by "an effeminate malice towards his colleagues." D'Arcy grabs every chance to show up his colleagues. Following suit, Fielding will serve the Hechts a fine meal but will then stop Charles from enjoying his longed-for after-dinner pipe. He continues to frustrate his guests' ability to savor the afterglow of the food he has served them. At the end of Chapter 1, he sees the Hechts out of his house, closing and slyly bolting the door behind them "perhaps a fraction earlier than courtesy required."

Those accustomed to such slights will always be on guard against detractors real or imagined. The failure of the Carne set to counter Stella's rejection of their snobbery conveys a failure to cope. Stella's attendance at the local Baptist church and her charity work within the village have broken the town-gown barrier for the first time. But these activities have also angered Carne die-hards. The associations called forth with interchange by Stella's murder weapon, a length of coaxial cable, symbolize the hopelessness of overcoming class barriers in England. When used to join members of different social backgrounds, this aid to electronic communication causes death. Le Carré shares the worries of the Carne set but without extending sympathy. The quality that Carne claims to uphold is a sham, which, ironically, damages its upholders most of all.

Le Carré wouldn't endorse this self-inflicted hurt any more than he would Stella's reform projects, poisoned, as they are, by the primeval ooze humanity has worked so hard to crawl out of. Her death is inevitable; anything built upon ooze and slime will sink into its own quagmire. Yet she does forecast the change that will refresh an England gone tired, sordid, and monotonous. She represents a vital first step toward renewal. Yet neither she nor her kind will inherit England, insists le Carré. By razing barriers and exposing the rottenness of foundations, she has served posterity well. Her death confirms the value of her service. Like a Hegelian heroine, she destroys outmoded social forms. But even though this destruction helps the commonweal, it violates the law and thus calls for punishment; as flawed as it is, the law must be squared. The length of coaxial cable that kills her also expresses the electronic future from which she'll be excluded. But the depravity that fuels her power lust disqualifies her from membership in *any* sane, responsible society. By keeping it in view, le Carré has dovetailed abnormal psychology, social change, and politics within the framework of Hegelian myth. Change won't stampede through dowdy England. Rather than surging forward, it will observe a waddling, crablike rhythm. The old ways will be supplanted slowly. Representatives of alien orders like Stella and Fielding will enact this supplanting. Although a cautious social historian, le Carré does speak thoughtfully and accurately. His caution is well judged. Even Nietzsche located his *Übermensch*, or Superman, generations in the future.

Described as "massive and genial, with his splendid mane of gray hair," Terence Fielding looks like the deliverer England needs to rouse it from its lethargy. But the grim reality governing Carne's senior housemaster belies the god-like assurance and ease he exudes. Fielding plans to retire from Carne after the end of the Lenten half of the academic year, which has just begun. The promise put forth by the transit from Lent to Easter, and from winter to spring, never graces him. His wrongdoing will stop him from retiring with honor. Rather than rising to the dignity his age and service would normally confer, he sinks to defeat. His arrest by the police at the end will turn his mind to the harsher aspects of the Lenten season—abstinence and cold. And spiritual self-reflection? The possibility of his being hanged for a murderer before Easter points him to the ranks of the damned; he'll not celebrate resurrection. The hell that beckons would be familiar to him. Short of funds and lacking in job security, he has known no peace for decades. His calling himself a fraud and insisting that he has ruined his life perverts the offhanded self-disparagement affected by the English public school man. Although his fine phrases and godlike looks mask the harshness of his words, they can't hide the truth that he takes every chance to demean himself, Carne, and the traditions it rests on. "None of us has read a word on any subject since we left University," he says of himself and his colleagues.

Illuminating his self-scorn is a remark from le Carré's 1972 novel, *The Naive and Sentimental Lover*, made by a mother to her small son: "You can't really spread much love around unless, in a funny way, you love yourself as well," *Murder* would have taken on artistic strength had it applied this remark more rigorously to Fielding. Le Carré does include the survivor's guilt plaguing Fielding since the death of his brother Adrian in the war. But his treatment is brief and casual. He doesn't show Fielding's inner drama advancing or retarding the present-tense action as much as he might have. Character is thinly drawn in *Murder*. For instance, le Carré refers to the "great ugly body" of Shane Hecht and "the slow rotten smile of a whore" she turns on Fielding in Chapter 1. But he restricts her whorish malice to the drawing room and reduces it to a handful of nasty remarks. Fielding, too, is assigned intriguing qualities; in Chapter 5, Smiley sees him as "changeful but sterile, daring but fugitive; unbounded, ingenuous, yet deceitful and perverse." Though Fielding displays himself more than did Dieter Frey, his loose counterpart in *Call for the Dead*, little of his asserted range of personality comes through. The key event of his life had to be an indiscreet homosexual incident with "some Air Force Boy" during the war. The scandal caused by the incident has poisoned his career. Because of it, he has never had a regular contract at Carne. And since he must be hired each year as a temporary, he will have no pension, either. His shameful past, low pay, and lack of job security could have indeed gorged him with self-hatred. But these privations could have also strengthened him; having survived his trauma, he should respect himself. But where would such self-esteem leave the novel? Le Carré couldn't have shown it sinking his self-hatred or he'd have removed the hurt that drove Fielding to commit murder. But he could have given Fielding a depth and complexity he now lacks by showing his day and night sides in conflict. Such a clash would have made both him and his crimes more believable.

Most sadly neglected is the tie between his guilty past and his hectic present. Stella Rode has been torturing him with threats of scandal and ruin. Yet Carne's senior tutor, Felix D'Arcy, another Oxbridge-Mayfair type, has been squeezing Fielding much longer than Stella; D'Arcy it is who hires him anew every year and then overworks him for a low wage. Sex provides no criminal motives. According to Fielding, D'Arcy, who lives with his sister, is a "sublimated pansy." Fielding might have been describing himself. Though he claims to love his head prefect, Tim Perkins, he doesn't flinch from murdering Tim when Tim finds evidence linking him to Stella's death. Nor is there any indication that he ever approached Tim sexually, although he might have wanted to. His strongest motives are those of self-preservation. Any sexual overture coming from Stella, his victim, wouldn't be aimed at the boudoir, either; in Chapter 19, we learn how she flirted with an ex-schoolmate of Stanley in order to insult him. Stanley also says that she enjoyed kissing him during evening walks in the country when they were newlyweds. But because her sexuality is probably as distorted as the rest of her, she'd most likely use it only as she did with her husband's ex-schoolmate—to manipulate or control. This childless woman's brutal whipping of her dog, her surrogate child, conveys her hostility to the natural flow and function of sex.

Another hideous portent that materializes as an anatomical image occurs in Fielding's statement in Chapter 5, "You see before you a dead soul, and Carne is the body I live in." Would that le Carré had invested more artistic energy in this striking image. He does try to make the image thematic in Chapter 16 when he has Fielding say of Stella and Tim, "Carne killed them; it was Carne." His words compel our attention. Though no one suspects him as he speaks, he has killed both Tim and Stella. But how do the thirty years he has spent at Carne as a second-class citizen make him the school's avatar? His comment later in the chapter, "The very name Carne means quality," offers little help. With his usual self-disparagement, he had called himself a parasite when he claimed to inhabit the body of Carne. No clear connection emerges joining Carne, quality, and this old self-hater who is stumbling toward a lonely, threadbare future. One wouldn't emerge any more clearly either if his tie to Carne were stronger or more legitimate. If the school epitomized quality, as he claims, it wouldn't have hired him in the first place, let alone kept him on its faculty for thirty years. Anyone cursed with such a bad self-image couldn't teach or do anything else well. He'd also be an awful role model for the boys. Perhaps the quality he ascribes to Carne was never there. Perhaps Carne is a parasite feeding upon the English body politic just as he feeds upon Carne. The correspondence merits more attention than le Carré directs to it.

The attention he *has* given the correspondence implies that Fielding named Carne as the killer of Stella and Tim to foil the investigation and thus shield himself. Stella and Tim have nothing in common, differing in age, sex, temperament, values, and background. Though both died because they knew too much— ironically, in a school setting, where the acquisition of knowledge should be the greatest goal—Fielding kills one of them with relish and the other with a sense of loss and grief. Quality isn't being murdered in either case. The two victims are far from exceptional. Tim fares badly both as a student and a head prefect; the scheming Stella degrades herself anew every time she plots to hurt someone; Fielding, the book's other major casualty, thinks too little of himself to attain any height. Neither could le Carré's title refer to the upper-class origins and people involved in the case. Stella, the first murder victim, scoffed at Carne's aristocratic heritage. Her highborn successor, Tim Perkins, might have enhanced and extended it on the cello he was learning to play so well. Fielding appreciates the beauty of Carne's heritage, buildings, and flora but lacks the talent to capture them in art. Unfortunately, the tendencies and foibles of Fielding, Tim, and Stella form no coherent pattern that justifies the title, *A Murder of Quality*. Unless the title of his second novel conveys some special meaning le Carré isn't sharing, it makes little sense. In fact, together with the book's orthodoxy of subject, setting, and technique, it tempts us to ask whether it was written before *Call for the Dead*.

II

What dates the writing of *Murder* later than that of *Call* is le Carré's treatment of Smiley. The George Smiley of *Murder* is more developed and reflects more authorial care. As cautious as before, he still thinks on paper—weighing evidence, reviewing what he knows, and pondering the value of different clues and leads. His prose comes before us at crucial moments. He shares his insights with Brim in a letter in Chapter 4, and he uses what he has unearthed to find a motive for murder in Chapter 11. No armchair sleuth, he also performs well in the field. He impersonates both a journalist and a prospective dog buyer to get witnesses to talk. To coax a confession out of Fielding in the last chapter, he twice uses the phrase, "For Adrian's sake." This appeal is blatant opportunism. Fielding's brother Adrian, long dead, has nothing to do with the deaths of Stella and Tim. Yet Smiley's scheming costs him no guilt pangs. First, his long career as a spy has taught him that crime stoppers can't worry about squaring means and ends if they want results. He also has to ignore morality because of the mystery hemming him in. Neither smug nor knowing, the Smiley of *Murder* keeps pronouncing on the unknowability of life. "I don't believe ... that we can ever entirely know what makes anyone do anything," he muses, while pondering "the obscurity of motive in human action." Wrapped in darkness, he probably can't be blamed for snatching at the few points of light that break up the void.

The void rules. Displaying the city man's fear of wild, lonely landscapes, he panics when he visits Stella's murder site by himself on a dark evening. Earlier, he had admitted that he was frightened of Jane Lyn, who would soon appear at the murder site and claim to have seen the devil careening through the skies. Nor did this modest man anticipate having to sink his fears in order to approach Jane within moments of catching sight of her. The self-mastery he demonstrates here will also help him confront Fielding at the end with his guilt, even though his modesty deters him from claiming credit. Outmaneuvering, cornering, and then apprehending Fielding, in fact, gives him more grief than pride. Fielding has already suffered more than he deserves. In arresting him, Smiley is also smirching one of the few honorable ties the service has provided him. The regret he feels for betraying the memory of Adrian may not jolt him as sharply as did his killing of Dieter Frey in *Call.* But it jars him enough to ruin any sense of victory he might have enjoyed in apprehending a murderer. No avenger or angry justicer, he. Le Carré describes him preparing to confront Fielding as "already sickened by the kill" he's getting ready to enact. The enactment of the kill doesn't lift his spirits; as in *Call,* he's killing a past he had been idealizing as a refuge from the squalor and drabness of postwar England.

The book's closing sentences, "But there was nothing to see. Only the half-lit street, and the shadows moving along with it," deny him both vision and achievement. Capturing this letdown, le Carré's imagery also recalls the ravaged landscape where Stella was murdered. The shadowy figures drifting in London's half light seem as marginal as Stella or Jane Lyn, the people Smiley associates with the brooding morbid countryside he wanders in Chapter 7. Needless to say, nothing he has seen or done the past week will enrich these cardboard existences, either, in his opinion.

The blend in him of rationality and obsession marks an advance from the Smiley of *Call.* His careful, systematic reasoning as an investigator can't protect him from the Kafkaesque plight of guilt without crime. Most dramatically, he can't stop hurting or slandering Stanley Rode. Not only does he misrepresent himself as an obituary columnist so that he can pry evidence from Rode that will convict him as Stella's killer. He has already condemned Rode in his own mind. Without a scrap of proof, he discredits this recent widower to both Stella's minister and her father; then he tells Inspector Rigby to arrest him. He's driven to damage Rode. Incredibly, he shows her stern magistrate father, a figure of Calvinist justice, the letter in which Stella claimed that Rode wanted to kill her. But why is Smiley trying to bring Rode down? What could have robbed this prudent, humane man of his honor, justice, and fairness? As has been noted, a possible explanation for his wildness lies in Chapter 24 of *Smiley's People,* where he brings the Soviet attaché officer, Anton Grigoriev, to his knees. Like the former academic Smiley, Grigoriev and Rode are both short, stubby teachers with marital troubles. By turning his wrath on them in the name of justice, he's declaring his superiority over them. He's also indirectly punishing himself for having become Ann's victim. His enslavement to Ann has ruled out all other forms of protest.

The opening scenes of *Murder* find him in familiar straits; he's both unemployed and living alone. He's also restless. He tells his friend Brim at the *Christian Voice* that being out of work has given him the time to investigate Stella Rode's murder in Carne. He *will* enjoy the change that going out of town will bring. But the change is actuated by motives he hasn't voiced. If Ann did come back to Bywater Street with him from Zurich, as he was expecting at the end of *Call*, she couldn't have stayed long. Nor could he be leaving home to bury thoughts of her. If anything, his trip to Carne sharpens his awareness of her. His private and professional selves meet at Carne, Ann being the cousin of a Dorset peer, Lord Sawley, whose family has been connected to Carne for 400 years. Also, during his investigation, Smiley stays at the Sawley Arms. His departure from Carne by train in Chapter 18 reveals that he went there to confront an image of Ann:

He hadn't wanted to come.... He'd been afraid of the place where his wife had spent her childhood, afraid to see the fields where she had lived. But he had found nothing, not the faintest memory ... to remind him of her.

Smiley isn't telling all. During his stay in Carne, he put up at the Sawley Arms despite having always hated it. He won't face his purpose for visiting Carne directly. The purpose takes the form of his grammar school *alter ego*, Stanley Rode. Like Grigoriev after him, Rode bears the brunt of Smiley's refusal to cope with his marriage. In his role of whipping boy, Rode allows Smiley to scourge himself for failing with Ann and to feel that he has served justice.

Any pangs of conscience he suffers for abusing Rode he keeps to himself. But the Lenten setting of the action conduces to the spiritual self-reflection that might well lead to repentance. Le Carré's many references to the February gusts, snows, and chill of Dorset put the redemption brought by Easter a long way off. Smiley belongs with the unredeemed. Both he and the culprit Fielding have female aides known by shortened versions of their last names. Balancing Brim, Smiley's one-time colleague in Intelligence, is Fielding's house servant, Miss Truebody, who is usually called True. Le Carré keeps reminding us that such identities may be religious as well as moral. Not only was Carne founded as a religious community; its boys always seem to be marching off to mandatory prayers at the college chapel, as well. Then there is mad Janie living in a disused chapel. The book's most powerful scene, in fact, occurs at the chapel at the end of Chapter 7 amid an atmosphere of terror and foreboding. The patchy snow, the torn ground, and the gaunt, dingy house nearby, its ivy vines making crazy patterns under a pale winter sky, set the mood for Janie's insistence that she recently saw the devil flying in the wind. But nothing prepares Smiley for the shock awaiting him inside the chapel:

> Two candles and an oil lamp on the bare altar shed a dim light over the tiny chapel. In front of the altar, on the sanctuary step, sat Jane, looking vaguely towards them. Her vacuous face was daubed with strains of green and blue, her filthy clothes were threaded with sprigs of evergreen and all about her on the floor were the bodies of small animals and birds.

This barbarism, no stylistic indulgence, tallies with the novel's deep structure. Its religious context refers to the evil that Smiley has been perpetrating on Stanley Rode and that the Carne community has been perpetrating on itself. Le Carré's flinging this barbarism before us amid February gloom and ice enforces the idea that the resurgence connected with Easter may exceed the characters' reach.

Deepening this pessimism is the deftness of the plotting. In its best moments, *Murder* is neither shallow nor mechanical. After opening in Carne, it cuts, in Chapter 2, to the Fleet Street Office of the *Christian Voice*. The practices, policies, and people of London's Fleet Street, where many of Britain's newspapers and magazines have their homes, look far removed from those of Carne. A letter has joined the two worlds. Stella Rode, who descends from one of the *Voice's* original patrons, has written to say that her husband wants to kill her. Because of her family's fifty-year tie to the *Voice*, Brim, the magazine's editor for the past fourteen years, calls in Smiley. Ironically, Smiley will hear about Stella's murder on the telephone from Fielding, her murderer and his only contact at Carne. A clever plot turn of a different sort comes at the end of Chapter 17, when Stanley Rode, the most likely suspect, disappears. But the impression of guilt he has given goes away quickly. The next chapter reveals that he went straight from Carne to the *Voice*. His behavior on Fleet Street goes against what might normally be expected of a murder suspect. And so does his reason for coming to London. So malignant was Stella that he wants to stop the *Voice* from running the flattering obituary of her they had prepared. His plea for justice bespeaks innocence. Had he murdered her, he'd have carefully avoided publicizing any bitterness he might still feel.

Moments like his account of Stella's malignancy draw us into the quest for the culprit. Just as intriguingly, le Carré connects betrayal, capture, and death with food. The Rodes dined at Fielding's the night of Stella's death. Echoing Shakespeare's Macbeth and T. S. Eliot's *Murder in the Cathedral*, Fielding feeds Stella and then carves her. The motif recurs at the end. Just before leaving Carne, Smiley invites Fielding to dine with him in London. His heart seems to have opened to the lonely, broken man. Yet his words at the end of Chapter 16, spoken inwardly after his dinner invitation, "Terence Fielding was the most accomplished liar he had met for a long time," suggest that he had comforted Fielding in order to lower his guard. The impression carries into Chapter 20, the book's last, in which the two men dine with Miss Brimley. Just before accusing Fielding of murdering two people, Smiley refills his wine glass and speaks tenderly of Adrian. In view of his intentions, his geniality smacks of sadism. He knows that he has cornered Fielding, just as Fielding anticipated killing Stella while feeding and exchanging pleasantries with *her*.

Until Rode's visit to the *Voice* a chapter from the end, Stella's evil and thus her murderability both remain open questions. The new faculty family at Carne, mathematician Simon Snow and his wife Anne, praise Stella to Smiley for helping them settle into their house. The esteem in which they hold her impresses us. They're the only likable faculty couple at Carne whom we meet. They also find the place stuffy and plan to leave. Such moral clarity dignifies their high opinion of Stella. Yet le Carré has engineered this dignity to manipulate our responses. The Snows' approval of Stella, it later turns out, was based on incomplete information; the furniture mover they found so frustrating only bestirred himself in their favor because Stella was blackmailing him. Le Carré sustains our interest in the Snows' praise of Stella. Whereas he doesn't discredit them with the traditional association of snow and death, he does call attention to the negative aspects of snow. Snow is on the ground the bleak, cold day Smiley arrives in Carne; it patches the earth near Jane Lyn's chapel on the evening when the chapel is strewn with dead birds and animals; the ground was also snowy when Stella dies.

Less sympathetic than the Snows to begin with, Carne's effete, mincing senior tutor Felix D'Arcy recovers little of our favor by puling about Stella's clothes, her religion, and her frequenting the public laundry. But his statement that she enjoyed ridiculing her husband in public discloses an important truth; Rode confirms the story himself later in the book. Shrewdly, le Carré has used an obnoxious character as a truthsayer in order to lure us into discrediting both the character and his words before testing other explanations. One of these comes from the veterinarian Stella had ordered to put down her dog. Two chapters after hearing the Snows praise Stella, Smiley listens to the vet say of her, "She was trouble." Twelve chapters into the twenty-chapter book, she's still an enigma. Though a case seems to be building against her, it's still too shaky and unformulated to win our assent. Le Carré, meanwhile, has encouraged us to read on while tempting us to mix reason and sentiment. Without more supporting evidence than we have, we can't form an opinion of the controversial Stella. And what we think of her matters a great deal because it determines our attitude toward both her slayer and his apprehension.

Unfortunately, our attitude sours before the investigation gains momentum. The novel never recovers from le Carré's mishandling of the murder. As soon as the Rodes leave Fielding's dinner party, the interior logic of the plot comes adrift. This disintegration is predictable. Rode had given an examination the afternoon of the party. After proctoring it, he had chapel duty. "As an expediency," he gave the exams to Tim Perkins, Fielding's head of house, so that he could later collect them and take them home. This arrangement makes no sense. The only expediency it creates is temporary, and the gains it brings reverse themselves quickly. Before delivering the exams, Tim removes his from the rest, fills in the answers he had left out, and then replaces it. His dishonesty will cost him his life, even though le Carré never shows us convincingly how. Other problems move to the fore. Why didn't Rode lock his exam case before giving it to Tim? And why did he go back to Fielding's to pick it up after he had forgotten it on his way home from the party? Even after conceding the point that the exams had to be graded quickly, we can't see merit in Rode's zeal to recover them. He'd have had to stay up all night to finish grading the batch by morning. The reason given in the text, that Stella sent him back so that she could later taunt Fielding in private, won't pass muster, either. Fielding would have had to receive Rode at home to give him the case, then overtaken him on bicycle on his return trip without being recognized, murdered Stella, and hidden the evidence before Rode's return.

To assume that all these events could have happened within a short time span is preposterous. To begin with, Rode would have certainly recognized the distinctive-looking Fielding; the local madwoman, Jane Lyn, who knew him less well, identified him straightaway. Not only was the moon full the night of Stella's murder, helping visibility. The snow on the ground provided still more brightness. Then there's the problem with the Rodes' dog. Stella had just beaten the dog (as Fielding would beat her). Then she ordered a veterinarian to kill it after telling him falsely that the dog had bitten a mailman. It's hard to know what she was thinking when she gave this order because the death of the dog left her unprotected. The dog wouldn't have let Fielding pound her; as "a large mongrel, quite an intelligent animal," it may have kept Fielding away from her altogether. She miscalculated fatally by destroying the dog. Though accustomed to meeting Fielding late at night, she never expected him to attack her. Rode's behavior around the time of her death is also puzzling. Why did he insist that she kill the dog after seeing it covered with bruises and welts? Was he deliberately removing her protection from intruders so that one might kill her? While inviting these questions, le Carré withholds evidence on which answers can be based. Stella he associates with night and darkness throughout. This doer of dark deeds enjoyed midnight vigils; Stanley recalls walking with her in the dark during their youth; her letter to the *Christian Voice* is read at night; she dies in darkness. But most of the darkness that hides her from us comes from le Carré's inexperience. Stella carries a disproportionately heavy load of guilt for a character who never appears. Even Smiley, who never met her, refers to "her twisted will" and "her twisted little mind." Such attacks would mean more if she had come before us—either to defend herself or to confirm her wickedness. Her self-defeating acts might have declared themselves as symptoms of moral conflict or suppressed guilt, giving the plot an inwardness it now lacks.

But if *Murder* suffers from thinness of execution, it's also marred by inconsistency and, perhaps, lack of authorial concentration. "Massive and enveloping," Shane Hecht is compared to "a faded Valkyrie." Yet the next sentence refers to "all the black hair on her head." Having lived in Germany for several years, le Carré should have known that Wagner's Valkyries are blond. He also has trouble with the footing around Carne. At the start of Chapter 12, Smiley walks through some "thick mud" leading to a kennel. Yet later in the chapter, on the very same day, he notes, outside a local church, that "the ground was hard despite last night's rain." A villager in the next chapter, which unfolds, presumably, several hours later, warns a visitor, "The lane's still quite slippery from the snow," and, later that night, a policeman recalls that "the snow was hard and showed no prints" near the Rodes the night of Stella's murder. Such radical changes in both the atmosphere and the earth's surface could foil any police investigation. Perhaps le Carré intended these changes to reflect his portrayal of the human character as deceptive and obscure. Smiley, we recall, keeps saying such things as, "We just don't know what people are like." While reviewing the various suspects in Chapter 11, he also writes, "Terence Fielding—in a sane world, no conceivable motive." But he helps his author cover his tracks by adding immediately, "Yet was it a sane world?" This mystification is included to mitigate the shoddiness of the motivation; Carne's turf, now spongy, now hard, now slick, offers no reliable footholds. Although his own wrong-footedness gives no hint of it, the le Carré of *Murder* could know more than he's telling; he was born and then studied in Dorset. His failure either to include accurate information about Dorset's weather and underfooting or to treat consistently the information he does include characterizes the book.

Later in his career, he learned how to touch in vital data while avoiding the dead hand of overexplicitness. But overexplicitness isn't best avoided by failing to buttress one's plot with concrete detail and direct statement. *A Murder of Quality* errs in this direction, much of its vitality leaking into the vagueness caused by scamped or flawed development.

Chapter Seven
Turning the World Upside Down

The Spy Who Came in from the Cold tested le Carré's creativity more than either of his earlier two books did. Returning to the intelligence work that actuated *Call*, it also updated the German setting of his first novel. The Germany of *Spy* is post-World War II; it comes before us as part of the present-tense action rather than in retrospect; it takes its savor from East Berlin rather than Dresden. Jews once again play the roles of victims; in place of Dieter Frey and the Fennans are Elizabeth Gold and Jens Fiedler. Responsible for their deaths is Sam Fennan's assassin, Hans-Dieter Mundt. Soon after murdering Fennan, Mundt flew back to East Germany and rose to prominence in his country's security network. It also comes out that he was recruited by the Circus before leaving England; Mundt is London's man in East Berlin. But his tie to London has been inferred by a colleague, who accuses him, before a special tribunal, of treason and conspiracy. The tribunal restores the double-solution device of *Murder*, where one logical explanation of guilt yields to another—still tighter, better documented, and more logically satisfying. By building the device into the machinery of a formal trial, the novel creates exciting surprises together with sharp insights into the spying profession. The artistry that unearths these riches and makes them thematic has accounted for the book's great popularity. Boucher is one of the book's many reviewers whose high praise won so many friends for le Carré's 1963 novel; Boucher said of *Spy* in the *New York Times Book Review*, "Here is a book light years removed from the sometimes entertaining trivia which have (in the guise of spy novels) cluttered the publishers' lists for the past year."[1]

To supply the benefits of stability and continuity, George Smiley plays an important, but small, part. How small, though, we can't say. At a London restaurant in Chapter 6 where Alec Leamas, the book's main figure, talks to a Communist agent, a "little sad man with spectacles" is sitting alone at the next table. Also unidentified at a Dutch airport where Leamas disembarks in Chapter 8 is "a small frog-like figure in glasses, an earnest, worried little man" reading a newspaper. Smiley could well be watching Leamas's movements considering the stake he has in them. Leamas goes to his home the day he leaves jail; Smiley pays Leamas's debts after Leamas leaves the country; he's on the other side of the Berlin Wall exhorting Leamas to jump in the book's last scene; in Chapter 11, together with Peter Guillam, he had visited Liz Gold, who saw him as "a kindly worried little man" while he questioned her gently about her tie with Leamas. Withal, Smiley appears on stage less than five per cent of the time of the action. The tactic of supplanting him with Leamas, whom le Carré had fewer qualms about killing, helps the novel's moral theme attain a darkness commensurate with its politics.

Pessimism is also a function of imagery in *Spy*. The book is full of interiors that are cold and grubby or dingy and smelly. There's no escaping the stenches the book gives off. Dirty dishes, half-empty coffee cups, ashtrays brimming with cold cigarette butts, and the reek of stale whiskey assault the reader in the novel's first half. The bare-bones effect achieved by le Carré's description of the border between the two Berlins in Chapter 1 foreshadows this harshness. The cinder blocks, barbed wire fencing, and glare from the arc lights of the sentries' towers, all of which will reappear at the end, are galaxies removed from the relaxed amplitude characterizing le Carré's description of Carne School early in *Call*. The dark and the chill aggravate the desperation gripping the characters as they await a friendly spy who is nine hours late arriving at the checkpoint. One-line dialogue predominates, as if those waiting in the cold and dark had run out of conversation hours before. Perhaps humanity itself has thinned and hardened in the October chill. The characters move mechanically in and out of the shadows surrounding the checkpoint hut, and none of them besides Leamas is named.

This desolation builds the mood le Carré wants to build. Writing in 1982, John Gardner called *Spy* "a brilliant, dark, economically written book which seemed, almost for the first time, to take us to the heart of the true clandestine world" of spies.[2] Revealing a new inclusiveness, assurance, and control, *Spy* sets before us the language, the moral code, and the subtext governing the intelligence world. This inside view of spying includes information about hand-to-hand combat, techniques of shadowing and questioning, the fabricating and issuing of false passports, and the arrangements for exchanging information and money. Most dramatically, the novel shows how lies and other concealments serve the spy better than the truth. Near the end of the action, Leamas says that spies everywhere follow Lenin's maxim, the expediency of temporary alliances. Based on the assumption that good results justify any means, the maxim condones practices like betraying one's field agents and using the agents' best qualities as weapons against them.

The gap between expediency and decency swallows everyone linked to spying. Tough-minded, spies are taught to resist giving in to emergencies, simple solutions, or humane impulses. Life for them is shaped by will, brains, and a respect for power. They know that the rules governing them are complex and that behavior isn't a function of action but of the reasons lurking behind action. These reasons, they also recognize, rest on the intricate, shadowy maneuverings of the powerful. Acknowledging this deviousness, Leamas says inwardly of his chief, "Control had his reasons; they were usually so bloody tortuous it took you a week to work them out." Monaghan carries the point forward. So secretive is Control that he acts like a man in hiding from himself. Neither his wife nor the woman he lives with after leaving home knows how he supports himself; his live-in lover never even learns of his wife's death from him. Monaghan shows how this exaggerated self-protectiveness tallies with the inhumanity of spying: "Just as he has replaced his real name with one describing his function, so Control appears to have yielded up all human considerations to the pursuit of successful technique, and for him ends have come totally to justify means."[3]

Both the immorality and the Byzantine thought processes governing spying emit shock waves. Fiedler, the East German security expert, has detected and accurately explained the treachery of his chief, Mundt. Yet by distorting and lying, Mundt both clears himself and destroys his accuser. Fiedler's full and logical explanation of Mundt's guilt recoils fatally; like their western counterparts, the spies that condemn Fiedler reject the truth when it's in front of their noses. Mundt survives because he knows how to protect himself. He had given Karl Riemeck, another double agent working for the British, access to secret files; then he helped Riemeck deliver these materials to the special branch. But as soon as Riemeck came under the suspicion of his East German colleagues, Mundt shot both him and the woman he was living with. He couldn't risk Riemeck's being blown, caught, and then exposing *him* as a British spy. The Circus would commend this ruthlessness, having themselves sacrificed Leamas to defeat Fiedler, who had climbed too high in GDR security to be brought down by Mundt alone. Never mind that Fiedler is kind, decent, and innocent of the conspiracy charges that lead to his death. Never mind either that Leamas testifies against his ally Mundt or that he hates Mundt. Without knowing it, he has served a master plan devised by his superiors. The plan succeeds. Fiedler dies, and Mundt arranges Leamas's escape from East Berlin.

Leamas seems the novel's main victim, narrative structure developing the truth that this stalwart who has served his chiefs loyally for decades never enjoyed their confidence. Not only was he unwittingly helping Mundt destroy Fiedler when he was trying to help Fiedler; the Circus also broke faith with him during his four years as head of its Berlin station. Time and again, he insists that, as the chief of the Berlin command, he'd have been told of the Mundt defection. He's very naive for a veteran hand. Much of the shock value of *Spy* stems from his piecemeal discovery that Control has always used him in secret operations without letting him know the operations' goals. Control even makes sure that he follows through in his masquerade as a Communist defector. Using his power as the head of the British Secret Service, he gets London's newspapers to print a release, with a photo alongside, declaring Leamas wanted by the police for violating the Official Secrets Act; the widely published news story would negate any reason he could give to his Communist overseers in Holland for returning home.

I

Commenting on the art of spy fiction, Bruce Merry claims, "A well-made spy thriller aims at the elusive quality of 'unputdownability.' It wants to be read all at once, or at a minimum of sittings."[4] What makes *Spy* so riveting are the personality and plight of its main figure. Conducting his last mission before retirement, Leamas never does come in from the cold. One can see why. Whereas the Smiley of *Call* and *Murder* had helpers, Leamas works alone; rather than helping him, his paymasters step up the pressure on him, hold back vital information, and betray him. Much of this deceit comes, moreover, when he needs help most, i.e., when he's in unfriendly hands. Can he withstand it? One reason he has survived so long in his dangerous trade is his physical strength. Despite his excessive smoking and drinking, this fifty-year-old with a swimmer's build is very strong. He spends most of the night walking the cold streets of West Berlin after the shooting death of Karl Riemeck despite the nervous and physical wear of having waited nine hours for Riemeck to turn up. Again, he walks great distances to recover grip, covering miles of

London on foot, the day of his prison release. During his outdoor briefing sessions in East Germany, his interrogator, Fiedler, though much younger, can't keep pace with him.

Nor is his athletic prowess confined to walking. A swift fist-and-elbow combination knocks out a London grocer, fracturing his cheek bone and dislocating his jaw. Leamas's list of victims goes on. Later, he kills a young German sentry in the dark with the same swift resolve he had directed to the grocer. Plucky and restless, he then butts a guard in the stomach with his head despite being bound, outnumbered, and semi-conscious. His adrenalin keeps spurting. At the end, he climbs the Wall near the Brandenburg Gate and would have pulled Liz Gold to safety, too, if the Vopos, or East German guards, hadn't shot her in her ascent. He also knows the uses of passiveness. Le Carré said of him in 1974, "Alec Leamas is a very commonplace chap, with banal inadequacies precipitated into a situation of fantasy and conditioned to respond in a special way."[5] Perhaps le Carré underrated his man. A thoroughgoing, well-tested pro who deserves the trust of his chiefs, Leamas has taught himself how to adapt to his surroundings. Though capable of violence, this nervy, irritable man displays much more passiveness than most thriller heroes. Control's not confiding in him means that the major developments of the novel occur to the side of him. The days he spends both feverish at home and languishing from his wounds in hospital also mean that many of these developments take place while he's unconscious. Then his debriefing by the Communists in London, the Hague, and East Berlin occupies much of the book. Not knowing the questions being put to him beforehand, he's again out of control. He's also being exploited. Whereas Fiedler believes Leamas can help him convict Mundt of treason, both Mundt and Control are using him to discredit and thus eliminate Fiedler.

But he couldn't serve anybody's cause unless he had the skill, experience, and instinct of a good spy. Though his years in the field have worn him down, making him liken himself to an airplane suffering from metal fatigue, he still retains the professionalism to perform well over a broad range. The performance looks deceptive. He tailspins into debt, drunkenness, and moral degeneracy to convince the Communists that he has cut all ties with the Circus. His small pension, reduced from what he had expected by a break in service, has made him want to settle a score. That the sworn enemies of the service that cheated him of his retirement allowance have offered to help him sweetens his drive to vengeance. Such is the scenario Leamas must write, act, and direct. But he can't play it straight. To trick his interrogators, he'll act unpredictably. He'll offer solid information willingly. At other times, he'll turn moody and quarrelsome, offering nothing. To live a lie, he learns, takes both insight and timing. He must assess the psychological climate of every moment to know when to hold back and when to come forth. At all times, he must stay within the bounds of probability. This, he has been trained to do. A spy's cover, no violation of self, extends or carries forward the spy's values, traits, and personality quirks. Le Carré says of Leamas in Chapter 2, "Leamas was not a reflective man and not a particularly philosophical one." He has omitted his man's ability to spot danger quickly and to improvise a plausible self that can deflect or defuse it.

Closer to the mark is his calling Leamas, later in the chapter, "stubborn, willful, contemptuous of instruction." Basically anti-social while remaining perforce a shrewd social observer, Leamas prefers danger to the workaday suburban routine of commuter trains, paper clips, and mortgage payments. As his total disregard of his former wife and children imply, he keeps people at bay. He hates being touched; rudely, he rejects the handshake of the Communist spy who delivers him to a contact in The Hague. Such rudeness will occur often. Brutally cynical, he holds no brief with friendship or religion; he reads no books and supports no political ideologies. Perhaps he does his loveless job so well because he sees it as a technical exercise rather than a blow for morality. Orlov points out that intelligence operatives often court danger out of pride.[6] A sour, inverted pride it may be that makes Leamas ridicule transcendent goals like justice, equality, and love. It probably also explains his sullen independence, a trait that will manifest itself as defiance of authority. Neither well born nor university educated, he has nonetheless acquired, within the service, a position of high trust. He has a gift for languages, speaking decent French along with fluent German and Dutch. But he's too surly, edgy, and contemptuous of office politics to opt for a desk job. The clubby, donnish ways of the Circus' executive branch annoy him, and he lacks the patience to follow regulations. When he returns from Berlin to the Circus after Riemeck's death, he refuses to comply with a new rule obligating those without a pass to file a slip. Talking to Control doesn't improve his contempt for protocol—or his manners. He'll nod or shrug his shoulders to avoid speaking to his chief. At other times, he'll act bored, speak evasively, and even snap at Control to show his impatience. He has too much pride to leaven his truculence; he's selling his skill, not his manner. And his skill was shaped in the cold rather than in committee rooms panelled in fumed oak and decorated with sporting prints.

Suitably, he first appears in the cold, conducting an operation. A man of duty, faith, and courage, he's waiting at one of the crossing points between the two Berlins for Karl Riemeck. Blown, scared, and alone, Riemeck is already nine hours late. Neither his lateness nor the pleas of an American sentry that Leamas go home to sleep can budge Leamas. Testy and sullen from the long wait, he snarls at the sentry to shut up. But if the hours of waiting have made him tense and curt, they haven't jaded his humanity. He apologizes to Elvira, Riemeck's woman, after scolding her for neglecting security. What has upset him is Riemeck's having told her of his plans to cross into the West; spies can't leak such operational disclosures if they want to survive, as the deaths of Riemeck and Elvira will show. Ironically, Leamas will make the same mistake and pay the same fatal price. Though his aims are austere, feelings keep intruding upon them and smudging their stark purity. This purity wears unusual garb. He drinks, neglects his appearance, ignores other people, and embezzles funds after his supposed resignation from the secret service; in Chapter 5, he's found dirty, feverish, and hung over in his squalid, icy room; the next chapter shows him assaulting a grocer who denied him credit.

None of these depredations, which he enacts to lure the East Germans into approaching him, hurts him as much as does opening his heart to Liz. The word ending Chapter 13 and marking the midway point of the twenty-six-chapter *Spy*, "home," proves ironical. Leamas will never come in from the cold to enjoy the cozy, anchoring warmth of home. As his unusual last name suggests, he's fated to play the sacrificial lamb. But he also contributes to his sad fate. This smart alec has the knowledge and the experience to know that he should avoid sexual intimacy while operational; as has been seen, the book's first victim, a brother spy, dies because he confides in a woman. Witnessing Riemeck's death should have sharpened Leamas's awareness of the dangers of forming a sexual tie, as should the news that Elvira was shot leaving her flat, since Leamas once lived there himself. He comes close to death several times before dying, and the death he grazes has a sexual aura. It's as if his long career of deception and denial has stirred in him the countering romantic dream of achieving love's fulfillment in death. Smiley worries about his discretion after hearing what he had told Liz before leaving her. As well he might; by confiding in Liz, Leamas has broken the foundation tenet of the spy trade. The first law of survival taught to recruits in spy academies all over the world is the need to shun emotional entanglements. The consolations of human contact are all too often paid for with the loss of both operations and lives.

The success enjoyed by the heartless Mundt also shows how the suppression of warmth can aid a spy. "A very distasteful man. Ex-Hitler youth" is how Control describes this vicious anti-Semite and murderer. Though accurate, his description omits two key facts—that Mundt does his job well and that British Intelligence both turned him and whisked him out of the country before he could be tried for murdering Sam Fennan. His killing of Riemeck at the start of *Spy* sends Leamas back to London whipped and forlorn. Leamas's fangs have been drawn. Whereas he has failed to probe Mundt's East Berlin network, his own operations have been dismantled and his top sources, murdered. This devastation emanated from the Circus. In order to protect Mundt, Control concocted it. Like the two archfoes Smiley and Karla, Mundt and Leamas end up on the same side. But the bond joining them is tighter. Ironically, the two men have already been allies for years, though Leamas was never told. Perhaps he should have foreseen the alliance. The ruthlessness of all spies everywhere razes moral guidelines and subverts traditional values. Much of Mundt's effectiveness, in fact, stems from the excellent cover furnished by his well-known scorn for the civilized decencies. The Circus's man in East Berlin, therefore, is a devil. His foil in GDR Intelligence, the dedicated, idealistic Fiedler, has served his masters faithfully. But such honor has no place in the realm of spies. In an irony typical of the book, Fiedler's masters believe him to be London's source and put him to death.

His conviction occurs at the special tribunal he had called for the purpose of stopping his superior, Mundt. As head of GDR counterintelligence, Fiedler found out that British security had been paying large sums of cash into banks in Copenhagen and Helsinki and that the withdrawal of these sums coincided with Mundt's visits. His zeal to bring Mundt down quickened by his Jewishness, Fiedler builds a strong case. The verdict might have even gone his way if the Circus hadn't stepped in. Control authorized his agents to pay Leamas's outstanding debts, to compensate the grocer Leamas had beaten up, and even to buy up the unpaid part of Liz's apartment lease. His purpose? To spend this money openly so that East German security would learn about it and yoke it to Leamas's ongoing tie with the Circus. In making their payments, the agents left their footprints everywhere. Control is deliberately wrecking the operation he sent Leamas to Germany to perform.

The wreckage goes beyond the operation. Fiedler's kindness, decency, and patriotism do him in. He dies because he argues so well against Mundt; were he less effective, here and elsewhere, the Circus wouldn't have had to bring him down. The meaning of his downfall transcends politics. When he asks Leamas in Chapter 13 what his philosophy is, he's answered, "I just think the whole lot of you are bastards." Fiedler's question means nothing to Leamas because he has never been stirred by motives of justice, reason, or love; no fighter for humanity, he. The previous chapter ended with Fiedler looking out of a window and saying, "You should see it in the Autumn ... it's magnificent when the beeches are on the turn." The chapter ends here, as it should, le Carré's point needing no embellishment. Fiedler possesses a poetic streak. His lyrical response to nature is lost on the prosaic Leamas, whom le Carré gives nothing to say in reply because he'd have seen nothing out of the window worth noting. The fact-ridden opportunist Mundt would dismiss Fiedler's effusion faster still than Leamas. The hardness and the cynicism that help him triumph as a spy have also blinded him to the beauties his triumph has spread before him. Here is the crowning irony of this irony-packed novel; the skills that help a spy win the day also leach his/her victory of meaning; a spy's survival labels him/her a moral and aesthetic dwarf. Unfortunately, the converse also applies; to be warm and human is to invite disaster, leaving the field to those too shrunken, coarse, and warped to do it justice.

II

This topsy-turvy morality finds voice in the book's rhythm. In *Spy*, le Carré confirmed his mastery as a structuralist before moving on to his later, more meditative fiction, where incident yields to inwardness. Not only do the right things happen in *Spy*; they also happen at the right time. Le Carré's intrusions remind us that we know more about the developing action than any of the characters. But our smugness is short lived. No sooner do we savor our privileged information than we are shown to have known less than we had thought; the novel we're reading differs from the one that's developing. Unhurried and precise, le Carré keeps changing, reversing, and subverting our expectations of where things are heading. Our involvement sharpens at the end of Chapter 10, for instance, the last sentence of which reads, "For the first time since it all began, Leamas was frightened." We've seen enough of Leamas to know that only something dire would scare such a seasoned veteran. Yet le Carré justifies his fears. The end of Chapter 10 finds Leamas boarding a plane for East Berlin, where he'll be beyond shouting range of help. Also disconcerting him is the question whether any pleas for help he might utter would be answered. Wanted by the police in England and feeling betrayed by Control, he has put himself in the hands of Eastern bloc spies.

But rather than probing his psyche, le Carré starts the next chapter with the short paragraph, "The men called on Liz the same evening." In no haste to dispel the tension created at the end of the last chapter, he has cut to Liz's London bedsitter in order to deepen and extend it. Liz's male visitors turn out to be Smiley and Peter Guillam, neither of whom browbeats her. But their very presence in her room, benign as it is, sharpens our concern for both her and Leamas's welfare. If Leamas's relationship with Liz hadn't compromised their safety, Circus operatives wouldn't have come calling. The scene at Liz's has done its job quietly and economically. Having already committed us to Leamas, le Carré then shows him in danger at the end of Chapter 10. The interlude at Liz's intensifies this danger in several ways— by implicating another person in it, by infusing it with emotion, and by channelling it into the operation Leamas is performing blindfolded. This dovetailing and deepening convinces us that his danger will increase as long as he stays operational. Because of her love for him, Liz remains a force even when she's off stage. But the le Carré of *Spy* prefers straight-forwardness to indirection. Carefully waiting his chance, he materializes her at the tribunal, fusing the love interest with the political intrigue. Leamas's fraught response to seeing her at the start of Chapter 22, "You bastards! Leave her alone!" enhanced by his bedraggled clothes and smashed face, gives the fusion emotional force.

Rarely will the force subside. We shall commit ourselves to a pattern of behavior or meaning only to see our commitment overturned, as safety slides, melts, or lurches into danger without warning. Threats come from surprising sources. Leamas will impress us by fielding these threats, in his degradation, better than we'd have expected him to. Notwithstanding, he's drawn even further into the web of conspiracy following his release from jail. Each succeeding phase of his supposed defection, taking him from London to The Hague and then to East Berlin, robs him of options; each phase challenges anew his wit and integrity. Both the Circus and GDR security have been working in

London, and their efforts have heated the trail to him. While Smiley pays Leamas's debts in clear view of anyone who wants to watch, the East Germans lure Liz to the GDR, allegedly to take part in a cultural exchange program but in reality to question her at the tribunal. At the end of Chapter 15, playfully called "Come to the Ball," she consoles herself with the belief that going to Leipzig will ease the pain of losing Leamas. The Leipzig invitation, ironically, will restore him to her, but in a way that sharpens the pain she had sought to ease.

But before stinging her anew, the plot offers temporary relief. Chapter 24, which unfolds after the tribunal, contains this description of Liz's passage through the prison where she had been stowed:

Liz followed ... along endless corridors, through grilles manned by sentries, past iron doors from which no sound came, down endless stairs, across whole courtyards far beneath the ground, until she had descended to the bowels of hell itself, and no one would even tell her when Leamas was dead.

Out of this Gothic labyrinth comes hope. In still another reversal of expectation, Mundt, her foe, meets her outside the prison—but to offer help, not the torment she has been awaiting. Walking with him through "the sweet, cold air of a winter's evening," she sees Leamas standing by a car. Danger and the prospect of safety had also oscillated in *his* favor. He was chained, beaten, and shouted at after killing the guard in Chapter 16. Dizzy with pain and nervous stress, he fainted. When he woke up, Mundt, his interrogator, was gone. Instead, Fiedler, thought by Leamas to be in jail, was standing nonchalantly at the foot of Leamas's hospital bed smoking a cigarette.

Bright and exhilarating, *Spy* deserves the great popularity it has enjoyed. Its wealth of plot and incident puts forth many intriguing speculations about behavior and motivation. Thanks to its timing and atmosphere, these speculations take hold. The first chapter ends with a jarring physical image—the lurching, bullet-ridden body of Karl Riemeck falling dead to the ground alongside his clattering bicycle. Using adumbration and symmetry to clinch its presentation of the inhumanity of spying, the novel ends by showing Leamas also shot dead by border guards near another of the checkpoints dividing the two Berlins. Spying is a closed circle whose end copies its deathly beginning.

The dramatic focus of this inhumanity is the tribunal. Le Carré's first two novels shared a common fault; everyone in *Call* and *Murder* took the witness stand but the culprit. *Spy* corrects this fault by developing its central idea in a gripping courtroom trial extending over four chapters, in which everyone has his/her say. Television series from the 1950s and '60s like *Perry Mason* and *The Defenders* and the films/Broadway hits, *Twelve Angry Men, The Caine Mutiny Court Martial, Witness for the Prosecution,* and *Inherit the Wind,* had made the courtroom a unified setting for the give-and-take of dazzling rhetoric, the springing of surprise disclosures, and the sudden reversal of advantage. The tribunal in *Spy* exploits much of this dramatic potential. At the outset, the odds weigh heavily against the defendant Mundt, who is clad in a gray prison uniform and flanked by guards. But the spectacular manifestation of Liz and her relentless questioning by the defense attorney, improbably "a benign figure, a little rustic," swings the balance toward Mundt. The mild, fatherly-looking defense counsel catches Liz in so many lies and inconsistencies that he demolishes what looked like a solid case against his client.

The admittedly cinematic closing sequence[7] speeds the rhythm of reversal. Liz and Leamas are driven to the Wall, which, by prior arrangement, they have ninety seconds to scale, Leamas going first and then pulling Liz to the top. But the escape can't look managed; to avert suspicion, the sentries guarding the escape route must give the impression that they tried to stop the two runaways. This arrangement contains a surprise. Again, Leamas is betrayed by his chiefs. Though the sentries permit him to reach the top of the Wall, they open fire on Liz as she's being helped up. The vividness of le Carré's description of this assault combines choking immediacy with moral revulsion. Leamas recoils in disgust from his discovery of the meaning of the bullets lodging inside Liz. Taking an operational view, Control has underrated him; Leamas won't buy his freedom with Liz's life. Grella shows how his refusal to survive on Control's terms proclaims his triumph as a man:

Alec Leamas discovers that both his love and his loyalty have been betrayed by an intricate British plot to uphold the position of a hated East German official who also happens to be a British agent—the horrible enemy is really the ally. Sickened by the betrayal ... he [Leamas] rejects the alliance and turns back.... He comes in from the cold only by choosing to die at the foot of the Berlin Wall, the only way out of his underworld.[8]

Leamas was not sent to East Germany to die. But the survival offered him rests on terms he rejects, viz., the killing of Liz to protect the operation. Thus he climbs back down the Wall to die with Liz rather than jumping to safety on the western side. Andrew Rutherford judges well to call his act of moral protest an affirmation.[9] Liz's death suited the Circus. Had she lived, she might have blabbed; her words would have blown Mundt's cover and robbed the Circus of its most vital East German source. Next, her death silences those who might accuse Mundt of helping her escape. The ending of *Spy* is as nasty and bitter as any le Carré ever wrote; the only noble impulse Leamas displays in the novel both causes and coincides with his death. Neither Mundt nor Control foresaw his dramatic protest against Liz's death. Even though he spent much of their last rendez-vous growling at her, his dying vision, of children "waving cheerfully" through a car window, expresses his conversion to the love, warmth, and wholeness she represented. His willingness to back his conversion with his death, the rebellious style of his death, and his matching his moral protest to the end of his career as a spy all negate Kenner's complaint that the "message" of *Spy* is pedestrian: "One can value nothing but immediate human relations: Leamas loves Liz, food is good, bed is warm. Under the narrative intricacies of espionage and politics is concealed the Playboy Philosophy, nothing more, and even that devoid of its jungle allure."[10]

A lifetime of denial and deceit does, indeed, prime a spy's appetite for the "immediate human relations" Kenner scoffs at. Leamas's death, elected in favor of coming in from the cold at Liz's expense, raises their value still more. Le Carré has the artistry to dramatize his ideas rather than presenting them as preachments. One of these ideas he invites without laboring is that Leamas's death helps the Circus more than his escape would have; the death solidifies Mundt's power by freeing the East German from his promise to spare Leamas. Such is the power of the heart's truth. Control misled and betrayed Leamas every step of the way of his East German mission. But in his most ruthless fantasies, he'd not have ordered the death Leamas inflicts on himself. The success the mission finally enjoys would make even the hardest spymaster wince.

Le Carré's ending his novel by confronting the Circus bureaucrats waiting for Leamas on the other side of the Wall with their own hardheartedness gives this remarkable, original novel the concluding sting it deserves. Leamas's death both intensifies and sheds fresh, revealing light on the brutal expediency le Carré had shown governing the spy trade. What is more, it does this excellent work in a context both forceful and luminous. Leamas's descending the Wall to stand by Liz's dead, faceless corpse gives the border guards no choice but to shoot him. The silence during which they hold their fire, mutely begging him to climb back to safety, clamors louder in our ears than any other sound in this busy, noisy book. In view of the dread it builds, it's also one of the most eloquent silences in the decade's popular literature.

Chapter Eight
Trespasses

The Looking-Glass War (1965) both extends and deepens le Carré's dramatized sermon on the inhumanity of spying. As Mundt showed in *Spy*, agents aren't chosen by intelligence organizations for their congeniality. Activities, the performance of which often sink the rest of us, like blackmail, treachery, and murder, earn *them* money and promotions. As in *Call* and *Spy, The Looking-Glass War* shows dirty deeds enacted under executive order. Again, spymasters risk or even destroy agents in the field. They do so not to protect the operations they have launched but to protect themselves. Their guile is a function of both sinking-lid budgets and personnel cutbacks. Security agencies would rather lie to both their sister branches and the Ministry itself than surrender a brief. This bureaucratic chicanery can leave the field agent where he doesn't want to be—unprotected and alone in a dangerous place. Writing in a voice more analytic than dramatic, le Carré shows in *War* the moral stagnancy that overtook British Intelligence in the two decades following the end of Hitler's War. No larger-than-life villains like Dieter Frey or Mundt irradiate the book. Unlike Control's elaborate scheme to protect Mundt in East Berlin, the machinations recounted in the plot are both predictable and transparent. An anonymous review in *Time,* called "More Le Carré Capers," discusses how *War* depicts a spying operation less efficient and thus more realistic than the one in *Spy*.[1]

This assessment is correct. Despite their pretension and self-righteousness, most of the spyrunners in le Carré's fourth novel barely muddle through on a moronic level. Let's see why. The action centers on a minor branch of the Defense Ministry called only The Department. Having dwindled in both manpower and prestige, The Department also lacks a clear purpose. Its executive branch consists of men who fought in the 1940s but who lack the youth, technology and bureaucratic skill to cope in the '60s. Their only victory is won over Fred Leiser, the naturalized Pole they slip into East Germany near Lübeck to photograph whatever launching pads are being built nearby to fit Soviet nuclear rockets. But they only defeat him because they cheat, perverting the values of camaraderie and fair play that helped them beat Hitler a generation before. Not for a moment do these cowards, liars, and snobs accept Leiser as one of them. Not for a moment do their capabilities impress us. Book Two of *War* opens with the Department's head, Leclerc, phoning his junior officer, John Avery. Wilf Taylor, the courier the Department sent to Finland to collect a roll of film, is dead, and Leclerc wants Avery to meet him at the office straight away, even though it's three o'clock in the morning.

Leclerc's phone call is disruptive, fatuous, and wholly in character. The Department, housed, suitably, in a "crabbed sooty villa" with grimy windows and a stained facade, will gain nothing from Avery's loss of a half night's sleep. Wilf Taylor will still be dead. Nor can any amount of scheming hide the truth that Taylor should have never been sent to Finland in the first place. He lacked the training and experience for courier work, as Leclerc knows; in a blunder caused by Leclerc's negligence, he was carrying a passport the Foreign Office had revoked; finally, the Circus already had some reliable couriers stationed in Finland that Leclerc could have used had he not hogged the operation. From what we see of him, Leclerc wouldn't flinch at sacrificing a colleague to his ego, either. Sarah Avery puts the right construction on his 3:00 a.m. wake-up call when she tells her husband, "For God's sake, stop talking like a cowboy." Spies whip up intrigue, bang around, and upset others to show off—mostly to themselves and each other. Only the mannish triteness of cowboy talk could explain their behavior. Without compunction, Leclerc pulls Avery from his bed, neglects to provide transport for him, and then grumbles when Avery doesn't show up quickly enough to suit him. Bloodless and heartless, he won't provide either a fire or a towel for Avery at the office.

He doesn't care any more about straining Avery's marriage than he does about his comfort. Besides feeling free to summon Avery to the office at any hour, he fails to protect his agent's family; later, the police wake Sarah in the middle of the night when they suspect Avery's complicity in the dead Taylor's having carried a revoked passport made out to someone else. Moreover, when Avery complains about the police's harassment of Sarah, which Leclerc could have precluded with a phone call, he's answered rudely and dismissively. Like Kafka's bureaucracy, the Department tolerates no criticism or dissent. Leclerc snaps, "Tell her she won't be troubled any more. Tell her it was a mistake ... tell her whatever you like. Get some hot food and come back in an hour." His vanity has blinded him to the worries he has needlessly inflicted upon Sarah. His heart shrivelled and died long ago. Our never being told his first name captures his incompleteness; having worked too long as a spy, he has let his hold on life slip. The last human tie felt by this arrogant, undersized bachelor who lives alone was to the flyers, long dead, he served with during the war (and whose deaths were caused by his miscues?)

His numerous omissions and mistakes disqualify him from the rigors of friendship; anyone so uncaring of others can't afford friendship's outgoings. They also show how far the Department has fallen from its wartime glory. How could an agency function, let alone flourish, we keep wondering, with such a pompous fool running it? Despite his experience and exalted self-image, Leclerc doesn't know his job. The following exchange with Avery betrays a carelessness inexcusable in a spymaster. What the exchange hides is that Leclerc has no business sending an untrained Avery to do basically the same job that killed Taylor, viz., bringing back to London a roll of clandestinely shot film. His slackness in planning both the operation and its execution, it's worth noting, endangers Avery, not himself:

Leclerc spoke cautiously.... "You can ring me here tonight from Finland. If you've got the film, just say the deal's come off."

"And if not?"

"Say the deal's off."

"It sounds rather alike," Avery objected. "If the line's bad, I mean. 'Off' and 'Come off.'"

"Then say they're not interested. Say something negative. You know what I mean."

His conduct with his peers reflects the same haughty ineptitude. Chapter Eleven shows him asking George Smiley for some technical help with Operation Mayfly, the mission being mounted to slip Leiser into East Germany. Smiley outmaneuvers and outclasses Leclerc throughout the interview. Catching him in a lie, Smiley gives him much less than he had come asking for. Leclerc had wanted a new wireless for a training exercise he claims to be mounting in Germany. But a training exercise doesn't merit new equipment, Smiley points out, arguing that, were the equipment taken by unfriendly forces, it couldn't be used later in military operations. Leclerc must eat his lie, for had he confessed the truth about Operation Mayfly to Smiley, he'd also have had to hand over the running of it to the Circus.

But the person who pays the most for his lies is Leiser. Rather than using a wireless that's light, new, easy to work, and hard for the enemy to detect, Leiser must carry an outdated fifty-pound unit. The technical dangers the unit has saddled him with come across in the second of the book's two epigraphs, from F. Tait's *Complete Morse Instructor:*

The carrying of a very heavy weight such as a large suitcase or trunk, immediately before sending practice, renders the muscles of the forearm, wrist and fingers too insensitive to produce good Morse.

The physical and moral dangers follow shortly. Leclerc had to know the risk he was exposing Leiser to by sending him into hostile turf with obsolete, overweight gear. If he wasn't sabotaging his agent's efforts, he certainly wasn't protecting the agent as he should—and could. The lesson pointed out by his negligence is clear. Power is all: the mistakes of those in charge are paid for by their juniors. What happens to Taylor tallies with the disaster that defeats Leiser. The harm stems, not from Leclerc's evil, but from his being as out of touch with reality as the Department he runs.

Because he refuses to breakfast in a nearby cafe the morning he sends for Avery, the two men walk a great distance to another, where the food costs more but tastes worse. After eating, the two set out for Wilf Taylor's home to break the bad news of Taylor's death to his widow. But again an otherwise simple undertaking defeats Leclerc. His refusal to queue for a bus at an hour when there are no taxis forces the two men to trudge another long distance, this time through a cold rain. Luckily, Avery escapes from the outing with only a chill. He will soon face worse dangers. En route to the Taylors, he had agreed to collect the dead man's body and effects from Finland. But when he brings up the subject of his welfare in the field, he's first ignored and then fobbed off with the all-purpose "Show your passport and play the rest by ear." Leclerc has played him false, just as he had done Taylor, who couldn't even pronounce the name on the phony passport issued to him. Hasty improvisations cause trouble in the field. Spies must provide beforehand for mistakes and accidents; they plan ahead to deflect or neutralize the unforeseen. Even the reminder of his peer and longtime colleague Adrian Haldane that Avery hasn't been trained for operational work elicits from Leclerc the unfeeling, "He can look after himself." A moral void, Leclerc cares so little about his own well-being that he could hardly be expected to look after others'.

That he's reproached by aloof, disdainful Haldane shows how far he has strayed from living values. Puny details rule Haldane. He's forever fiddling with petty cash vouchers and talking about reimbursements for expenses connected with the job. A believer in the idea that rank has its privileges, he travels first class to Oxford, where Leiser's training takes place. Yet when he learns that Leiser traveled first class himself, he says high-handedly that Leiser must have paid the difference himself. Haldane's practice of ignoring everything in the newspaper he buys each day except for the crossword puzzle shows how far his vision has narrowed. His persistent cough—severe enough to have barred his way to an outfit better than the Department—reminds us of the nastiness at his center. He resents John Avery because of Avery's youth. Cynical and sarcastic, he mocks the trust Leiser extends to the Department by taking on Operation Mayfly after having been betrayed by his British chiefs during the war. Later, when asked if he thinks that Leiser has crossed safely into the GDR, he yawns and says with relief that Leiser is now beyond the Department's care. Within minutes, his face radiating peace, he claims that Leiser is on his deathbed, and he defines love as whatever can still be betrayed. His mind has turned to transcendent matters; it's suitable that he, the sickliest character in the book, is also the most visionary.

But because the robust Leiser can commit himself to the loftiness Haldane only talks about, he stands as a reproach to the older man. The spying profession would go smash with more Haldanes and Leclercs running it. But perhaps this is one of the novel's main points. What keeps spies in business is the presence of such ineffectuals on both sides of the Cold War. The title of le Carré's 1965 novel describes undercover activity as self-cancelling. According to Nigel West, such wastefulness can't be corrected. West argues in *The Circus* that deskmen disregard both their field agents and the public interest more grievously in times of stress than in calm:

All the Directors [of British Security] are a part of the same intelligence bureaucracy and all have a vested interest. When it comes to an internal foul-up, history tells us that their instinct is one of self-preservation. As we have seen, the structure and constitution of the organization tends to encourage, not inhibit, this behavior. It is a flaw that can only benefit the opposition.[2]

I

West might have been thinking about *The Looking-Glass War* when he framed his argument. The brutality described in the book may not be entertaining, but the truth, no matter how it's told, enriches us more than entertainment. The pleasure the book gives comes from its artistry, the severity of which challenges and alienates as it pleases. Like *Spy,* the book opens in October. Its autumnal quality stems also from its aging characters, its moodiness, and the sense if gives of wheeling in tired circles. Had le Carré not let on early that the book was opening in Finland, we'd have imagined ourselves trapped in the dead of an unusually hard English winter. It's difficult to imagine a bleaker, colder, more unfeatured landscape than that shown at the outset of *War:*

Snow covered the airfield.
    It had come from the north, in the mist, driven by the night wind, smelling of the sea. There it would stay all Winter, threadbare on the gray earth, an icy, sharp dust.... The changing mist, like the smoke of war, would hang over it, swallow up now a hangar, now the radar hut, now the machines; release them piece by piece, drained of color, black carrion on a white desert.
    It was a scene of no depth, no recession and no shadows. The land was one with the sky; figures and buildings locked in the cold like bodies in an icefloe.
    Beyond the airfield there was nothing; no house, no hill, no road; not even a fence, a tree, only the sky pressing on the dunes.... Somewhere inland were the mountains.

The menacing weather sets the tone for the novel, its northern source creating a dread reminiscent of the arctic imagery of Lawrence's *Women in Love* (1920) and Thomas Pynchon's *Gravity's Rainbow* (1974). The snow beating down from the north merges with the mist, the darkness, and the sea's harsh smell. The dagger-like snowflakes evoke both the pain and desolation of war. But it's a war whose horrors haven't yet been imagined. With its snowy mists draining everything of vitality, this polar desert defeats the eye. The only objects permitted autonomy are the machines strewn about the airfield, and even they look like carrion—too hard, stiff, and cold to be of use. The implacable northern sky has conquered all, locking everything in sight in its deathlike clamp. The blanketing snow and mist have erased the marks that define and distinguish. Except for the pathetic machinery peering hopelessly through the barrens, singleness has been lost.

    By extending and then fusing his highly inventive images within a controlled context, le Carré develops their ramifications with a new skill and verve. Reality itself seems disordered. A glacial landscape looks like a desert. The sky has become darker than the ground in the tricky light. Fog, snow, and winds add to the clamor and confusion. The plane flying from Düsseldorf over the Baltic that Taylor has come to meet is late, and no new arrival time has been set. Understandably, Taylor is fretting about his task. He has come to Finland to collect some film snapped above a putative East German rocket site. "This was a job for those swine in the Circus, not for his outfit at all," he fumes, "stuck out on a limb, miles from nowhere." The cold, the dark, the waiting, and the cacophony of foreign voices in the waiting lounge all rattle him. Nor does the arrival of Captain Lansen, the pilot who violated GDR airspace to fly within camera range of his target, lift his drooping spirits. Weary and disgusted, Lansen neglects all the prearranged signals by which he and Taylor were to know each other. His lack of caution can be explained. His overflight risked the lives of twenty-five children aboard his plane. The two Soviet MIGs that intercepted, buzzed, and escorted him out of GDR airspace could have also shot him down. He feels more angry than lucky. "It's not even my job, this kind of thing," he says, alluding to the pattern later developed by Taylor, Avery, and Leiser, other untrained, unequipped people sent by Leclerc to do jobs beyond their capabilities.

Le Carré bypasses his motives for accepting the assignment. The tax-free $5,000 Lansen was paid to lose his way and take some pictures obviously helped buy him. But his reasons for courting danger might have gone beyond money or praise. Le Carré doesn't portray flyers as heroically as did his fellow Oxonian of the previous generation, W. H. Auden. Like Charlie Marshall, the opium-addict pilot of *Schoolboy*, Captain Lansen may be looking in space for joys he hasn't yet found on earth. Whether his $5,000 fee buys him the thrills or the peace he was seeking remains unknown; after pocketing his fee and walking away from Taylor, he never reappears. Taylor's motives prove just as opaque. Taylor achieves only the death he may have unconsciously flirted with by coming to Finland. The chapter's final disorder, or ravage, shows him killed en route from the airport to the nearby Regina Hotel; the car that kills him on the deserted road prevents the consummation whose importance comes across in the regal-sounding name of his destination. In tune with this nastiness and futility, le Carré reports Taylor's death in a flat, deadpan prose; both atmospherically and morally, we've moved into a region where all heightening is suppressed. The screaming agony of death— significantly, enacted from behind in a vivid image of betrayal—exists on a par with the rolling, enveloping mists. All is padded and muffled. The thud of the death car breaking Taylor's spine and flinging him aloft can't be distinguished from the sound of the loose snow being swept aside by the car's axle. Recalling Leamas's dying fantasy in *Spy*, the mob of chattering children waiting at the airport with Taylor for the Düsseldorf flight symbolizes the innocent communal joy the stricken Taylor will never again know.

No aberrations, the waste and agony depicted in Chapter 1 prefigure the following action. *War* is a work of outstanding nastiness. The secrecy, duplicity, and treachery it recounts are so devastating that they strain the bounds of narrative convention. In his attempt to mount Operation Mayfly, Leclerc lies to the Under Secretary, the Defense Minister's aide de camp, while asking his help in fabricating a lie to tell the Circus. Then Haldane, whose deceit shows in his withholding from Leiser his real name, orders the Pole to conceal the purpose of his training regimen from the various technicians, photographers, and medical officers who visit the training site. Haldane and Leclerc, the old pros in charge of the operation, besides lacking patriotic fervor and idealism, have insulted Leiser. They've told him to dupe the operation's auxiliary workers so that he may be more easily duped himself. What they never learn is that he transcends their knavery. A sign of his transcendent idealism comes early. Unlike the career professionals Taylor, Avery, and Bruce Woodford, he keeps the operation a secret from his woman.

But like that of the tragic Leamas, his success in the human sphere correlates negatively to his prowess as a spy. Acts of generosity and compassion always recoil on the field agent in le Carré. The closing pages of *War* find Leiser cabined with a young woman of eighteen in a rundown East German inn. He knows that the Vopos have worked out his location from the signals he has been transmitting to his friends just over the border. His discovery and arrest are both imminent. In an act of moral genius, he rejects the young woman's sexual overture. He knows he'll be leaving her soon, probably forever, and he doesn't want her to get too fond of him beforehand. Also to protect her, he makes her look like his victim rather than the accomplice she has been. The soldiers bursting into the room see him with his knife at her throat, held in the classic manner, "thumb uppermost, the blade parallel to the ground." To all appearances, he's the ruthless, disciplined undercover spy. But how accurately does his appearance reflect reality? Purpose and technique have harmonized. The menace he represents is a fiction, enacted to absolve the young woman from guilt. By pretending to attack her, he's extending the love she wanted from him sexually. His sacrifice shows that a spy can't love normally.

Leiser needn't opt for a career in intelligence to forfeit the joys that excite and sustain others; one mission in the field ensures his deprivation.

Ironically, his heroism will go unnoticed and unsung. He does scale the heights consistent with popular notions about spy missions, but in a way alien to all formulas. Just before his capture, he plucks up the self-presence to recount the following anecdote:

I'll tell you about London ... I went for a walk, once, it was raining and there was this man by the river, drawing on the pavement in the rain. Fancy that! Drawing with chalk in the rain, and the rain just washing it away.

The anecdote symbolizes Leiser's own plight. Leamas-like, he conquers fear in the moments before his arrest both to see and to do what must be done. Yet his controllers Haldane and Leclerc will never learn of his brilliance. The operation has been called off. They're already dismantling their wireless and have started to concoct a story that will both disclaim Leiser and block any trail leading from him to London. The only people listening to the signals he's putting out are the East Germans and the Soviets. Having accepted the desertion of Leiser behind unfriendly lines as an operational necessity, Leclerc, always the cool opportunist, asks Smiley about acquiring a new copier for the Department.

The moral poverty informing opportunism like his has caught the attention of Graham Greene: "The spy takes more interest in the mechanics of his calling than in its ultimate goal—the defense of his country," said Greene in 1983. "The 'game' (a serious game) achieves such a degree of sophistication that the player loses sight of his moral values."[3] Smiley endorses Greene's skepticism when he says in Chapter 5, "It's such a mistake, I always feel, to put one's trust in *technique*." His attitude sharpens in the next-to-last chapter when he accuses Haldane of having sacrificed all to technique: "You've made technique a way of life ... like a whore, technique replacing love." If expediency justifies the cruelty of abandoning Leiser, then Smiley has spoken true. Avery's cries that Leiser be rescued go ignored. From an operational standpoint, Avery is deluding himself. The more experienced agents, whose hearts have calcified, see the issues more clearly. At the end of the operation, Leclerc invites Haldane to dine at his club, presumably to celebrate their mutual success. Our last glimpse of the team of British spies housed with their now dismantled radio gear in a remote farmhouse focuses on Avery, "sobbing like a child. No one heeded him."

At this far point in the action, the ruthlessness of his chiefs no longer surprises us. Before Leiser crossed into East Germany, Leclerc had put both Taylor and Avery at risk in a foreign country without a scrap of remorse. The extent to which the spy trade had exorcised humane impulses shows in le Carré's handworking of the motif of the apology. When Leclerc ignores Avery's questions in Chapter 2, "What happened to Taylor? Who killed him?" the junior officer apologizes, as if his concern violated professional etiquette. Throughout the work, such expressions of caring are made to embarrass those who utter them. Avery feels clumsy and stupid again in Chapter 4 when he asks Leclerc about the dead Taylor's ten-year-old daughter. His apologizing four times at the end of Chapter 9, the last of Book Two, shows humanity yielding again to the arrogance of power; he has broken an unwritten law. His words also reveal that he has come to resemble his superiors more than he knows. Unconsciously, he's assuming their authority, confidence, and persona. In spite of his moral principles, he's going to end up like them. Their voices echo in his speech; his pedantry and deceit copy theirs. His goals are theirs, too. If his failure was unique, they'd pity him. What began in Chapter 9 as an objection to the police's grilling Sarah in the middle of the night about Taylor's illegal passport ends in truckling and fawning. Leclerc naturally overlooks the truth that the passport's illegality came about from his failure to connect with the Foreign Office. Amid vulgarity and sanctimoniousness, virtue alone apologizes for itself.

Some of the background for the process by which virtue surrenders to officialism has already been filled in. The roll of film that Captain Lansen gave Taylor never appeared in Taylor's personal effects after his death. In order to avoid angering the GDR, the Federal Republic of Germany, the Soviets, and even the Americans, the Department will have to use a man rather than an overflight to determine the presence of Soviet rocket pads near the East German towns of Rostock and Kalkstadt. Book One, called "Taylor's Run" and extending but one chapter, is the shortest of the book's three major units. Le Carré's implied Joycean pun has made its desired point. The book's opening scene unfolds in Finland. Occurring at day's end, it describes still another finish—that of Taylor. But it also marks a beginning, each of the novel's remaining two books (entitled "Avery's Run" and "Leiser's Run") extending progressively longer. Events in *War* beget others. Avery hasn't been in Leclerc's office for half an hour before being told, in the offhand, donnish way le Carré's bureaucrats have of demanding the unspeakable, to collect Taylor's things.

Smiley's longest single appearance shows him preparing Avery for his errand to Finland. Noting the older spy's "curious air of indirection," Avery finds him tired, slow, and absentminded. But no sooner has he written him off as a doddering eccentric than he finds in Smiley rich stores of sense, mental agility, and compassion. (That the two men apologize to each other during their exchange confirms their humanity.) What he doesn't know is that Smiley has seen through his lies about the Department's plans to conduct a training operation. So poorly did Leclerc brief him before sending him to Smiley for help that Smiley and Control both knew all about Operation Mayfly before its launching. In fact, Control believes the operation foredoomed. Any doubts he may have of its failure he scotches by sabotaging it. And though Smiley denies the charge, when it's made by the Department, Andrew Rutherford also believes that Smiley aborts the operation under Control's orders.[4]

The operation never stood a chance from the start. As we've seen, the deskmen running Operation Mayfly aren't just ruthless but incompetent, too. The title of Stephen Marcus's review of the novel in the *New York Review of Books*, "Grand Illusions," refers to the misconception and muffed execution of the mission. And why shouldn't it? Moral failures both, Leclerc and Haldane also slump badly in the areas of judgment and technique. Had they respected the limits of their charter, they'd never have undertaken the operation to begin with. Using a man to get information about a military target falls outside the Department's competence. By infiltrating Leiser into East Germany, the Department isn't merely straying from its brief; it's also sending Leiser to his death, since it lacks both the facilities and time to prepare him. He's given only four weeks to learn ciphers, photography, cover, armed and unarmed combat, and techniques in encoding, sending, and receiving radio messages. The terminology le Carré uses to describe the recondite sequence of movements Leiser must perform with the crystals, dials, power amplifier, and meter selector on his wireless both conveys the rigor of the crash course and adds to the growing gloom. No one is surprised with the poor fingering technique and the memory lapses Leiser displays in his first message from East Germany.

But besides transmitting slowly and clumsily, Leiser also forgets to change both his call signals and frequencies. Signifying the Department's disarray and obsolescence is their calling upon Leiser in the first place. Twenty years away from soldiering and radio work, this garage mechanic of forty lacks both the manual dexterity and athletic skills to carry out his job. Besides, he hasn't kept up with developments in weaponry and communications. Even dry, contemptuous Haldane views the operation realistically. Of Taylor's fatal run, he admits. "We should have never used him.... We broke a first principle of intelligence." He also scathes Leclerc for sending Avery to collect Taylor's effects: "We've no business to use him for a job like that," he says at the end of Chapter 5. Yet he fails to act on his words. At the outset of the next chapter, Avery is flying to Finland improperly briefed. Avery can't tell the Finnish police the age of Taylor, whose brother he's pretending to be; he knows nothing either about the formalities pertaining to the release and transport of the body; he doesn't know how to get a medical certificate or police clearance; he can't explain why Taylor was traveling on an illegal passport.

Leiser is even more hamstrung for *his* run. Carrying an outdated and overweight radio is just one of his worries. Before he sets out, the Department even takes away the handgun they had told him to cherish as his most vital aid, Haldane and Leclerc giving Avery the job of relaying this heavy news to Leiser. This last deprivation cuts the tie between Operation Mayfly and any chance for success. At the last minute, Leiser has found out that he's going to be at greater risk than he was led to believe—and all for the sake of policy. To avert a political problem, he's going behind unfriendly lines without the means to protect himself as he was trained and, what is more important, with his morale shattered. The Ministry and the Department remain unmoved; they'll sacrifice their field agents every time to protect themselves.

This loveless expediency makes us wonder why Leclerc has bothered to undertake the operation, having done so much to subvert it. Part of the explanation lies in Avery's calling the Department a dream factory. Like Taylor's and then Avery's going to Finland unprepared for what awaited them there, Leclerc's many references to the heyday of his service, a generation before, shows how far afield of reality the Department has strayed. Leclerc and Haldane will support any fiction that makes them feel big. Politics within the Defense Ministry gives them their chance. If the Minister forbids the Department from running an agent into the GDR, he'll have to give the job to the Circus, who, in turn, will bring in the F.O., thus endangering the operation with publicity. The Department has shrunk so much since the war that Leclerc quickly grabs the chance to go operational. But decades of disuse have weakened his grip. The success of the operation counts less with him than returning to the lists of clandestine warfare. As soon as Leiser crosses into the GDR, both he and Haldane lose all interest in him; the Department has carried out its task. Although no war has been declared—an exigency that could reduce the pension of Taylor's widow—Leiser will have to rely on war rules to pick his way through hostile ground.

William Barrett, writing for *Atlantic,* calls Leiser "a wonderfully portrayed Middle European, the little man par excellence, a bit ridiculous in his small vanities and always humbly eager to be admired."[5] The admiration he covets never comes his way. With his long pomaded hair and his silk shirts, he reminds Haldane of a waiter or a bookie. The elegance and refinement he affects enhances, rather than detracts from, the garishness of his appearance. He'll never be accepted as an equal by his senior colleagues, and he knows it. His feelings of inferiority before the English gentleman class lure him into spying for British Intelligence. But Granville Hicks was wrong to call him an anachronism in *Saturday Review.*[6] He has adapted much better to postwar England than the nostalgic, snobbish paymasters who mistreat him. He owns a garage, employs at least two workers, earns enough to maintain a bank balance along with an expensive wardrobe, and has a steady girlfriend. But his awe for English breeding and style negates these gains. The novel's first epigraph, from Lewis Carroll's *Alice,* refers directly to his plight as an inferior-outsider: "I wouldn't mind being a Pawn, if only I might join." But it would oversimplify his complex response to his chiefs to say that he wants to become a modern English knight, plume and all. Yes, those chiefs are dragons, and they do scorn him as a foreigner. Like Kafka's hero, he never makes it to the castle; his goal is always out of reach. Yet he also seeks union with that goal, and, like another Kafka hero, that of "The Penal Colony," he confirms its sovereignty by dying for it.

Remember that he could walk away from the operation at any time, as he has good reason to do. Haldane condescends to him throughout; besides being overage and out of training, he lacks the memory, aptitude, and patience to transmit effectively on a wireless. He has flouted both his finer feelings and motives of self-preservation to undertake his assignment. He's not alone in his distress, either. Spying both appeals to and brings out bad traits elsewhere in the book. Leiser's recruitment by Haldane shows victim and victimizer meeting as mirror images with each party touching the other's hidden self. Haldane judges well when he says later that the Department gave

Leiser what he wanted most—love, i.e., a cause to invest his heart in. But what about Haldane's heart? If Smiley is right in saying that Haldane has replaced love with technique, then it becomes clear why he sends Leiser to his death. Committed to waste and ugliness, spying feeds on death. Also, Haldane, the veteran spy, envies Leiser his ability to love just as he envies Avery his youth. But envy cramps and confines. It stops him from learning how his definition of love, framed in Chapter 18, as whatever you can still betray, applies to his doomed agent.

The many things that go wrong for Leiser as soon as he passes into East Germany destroy all hope for his success. His morale has never been lower. Le Carré enters the stream of his thoughts to register his dismay at being both deprived of his handgun and discovering that Avery, his only friend during the training session, had lied to him every step of the way. His very equipment defeats him. "He tripped and the rucksack brought him down . . . and the suitcase swung him round," le Carré says of him about a half hour after his infiltration to show how out of control he is. Then, in a major looking-glass concurrence, Leiser kills a young sentry at the same time Haldane is pronouncing the death sentence on *him*. Like someone led by an unseen hand, Leiser seems to be trying to vindicate Haldane's pronouncement. He steals a motorcycle; his indiscreet questions frighten some villagers; he forms a sexual tie; his mistakes in transmitting lead to his early detection. The first message he sends reveals his unreadiness and incompetence; so poor is his transmitting technique that the Vopo sergeant who picks up his signal thinks that it's coming from a child. Rarely has an agent radioed so amateurishly. An American receiving station miles away uses his signal to place his whereabouts. What is more, the death of the young sentry he killed has been reported both on the radio and in the East German newspapers. Leiser hasn't only failed to protect himself; he's also acting like a man begging to be caught. In one of the book's more ironical looking-glass patterns, he finds himself surrounded by soldiers at the same time his controllers are rejoicing over the success of the operation. Poetic justice intervenes quickly. Just as the controllers are indulging the grandiose fantasy of requisitioning a training center for the Department, Smiley surprises them with orders from the Minister to cancel Operation Mayfly. The signals Leiser sends after this point will only be heard by the East Germans.

Smiley's intervention confirms le Carré's belief that anyone bent on self-destruction will always find willing helpers. The last section of the book, comprising Chapters 20-23 and covering the time from

Leiser's first wireless messages to his capture, is called "Homecoming."
The consummation inferred by this title develops Haldane's two
memorable insights of Chapter 18, i.e., that Operation Mayfly gave
Leiser the love he had heretofore lacked and that this love, like all
others, is eminently betrayable. The development outstrips Haldane's
formula. To begin with, Leiser's dedication goes beyond the
Kierkegaardian act of faith implied by Avery's description of him
crossing the East German border: "He just went into the dark." Leiser's
moral imagination has risen above the knowledge that his paymasters
have sold him out. In erring so flagrantly as soon as he sets foot
in the GDR, he's not merely defeating himself. Practicing the self-
detachment of an Eastern mystic, he's also defeating the intelligence
system in order to submit to it.

A series of mirror images clinches this important point. In Chapter
1, Taylor assumes "a classic posture of death" as the car that kills
him hurls him "violently backwards." This fusion of the classic and
the deathly characterizes the action. And it refers most pointedly to
spying. That which is classic forfeits vibrancy and mobility. Avery's
words to himself in Chapter 6, "A man must steel himself against
sentiment," yokes the classic to that which is implacable, even frozen;
coldness and cruelty are the logical consequences of the detachment
Avery wants to cultivate. The prearranged, the supervised, and the
derived always take on in the book a statuesque formality that opposes
immediacy and compassion. Some dartplayers in a London pub in
Chapter 13 play their game "with quiet devotion as if they were deeply
conscious of tradition." The juncture of tradition with ritual and
obedience recurs in our last glimpse of Leclerc as a "man intent upon
appearances, conscious of tradition."

Leiser is described as "intent upon appearances, conscious of
tradition" while pretending to kill the East German girl who has
befriended him in Kalkstadt. Practicing perfect combat technique with
his knife, he resembles a classic textbook spy. His impersonation of
a trained, ruthless field agent joins his beginning to his end and also
his dream of becoming an English knight errant to the reality of being
treated like one. Such closedendedness chokes off life. Executing his
drill perfectly, Leiser has submitted to a harsh discipline. His
willingness to die for the discipline reflects an adaptation beyond
Haldane's imagining. What it also evokes is the archetype in classical
literature of the consenting death of the king: the king is dead, long
live the king. The continuance of the realm requires the death of
the realm's ruler. Leiser resembles the regal suicides of antiquity in

the selflessness he attains. But selflessness carried to this extreme also denies life. Rejecting spontaneity and impulse, Leiser merges with the formalized deadness of his job. Perfectly expressive of the moment is the absence of anybody on the scene capable of appreciating his astute blends of fiction and reality and of creator and creation. Leiser's passage from the moral to the aesthetic sphere is complete. And le Carré celebrates it with another aesthetic event, the novel itself.

After steering Leiser's last-chapter masterstroke of vision and execution into one void, le Carré cuts to another—the farmhouse which had housed the team of agents that, perhaps only moments before, abandoned both the operation and Leiser. The Tennysonian quiet of the book's last two paragraphs both sharpens and realigns the motifs of noncommunication, waste, and cold, all of which carry forward from the first chapter. Much of le Carré's skill as a constructionist rests on his endings. The outstanding unity and understated force conveyed by the finale of *Looking-Glass War* tallies with the work's structure, mood, character development, and moral outlook:

> The farmhouse lay in darkness, blind and not hearing, motionless against the swaying larches and the running sky.
> They had left a shutter open and it banged slowly without rhythm, according to the strength of the storm. Snow gathered like ash and was dispersed. They had gone, leaving nothing behind them but tire tracks in the hardening mud, a twist of wire, and the sleepless tapping of the north wind.

II

This brilliant ending discredits George P. Elliott's complaint that the novel lacks balance.[7] Conveying a moral void consistent with a breakdown of communication both electronic and human, the ending also shows the distress of an agent who is deserted by his chiefs. This bleakness refers to the opening sequence. *War* both starts and ends in snow, darkness, and wind. Both the death of Taylor and the arrest of Leiser depict the statuelike rigidness and formality consistent with spying. Although the spy trade promises adventure and excitement, it delivers stagnation and decay. Our parting glimpse of both Leiser and Taylor show these victims being swept into the arbitrariness and artifice of the dream factory. In their first operational assignments, they learn a cardinal truth of their trade, viz., that the actualization of the dream kills both dream and dreamer.

But if Books One and Three are named for Taylor and Leiser, Book Two gets its title from Avery. Avery is both the luckiest of the three agents sent out by Leclerc on a solo run and the youngest of the team of spies that trains Leiser, takes him to the GDR border, and awaits his signals in the farmhouse nearby. At thirty-two, he hasn't yet sorted out his priorities. His status as an Arts graduate in a science-dominated culture helps describe his alienation. As his introduction into the novel shows—Leclerc's 3:00 a.m. order to report immediately to the office—the demands of work have been encroaching dangerously upon his family life. His heart has already hardened more than he knows. He omits kissing Sarah goodbye on his way out of the flat after Leclerc's wake-up call, despite knowing that his omission will sadden her. He can relax and feel more at home with his co-workers than with her and their small son, Anthony. Then he forgets to buy the toy he had promised to get Anthony in Finland.

The trip to Finland, in fact, settles the split in loyalties between home and work that was plaguing him. Despite Leclerc's incompetence and inhumanity in handling the trip, Avery returns to the Department. Leclerc takes his loyalty for granted. Perhaps he knows Avery better than Avery knows himself. Understanding the subtlety of the claims spying makes on any agent's psyche, he responds to Avery's angry announcement that he's quitting his job with the sublime arrogance of the cocksure—telling Avery that the Department's financial section has disallowed his claim for cabfare the night of the wake-up call. He can afford to fuel Avery's anger. Within pages of Avery's outburst, Sarah says that his job is taking him from his family. But rather than reinforcing his disgust with the job, her well-grounded complaint stirs his defensiveness, and, in another flare-up of temper, he resolves to stay with the Department. Truth of mood has triumphed over common sense and simple humanity. His resolve also generates behavior consistent with it. When Leiser asks him later about the practical details of his East German mission, Avery replies with the same dodges Leclerc had previously used with *him*.

Yet spying hasn't routed all his decency. Like Stevie, Winnie Verloc's retarded younger brother in Conrad's *Secret Agent* (1907), he possesses a fund of humanity the others either ignore or pervert. Part of the impact made by the book's bitter, shocking, yet wholly credible last sequence comes from our last glimpse of him. "Sobbing like a child," he has failed to convince his colleagues to rescue Leiser. His grief and dismay are smothered inside official policy. The others ignore him. One simple truth underlay the whole operation he participated in: Power is all; the small man risks and pays the most if anything goes wrong. Sentiment can't wrench this tenet of espionage, despite what the self-deluded Avery thinks. Operational considerations sent Leiser into the GDR; the same criteria dictate leaving him there.

But if Leclerc and Haldane lack the love to charm Leiser into executing his assignment, they do recognize it in others. No value or bond is too sacred to be violated by spymasters. A section in the opening chapter of Book 3, "Leiser's Run." begins, "Haldane and Leiser took their places at a corner table, like lovers in a coffee bar." Other reminders that all's fair in spying relate to the operation itself. In Chapter 11, le Carré says of Avery, "He lay awake, wondering about Leiser; it was like waiting for a girl." The deep, obscure flow of feeling joining the two men is reversible. In Chapter 17, Leiser says, with a grin, of his last training session, "It was the best ever, that week, John. It's funny, isn't it: we spend all our time chasing girls, and it's the men who matter." His commitment to the spying mystique he has been indirectly referring to surfaces immediately. Just before crossing the frontier, he asks Avery to give him something. We're back in the sphere of courtly valor and romance. The inverted logic of spying has turned him into a medieval knight who takes his ladylove's token into battle. Spying appeals to motives deeper than reason or common sense can ever probe. And nobody knows this truth better than Haldane and Leclerc. Avery speaks home when he indicts them for making him love Leiser. They used whatever humanity spying hadn't already curdled in him to play Leiser for a victim. According to them, the love he extended to Leiser was merely a tool, not something to be known or cherished.

The ease with which they trick Avery lends meaning to the novel's title, since they see him as a reflection of their earlier selves. The many mirror images in *War* reduce life to a battle fought with the ugliest of weapons for the most dubious of prizes. Control's sabotaging of Operation Mayfly shows that intelligence workers have as much to fear from their colleagues as from the opposition. Not only does this maxim echo in the Department's treatment of Taylor, Avery, and Leiser. Le Carré also implies that partisans of both sides in the Cold War use the same methods in the service of the same loveless moral code. The description of the East German border guards converging on Leiser, "Softly, like animals, the Vopos dismounted from the two trucks ... advancing in a ragged line," erases any moral preference that may have been building in us for the Soviet bloc. The parallels, repetitions, and correspondences lacing the book, besides imparting a throwaway brilliance, describe the spy's world as a shrunken place where freedom is denied. Leiser's options having dried up, he can only repeat the stock gestures of his trade at the end. Though spying whets the appetite for danger and romance, its glamor fades and coarsens in direct ratio to the agent's experience of it. What's more, this degeneration infects the agent. Statue-like, Leiser appeals to our aesthetic faculties, having left the moral sphere. And le Carré extends the process by making his distress the subject of imaginative art.

The process by which vitality drains out of the living is carefully foreshadowed. During his training, Leiser observed that the forearm extends in the same way in keying a wireless message as in knife fighting. The next chapter (Chapter 16) opens by saying that the wind that pulled at Taylor's corpse in Finland was the same wind that pounded both the operation's training base in Oxford and the West German farmhouse where the operation will move. Earlier, both Haldane and Leiser referred to the nine-millimeter handgun as a three-eight. Later, Leiser will twice face the problem of distinguishing between the sound of a door latch with that made by the bolt-action of a firearm. Integrated in its details and relentless in its follow-through, *The Looking-Glass War* impressed Eric Ambler as "very well written and very exciting" when it first came out.[8] The years have vindicated his tribute. In 1976, George Grella called *War* "le Carré's most eloquent novel."[9] The work's moral passion, sustained central metaphor, and deep interconnectedness all justify his having extended his praise beyond Ambler's. These virtues might encourage future readers to agree with him, as well.

Chapter Nine
Goddesses and Warriors

Another tale of stunted hopes and blighted chances, *A Small Town in Germany* (1968) conveys the pain, upheaval, and demoralization usually found in le Carré. But it deals with diplomatic espionage; it also unfolds between two Fridays (in May 1969 or 1970), rather than over several months, and it forsakes the multi-setting format of *War*. Except for one scene, the action of *Small Town* occurs in and around Bonn, capital of the Federal Republic of Germany. Setting imposes itself straightaway. The book's opening pages disclose a hornet's nest of political fanaticism. Demonstrations and riots have broken out in Cologne, seventeen miles up river from Bonn; the books in Hanover's British Library have been burned and its librarian, beaten and killed. Hectic and violent just before a major speech by the FRG's chancellor, Bonn displays the vehemence whipping down from the north. Posters and banners festoon the city's packed, noisy streets, and only the most strenuous efforts of the local police have been holding the crowds in check. The police are taking no chances. Both a curfew and a travel ban have been placed on most British Embassy personnel; all disturbances by dissidents are to be quelled with haste; the roads leading in and out of Bonn are being watched. As he did in his previous two books, le Carré uses atmospheric effects to build tension. Unseasonable cold claws nerves at the outset of *Small Town* as it did in the opening passages of *Spy* and *War*. "The night ... [the Prologue unfolds] smelt of winter," and "On that [same] spring night the winter had come back to visit" and to chill the people of Bonn.

The main source of the clamor the cold weather has aggravated is Great Britain's application for membership in the Common Market. The anti-British West German Chancellor, Dr. Klaus Karfeld, has timed his speech in Bonn to coincide with a meeting in Brussels of the EEC nations to vote on the United Kingdom's candidacy. Knowing that the UK needs FRG support, Karfeld is both applying pressure and testing options. He has revived the question of German reunification; this goal, he has been implying, can be reached more

144

easily with the help of Moscow than with that of the West. But the UK faces another threat which could worsen the one posed by Karfeld. The British Embassy in Bonn is worried that one of its workers has stolen information, the divulgence of which could both destroy the UK's tie to the FRG and clear a road between the FRG and the Soviet Union. The British fears roused by the coincidence of Leo Harting's disappearance with that of some highly restricted papers makes sense. But, as is typical of le Carré's narrative strategy, the reasons behind the fears stay dark most of the way. The disclosure of these reasons vex us as they surprise us. Yes, Leo Harting has taken justice into his own hands. But he never gave away classified information from the British Embassy. The discoveries he made pertained to British policy. He found out that his chiefs already had enough proof in their files to convict Karfeld of war atrocities. They also knew that the Federal Republic was quickly becoming a dictatorship. But they preferred to let the statute of limitations run out on Karfeld in order to protect themselves. Should they be kept out of the EEC, they'll want to strengthen ties with the FRG, even if it means forming a London-Moscow pact.

I

The text's Bonn setting helps orchestrate plot, theme, and technique. The word, small, in the title, besides referring to the *Bundesdorf* of 125,000 where the action takes place, evokes pettiness and nastiness; a female diplomat says of her circle. "I've never known anywhere for such gossip." Le Carré will mention the Niebelungs, the Lorelei, and the seven hills of Konigswinter to contrast the grandeur of German landscape and legend with the moral squalor of postwar Germany. A product of thumping prosperity, this squalor resists all formulas. "Bonn isn't prewar, or even post-war. It's just a small town in Germany," says a British diplomat, adding, "You can no more slice it up than you can the Rhine. And the mist drains away the colors." The same character had said earlier of Bonn, "An island cut off by fog, that's us. It's a very metaphysical spot; the dreams have replaced reality." The synthesis of mist, fog, and dreams accounts for the novel's tone. The weather plays visual tricks and distorts sounds. Precedents will be overturned. Words and acts will take on new meanings. The diplomats themselves, familiars of the fog, have fled reality. One character calls his duty station a "dream box," and, in the plot's exciting climax, another describes all attempts to improve government as "chasing the dream."

The mists clinging to the landscape expedite Britain's policy of rationalization and accommodation. The remark, "The mist drains away the colors. There are no distinctions," describes the muffling of clarity and candor by the bureaucratic fog that has seeped into British diplomacy. Harting must be stopped because he has rejected his superiors' creed of apathy. The novel's imagery supports the idea that surfaces can't be probed because appearances count more than reality. Le Carré wants us to ask whether surfaces threatening to spew out poison *should* be left undisturbed. The houses of Bonn are "soiled like old uniforms." The word, scaffold, with all of its deathly associations, recurs often in both English and German *(Schaffott)*; as part of his revivalist preacher's strategy, Karfeld uses a scaffold as his speaking platform for his big speech. The gray buses carrying his gray-clad bodyguard to the town square augment the aura of grime and sludge put forth by his neo-Nazism. Le Carré's well-pitched, painful imagery continues to show what happens when moral principle and emotional impulse get trapped in the mists of political expediency. Allusions to sexual failure and sexual license describe Bonn's moral collapse. Karfeld incites his hearers by claiming that Germany is being treated like a whore by the NATO powers and that Bonn has become an American whore. His speaking these metaphors of bawdiness from a scaffold links death, sexuality, and politics in a way consistent with the times. An old friend of Harting's calls Bonn a bordello and pronounces himself a whore. Before leaving London to look for Harting, Alan Turner, the Foreign Office investigator, believes that his estranged wife can't tell him goodbye on the telephone because she's in bed with her lover. Hazel Bradfield, a diplomatic wife, says of herself and Harting, "We were two old tarts and fell in love."

Hazel made Harting her lover partly because she and her husband, the Embassy's Head of Chancery, haven't had sex for years; although important, Harting is but one of the many lovers she has had in the past decade. Another sexual outlaw attached to the Embassy is Myra Meadowes, daughter of the Registrar. In what may not be such a wild exaggeration, one Embassy staffer claims that Myra has had sex with half the drivers in Bonn. The claim jars us. Real people with private histories and emotional burdens inhabit the book. No authorial smirk, Myra's sexual looseness stems from pain and loss. She had a nervous breakdown after she and her father had to leave Warsaw. As it did in *War*, security work devastates families in *Small Town*. Myra had to abort her baby, depriving herself and her aging father of someone to love, a need they both shared, because the baby's Polish father had angered Whitehall. Man trouble also afflicts Jenny Partiger, a Chancery staffer, as two of her lovers, one her fiancé, have jilted her within the year. Brittle and fragile, Jenny dissolves into tears in her lone extended appearance in the book.

Sexual disorder expresses itself differently in "elegant, willowy, almost beautiful" Peter de Lisle, a homosexual in his early forties. His older colleague, Mickey Crabbe, is impotent. By his own admission, he hasn't been able to manage sex for years. Could a key to his impotence lie in his name? Le Carré invites us to wonder. A crab (be) is a pubic louse that attaches itself to people during sex. The incongruity between this venereal pest and Crabbe's public school offhandedness is no accident. Nor would Le Carré have overlooked the injustice implied by the idea of punishment without crime. As a sexual nonperformer, Crabbe couldn't have caught crabs. But as an Embassy worker, he can't escape the bureaucratic contamination infecting his colleagues. The book's many convergences between private and public impulse imply a tie between his sexual problems and his dehumanizing job. The one inhabitant of the dream factory, apart from the rebel-patriot, Harting, who enjoys normal sex is the astute albino Bill Cork; his wife, in fact, gives birth during the book. Yet he dreams as wildly as any of his colleagues. He wants to earn enough money from his stock investments to retire with his family at age forty-five to a Greek island. A sign of his intelligence is his knowledge that the dream won't come true. He harbors dreams, he admits, to pad the impact of life's brutality. Life without dreams might overwhelm him. But how much has dreaming helped him? This cipher clerk can't escape alienation any more than he can solve the riddle of his career as a bureaucrat. When he learns that his wife had her baby without first telling him, he's crushed.

Cork and the others suffer from intellectual and spiritual dislocation, a complaint worsened and perhaps created by ontological dislocation; knowing *where* you are means nothing unless you know *who* you are. John Gardner noted this malaise in le Carré's writing in 1982: "Le Carré presents a simple synergism and deceit at the center of all things secret. His forte lies in . . . encapsulating characters caught up in the doom-laden duplicity of their trade and time."[1] Remarks made by security staffers in *Small Town* disclose a surfeit of sentimentality. A believer in the supremacy of the non-available, Bill Cork finds life without illusions impossible. A member of the F. O. says in Chapter 9, "The best girl is the girl you don't have." This unreality extends to setting. Harting discovers both Karfeld's guilt and the Britons' knowledge of it by working secretly in a forgotten storage enclave of the Embassy called the Glory Hole, which is also, advisedly, a name given to the holes bored in the walls dividing toilets in homosexual meeting places. It's this inversion of normal sexuality that symbolizes the Glory Hole episode rather than the heterosexual promise le Carré connects to it. Harting's ability to disclose truth in a forgotten, overlooked place like the Glory Hole reflects his author's practice of finding value in seams and margins. The entry of Alan Turner, who has come from London to look for Harting, into the Glory Hole resembles an epic hero's descent into the underworld. Like an Odysseus, Turner must go underground to find the truth—the missing files Harting's chiefs had believed were in Soviet hands. His discovery takes the form of a sexual consummation, foreplay and all. He gets ready to penetrate a dark, moist tunnel where hidden riches lie; the light switch he presses to find it is "domed like a woman's breast." The sexual motif is reinforced. Perhaps at the same time Turner's spirit is coming to life, as he reads the lost files, Janet Cork has her baby. And while discussing his impending fatherhood, Cork hears a friend say, "It's the beds.... More beds," while "the squeak of springs," as if set in motion by love-making couples, fills the corridors.

Further promise of renewal that will meet grief comes in the name of the Green File, the top-secret report proving, first, Karfeld's murderousness and, next, the truth that the British have always known about it. Harting himself wrote part of the report, twenty-five years ago, when he arrested Karfeld while serving as a sergeant in the British Army. But Whitehall won't use this information to sink Karfeld, their current enemy but potential friend. When Turner mentions Harting's wish to reopen the case against Karfeld, he's told by a peeved bureaucrat, "I have no idea what you're referring to. You're sick; you are wandering and sick." Despite the Rhineland's association with the great northern gods and the fertility of the area's vineyards, a more accurate emblem of postwar Germany comes in the Petersberg, the mountain lodge where Neville Chamberlain stayed in the 1930s while appeasing Hitler and selling out western civilization. The sellout has recurred in a Germany where many speak English and where, because of the Nuremberg trials of 1945-46, much of the nation's identity was framed by Anglophones. This cultural drama carries forward in Leo Harting, a German-born British citizen whose professional ascent has passed as unwatched as that of Klaus Karfeld. Harting also proves that people aren't ruled by symbols. Though his cottage stands at the foot of the Petersberg, where Chamberlain stayed, his resolve and integrity brighten the gloom cast by Chamberlain's shadow. He doesn't compromise, make deals, or sell out, as the appeaser did.

Soon after arriving in Bonn, Alan Turner equates Harting's political protest with the search for a father. Did Harting betray his country, Turner wonders, to find a father he could believe in? The question goes beyond the novel. Having lacked a father worthy of trust himself, a point made in *A Perfect Spy* (1986), le Carré may have embraced fiction-writing as a perfect cause. Some of his people also view their undertakings as father or religion substitutes. What the British Secret Service is for Fred Leiser and what the Israeli and then the Palestinian causes represent for Charlie in *The Little Drummer Girl*, the stopping of Karfeld means for Harting. It's not just something he can invest his loyalty in; meriting his blind faith, it's also a means of self-purification and a sacred charge. The front part of his last name, Harting, like that of Fred Leiser's workname, Hartbeck, describes purpose in le Carré as a function of the feelings. Both Leiser and Harting are the only people in the books they inhabit who seek oneness with their physical settings, social circles, and a guiding morality that will give them a sense of mission beyond that of selfhood. Both have higher standards and work harder than their superiors. The defeat of both means victory for complacency, hypocrisy, and moral compromise. Le Carré addressed this issue in the *New York Times Magazine* when he said, "In 'A Small Town in Germany' I had this British diplomat, an idealistic sort of figure who wants to expose the new Hitler ethic, and is frustrated not by *them* but by us."[2]

In Chapter 13, Turner, fearing that Harting has defected to the East, says that he has cut his countrymen's throats. It comes out later that he has been acting with more courage, idealism, and decisiveness than all his Embassy colleagues combined. He saw his duty and did it, forgetting personal danger. Speaking more wisely than before, the Turner of Chapter 16 remarks upon his consistency: "Leo hasn't changed," he says. "For you and me there are always a dozen good reasons for doing nothing," Turner tells Rawley Bradfield, Harting's chief. "Leo's made the other way round. In Leo's book there's only one reason for doing something: because he must. Because he feels." The trust Leo has in his instincts makes him an anomaly, a self-reliant, free-standing individualist among bureaucrats. The stir he causes in the bureaucracy confirms in him the superiority of the personal over the collective and of the heart over what is expedient and supervised. Before the novel begins, he has already tried to kill Karfeld twice. His lonely rebellion points up the fear, dishonesty, and corruption of the diplomatic corps. When faced by an act of patriotism, his colleagues crush it together with the patriot. They have to. Heedless of caution and policy, his intensity exposes their slackness. They feel threatened. A man of physical and moral courage, he does his job better than they want him to. Yet le Carré describes this clash by implication, not direct statement. His obliqueness dramatizes bureaucratic paralysis and immorality. It also tallies the cost of these defects. The surfaces le Carré shows remain sterile because they disallow authenticity. Harting digs below them to find their meaning and dies for his efforts. Lacking his historical sense, the others stand by and watch Karfeld use the same demagoguery that Hitler did thirty-five years before to wrest power.

Idling around is a pastime of the British diplomats in Bonn; inertia promotes dreams better than activity does. Only noticed after he has left, Harting catches all his co-workers flatfooted. This inconsequential-looking man has created a big flap in a small town; resolve and purpose lift the obscure over the high and mighty. His success gives insight into le Carré's beliefs about the exceptional person. Although Harting's mission—killing a head of state—resembles that of Forsyth's Jackal, he lacks the Jackal's dashing wardrobe, other jet-set tastes, and personal magnetism. Turner describes him well when he calls him a "refugee, fringe-man, lover manqúe, and trader in third-rate artifices." The mousy and the marginal can go a long way in le Carré, stirring, as they often do, his fondness for incongruity. The nefarious Karla is small, frail, and aging. Though Terence Fielding of Call has to renew his contract each year, he has taught at Carne School for two decades; the crime he commits, a particularly bloody one requiring a strong stomach and swiftness of resolve, is investigated by George Smiley, himself a fringe figure with his many dubious retirements and a marriage that looks more like a separation or a divorce. The marginal man whose purity and intensity move him to center stage recurs in Leiser, whose knowledge that he'll never be accepted as an equal releases hidden impulses. The person who has nothing or nobody to rely on accepts the burden of self-responsibility, runs le Carré's existentialist argument. And he shoulders this burden so well because being dismissed by others has left him without stays or supports. The institution won't prop him up. In Harting's twenty years as a diplomat, he has never been vetted, or screened; so far is he beneath his colleagues' serious notice that his name hasn't even been submitted for a security check.

A function of his apparent nobodiness is the great range of response he elicits from those who know him. Like a vacuum through which interference rushes, he has projected such a blank self that others invest in him both their hopes and wishes. Arthur Meadowes views him as a surrogate son even though less than ten years divide him from Harting. "You and I could blow him over with one puff," Meadowes tells Turner. John Gaunt, a Welsh security guard at the Embassy, also wants to protect Harting. Jenny Partiger agrees that he's vulnerable, saying, "He was so *little*.... You could hurt him so easily." Yet Rawley Bradfield calls him "a very self-sufficient person." "When Leo had a grudge, I wouldn't fancy being on the other end of it," he says. Harry Praschko, who has known him longer than anyone, calls him "indestructible." He also sees in him ferocious dedication: "He's a monk. A crazy monk that won't forget," he says of Harting's fanatical allegiance to his lights. Jenny Partiger holds the opposite belief, claiming of Harting, "He had never taken much interest in his work.... He was idle at heart."

The only other person in the book who provokes so many contradictory judgments is Harting's nemesis, Dr. Klaus Karfeld. Also undersized, Karfeld appears to his listeners at the monster rally in Bonn as "tired ... fresh ... well ... ill, older, younger, taller, shorter." Bypassing simple definitions, he's the political vessel into which his followers have poured their hopes. He has thus demonstrated, along with Harting, the ability of the small to rise. The unlikely Harting leaves his mark in many places and touches many people intimately despite having been an outcast. Perhaps he outwits Karfeld's security guard because, as Karfeld's opposite number, he can anticipate what they'll do. The two men have known and hated each other for twenty-five years; they've been each other's tormentor and victim; experts in humility and modesty, they've both mastered the Satanic wile of sinking in order to rise. Their mortal combat foreshadows the alliance of the polar opposites, Smiley and Karla, at the end of *Smiley's People*. It also discloses echoes from *War*. Most of these refer more pointedly to Harting than to Karfeld, whom le Carré keeps mysterious in order to focus on issues rather than personalities. But much of what we infer about Harting also applies to Karfeld. Both men are moved by revenge; each insists on belated redress; although they approach the question from opposite sides, politically and morally, they understand the force generated by historical precedent. Harting's supposed inconsequentiality (Barfield calls him *"trivial* and "utterly light-weight") and his having to volunteer for ugly jobs in order to keep his Embassy post make him a perfect exponent of Alfred Adler's doctrine of masculine protest. He shows the chiefs he has truckled to for twenty years that he's not trivial, after all; that, in fact, he's a man of daring and danger who has been controlling Embassy affairs.

But this definition oversimplifies. Having both a Christian and a Jewish parent, he has spent most of his life serving the British government in his native Germany. He speaks German with a slight English accent, and his English bears more than a trace of German intonation. From the start of his career with the Rhine Army, he has kept a foot in both the German and the British camps; his first postwar job consisted of investigating the claims of German farmers against the occupation forces which damaged their lands and livestock.

His ombudsman's job redeemed his smothered identity; it taught him how to negotiate. It also showed him how to parlay his advantages in order to lift himself. Though knowing nothing about archives, he later becomes a skilled archivist. The monumental gift for scholarship he acquires also builds him a solid case against Karfeld out of the voluminous records, licenses, news clippings, and registers he sifts in the Glory Hole. That his efforts are both derided and suppressed conveys the intelligence establishment's hostility to what is sound, honest, and civilized. But bureaucratic stonewalling can't hide the splendor of Harting's achievement. As has been seen, Harting functions as a fringe operative: "Unpromotable, unpostable, unpensionable," is how Turner hears him described in London. Turner only learns later that Harting slowly made himself indispensable—selling items like radios, phonograph records, and hairdryers at cut rate, organizing social outings, and playing the organ for the chapel choir. The chaplain's inability to replace him the day he misses choir practice to hunt Karfeld proves his importance. If he occupies the fringe, he has entrenched himself there. Not only have others been literally singing his tune for the past two years; his departure also ends the singing.

But his life stops, too. Le Carré hasn't let his fascination with the contingent and the unsponsored cloud his politics. As the Fennans and then Liz Gold showed, those lacking official approval walk in danger when they stray under the shadow of national security. A sign of their vulnerability is their Jewishness; as Dieter Frey of *Call* and Liz Gold showed, having one Jewish parent suffices to doom a person in le Carré. The point is underscored, ironically, by a reference to an older adventure writer not noted for his friendly attitude toward Jews, John Buchan. Chapter Six of *Small Town* is called "The Memory Man," perhaps in honor of the London music hall performer from *The Thirty-Nine Steps*, Mr. Memory. Like him, Leo Harting, whom a friend nicknames the Memory Man, is short. He also follows Buchan's character in meeting grief because of his involvement in an international conspiracy. Nor is this dovetailing of names le Carré's lone reference to Buchan. In *Smiley's People*, Smiley uses Standfast as a workname. Book Two of *War* opens with an epigraph from Buchan's novel, *Mr. Standfast*, whose racist innuendo foreshadows Leo Harting's pain: "There are some things that no one has a right to ask of any white man." The upper-class establishment figures of *War* and *Small Town* do make outrageous demands on both outsiders like Leiser and Harting and the English-born neophyte spy, John Avery, all of whom are white. The racist-imperialist ethic of Rule Britannia associated with Buchan can still be dredged up to justify governmental cruelty today.

In spite of it, Harting stands as fast as any other person in the Embassy. He makes great demands on himself, and he executes most of them admirably. His triumph declares itself in his success with women. Though lacking the benefits of money, job status, and good looks, he shames the sexual nonstarters, dropouts, and inverts surrounding him with his prowess as a lover. This success stems from charm, gentleness, and heart knowledge, not rank sexuality. He cares about people and enjoys helping them. No one else in Bonn's diplomatic enclave can make the neurotic Myra Meadowes laugh. His former fiancé lets him into the Hanover library where she's working so that he can shoot at Karfeld from a window. Perhaps he got her her librarian's job, and she felt obligated to do him a favor in return. (People all over West Germany owe him favors.) Perhaps he still rules her heart. In any case, she ran the risk that Karfeld's thugs would seize her for helping Harting try to kill their chief. And seize her these angry avengers do. Margaret Eickmann/Gerda Eich is kicked, punched, forced to burn her own books, and then killed within hours of the time that Harting's bullet miscarries.

Jenny Partiger, Harting's senior officer at the Embassy, also takes grave risks for him. She acts out of love. He had won her heart through the tactic of approach-avoidance. After declaring his love for her and getting rebuffed, he ignored her. His tactic threw her completely off stride. She'd have given him anything when he came to her after several weeks of keeping away. Choking over her tears, she tells Turner how she broke a major rule of security for him. But she didn't merely give him the key he asked for; she presented him, rather, with an entire ring consisting of forty-seven keys to highly restricted desks and cupboards. Her resistance overcome by a flood of love, she didn't care that his reason for needing to unlock the Assembly Room was a lie. All that mattered was the chance to show her love. She had to let him know that her love for him overrode both official policy and ethics.

The association of keys with sexual potency denotes moral growth in Harting. In Hazel Bradfield, he tumbles one of the most beautiful women in Bonn. Just as indicative of his manhood is Hazel's local standing; she's married to Harting's immediate supervisor and, as head of Chancery, the supervisor of many others. Harting's bedding of Hazel shows him transcending the association of sex with power, control, and degradation so central in le Carré. Hazel's description of her liaison shows him growing through love: "Leo married me for money. For what he could get out of me.... He stayed with me for love." And love also moved *her* to stay with him. As an outsider-underdog, he always has to keep his eye on the main chance. But Hazel's greatest material gift to him, the key to the Glory Hole, had nothing to do with manipulation. His ability to make her happy also elevated him from being a prissy little underling in her eyes to where she told her husband to renew his contract. Harting's having touched her heart so deeply confirms our impression that this short man stands taller than anyone else in the book. Hazel tells the burly Alan Turner, his closest rival, "He's a man. He's ten times the man you are."

She says this to Turner on the Thursday he turns up in Leo's place for Leo's weekly tryst with Hazel. This identity of purpose calls to mind several other likenesses between the two physical opposites— dark, dapper, ferretlike Harting and the pale, bulky Turner, who has come to Bonn dreadfully clad to find him. Hazel provokes another contrast which time resolves; whereas Harting charmed her, Turner beats her up and wins only her contempt. Then there are the immediate parallels. The Yorkshireman Turner's former career as an academic evokes the massive scholarship Harting performs to build a case against Karfeld. But whereas Harting is an immigrant bachelor who has enjoyed a colorful career with women, the sexless Turner is watching his wife's love affair with an upper-class Englishman wreck his marriage. The identity glide evolving from this countering motif reaches full expression at the end. Turner started out hating Harting as a traitor. But his opinion of him improves the more he learns.

The man he called "Harting" in his first days in Bonn he comes to refer to as "Leo." In fact, "Leo!" is the last word he says in our hearing while "looking at his own life, his own face," in that of the dead patriot, which he sees in The Epilogue for the only time. And why shouldn't he see in Harting's corpse a mirror image of himself? The two men had faced the same dangers from the same enemies. Ludwig Siebkron, Bonn's chief of police and security head, orders his men to beat up Turner to stop him from investigating. The next day, Siebkron lures Harting out of his hiding place and kills him before he can get to Karfeld. Betrayal also maneuvers Harting and Turner to the scaffold which served as Karfeld's rostrum for their mirror meeting (in Chapter 14, Hazel had called Turner "the deadliest thing I ever met"). Balancing the adultery of Turner's wife is the treachery of Harry Praschko, Harting's oldest friend, and of Gerda Eich, his former fiancée, both of whom told Siebkron where to find Harting.

The trait that welds Turner most firmly to Harting is the retributive morality the men share. Seekers both, they hate bureaucracies because they're built on evasiveness, toadyism, and fear. "He'll never stop searching," Hazel says of Harting, whom she also calls a puritan. She has judged him well. For at least five years, he has been leaving the wooden buttons from the clothing worn by Karfeld's wartime victims to show his contempt for whatever offends him. Turner keeps the same strict accounts. "You want all the lines joined up and all the colors flat," Hazel says of his moral primitivism. Earlier she had complained to him, "You want things spelt out for you." She's not the only Bradfield to judge him. Her husband later calls him a mountaineer, yoking him to Sisyphus, the boulder pusher of ancient myth. Tightening the identification is Turner's statement to Jenny Partiger in Chapter 8 that Harting will never be found. His answer to her sensible retort, "Then why look for him?" invokes the existentialism threading the novel: "Why not? That's how we spend our lives, isn't it? Looking for people we'll never find."

This credo validates his discovery of Harting at the moment of Leo's death. Turner hasn't stopped searching for his "untamed half." His being ordered off the search by Bradfield and then pounded by Siebkron's thugs only increases his zeal. His pale eyes conveying his implacability, he represents a new direction in character portrayal for le Carré. This bruiser displays a wide array of social skills at a diplomatic dinner, parrying the attempts of others to wrest information from him with some well-bred evasions, pretenses of ignorance, and the tactic of answering questions with questions of his own. Yet he won't shrink from straight, hard talk. When Hazel prevaricates with him during their sole Thursday meeting, he tries to beat the information he has come for out of her. With the same alacrity, he insults her high-ranking husband to his face, attacking him both as a diplomat and a husband. His tough talk, ability to take punishment, slapping of Hazel Bradfield, and moral pride all put him closer to a hardboiled dick in an American private-eye yarn than to his fellow Londoner, George Smiley. Though pummelled hard enough in *Call* to need a month in the hospital, the sensitive technician-sleuth Smiley lacks the physical strength to survive the corruption of Bonn in 1969 or '70. The tough, sarcastic shamus functions better amid the desolation and depravity of an unredeemed world. And evil is no anomaly in *Small Town*. In view of its wholesale vulgarity, the betrayal-ridden Bonn of the novel stands closer to Raymond Chandler's Bay City than to the London of Conan Doyle, the Styles of Agatha Christie, or the Dorset of *A Murder of Quality*.

Yet even Turner can't tally the cost of this devastation. Rawley Bradfield, "upper-class academic" and head of Chancery, denies the truth constantly. His dishonesty has created an emotional crisis too complex for him to cope with. Though he both despises and resents Harting, he rehired him recently to please a wife he loves but can't communicate with verbally or physically. But his guilt cuts still deeper. He knows that his own apathy has enabled Harting to take on so many sensitive jobs in Chancery that the Embassy could never replace him. Thus the worst part of his crisis comes in his knowledge that, though he has caused it, he can't quiet it. Harting couldn't be fired at all, even if he weren't having an affair with Hazel. He controls the two main areas of his chief's life—his work and his home. But le Carré doesn't cast blame. Bradfield's summary of the accommodations and compromises he has made during the past generation leaves us not knowing whether to despise him or to cry:

I have controlled the processes of my own mind for eighteen years of marriage and twenty years of diplomacy. I have spent half my life learning not to look, and the other half learning not to feel. Do you think I cannot also learn to forget? God, sometimes I am bowed down by the things I do not know.... Do you think I take pleasure in what I have to do?

Karfeld lacks Bradfield's tender heart. Called by Merry "a revivalist Nazi demagogue,"[3] he preaches a new nationalism. Included in his pulpit-rattling cadences is hatred—for the United States, Great Britain, and NATO. Karfeld has two forebears, one real and one fictional. The theme of the main character's speech in le Carré's 1967 *Saturday Evening Post* story, "Dare I Weep, Dare I Mourn?" resembles that of Karfeld's, *viz.*, the failure of the West to honor the rights of Germany.[4] (But in the story the speech comes at the outset rather than at the end, where it appears in *Small Town.*) The second, and more vital, source goes back to Hitler's platform exhortations in the mid-1930s to restore German honor by breaking the fetters of Versailles. Karfeld rouses the same fervor in his hearers that Hitler did thirty-five years before, a point underscored by the leader of a military band standing across from Karfeld and holding his arm in a fascist salute before signalling his musicians to play.

Only Leo Harting tries to stop the neo-Nazism he sees threatening the FRG. The memory man is helped by his ability to infuse his recollections of the war with a keen sense of history. An industrial chemist by profession, Karfeld manufactured poison gas during the war. The human guinea pigs, mostly Jews, he experimented with came to his Hapstorf factory in gray buses whose windows were blackened from within. A gray bus with blackened windows also brings Karfeld's gray-garbed bodyguard from Hanover to Bonn for the big rally. This sludge that Karfeld pumps into Bonn's fog, mists, and exhaust fumes enriches the book's theme. In what may be the book's most explosive moment, Turner announces that the doctoral thesis Karfeld recently submitted dealt with the effect of poisonous gases upon thirty-one dead bodies. This evil carries into the town hall rally. As has been noted, both Bradfield and Siebkron knew all along of Karfeld's guilt. But now that expediency and complacency dictate overlooking it, neither they nor any of their charges will oppose Karfeld. The miasma he emits has snuffed out both independence and individualism. Le Carré records the inevitability of his triumph in an image whose power builds from its rhetoric, its apocalyptic allusion to W. B. Yeats's "The Second Coming," and its fusion of German fascism and British moral flab. Turner is observing the legion of Karfeld's backers move toward the town hall square in a drab gray wave:

Turner waited until he was out of sight before walking back.... As he went there rose suddenly behind him an unearthly rumble of feet and voices, the saddest, deepest sound he had ever heard in his life. The columns had begun to move; they were shuffling slowly forward, mediocre, ponderous and terrifying, a mindless gray monster that could no longer be held back, while beyond them, almost hidden in the mist stood the wooded outline of Chamberlain's hill.

II

This unfeatured menace conveys the twin idea that character itself is shadowy, leaden, and out of range and that, under fascism particularly, life is ruled by forces we can't see clearly enough to know or stop. No fast-paced action thriller, *Small Town* probes surfaces and examines issues in a sober, even-handed way. Turner's toughness hides his sharp intuition. Rather than tracing Harting through close observation of physical clues, he finds out what his quarry is like by looking for him in other people. The rich fabric of motives he weaves contains many strands. Having arrested and then testified against Karfeld, Harting has known of his guilt for twenty-five years. Now that the statute of limitations has expired, nobody will reopen the case. These realities make Harting more of a temporizer and reluctant justicer than a fire-eating avenger. He prefers talk to action despite his legacy of Old Testament retribution. Several of the people Turner talks to about him report him mouthing interminably about having been wronged. Though he's the only one who'll punish Karfeld, he waits till the last moment. Only after being shamed by his conscience does he take definite steps. But having moved forward, however grudgingly, he won't turn back. He has a more exacting code of justice than the officers of the Nuremberg Court, whose justice dribbled away in four years. Even the twenty-year statute of limitations falls short of his memory, ethics, and private hurt. The outsider, not the officially sanctioned body, presses for change. Like Alec Leamas before him, Harting kicks against the system in the only way left to him, by choosing death over apathy and moral paralysis.

The research operation he runs so secretly and effectively from the Glory Hole rests on the Kafkaesque motif of burrowing and finding tension in enclosures like tunnels, jails, and mazes. His efforts displace time and space, compressing events into a pure present. Dismembering rather than developing society, Harting also exposes both the confusion of roles and the decenteredness of contemporary life; his mining of seams and edges betrays the impotence and inertia of his paymasters. The novel's technique endorses both this Yeatsian loss of center and the Kafkaesque labors unearthing the loss. *Small Town* displays a reluctance in le Carré either to repeat himself or to accept limits. We've already seen both the book's investigative sleuth and moral corruption putting the book closer to American than to British mystery fiction. Also, le Carré moves from the GDR to the FRG; neither Smiley nor any of his colleagues from the Circus or the Department shows his face; diplomatic intrigue replaces field work. But le Carré builds upon, rather than rejecting, artistic strengths evolved in his earlier work. Both *War* and *Small Town* show the benefits of working margins and then pushing them toward the center. Virtual nobodies in both works attain heights beyond any set forth by official policy. Even though we don't yet know Harting, our first glimpse of him in the Prologue conveys a singlemindedness that will embarrass and reprove his chiefs throughout. Ignoring the banners draping the buildings nearby and the greetings of other pedestrians, Harting rivets his attention on Karfeld, "the plumper figure a hundred paces ahead of him."

Thus Harting angers his English superiors by defending cherished English values. Neither earlier nor later does he come so close to killing Karfeld, who has stolen into Bonn for a meeting so secret that he's travelling to it on foot, hoping to lose himself in the crowd. Luck sides with him. Just before he's about to be shot, he reaches the pick-up point and climbs into the car waiting to take him to his top-secret meeting. Yet because the Prologue, entitled "The Hunter and the Hunted," identifies neither of its eponyms, we don't know what's happening or what's at stake. The dismay registered at the end of the Prologue by the policeman who had questioned Harting but failed to remember him from his picture on the notice-board of the station house ends the chapter. It also foreshadows le Carré's portrayal of Harting as a cigar smoker who speaks German with a trace of an English accent together with the pact between the British Embassy and the local police to protect Karfeld from Harting. But such revelations only come later. Sometimes they come piecemeal. *Small Town* recounts events after they happen and/or from a distance. The meaning of these events may be disputed. Le Carré avoids pat answers. Oblique and elliptical in his approach, he won't connect events, often breaking into conversations without identifying the ideas or people being discussed. He'll bring in characters without defining their place in the narrative. Then he'll refer to unfamiliar people and ideas. The topic of a discussion may only surface after a page or two. It may then be shouldered aside by a digression. Then the digression may foreshadow a major development. A propos of nothing we can make sense of at the time, a Bonn journalist at a dinner party refers to Karfeld's gray buses having been important "about a thousand years ago."

And how better could le Carré yoke form and content than by joining his many disconnected surfaces with someone who doesn't appear? Novels like Virginia Woolf's *The Waves* and Anthony Powell's *What's Become of Waring* along with plays like Clifford Odets' *Waiting for Lefty* and Samuel Beckett's *Waiting for Godot* have proved the feasibility of writing a good literary work whose main figure is never seen. Le Carré's contribution to the tradition shows in his ability to win sympathy for Harting. Readers usually have trouble opening to a character they've not met, particularly a would-be assassin. But the reasons for stopping Harting and the motives of his pursuers have both earned our scorn. Turner is the exception. Though he starts out as Harting's tracker-antagonist, the more he learns about his quarry, the closer he moves to him. The process only stops when their identities fuse; the shattering of Turner's mirror image climaxes his looking-glass confrontation. But Harting isn't the only character whose appearance is delayed. That other mover of the plot, Karfeld, enters only in the Epilogue, after appearing in the Prologue with Harting, where both men went unnamed. Then Harry Praschko, Harting's oldest friend, ex-political ally, and Judas, comes in in the book's last chapter.

The novel's structure matches le Carré's strategy of character portrayal to idea. Anticipating the entry of tough, classless Alan Turner, *Small Town* begins like a novel by Hammett, Chandler, or Ross Macdonald—as a missing person's case. As has been seen, a wave of anti-British feeling, set in motion by Karfeld, is gaining force in the FRG at the same time that Great Britain's application for admission into the EEC is being voted on in Brussels. Harting's chiefs at the British Embassy fear that he has defected to the USSR, taking with him information the disclosure of which could wreck Britain's tie with the FRG. Turner is thwarted in his search for Harting as was Sam Spade in his for the Maltese falcon because his client is also the culprit. Although Harting must be found, the search for him can't damage the West German good will London needs to keep alive its chances to join the EEC. Thus Bradfield hides his guilty knowledge and thwarts the search. But he can't thwart it forever. As suppressed information comes to light, so does Harting's character. The process is slow but sure. At its completion, Harting hasn't only become the book's most fascinating figure. He has also described how the tame and the predictable can stir wonder and how apparently far-flung lives connect obscurely but inexorably. The action moves from the point where Harting's absence seems a minor irritant, barely deserving mention, to where it might decide the future of western Europe.

The novel's middle chapter, the ninth, called "Guilty Thursday," both speeds the investigation and brings issues into the open. Its second sentence says of Turner, "He stood in the first floor corridor where Leo had stood." As Poe's Dupin did in "The Purloined Letter" and as Smiley will do in *Smiley's People,* Turner is copying someone's physical movements in order to recreate his mental processes. His impersonation serves him well, leading him to Harting's two main haunts, the windy bluff where the weekly Thursday tryst with Hazel takes place and the Glory Hole. Turner's reconstruction of Harting's movements and thoughts also create narrative drive. Chapter Ten describes the Embassy dinner party, the only scene in the book in which high-ranking Germans and Britons appear together. Le Carré's dual eye for the public and the private lends the scene conviction and flair. As in a party scene written by Evelyn Waugh or Henry Green, Chapter 10 shows conversational glitter flashing its silver in a void. But the innuendoes and glancing slights of the socially accomplished dinner guests blur and fray as they did in *Murder.* The diplomatic chic the guests work so hard to affect soon sinks into pretension, rivalry, and loss of control. Piercing the alcoholic mists exuded at the dinner party, Turner sees that neither Siebkron nor Bradfield will help him find Harting. His recognizing that, in fact, those in power don't want Harting found prompts his illicit 4:30 a.m. visit to Harting's house in the next chapter, which opens several hours after the end of the party. And, as if this visit had produced an acausal connection, Harting is evoked; a minor diplomat reports having seen him drinking beer in a local train station in Chapter 12.

The novel's shrewd mixture of vigor and delicacy does full justice to the many changes recounted. Together with its heightened awareness of class differences, the ripeness of phrasing in *Small Town* looks ahead to *The Naive and Sentimental Lover,* le Carré taking special pains in both works to touch in details of landscape, weather, and artifact that create a local ambience. Yet he also brings back the stream-of-consciousness technique from *War* to convey distress; hallucinations of home mingle with Turner's present circumstances after he's beaten up for working harder at his job than those in charge want him to. In the early scenes, like those of *Drummer Girl,* which unfold in nearby Bad Godesberg, le Carré will move from the panoramic to the scenic and from the journalistic to the dramatic. Another way he brings Bonn to life is by lacing its political background with personal opinion: "The very choice of Bonn as the waiting house of Berlin has long been an anomoly; it is now an abuse," he says in Chapter 1. Certain passages satirize the diplomatic class in the vein of Forster's *A Passage to India;* others invoke the sparkle of Oscar Wilde. In Chapter 13, a well-travelled diplomat from England's upper classes quips dryly, "I had a violin once. It fell to pieces in Leopoldville. The glue melted. It's awfully hard ... to pursue culture when the glue melts."

The book's most noteworthy stylistic innovation also concerns dialogue. *Small Town* converts le Carré's oft-praised powers of impersonation to artistic capital for the first time. The donnish diplomat Rawley Bradfield, the Welsh security guard John Gaunt, and, particularly, the ex-war refugee Harry Praschko, whose English still bears the edginess and colloquialism of the American GI's from whom he learned it, show le Carré acting more like a recorder than a creator, content to listen in while a character takes over the narration. Praschko's long recitation, like those of Charlie Marshall and Ric Ricardo in *Schoolboy,* matches psychic identity to politics. Others add verisimilitude and flesh out motivation differently, sometimes with a joke. Seeing Turner again after Turner tore him and his daughter from Warsaw, Arthur Meadowes takes revenge—by talking. Nearly all of Chapter 6 consists of his interview with Turner. Although he's not long winded, he wants his say, and he won't let Turner rush him as he develops his thoughts. His talking to a captive audience constitutes perfect bureaucratic revenge. It also makes for a good laugh.

But was le Carré laughing when Karfeld combined the goal of German reunification with that of forging a Bonn-Moscow pact? These twin aims aren't feasible. Though the USSR has promoted the absorption of capitalist states by their Communist neighbors since the end of World War II, it has also frowned upon German nationalism. The idea of a unified Germany repels the Kremlin. Books are still being written and TV documentaries produced on subjects like the infamous Leningrad Blockade.[5] Here in the 1980s, Soviet republics like the Baltic states of Latvia, Lithuania, and Estonia have also celebrated forty years of freedom from Nazi oppression. Although the Soviets don't identify Hitler's Germany with today's, such public occasions fan whatever residue of anti-German feeling remains in their country. It's hard to see how Moscow would push for German reunification unless it were to occur on terms that very few German leaders would accept. But given the breadth and sweep of *Small Town,* this is a small cavil. Readable and relevant, well observed and resolved, the book outpaces by far Len Deighton's *Ipcress File* (1962), another novel about corruption in British security and featuring, in Harry Palmer, an uncouth but effective and sympathetic agent wrung by his superiors.

Then there's Leo Harting, whose colleagues will forget him sooner than we will. In building *Small Town* around him, le Carré awakens us to the murderous realities of diplomacy. He also celebrates the fiction writer's freedom and power. Virtue needn't win out in a novel to claim our attention, Harting reminds us. The reminder drives home. Writing about evil is an act of justice, preventing the evil from being buried. Writing about it as well as le Carré does in *Small Town* is a triumph of the spirit. Yet, lest we become dazzled by his *tour de force* of protesting against evil through a character who never appears, we should also honor his ability to locate human consciousness between history and anticipation. The consciousness he locates and engages, furthermore, is ours. Our anticipation of Leo Harting's entry into the action occupies us more and more till we reach the harrowing, inevitable finale. The shadows cast by Klaus Karfeld's scaffold define *A Small Town in Germany* as a work of reach and complexity by a deadly moralist who is also an exacting artist.

Chapter Ten
Reeling Around Parnassus

Beginning in twilight, *The Naive and Sentimental Lover* starts as a nostalgic evocation. Its opening chapters celebrate the cultural splendors of England's aristocratic heritage, mourn their decline, and mock their present perversions. Haverdown, the Somerset estate which supplies the name of the book's first section, symbolizes an upper-class life that has long since passed. Le Carré's affection for England's bygone glories reflects the lover's quarrel voiced elsewhere in his fiction. Other similarities to the spy books occur, too. From *Small Town* comes an appreciation for what might have happened, those energies that were sidetracked or stifled in the thwarted pursuit of a goal; *Lover* repeats several times the argument dramatized through Leo Harting, i.e., that a person must be judged by what he/she looks for rather than by what he/she finds. This energy excludes spying. Whatever shreds of literary intrigue the book contains stay clear of the plot. The two main characters check into a Paris hotel under the names of the notorious double agents, Burgess and Maclean. Later, the writer of an imaginative account of the men's Parisian frolics is identified as Chapman Pincher, future author of the 1981 study of spying, *Their Trade is Treachery*. Just as playfully, le Carré refers to two London theater ticket agents in Chapter 29 as Lacon and Ollier, Oliver Lacon being a cabinet officer in *Tinker, Tailor*.

Such allusions tempt us to look for other elements that join le Carré's 1972 work to the rest of the canon. We need not look far. One feature shared by all the work is the "preoccupation with moral values" noted by John Kirk in 1963.[1] But what supplied the impetus to explore morality through the medium of mainstream fiction? Perhaps le Carré wrote *Lover* in response to *Some Gorgeous Accident* (1967), another work dealing with two men who love the same woman, by his friend, James Kennaway.[2] Other influences include William Blake's doctrine of excess, the Nietzschean will to power, John Fowles's politics in *The Aristos* (1964), and the concept of intense male friendship put forth in D. H. Lawrence's *Women in Love* (1920) and

David Storey's *Radclyffe* (1963). Several strands join these sources. First is the belief that truth comes in terror, not fact. Terror liberates, refreshes, and renews; a sense of panic awakens us to first truths. The expanded, energized self will fare forth with new self-command after being terrified. Pushing forward without apologies or regrets, the brave, the free, and the noble will obey their impulses. They will take rather than give, the force of their example constituting a supreme gift of its own. "Feeling is knowledge," says someone in the text, invoking J. C. F. von Schiller's distinction between the naive and the sentimental. Advising us that these two dispositions or drives always interact, rather than existing independently, Schiller equates the naive with spontaneity and innocence, impulse and challenge. Whereas the *naif* has the ease, naturalness, and self-trust conveyed by the Old Testament, his sentimental counterpart follows the dictates of civilization and received morality. He's a slave to group values. Instead of imposing himself, he follows. He mouthes the stock phrases of whatever creed rules his society. In our Judeo-Christian epoch, his impulses have become suffocated by the New Testament ethic of sacrifice and humility. He's a sheeplike imitator, not a creator or leader.

Exemplifying Schiller's spectrum-split between the naive and the sentimental are the bland, cautious corporation executive Aldo Cassidy and the fiery, belligerent novelist Shamus (no last name given). Wild and uninhibited, Shamus defies many of his society's ideas, for instance, about indebtedness. He takes from others as he pleases without feeling any need to reciprocate. He even acts as if he's doing Aldo a favor by living free in his Thameside flat and Swiss chalet. The Water Closet, his pejorative term for the flat he uses but fails to clean when he leaves, shows his disdain for the mutuality and reciprocity most of us try to guide our lives by. This bold assertion of freedom and power grips us even while we reject it. His absence from the novel between Chapters 8-13, some eighty-three pages in the original clothbound edition (New York: Knopf), paralyzes the action. Explanations for this paralysis come easily. Polite, restrained Aldo can't hold our interest. Besides lacking Shamus's dynamism, he's so crushed by Shamus's sudden departure that he loses all purpose and drive.

But his submissiveness and resignation exert a charm of their own. His self-questioning decency, if incapable of propelling the novel, impresses his circle as much as it does us. His statement in Chapter 10, "I want to make people happy. ... That's all I care about," articulates a noble goal, one that any person could proudly direct his/her energies to. It's not surprising that Shamus's wife Helen falls in love with him and agrees to leave Shamus for him. Other fictional elements make the same claim on us while also reminding us that the naive and the sentimental in Schiller aren't distinct. There is, first, the strong tie that builds between the founder, board chairman, and managing director of a successful London firm and the nomadic bohemian artist. The doubling motif found in *War, Small Town,* and *Smiley's People* may reach its apogee in *Lover.* Shamus and Aldo are about the same height and age; roughly contemporaries at Oxford, they have the same body build. Besides loving both Helen and each other, both do ethnic vocal impersonations. Moreover, both men attained success early, Shamus having published a brilliant novel twenty years before the present action of the book and Aldo having earned enough through his industrial wizardry to retire at age thirty-eight. The first meeting between the two men prefigures their emergence as foils locked in a moral dialogue which gains depth from their burgeoning love tie. Shamus addresses Aldo immediately as "lover," an epithet he will use almost exclusively in the coming action. Aldo, in turn, is smitten straightaway. He finds Shamus "very handsome," shortly after which he shocks himself by getting an erection. This magnetism persists. The possibility that Shamus has phoned him after an absence of several months dries Aldo's mouth in Chapter 12. Then he quotes Shamus in a speech given to the directors and shareholders of his large firm. When the two men go to Paris together, it becomes difficult to tell whether their registering in a hotel as Burgess and Maclean refers to homosexuality (even though the reference would only be half true); accepting Shamus's valuation, Aldo calls himself Shamus's lover.

Or could the reference to Burgess and Maclean portend treason? A great deal of touching and stroking, hugging and kissing, goes on between the men. But not only are the men married and thus guilty of adultery; le Carré may also be using both the Paris interlude and Shamus's statement that the bed in the Thameside flat can sleep three people to rework sexual frontiers. Little positive reworking takes place, though. It's during this same time that Aldo and Helen become lovers behind Shamus's back, just as Shamus and Aldo exchanged "long embraces under . . . warm blankets" in Paris when Aldo's wife believed him to be busy working at a trade convention. *Lover* asserts far more than it demonstrates. Acts intended as major declarations of freedom and power drown in vanity, selfishness, and lies. As in Lawrence's silliest moments, the characters claim to be leading richer lives than they do lead. And they look more like hypocrites than like failed idealists or moral revolutionaries. This disconnectedness mars the novel throughout. It asserts itself most pithily in Shamus's many references to a forty-three-year-old taxi driver in County Cork named Flaherty who calls himself God. What Shamus loves in Flaherty is the daring with which he embraces his self-concept; the person who imagines himself God becomes God, runs the logic, bypassing both the ontological argument of Aquinas and the cosmological argument of Anselm; wishes, ideas, and beliefs aren't always facts. Built on a philosophical void, the Shamus-Flaherty God projection collapses before taking shape. Advisedly, Flaherty never appears. Perhaps he doesn't exist. But if his, or Shamus's, merging of the real and the imaginary bespeaks genius, it fails to elevate that genius from the pedestrian. Shamus's love for Flaherty is marred by an urge to kill him. Following the classical paradigm of Oedipal displacement, Shamus wants to push Flaherty out of his throne so he can snatch it for himself.

Might we have looked for a nobler response from the man touted by Cassidy as the best creative writer of his time? Shamus's blind selfishness would hurt the novel less if it were an aberration or an anomaly. But it isn't. He reaches out for whatever he fancies. Explaining the lifegiving power of the naive, in Schiller's sense, Helen uses him as her example: Shamus is naive, she claims, "because he lives life and doesn't imitate it." Wrong. His many vocal impersonations make him the book's arch-imitator. More damagingly, they show that, rather than facing life squarely, he's forever standing sideways or speaking through a mask. The free and the bold don't need this caution. Nor would they be so reactive. Helen describes Shamus as a challenger of "convention, morals, manners, life, God." His need for something to push against shows that he's not free standing or self acting, at all. Were he truly creative, he'd practice more self-reliance. Had he the philosopher's calm, he'd not waste himself looking for demons to rout. "He does so adore an audience," admits Helen of her show-off husband. Significantly, two pages after her rehearsal of Schiller's doctrine of the naive and the sentimental, Shamus appears playing dominoes, a game in which each move depends on earlier ones and whose pieces touch rather than standing free. These realities call to mind another dialectic from Schiller, that of the organic and the mechanical. The mechanical, claims Schiller, is that which is derived and arbitrary rather than spontaneous, free, and natural. This dialectic, ignored in the book, embarrasses Shamus more than the one that supplies the book's title, because he looks like a fool or a thug whenever he shakes off restraints. What is more, his self-assertions look too rehearsed. Brazenness as shrill as his can only bring loss of self, as if his many impersonations hadn't already eroded his personality.

The devastation he doesn't turn on himself he inflicts on his intimates. Although Helen calls him "the complete enchanter," she never says what's so enchanting about having her passport burned, being punched in the face, and getting locked in a closet. Aldo doesn't fare much better with Shamus, who throws a rock at his head, bloodies his nose, and makes him pull him up a hill on a dogsled under threat of death. The love Shamus gives is laced with great lashings of cruelty, deceit, and violence—as, indeed, love can be in real life. Perhaps the master-slave relationship *can* reorder love. Freud's belief that strict authority is the payment exacted for civilization may well have sexual ramifications; we lack the information to judge. Le Carré deserves our praise for disclosing the darkness released by love. Nor can he be faulted for pondering the fertility of this darkness. But his failure to understand Shamus any better than idolatrous Aldo does robs his excursions into sexuality's night side of import. Shamus's barbarities teach nothing and raise no spirits or hopes. Yet they carry the high cost of dividing Shamus ever further from himself, of damaging his intimates, and, at another level, of derailing the plot. There's something sad in all this. The John le Carré of *The Naive and Sentimental Lover* resembles the circus clown who, tired of his baggy pants and bashed hat, wants to play Hamlet. By trying to write a mainstream novel, le Carré hoped to broaden his art. Alas, *Lover* both narrowed his art and cramped his vision. The premises upon which the novel was built failed to stir the energies that make his spy books so provocative and original.

I

In Chapter I, Aldo ponders the correct pronunciation of Haverdown, the Somerset estate he covets: "Was the *a* long or short? To have or to haver?" The question resounds through what follows. The have-nots are deprived because of their indecisiveness and timidity; they lack the selftrust to take what they want. The Nietzchean will to power, on the other hand, gives the lucky few the resolve and constancy to prevail. But how does the novel measure their success against the supposed failure of the sheeplike majority? Nobody seems better off at the end of the book than he/she was at the start. Aldo's marriage is still weak; his retirement from business before the age of forty has sapped his purpose. He won't enter politics, as he had hoped; the mystery novel he started to write will remain unfinished; he'll never see Helen and Shamus again. Although Shamus fares somewhat better, he pays very heavily for his gains. While writing his first novel in twenty years, he loses his wife to another man. His winning her back at the end can't hide the breakdown of love that took her from him; nor can it restore the trust Shamus felt before she strayed. Why else would Shamus pound and shackle her in the concluding section? Absolutists like him both give and take offense easily. And they don't shrink from exacting revenge. We shudder to think what Helen's life will be like after she steps out of the novel. On no score does her future promise well. Our last glimpse of the reunited couple finds them as homeless as they were at the outset. Though tremendous effort has been exerted and many pints have been wept, the gains are small. The name, Haverdown, may well invoke the distinction between having and not-having. The illogicalities of the plot also remind us that *havers* is a British colloquialism for nonsense and rubbish.

Some intriguing premises keep this trumpery from sinking the novel. With its remoteness, banging winds, and screaming birds, Haverdown offers little of the protection and comfort Aldo had come there to find. Then, the "packing cases and mouldering books ... strewn over the floor of the Great Hall" stink of dry rot; a backed-up chimney in another room, reached by a network of "dismal corridors," gives out its own stench. But this rankness is mitigated. The park neighboring the estate has "a lush pastoral quality" Aldo finds "distinctly soothing." And his first meeting with Helen and Shamus suffuses him with a radiance he had never known before.

The running-together of positive and negative features in the book's opening chapters foreshadows a truth that will color all of Aldo's dealings with his two friends; representing values beyond ordinary good and evil, Helen and Shamus keep giving Aldo both more than he had expected and more than he can handle. His love of tradition, pedigrees, and old things in general stems from his yearning to belong to something greater than himself. Unable to communicate with his wife, he claims that, in its present impasse, all he and Sandra need to hold their marriage together is two telephones. The inability of the clinic she runs with her mother to attract patients has put the burden of her happiness on him. Deeply self-questioning, he blames himself for the marriage's failure. When Sandra accuses him of lacking "any scrap of decency or moral fiber or human compassion," he acquiesces, only muttering inwardly that she may be right. He has no reserves to fall back on. The self-doubt that stops him from defending himself stems from troubles boiling up from his family of origin. To begin with, he inherited a legacy of transience and homelessness from his oft-wed hotelier-father. Then his mother left the home when he was about six, making rejection, separation, and loss the model for his ties with women.

Among his many attempts to relieve his separation anxiety is his staying in a white hotel in Paris. The white hotel in both Freud and the excellent 1981 novel by D. M. Thomas of the same name represents maternal comfort and sustenance. The mother's breast, source of the white hotel symbol, provides the infant's first object relationship and thus eases the infant into the external world. Before experiencing the mother's breast, the infant knows only itself and its needs, forming the boundaries of its world. The idea of returning to this first source of objective reality and nourishment grips Aldo. A Parisian prostitute he meets later comes to him in a fantasy on "sheer white legs" rising "like a white candle" out of the clothes she sheds; anchoring the construct, he thinks of taking her to the Sacre Coeur, that whitest of all holy buildings. The religious symbolism carries forward. The very presence of a prostitute in the white hotel is a defilement, which ushers in many others. Shamus ruins a bathtub, moves furniture, and destroys some of the hotel's property during a fight with the prostitute; then he makes a two-hour phone call to London which he doesn't pay for. These defilements worsen Aldo's sense of rootlessness and deprivation. Three straight sentences in Chapter 34, which takes place some months later, begin with Aldo saying, "I need a bed." Having seen the welcoming warmth of the white hotel chill and curdle, he's also turned away by his father and his lover-secretary. The Swiss business colleague who gives him a bed also accuses him of being homosexual, voicing an opinion expressed earlier by Sandra and Aldo himself. Though he buys Haverdown, fulfilling the dream that claimed him at the outset, he feels more cut off from a source of nurture and comfort in the Epilogue than at any other time in the book. His total silence in the Epilogue shows how much this soft, sociable man's futile quest for lost unity with the white hotel has devastated him.

A more direct hurt comes from his erratic, scolding father's rejection of him. The importance of winning old Hugo's approval shows in his surprising reference to the "fatherly gentleness" of Haverdown's trees; with their leafy tunnels, sheltering and nesting places, and rootedness in the earth, trees are usually associated with the female, not the male, principle. The closure Aldo craves with his father never comes, perhaps because it asserts itself so insistently. The more Aldo gives, the more Hugo withdraws. And Aldo gives a great deal. Buying in on the historical and architectural splendors of Haverdown pales before the hope of gaining his father's love. His thwarted need for unity with Hugo can be easily sensed. Intuiting it, Shamus calls himself "Daddy" to Aldo in Chapter 14. And he often acts like a stern, disapproving father who exacts stiff demands before smiling on his anxious, accommodating son. Aldo responds to him as to his literal father, surrendering everything—his volition, sense of right and wrong, property, time, and money. Incredibly, after Shamus tells him, "There's so much of you I could *use,*" Aldo chides himself for not being more generous to this demanding ingrate. Hugo is just as demanding and even more ungrateful. Like Shamus, he battens on Aldo's kindness and then insults him. Neither man can dispense simple humanity to Aldo, let alone fatherly love. And Aldo knows it. He dreams of Hugo walking over his skull just as he acquiesces when Shamus hits him in the head with a rock.

But why *should* Shamus or Hugo treat him decently? To do so would be to kill the golden calf. Aldo forces money on Shamus, pays his bills, lets him use his credit cards, and houses him in grand style. His immense generosity even rankles his eleven-year-old son, Mark. It doesn't stop there, either. His having named his younger son Hugo looks like another reaching-out for love that recoils on him; in trying to redeem a nasty relationship with a nasty man, he merely compounds his losses (he should have obeyed his first impulses, when he named Mark). Aldo's bilked intention smacks of the wish to control his family members, and the moral inertia and imbalance it infers merely prolong the tyranny it had set into motion. Unfailingly, Aldo brings out the worst in his intimates. Both the peritonitis that brought Mark down before the time of the book and the break in young Hugo's leg that refuses to mend suggest trouble in the Cassidy male line. Aldo is as bad a father to his sons as his father was to him. He sends Mark to a school, Sherborne in Dorset, which he (and le Carré) also attended and which Mark hates. Then he goes to Paris with Shamus rather than helping little Hugo recover. The broken leg suffered by the boy raises an intriguing possibility that bears on Aldo's psyche. The seven-year-old's grandfather-namesake bullyrags Aldo every time he appears in the book. Although Aldo had nothing to do with the accident that broke his son's leg after a fall from a tree, the similarity in names between that son and his grandfather makes us wonder if Aldo, too weak to resist passing on grief, didn't wish the injury on his persecutor's namesake as an act of revenge. Aldo's fear of heights gives the idea a resonance that chimes with both his blocked hopes and resentments.

The tension between Aldo's conscious and unconscious selves stirs currents elsewhere. Aldo makes accessories for prams, his reputation as an industrial genius having come from a footbrake he invented with a revolutionary safety device. We're meant to admire this breakthrough; Aldo's footbrake protects the innocent, serves the future, and helps continuity. But this champion of the helpless and the innocent is himself childlike, so much so that he makes us doubt le Carré's portrayal of him as a man of technological skill, leadership, and drive. His love for Shamus silences him ("love has no language"). Yet he goes mute after his beloved has just acted with rudeness, vanity, and malevolence. This harshness makes Aldo cower as he begs for more. After stopping Shamus's rock, Aldo apologizes to *him*. Such truckling strains our belief. This "louche criminal" and philanthropist includes enough inconsistencies and contradictions to qualify as an Everyman figure. Yet he has no middle ground. The hidden, lawless self that erupts so suddenly clashes with the shrewd, successful businessman that takes on the world; his revolutionary footbrake is so cunning that the Japanese can't even copy it. Nor can it be argued that his industrial prowess rose from a need to impress his father.

His name, Aldo, infers an abstract ability (All-do) that misleads and misrepresents. As long-suffering and self-debasing as he is, he towers even further above the ordinary than Shamus does. He has not only won fame as a businessman and an inventor; he's also a world-class mountain climber, bobsledder, and ski jumper. What's more, he's too modest to own to his laurels. Yet this over-achiever is also helpless, pampered, and effeminate. One of his schoolteachers called him "Doubtful" because of his wavering; at the end, a long-term friend accuses him of resorting to his customary practice of dithering. Sandra's calling him Pailthorpe, Shamus's addressing him as Lover, and his referring to himself as (Guy) Burgess also bespeak irresolution. He's so many things to others because he's so shakily seated in himself. This insecurity makes his problem ontological; either he doesn't know or want to be himself. The end of the novel finds him acting in character when he concocts his own downfall by missing the train slated to take him and Helen to their new life together; he replies "jovially" to a station guard after learning that the train has "indisputably gone."

But doesn't this self-imposed defeat make us doubt his many triumphs? Wouldn't someone as self-destructive as he reveals himself to be in the closing chapters have foiled himself earlier? Lacking self-confidence and beset by demons unleashed by parental rejection, he could never have succeeded as wildly in business as is claimed. Either le Carré doesn't know how hard it is to acquire money and power in competitive industry or he has misrepresented Aldo. Another alternative argues in favor of misrepresentation. Aldo has enjoyed a brilliant career. Either his accomplishments should have scotched his self-doubts or those self-doubts would have long ago clipped his wings, putting his accomplishments beyond reach. Whereas his vocational and public selves leap from triumph to triumph, his private side has bogged down in stagnancy and setback. This is what le Carré dwells on. As if Aldo doesn't have worries enough, he's also suffering from midlife crisis. His family is falling apart; the greed and selfishness of the business world sickens him; he feels empty, puzzled, and cheated. The goals he worked so hard to attain lack meaning, and their attainment hasn't improved his self-image. Viewing his office as a "sweet deep casket," he idles away his time going to the movies and dabbling at genealogy.

Now that he has created, in his firm, a self-perpetuating machine, he's no more needed at the office than he is by Sandra. And he knows it. His life is so barren that he welcomes the first distraction from it. Besides embracing mad, flamboyant Shamus, he defers completely to him. For instance, he introduces into his vocabulary the word, "bosscow," which Shamus calls Sandra. As soon as he hears the epithet from Shamus, he rarely refers to Sandra in any other way. This mindless adoption of Shamus's redefinition of Sandra, heretofore the most important person in Aldo's life, is richly symptomatic. Aldo lets himself be bullied, beaten, and humiliated, and he loves it all. But the alleged love that prompts this self-abasement rests on self-hatred. Aldo changes completely after meeting Shamus and Helen. His belief that they must be "either a dream or a pair of fakes posing as celebrities" to have granted him their friendship is both desperate and insulting. His having reached the point where he welcomes mystery and danger needn't entail getting fleeced, lying to himself, and overhauling his soft life.

Shamus forfeits our trust even more quickly than Aldo—and for the same reason. Once again, le Carré's artistic intent has failed to stir the treatment it deserved. There's no disputing the book's main premise, i.e., that perversity can lead to wisdom. Major writers like

Thomas Mann and Patrick White have described mischief and malice as better masters than sweetness and order: to stamp out Shamus's devils would also be to squelch his angels. But what angels are there? we begin wondering in the early chapters. And hasn't Shamus exorcised them already himself? This demonic creator reveals himself quickly to be narrow, dogmatic, and childish. The belief that anything can be wished into reality perverts romanticism; the man who believes himself a king can strew a great deal of pain without becoming kingly. Intriguingly, in Shamus, le Carré is testing his artistic limits by writing about another writer who constantly pushes out from the edges of self. It should also be said that the book's key relationship involves an inventor of a new braking system and someone who scorns all brakes, or restraints. Yet Shamus isn't free, at all. His extreme self-consciousness, manifested in his mania for performance, precludes freedom; he can't let himself go. He's no more spontaneous than Aldo. What looks like impulse in him often stems from calculation. And this man who tries so hard to shock or offend others is easily shaken himself. "How can I write if all the proles are growing long hair?" he asks in Chapter 22. If his words mean anything, they show that he's less instinctive and intuitive than he pretends. How else can his outstanding churlishness be explained. In Chapter 25, Aldo takes him to a movie because Shamus tends to shout at the actors in live theater. But Shamus won't be cheated of his chance to impose himself. On the way home, he interrupts Aldo's "spirited" interpretation of the movie by shouting the name of a mutual friend. Now Shamus knows that the woman across the street isn't who he claims. He just can't stand to hear anyone else hold forth, especially if the speaker is distinguishing himself.

It follows that a person so easily cowed should hate anything or anybody that resists him. Or might resist him; rather than viewing people as unique and sacred, he rejoices in collective terms. Easily threatened, he dismisses people by calling them proles or bourgeoisie. He has a catch-all judgment or cliché for nearly every occasion. To get a passport ironed, go to a whore; their highly sensitive fingers make whores the best ironers. Such judgments, allegedly directed to his soulless Philistine society, betray his failure to see clearly. He needs the daily, conventional world to rebel against, just as he needs an audience to shock and outrage. But what he views as rebellion is a denial both of himself and the creative forces that galvanize his art. His hatred of property robs him of a fixed residence. But the fear of middle-class conformity, mediocrity, and sham expressed by a home has also denied him the stability and assurance needed to focus his energies. Shamus is an eccentric, not an original. His tendency to exalt things or to kick them into the gutter ignores the degrees and gradations that make up humanity. Nobody so judgmental could thrill to the material spectacle of life. His calling Aldo Butch Cassidy, Paris Paristown, and champagne shampoo betrays a dwarfed sensibility. His hatred of the past has pushed him into the shrill present, where a harsh glare has ruled out the imaginative enticements of shadows, recesses, and echoes.

He's at odds with himself both as a person and an artist. Unless his every whim is obeyed, he'll erupt into violence. His constant bleats that Aldo forgive him his outbursts show his failure to live up to his own standards. A superior person who followed his instincts wouldn't ask for forgiveness because he'd be in tune with his dark gods. Yet the book is full of Shamus's sticky, slobbering pleas of remorse. They don't surprise us. He has routed his creative demons by jumping from pose to pose, outrage to outrage, and cliché to cliché. He can't hold a normal conversation; he has forsaken consistency. After extolling love's dynamism, he calls his beautiful wife "a fifth-rate concubine." No wonder he hasn't written anything for twenty years. But the real miracle is that he ever wrote anything at all. Someone so emotionally knotted and immature can't respond intuitively. And le Carré knows it. Though touted by Aldo as the chief literary artist of the age, Shamus writes nothing that we see. This is odd and unconvincing. He demands obedience, adoration, and unlimited material benefits while offering nothing in return. The few ideas he does have, he explains too much. We keep wondering where he has hidden his art. Or the humanity needed to fuel it; someone so intent on advertising himself that he shouts obscenities at strangers and threatens children could only repel, not charm, as Aldo insists. On the subject of Shamus's art le Carré is so shaky that, in the following passage, he wavers between a misplaced Swiftian irony and the possibility that Aldo has invented Shamus:

Someone gave Shamus his own book to sign ... and he stood in a pulpit reading aloud from it.... He read very quietly so that Cassidy ... could not have heard the words, but he knew from the rhythm and fall of them that they were the most beautiful words he had ever heard, more beautiful than Shakespeare of Kahil Gibran or the German High Command.

II

The uncanniness with which Shamus animates Aldo's psyche keeps alive the possibility that he's more of an imaginative creation than a person. Aldo may have invented him and Helen to fill a need greater than any that could be filled by Haverdown. Le Carré's hiding their last name from us puts them in a special category. And like creatures of myth, they keep eluding while presumably enriching Aldo. Mistakenly, he believes them the owners of Haverdown, rather than just squatters. Helen first appears to him naked, coming from a shower, the transistor in her hand playing Frank Sinatra (le Carré's later naming Aldo's mother Ella shows that he's not afraid to make known his preferences in popular music). This unlikely manifestation makes him wonder, "Had the girl existed, or was she the creation of his lively erotic fantasy?" Later, Aldo's affaire with Helen will supply the plot of Shamus's novel-in-progress. This pattern of concentric novels represents an easy way out for le Carré, freeing him from the rigors of narrative consistency. *Lover* is mannered, overdone, and exorbitant. Its unevenness and incoherence dictate its weak ending. The elaborateness with which Shamus, holding a loaded pistol with the safety off, conducts the wedding joining Helen and Aldo defies belief. For all his supposed heart knowledge, Shamus lacks warmth, compassion, and insight. Sadistically, he metes out punishment at the slightest excuse, and sex for him is always cruel and violent.

His performing a wedding whose reality is private and emotional rather than legal suits the novel's reassessment of conventional love (earlier, Aldo had called his son Mark "my lover"). But his defensiveness denies the wedding any uplift. The love that joined him to Helen and Aldo has run afoul of his possessiveness. Resorting to his throw-it-all-in style, he has determined to divide Helen and Aldo, even as he confirms and blesses their union. Helen leaves the chalet where her union with Sandra's husband was formalized while wearing Sandra's expensive hat along with a pair of sealskin boots, "though she did not approve of killing seals." This want of principle taints the whole enterprise. But the taint didn't emerge spontaneously. Both Aldo's dithering away precious time while supposedly looking for his lost watch and Shamus's materializing at the train station "hugging the clock [on the station roof] as if it were his latest friend" reveal a deep-seated unspoken collusion. It also turns the novel into a broken machine. Everything before this moment loses meaning, and nothing after it can acquire any. If Aldo failed to convince us of his powers as an athlete and an industrial magnate, he shrinks to nothing after he parts company with Helen and Shamus. Le Carré mentions his "spiritual death." And rather than asking whether Aldo's withdrawal from his city business brings him any wisdom, he resorts to blanket summary couched in a clinical, withdrawn style based on the "Ithaca" section of Joyce's *Ulysses:*

> How did they live ... Sandra and Aldo, for the rest of their natural lives? Did the marriage prosper? At first, they talked over their problem with great frankness.... Sandra had accepted that Cassidy had suffered spiritual death, but she was prepared, for the children's sake, to overlook it.

This information comes from such a distance that it scarcely grazes us. But perhaps it couldn't have come otherwise. The departure of Helen and Shamus has taken so much out of Aldo that he can no longer provide a dramatic focus. Le Carré's ideas have sunk his art. The novel extends only five disconnected pages after Helen and Shamus abandon Aldo in Switzerland. These pages must have been brutal to write. Le Carré hints at his displeasure with them by stowing them in an epilogue. Since the text has no matching prologue, he can't claim that the epilogue helped provide symmetry. It's here because the last chapter leaves too many questions unanswered. But it fills no void. The poor answers that these questions provoke are predictable. The failure of the three main characters to hold us leaves a gap which remains unfilled because the book portrays no casual, everyday life. Its *menage à trois* is too stylized and eccentric to admit the reality represented by Aldo's wife and children, all of whom play very small parts. Geoffrey Stokes is right to call *Lover* "an embarrassment."[3] The book shows le Carré writing against the grain of his talent. "He has chosen to relinquish his fundamental perception ... the truth that in this world of gray little men, gray little men shake the world," says Geoffrey Wolff, regretting that, in *Lover,* le Carré deserted Checkpoint Charlie for the Parnassus of Gide, Joyce, and Mann.[4] His regrets are well judged. Whereas the vision permeating the spy novels is strong, ironic, and controlled, *Lover* has a soft, runny core.

Its many blunders could make anyone wince. A Marxist reader, for instance, would object to the way Aldo both insists upon and apologizes for his fine trappings. Even more objectionable would be his way of amassing them. He calls his sumptuous Bentley "a present from the taxpayer, I'm afraid." The taxpayer treats him better than he/she knows. Old Hugo lives in a penthouse at company expense. The company also pays for Aldo's trip with Shamus to the pramsellers' convention in Paris, an unproductive enterprise deducted from the company's tax debt as a business expense. Finally, the posh Thameside flat which Aldo loans to Helen and Shamus belongs to the company. If anyone pays for it, it's the taxpayer again. And how about our own investment of time and energy? Shamus's profligacy, his ingratitude, and the chaos he leaves the flat in when he moves out provide occasions other than economic for growls and grumbles. The book's style will also offend readers accustomed to the concise elegance of the spy books. In line with the flat tone and technical vocabulary le Carré lifts from Joyce's "Ithaca" episode, he'll often use epithets, like "the discarded writer" for Shamus and "the Managing Director and Founder of Cassidy's Universal Fastenings" for Aldo, to dignify the action. These epithets stand as veiled confessions of defeat; a well-managed action wouldn't need such artificial heightening. Other attempts to blend the witty and the voluptuous fall just as flat. The reference to Shamus as a magus in Chapter 21 and terms like "the Few" and "the Many-too-Many" in Chapter 22, adapted from John Fowles's *Aristos,* sound more mechanical than organic, violating a major credo of Schiller, who supplies the novel's title.

Such tag terms occur often. Because *Lover* represents such a wrong direction for le Carré, the book's language wobbles along with the plot. The shakes set in early. When le Carré says in Chapter 1 that the door handles of Aldo's Bentley are recessed "in succulent cavities of felt," he has forgotten that his metaphor will repel his readers, none of whom care to suck felt. Metaphor isn't his only stylistic problem. The dialogue rings false. Prearranged and pretentious, it can smack of conscious literary performance:

> Shamus needed water, and he had heard from reliable sources that Bristol was a port.
> "He can't survive without it," Helen explained.
> "It's the sound," said Cassidy. "The lapping sound."
> "*And* the permanence," Helen reminded him.
> "Think of undulating waves, going on forever."

At other times, curiously, the dialogue needs closer supervision. Witness this infantile exchange between Aldo and Sandra:

> "It's not your fault," said Sandra. "It's the Mayor's, isn't it? After all," she added speculatively, "he *runs* the town, doesn't he?"
> "Naughty Mayor," said Cassidy.
> "Naughty Mayor," Sandra agreed.
> "Spank him," Cassidy suggested.
> "Spank, spank," gaily said Sandra, wife to Aldo.

There's also a problem with names. It's never clear why le Carré calls his writer Shamus, after the jargon term for an American private detective, or why the Englishman Aldo Cassidy has an Italian and then an Irish name. Inconsistency bedevils le Carré throughout. The action sags and sprawls, irrelevances and non sequitur leak in, and the theme gets lost. These problems weren't unknown to le Carré. Having blocked lines of plot growth, he will try to squeeze more out of his material than the material warrants: *"Cassidy divided by Shamus equals Helen.* Or was it the other way round? *Helen over Cassidy equals Shamus.* Try again. *Cassidy over Helen. . . ."* If there's a point where love and ruin meet, consume each other, and become something new, the book hasn't disclosed it. The knocks and bruises absorbed by submissive, resigned Aldo lack meaning. No dialectic ennobles them. All attempts at elevation in the novel, in fact, come to nothing. Selfishness and secrecy quickly poison the three-way love tie joining Shamus, Helen, and Aldo. While Shamus is writing his novel, Aldo and Helen spend more and more time together, they deceive Shamus about how close they've become, and they begin sleeping together. It's ironically appropriate that they forsake the Savoy, site of their first rut, for sleazy Paddington boarding houses; sleaze is their true element. Shrewdly, le Carré humanizes their sexual tie by delaying the magnetism it exerts on Aldo. Aldo's first sexual encounter with Helen leaves him feeling repelled and wondering if he's homosexual. But as soon as his passion surges forth, it channels itself through the classic Freudian outlets of love and work. Not content to take Shamus's woman, he announces that he also wants to write a book. Le Carré relies on Freud's formula because he hasn't found one of his own.

He had more ambitious hopes for the book. The idea is here but not the plotting to support it. What's good about *Lover*—the boldness with which it sets out to extend the love bond—is also what makes it not good enough. In extenuation, it taught le Carré the importance of deciding both how much to invest in his materials and how to deploy them to their best advantage. What follows it proves that the novel represents only a temporary loss of form. The renewal and development of this form show that *The Naive and Sentimental Lover* also cleared his mind for the writing of his major achievement, the Karla trilogy.

Chapter Eleven
Grand Designs, Old Miseries

Tinker, Tailor, Soldier, Spy (1974) finds le Carré back on solid, friendly ground. The book surpasses its predecessors in fullness and density because it explores themes consistent with his unusual artistic reach and complexity. Confronting his intricate individuality, he slows narrative pace in order to show how fascinating intelligence work looks from a slow tempo. As in much of his work, the pleasure given by *Tinker, Tailor* comes less from the resolution of the plot than from the insights. He's particularly astute describing the nuances of spying—the obstacles, tensions, and threats under which spies work and live. His people are caught up in problems so numbing that they make us doubt whether they can survive the novel. Hedonistic Ann Smiley has left George again, this time with an unemployed actor whose clothing and gasoline bills George is expected to pay. There's also a reference to a Welsh ballet dancer of twenty who had a romp with Ann in the mid-1950s.

But le Carré shows a side of her infidelity he has heretofore kept dark. Ann needs more than thrills, and she's more than a sensual creature. Smiley notes of her after she has been discarded by Bill Haydon, "that she was deeply unhappy." Haydon, who may have cast her off against his will, has worries of his own. He's the mole, or deep cover agent, planted by Moscow in the Circus in order to wreck it. He only started sleeping with Ann because he was told to by Karla, director of Moscow Center. Fearing Smiley's discovery of Haydon's Kremlin link, Karla believed that he could discredit Smiley if his Circus colleagues suspected his motives in incriminating Haydon. Perhaps Haydon ended the affaire under orders, too, having fulfilled his mission of raising doubts at the Circus in Smiley's credibility *vis-à-vis* himself. Such a privation would matter little alongside the terror he lives with each day. This terror is left to our imaginations. The main action of *Tinker, Tailor* consists of finding him and then burrowing into his stronghold in order to stop him. But le Carré records this search from the standpoint of the infiltrated security network, not from that of the mole, Bill Haydon, for whom the threat of capture never relents. The risks and pressures faced by Haydon are nearly unbearable, since the capture of a highranking double agent like him usually entails a quick trial and execution for treason.

Haydon's distress is mirrored by that of his pursuer, Smiley. Finding himself assailed by ambiguities, as usual, Smiley struggles against the sterility and falseness of a corrupt system while protecting it from further corruption. That this evil stems from his own generation, till now prized by him and his colleagues as the elite of the service, makes his job all the harder. He doesn't grieve alone. Hearts crack all through *Tinker, Tailor* and its two successors. The Karla trilogy takes us inside the special branch and describes the ruthlessness that rules it. These novels aren't just about spies, but about the world of spying. They describe a condition. Rather than distinguishing between NATO and Warsaw Pact nations, they connect spies everywhere. Both the points of connection and the dialectic generated by their interplay lend motives, choices, and convergences new weight. H. R. F. Keating has shown how the spy trade stands as a microcosm of life today in the Karla trilogy:

He [le Carré] used the form to penetrate a whole world in a way that can be compared to the great novels of the nineteenth century. He sought to show the spy ethos, and all the complications that it gives rise to seeping through whole societies. He produced espionage novels that had both sweep and vision. He asked on a massive scale a question that goes to the heart of Western democracy today ... how is it possible to defend humanity in inhuman ways?[1]

That this question inspires le Carré is seen in his lyrical response to the English countryside. Rooks clatter in elms, sunshine glances off the thatched roofs of rectories, and rain runs like gunsmoke across cricket fields in *Tinker, Tailor*. The English origins of this scene-painting enrich the action. Smiley, who has returned to a le Carré novel as a major figure for the first time since *Murder* (1962), calls himself "out of date, but loyal to his own time." Renowned in his circle for his patriotism, he's asked by a colleague in Chapter 2, "Do you love England still?" Several hours later, he recalls a former colleague's hatred for everywhere "except Surrey, the Circus, and Lords Cricket Ground." This reverence for things English extends to Jim Prideaux, the ex-Circus operative who was ambushed, caught, and then tortured by Soviet forces. Now teaching at a boys' school, Prideaux will gladly interrupt his classes to lecture his pupils on the glories of England. Yet *Tinker, Tailor* doesn't celebrate or recreate England's past. Nobody in the novel, except perhaps Connie Sachs, the ousted specialist in Soviet affairs, wants to go back in time. What occupies the people's attention is the weight of the past. Haydon, Moscow's man in the Circus, also belongs to an era redolent of English grace, charm, and culture. Ever mindful of the wreckage he has strewn, *Tinker, Tailor* roots itself solidly in England's place-settings, institutions, and personalities.

Many of these references tie in with the special branch, historically that most English of English institutions. In Chapter 28, Smiley and Jerry Westerby, who will come back as the title character of le Carré's next novel, *The Honourable Schoolboy*, recall bygone Circus cronies over curry and beer. The cameo appearance of Miss Ailsa Brimley of *Murder,* in Chapter 22, also expresses le Carré's delight in returning to the friendly purviews of Cambridge Circus and environs. The profusion of the jargon terms (i.e., lamplighters, scalp hunters, and mailfist jobs) and references to different branches of Intelligence create still more chances for le Carré to make the Circus a metaphor of the English psyche. One of the joys of reading *Tinker, Tailor* consists of the intimate inside look the novel provides into the realities of spying, both in the field and in the office. Le Carré recounts the steps by which old records may be identified in Circus archives and the restrictions governing their being read. He shows how spies arrange clandestine meetings in the field and how they use body codes (shirt collar worn open or shut, handbag carried in right or left hand) as safety signals. The following description of a spy seated in a Hong Kong bar by a fellow pro conveys the vigilance spies must observe simply to survive. The brevity of the description underscores the potential danger of lowering one's guard. Here is a society where a small mistake can be fatal: "Just the way he sat.... He had the pick of the exits and the stairway; he had a fine view of the main entrance and the action; he was right-handed and he was covered by a left-hand wall."

I

Gripping in its own right, information like this reveals the pressure spies face daily. *Tinker, Tailor* compounds this pressure by taking away the agents' relief from it. The presence of a mole in the home office heightens, rather than lessens, the dangers of field work. "A penetrated secret service is not just a bad one: it is an appalling liability," said le Carré in 1968; "In place of an all-seeing eye, it becomes a credulous ear and misleading voice."² This liability increases in

Tinker, Tailor, Haydon's having been recruited by Moscow long before he became a Circus chief. Like his acquired position of power and trust, his longterm familiarity with Circus procedures has thrown security into confusion and crippled its capability. "The higher a secret informant is placed in the government department [of the nation whose security he has penetrated], the more valuable he is," Orlov, the former KGB chief, reminds us.[3] This value asserts itself in several big ways. The high-ranking mole can inspect his host government's secret files for materials which he may copy (but not steal) and then give to his friends. He can mislead his supposed colleagues with false information. He can also lower their morale. Besides having access to secrets, the mole breeds self-doubt and internal strife; outfits like MI5, the CIA, and the French SDECE start to panic when they feel his breath upon them. Suspicion, always a hazard in security work, infects everyone. The bureau stops producing intelligence. Because the mole can destroy thousands of his countrymen, the search for him consumes monumental time, money, and personnel. Every lead, however unpromising, must be traced; far-flung occurrences must be compared on the off-chance that they'll connect.

The primacy of stopping the mole also gives his colleagues, and often the mole himself, extraordinary police powers. The threat he poses dictates the invasion of private lives in the national interest. This invasion creates casualties. What survives the mole's capture, if, indeed, any capture takes place, may be so feeble and frayed that the next wind will tear it apart; like Agatha Christie's people, nearly everyone in le Carré has something to hide. As le Carré's career moves forward, his vision darkens, giving his books a sharpness that both controls and shapes their increased length. This unity declares itself in intriguing ways. As spies' private motives encroach upon professional decisions, disloyalty and betrayal move to the fore. The family comes within the line of fire. Because a spy's effectiveness operates inversely to his/her personal integrity, intelligence agents in the Karla trilogy will attack the commitments of the person they're applying pressure to—a wife, a brother, or a daughter. There's an irony here that needs pointing out. The family ties under fire have often snapped long before being targeted as attack zones. Smiley and Ann are estranged in *Tinker, Tailor;* Drake and Nelson Ko of *Schoolboy* haven't seen each other for twenty-five years; the closing chapters of *Smiley's People* reveal that Karla has never spoken to his daughter. Yet these ties win top priority. The mounting alienation they foster carries the dreamlike quality attributed to spying in *War* and *Small*

Town into the private sphere. Not content to pursue imaginary
professional goals, the kingpin spies in the trilogy may also be wasting
themselves on dreams. The contagion has spread in open view. Though
played for deadly high stakes, spying relaxes its practitioners' hold
on reality to the point of self-extinction. It's no wonder that, despite
their craft, Smiley, Drake Ko, and Karla all buckle under the pressures
applied to their private vulnerabilities.

The pressures come from the bureau. Setbacks have hobbled and
nearly crushed the Circus at the start of *Tinker, Tailor,* a scandal
and a shakeup in the executive branch having occurred a year before
the present-tense action. A plot to win the defection of a Soviet spy
in Hong Kong to Britain has miscarried. In an unsigned telegram,
London Station sent its Hong Kong operative a stall rather than the
confirmation he needed to move forward with the defection plot. Smiley
and several of his former security colleagues determine, in a secret
late-night conference, that an alert, fast-stepping Circus chief could
have warned Moscow about the plot. The blowing of another top-
secret operation in Czechoslovakia some months later has persuaded
Smiley and his friends to look for the mole in London Station. But
the mole has already armed himself against such searches. Knowing
that Control was watching him, Haydon sabotaged many of his boss's
projects in order to smirch him. Though Haydon wrecked the
Czechoslovakian operation himself, for instance, he saw to it that
Control took the blame. His timing was excellent. After Control's
death, which was hastened by the defeats he suffered in his last months
running the Circus, Haydon removed other threats like Smiley, Jerry
Westerby, and Connie Sachs. Then, adding to his cover, he used his
power to replace Control with Percy Alleline (when Alleline's mistake
in trusting Haydon surfaces later on, he's quickly dropped as Circus
chief). Finally, Haydon instituted a new operational policy called
lateralism. Belying its democratic-sounding name, lateralism has
paralyzed British Intelligence by concentrating all official power in
London Station. The special branch has been reorganized to speed
the flow of secrets from London to the Kremlin.

But the reorganization decreed by lateralism also includes safety
features, Haydon having taken steps to thwart any search leading to
him. When Smiley and his friends learn that the Circus's investigative
resources are being held by those under investigation, they have to
plan anew. Their discovery that the mole must be a Circus chief has
stalled them. "Who can spy on the spies?" asks a worried cabinet

officer. The mole controls both the materials and the personnel his hunters need to trap him:

> We can't move. We can't investigate because all the instruments of enquiry are in the Circus's hands, perhaps in the mole Gerald's. We can't watch, or listen, or open mail.... We can't interrogate; we can't take steps to limit a particular person's access to delicate secrets. To do any of these things would be to run the risk of alarming the mole.

Put in charge of the investigation because of his experience and his skill, Smiley knows that he must be cunning if he hopes to catch the mole. Thus he has Peter Guillam, last seen briefly in *War,* invade and burgle a Circus archive; the file Guillam takes from an archive shelf is *not* the one he had requisitioned. Then Smiley stays up all night in a Paddington hotel reading the filched file so that Guillam can return it early the next morning. Le Carré conveys structurally his belief in using criminal means to catch criminals. Guillam steals the top-secret file from its archive, "a warren of dingy rooms and half-landings," in Chapter 20, the book's middle chapter. This parody of the epic hero's descent into the underworld puts deceit at the heart of the action. Nobody who drifts into the shadow of intelligence work can afford decency, honesty, or the outgoings of love. This book, the main actions of which occur in the dark hours, doesn't show darkness being defeated by light. It describes, instead, the absorption of political and moral darkness into a fogbelt of ambiguity and compromise. As Smiley's loneliness and pain show, the novel's sensitive, intimate portrayal of an attempt to salvage something from grief and waste includes the defeat of kindness and compassion.

Smiley will make every allowance for both Ann and Haydon. But his charity keeps recoiling on him. His refusal to stop Haydon when morally certain of his guilt months before the time of the novel has caused the dismantling of operations and the rolling up of networks all over the service. His habit of inviting Ann back to 9 Bywater Street always reinstates the marriage on *her* terms, i.e., the same ones that led her to leave him in the first place. He also feels the recoil action of his devotion to his job. Though tight, comprehensive, and incisive, his labors can't soothe him. He can't savor victory; perhaps, he can't even recognize it. As is shown in the remorse that grips him after he collars Haydon, his professional triumphs confound his heart; also, every reunion with Ann presumes a new parting *(Tinker, Tailor* ends before she notices him at their prearranged meeting place). This bleakness vindicates Merry's reading of the novel's moral, i.e., "spying destroys a man's capacity for self-appraisal. It nearly destroys his capacity for loving."[4]

Love gives Smiley more grief than pleasure, his main commitments still being England, the service, and Ann. These bonds are all in disarray at the novel's opening. As has been seen, Ann is living with another man, and changes in the Circus hierarchy caused by Control's death have ousted Smiley from his job. He seems to have lost his chance to protect England. The resentment caused by his ouster comes across in the sarcasm he directs to Peter Guillam. Instead of being sacked by the Circus's new high command, Guillam was merely reassigned: "I'm surprised they didn't throw you out with the rest of us," Smiley tells Guillam, "not very pleasantly," in Chapter 3, adding, "You had all the qualifications: good at your work, loyal, discreet." Perhaps this bitterness against the service that misused him so badly has heightened Smiley's sense of moral responsibility; in 1974, le Carré said that the George Smiley of *Tinker, Tailor* was "in a state of total ideological disorientation."[5] Despite or perhaps because of this confusion, Smiley shows exemplary tact and comprehension together with a brutal capacity for hard work. One character reminds him to sleep; another tells him that he looks a wreck. He deserves to be reproved. For a jobless man, he stays obsessively busy. After talking to colleagues during the day, he stays up all night in a rundown rooming house, reading the stolen files that must be returned the next morning. This work, so sensitive that it can't be taken home, includes backtracking, annotating, and comparing leave rosters with sick-leave lists from different service branches. The following morning will find him out in the streets, doing legwork and interviewing witnesses. He moves in an ever-tightening spiral. After learning all he can from official records, he narrows his search to the man who was duty officer the night of Jim Prideaux's capture in Czechoslovakia. Then he goes to Thursgood's School to interview Prideaux himself. From what he discovers of in-house rivalries and information leaks, he learns how the mole tricked his Circus colleagues into supporting him at Prideaux's expense.

Smiley may be the only person capable of snaring Haydon. The wall of security—money, planted documents, and aides—shielding Haydon consists of the sturdiest bricks and mortar the Kremlin can find. Next, he has won the support of Percy Alleline, acting head of British Intelligence. The ambitious Alleline, feeling maligned and eager to make his mark, becomes Haydon's easy dupe. Haydon backs his claim of having access to a rich vein of Soviet intelligence by producing some excellent samples, advisedly, in Alleline's field of expertise. All he allegedly wants for such treasure is protection from bureaucratic meddling. So while throwing Alleline chicken feed, he surreptitiously gives Karla the Circus's prize gems. He hadn't reckoned on Smiley. The deposed Smiley both catches him and, having blocked his lines of retreat, dismantles his network. Suitably, besides baiting the trap that ensnares Haydon, Smiley is also a member of the arresting team that pulls him in. The arrest sequence stirs in him motives deeper than those of patriotism. Though Smiley hadn't appeared in a le Carré novel for nine years, he had stayed on his author's mind. Like him, the narrator of le Carré's November 1968 *Saturday Evening Post* story, "What Ritual Is Being Observed Tonight?" read German literature at Oxford and loves a beautiful, sluttish woman (he also writes about Schiller's doctrine of the naive and the sentimental).[6] His pain prefigures that of the Smiley of *Tinker, Tailor,* a more developed figure than the one featured in *Call* and *Murder.*

Ann's affaire with Haydon yokes Smiley's private pain to larger ones. The collision of his two worlds intensifies his grief because it shows him his insignificance; his marriage can be manipulated at will by the power brokers. Ann violated two rules by fouling the Bywater Street nest with a member of her and Smiley's set. It's even more insulting to Smiley that Haydon made love to her out of political, not personal, motives. The background of the insult is worth pondering. Perhaps Smiley himself cleared a path for the mole to her bed. When he had tried to persuade Karla to defect to the West, some fifteen years before the time of the novel, he used arguments that pertained more strictly to his own marriage than to Karla's. His attempts to break Karla's composure had the reverse effect of exposing his own flank. Unwittingly, he showed Karla exactly how to knock him down. Karla's keeping of the cigarette lighter, inscribed, "To George from Ann with all my love," that Smiley had tossed on the table of the Delhi prison cell where he talked to Karla, expresses the bond that builds between the two master spies. First comes the element of heat. The jail in which the men meet is sweltering, and the flames rising from the ignited cigarette lighter refer directly to the obsessiveness joining the men, who quickly become experts on the subjects of one another. If Karla manipulates Smiley's love for Ann in *Tinker, Tailor,* Smiley will trade on Karla's love for his daughter, Alexandra, in *Smiley's People.* The fire metaphor conveyed by the cigarette lighter persists. Symbolizing the irony by which the attainment of a spy's hopes can defeat, rather than gladden, the spy, the flame-producing lighter serves as a counter in the Cold War, and it's next seen, in *Smiley's People,* on a freezing winter night.

In the same 1980 work, Smiley calls Haydon "the flower of their generation, the jester, the enchanter, the iconoclastic reformer; Bill the born deceiver whose quest for the ultimate betrayal led him into the Russians' bed, and Ann's." The high colors inferred by this recollection flit across *Tinker, Tailor.* Le Carré's selectivity will inspire a good deal of speculation among future readers as to the mole's real-life model. Several Soviet double agents had Haydon's *élan* and flair. Like him, Sir Roger Hollis, the Kremlin spy who served as Director General of MI5, spent time in the East. There's also a resemblance to Sir Anthony Blunt, who, like Hollis, was born in 1905. But whereas Blunt was a distinguished art historian who became Deputy Director of the Cortauld Institute of Art in London's Portman Square and then Surveyor of the Queen's Pictures, Haydon was a painter. Smiley recalls attending showings of his work in both Oxford and London. The resemblance between Haydon and Harold "Kim" Philby has also been noted. In his review of *Tinker, Tailor,* Karl Miller listed some similarities between the two spies. Le Carré himself called Philby "an embittered solitary" who was "at war with his own shadow."[7] These words also describe Haydon, an upper-class cheat and traitor endowed with breeding, boyish charm, a zest for adventure, and social influence. Le Carré hints at his malaise by calling his last, unfinished paintings "cramped, over-worked, and condemned." Displaying what le Carré saw in Philby as "the self-hate of a vain misfit,"[8] these claustral canvases betray a lack of freedom and freshness.

One can't forget Haydon's notorious magnetism, which he exploits and abuses and which plays such a vital role in both his sexual and professional lives. His various careers, as aristocrat, explorer, spy, and linguist, have, along with his art, evoked comparisons with Rupert Brooke and Lawrence of Arabia. With grudging admiration, Smiley mentions his "dazzling war." The homage continues: "He was ubiquitous and charming; he was unorthodox and occasionally outrageous. He was probably heroic. The comparison with Lawrence was inevitable." Yet, like the T.E. Lawrence figure of W. H. Auden's early poems, like "Watch Any Day His Nonchalant Pauses" (also called "We All Make Mistakes"), Haydon harbors a secret, haunted self. The weary undergraduate decadence that sometimes overtakes him calls to mind Oscar Wilde's Dorian Gray. His having been designated Tailor, by the mole hunters who gave their other suspects the code names Tinker, Soldier, Poorman, and Beggarman, refers to his sartorial grace. After his arrest, he insists upon arriving in Moscow in his own clothes: "Those Moscow tailors are unspeakable. Dress you up like a bloody beadle," he protests. Yet this man who's so attentive to his dress also works hard to unstitch and tear apart England's social fabric. The discovery that the elegance, beauty, and derring-do called forth by him rested on treason ends a way of both thinking and living for two generations of English people. "To understand Haydon's betrayal of his country," says Rutherford, "is to see that it involves the betrayal of his class, his profession, his own past—but also of his colleagues, friends, and intimates."[9]

Le Carré omits Haydon's rise to power and how he managed it—the skills he used both to build an organization and to fool his colleagues. The internal shadings, ambiguities, and contradictions of his character also develop off stage. One sometimes wishes that le Carré gave more space to the foibles, eccentricities, and neuroses that destroyed him—and to his moral objections to what he saw happening to the British nation. This defector who beds Ann Smiley destroys her husband's peace along with a lot else. Yet time and again England's failure to live up to the standards it preaches makes Smiley wince. When Haydon calls his nation's part in the world trivial and irrelevant, Smiley doesn't protest. His silence jogs our imaginations. It makes us wonder whether the taste for excellence Haydon acquired at Oxford and then developed through his artistic sensibility hasn't itself been betrayed. His being an artist is material; as Plato said in *The Republic*, artists endanger the political status quo because they can imagine a better reality than the one at hand. Smiley's winces prove that an artistic sensibility isn't required to perceive postwar England's failings. And even if le Carré does describe Haydon's treachery as poisonous and self-negating, he doesn't quarrel with the convictions undergirding it.

One thing le Carré's tangential approach does do is to tally the cost Haydon must pay to turn his convictions into conduct. The unusually sharp Circus chief, Roy Bland, calls an artist "a bloke who can hold two fundamentally opposing views and still function." The idea, which Smiley attributes to Scott Fitzgerald (who probably adapted it from Keats), refers to Haydon. Haydon explodes into real grief and outrage after learning that Prideaux was shot conducting a mission that Haydon himself sabotaged. The inner turmoil gnawing his victim, Prideaux, whom Smiley calls Haydon's "oldest, closest friend," may be just as fierce. Spies spend as much time in the realm of the imaginary as do creative artists. Like Smiley himself, Prideaux will also excuse Haydon's wrongdoing. "You never were one to see him [Haydon] straight," he barks in Chapter 22. His earlier disclaimer to Karla, "You can't judge Bill.... Artists have totally different standards. See things we can't see. Feel things that are beyond us," sounds as if he's trying to condone Haydon's betrayal of him. The irony of his growling at Karla, "Go to bloody hell. If you had one Bill Haydon in your damned outfit, you could call it set and match," only recoils on him later. Like Smiley, Prideaux was morally certain all along of Haydon's guilt. Yet the pain caused in him by the rift between what he feels and what he knows probably falls short of that experienced by his more delicately organized traitor-friend, a man whose politics, enacted in the name of freedom, have denied him freedom.

This denial intensifies. As his fussy, crowded last paintings show, the spy in Bill Haydon drives out the artist together with the person. Replacing him in the spy trade, and thus assuring the trade's continuance, is fat, lonely, asthmatic Bill Roach, a new boy at Thursgood's prep school, "graded dull, if not actually deficient." Bill's teachers and fellow students misjudge him as badly as Haydon's colleagues in the service do him. Other similarities come to mind. Like his older namesake, Bill Roach loves Jim Prideaux. He's also a "natural watcher," having learned early in life the importance of observing closely one's friends. His teaching himself concealment and cover justifies Prideaux's calling him the "best watcher in the whole damn unit." Bill Haydon's vigilance was also formidable, or he'd not survived as long as he did serving two masters. Perhaps skill in spying stems from loneliness, anyway. One can only imagine the dreadful apartness created by Haydon's constant need to stay alert; a person who can't lower his/her guard can never relax and have a good time. Perhaps le Carré prepared for this isolation by making Haydon a person of extremes—a man of genius, daring, and charisma, of whom a colleague says, "Fantastic fellow.... Incredible ability. Incredible record. Brilliant," and also a badgered hater of his kind. Le Carré makes Bill Roach's loneliness, as well, a function of living on the extremes rather than in the comfortable middle. Bill has the richest father of any boy in the school. But this blessing is offset by his having the scurviest name and perhaps the fewest friends and the worst health. There's a good chance that he's the most guilt plagued, too, the source of his guilt being the breakup of his parents' marriage.

But it comes out in Chapter 29 that Jim Prideaux's parents also lived apart. This parallel with young Bill's family of origin matters because Bill spots Prideaux as a fellow solitary and fastens on to him as soon as he arrives at Thursgood's as an emergency faculty replacement. Not only does Prideaux's hunchback exteriorize Bill's inner hurt; it also shows Bill the benefits of being different. Included in these benefits is growth. "Known a lot of Bills. They've all been good'uns," says Prideaux in Chapter 1 soon after comparing himself to Rip van Winkle. The comparison is vindicated by his killing of Haydon a couple of months later. Like someone who has been sleeping for twenty years or has never grown up, Prideaux gives up his adolescent hero worship in favor of punishing a crime that would otherwise go unpunished. The pain accompanying his assumption of adult responsibility reaches us in a startling image: the hunchback killing the golden Adonis. The quick death Prideaux inflicts upon his old friend and hero, Bill Haydon, foreshadows the slow death he visits upon his new friend, the hero-worshipping Bill Roach. There's little doubt that young Bill will earn his living as a spy. His two-months' association with Prideaux has started him on his future career. Besides honing his surveillance techniques, he also speaks of mixing dreams with reality. And, in his discovery that Prideaux's heroism has been smirched, he awakens to the inescapability of moral ambiguity and pain—those constants of any spy's existence. To clinch the point that Bill has found his vocation in espionage, le Carré gives his embryo spy the body build of George Smiley.

Closer in time to the perimeters of the Intelligence community than Bill Roach is Connie Sachs, the bloated old infant with a photographic memory who was dismissed from the Circus in the blanket catch of spies which had threatened Haydon. An expert in Kremlin affairs, Connie has a memory so accurate and retentive that she can produce a detailed case history of almost any Soviet spy who came under the Circus's eye during her long tenure. She only shows her face in *Tinker, Tailor* for one chapter, when Smiley visits her Oxford home to learn about the then unidentified mole's London link to Moscow. A fascinating mixture of brilliance and whimsicality, she enriches *Tinker, Tailor*. Le Carré was to show excellent judgment by bringing her and her piquant incisive talk back for longer spells in his next two books.

But the restoration of the service to old pros like Connie and Smiley in *Schoolboy* can't block the changes overtaking the spy community, particularly the community's decline in tone, style, and prestige. The ousting of Smiley and his circle also signals a drop in effectiveness. How sharp the drop is le Carré never says. The aggressively ambitious Percy Alleline, the Hungarian refugee Toby Esterhase, and the brilliant working-class Londoner Roy Bland have certainly lowered the social tone in Circus leadership from its prewar eminence. But to say that British Intelligence has given way to nastiness, venality, and self-seeking is unfair. Maston, director of the Circus in the late 1950s in *Call,* was stupendously inept. And nobody wrecks the Circus more than its most shining example of mandarin supremacy, Bill Haydon. And Haydon it is who grouses the most about the service's degeneracy. Included among the few scraps of self-disclosure he offers after his arrest is that his objections to contemporary Britain are more aesthetic than moral (like Dieter Frey of *Call,* he's most offended by America's influence on British policy). His voicing his moral objections as an afterthought reflects the extreme detachment of the decadent. Little more than his sense of good form seems to have been offended: " 'It's an aesthetic judgment as much as anything,' he explained, looking up. 'Partly a moral one, of course.' " His gross misconduct dictates his downgrading of morality. He's not only saving face. It's nearly as if he rehearsed what he would say if ever brought to boot as a traitor. Maintaining the well-bred nonchalance of the public-school man, he treats his capture with an air of aloofness, even of boredom. Nor do his ensuing talks with Smiley show him either defending or apologizing for himself. The only time he forsakes his upper-class indifference to his personal fate is to tell Smiley what to do with his mail, salary, and personal effects.

Sharpening le Carré's presentation of his patrician traitor is his treatment of ill-favored Ricki Tarr. As scroungy and marginal as Haydon is privileged and commanding, Tarr, the Malaysian-born son of an Australian father, traces a reverse course from that of his prominent foil. Tarr's instrumentality in bringing that foil down reflects both le Carré's acceptance of change and his distrust of nostalgia. Tarr adds significantly to the undermining of conventional authority so central to the book. While he's in Paris helping his colleagues defeat Haydon in London, he's also holding at gunpoint the head of the Paris command, advisedly the "Circus elder" who recruited Tarr years before. The authority under attack in this scene is aesthetic as well as political and social. Intriguingly, *Tinker, Tailor* challenges aesthetic conventions while discouraging a preoccupation with art. Dispersing its elements rather than developing them consistently, the book immerses us in narrative technique, perhaps at the expense of content. But the imbalance is soon redressed. Le Carré's leaving both Tarr and Haydon out of the action most of the way realigns our attitude toward the form-content interplay. By thwarting our expectations, le Carré also invites us to question received notions about the order of events. These notions are social and political as well as artistic, absolving him of any charge that he has indulged artistic form for its own sake. The moving of narrative elements between center and edge, mostly off stage, strikes a liberating note besides charting new directions for adventure fiction.

II

The novel's technique in general supports the idea that life eludes straightforward modes of narration. Images of imbalance abound, beginning with Jim Prideaux's bent back and lopsided gait. The trailer Prideaux lives in while teaching at Thursgood's tilts to the side until he props up its low end. His levelling of his trailer looks ahead to the novel's main activity, that of righting a wrong. Haydon's double agency has knocked many things off true. The difficulty facing the attempts of Prideaux and his friends to restore balance shows in the parking place he chooses for his trailer, an uneven break in the school grounds called the Dip. Other skewed apparitions in the novel include the jowl of the Defense Minister, which looks "as though it had been knocked off true," and the immobilized head of Haydon, "propped unnaturally to one side" and later called "Bill Haydon's crooked death mask." (Prideaux's wishing he had broken the neck of the man who drove him to his ambush in Czechoslovakia shows that Prideaux goes for his foes' necks, just as Peter Guillam attacks their arms.) The novel ends with Bill Roach wondering about the handgun belonging to Prideaux that frightened him so much. Here's another decentering motif. The handgun that provokes so much terror in Bill is never fired, Prideaux snapping Haydon's neck (in another off-stage action) rather than shooting him to death. The many broken circuits, missed connections, and out-of-kilter images in the novel describe life limping pathetically along. And limping blindly? Like a beheading, the breaking of a neck, particularly that of an ex-lover, which Haydon was to Prideaux, depicts the loss of direction and vitality hinted at by the unfired handgun.

Rutherford's summary of this malaise makes betrayal the crutch most often used by people to stay afoot:

The world it [the novel] presents . . . is one of multiple betrayals—of treason, infidelity, disloyalty, and broken faith. Bill Roach, the pathetically vulnerable schoolboy of the sub-plot, suffers from his parents' broken marriage. His case is juxtaposed with the absurd one of the headmaster's father, who has run away with a receptionist from the nearby hotel, gladly abandoning wife, son, and school. . . . The unfaithfulness of Smiley's wife, especially her liaison with Bill Haydon . . . recurs in conversation after conversation, as well as in Smiley's own tortured awareness. Sexual infidelity is paralleled by professional disloyalty. Networks are blown, operations aborted, and agents liquidated by covert trickery. . . . Above all, Jim Prideaux . . . was shot in the back, literally and metaphorically, on a mission which turned out to be a baited trap.[10]

Betrayal joins the people in the book. As Rutherford's catalog of treacheries shows, the dynamic must play itself out. Soon there will be nothing left to betray, and people will drop to all fours and start wallowing in the primeval ooze. Besides including a reference to Judas (at the end of Chapter 21), the novel teems with images of betrayal. Recalling how the identity of the mole was narrowed to five possibilities, Prideaux adds, "It's one of the top five. . . . Five fingers to a hand." Belonging to the executive arm of the Circus, the hand supposedly offering help, comfort, or relief is actually poised to strike. The damage caused by the treacherous hand can be irreversible. Invoking the religious context created by the reference to Judas and the two church settings where key events occur, a character says of Prideaux's entrapment in Czechoslovakia, "A bullet in the back is held to be quite a sacrifice." Eleven chapters later, in Chapter 21, Percy Alleline accuses Guillam of stabbing him in the back. In line with Rutherford's demonstration of the many forms of betrayal featured in the novel, le Carré follows his reference at the end of Chapter 21 by starting the next chapter with the words, "The bedroom was long and low." The sexuality evoked by the bedroom reference asserts itself quickly and thematically. The live-in girl friend of the first character mentioned in Chapter 22 is also sleeping with her music teacher. To show how betrayal has destroyed traditional guidelines, she may even be the teacher's wife; the roles of lover and cuckold have either blurred or been displaced. Le Carré wants us to remember this reworking of the classic love triangle. Three people figure later in the chapter in still another treachery; then three Kremlin functionaries suspected of conspiring with British Intelligence in Hong Kong are "all . . . shot in the back of the neck." Finally, Ricki Tarr, who ran the aborted Hong Kong operation, says of Alleline in Chapter 26, "He's sizing up to shoot me in the bloody back!"

Le Carré blocks all outlets from this tangle of treachery; the insularity of English society both seals off escape routes and stops the flow of oxygen needed to kindle organic change. Haydon's double agency, a desperate attack upon English civilization, may be the only form of protest available to someone wanting to change the system. Le Carré portrays the closedendedness of his society in several ways. Haydon and Miles Sercombe, the Minister, are both Ann Smiley's cousins. Then Haydon's conspiracy against Control also brought down Control's lieutenants, all of whom threatened Haydon. And could the mole have jeopardized his own safety, as well? Smiley's speculation in *Smiley's People,* noted by Michael Wood, "whether a good double agent is not in some ways true to *both* his causes, *both* his loves,"[11] touches the quick of Haydon's drastic revolt. It also makes us wonder about the turmoil gripping Haydon after trapping Prideaux, when he heard that Prideaux was shot, and perhaps even when he sensed that Prideaux was preparing to kill him. First documented in a letter written by Haydon from Oxford in 1937, nearly thirty-five years before the novel's present-tense action, the friendship of the two men shows both the range and the depth of the treachery infecting England. It also alludes to the insularity that makes orderly internal change so difficult to achieve. Besides introducing Prideaux to his future Intelligence recruiter (the recipient of the 1937 letter), Haydon went through Oxford and the army together with Prideaux, served as his Circus colleague, and was also his lover. How can such a bond be broken other than by death? Haydon's deep loyalty to the bond makes his unreported perceptions, just before the death he knows he deserves, so intriguing.

Neither Haydon's panic nor his pain could have blinded him to the poetic justice of his murder. But his double agent's mind, sensitized, as has been seen, by both his artistic sensibility and his upper-class attraction to quality, may have also condoned his treachery to the end. The insularity of the English public school mentality opposes growth and other forms of natural process. This inertia takes away the reformer's chance to contribute to tradition; he must fight tradition. Le Carré conveys the stalemate by describing time as stasis. Instead of rolling forward, time in the novel seems to have stopped. While walking the grounds of Oliver Lacon's Berkshire estate, setting for the top-secret meeting of the security officers who want to launch a mole hunt, Smiley muses, "Perhaps I never left the place. . . . Perhaps we're still here from the last time." Time again reorders itself for him a week later after a long session of combing and sifting Circus archives: "He was back on the top floor of the Circus, in his old plain office ... just as he had left it a year ago." The loss of reality attending such dislocations breaks Prideaux down during his solitary confinement in a Soviet jail. To make him talk, his jailers scramble his sense of natural sequence: "Time, said Jim, at this stage lost him completely. He lived either in the darkness of the hood, or in the white light of the cells. There was no night or day, and to make it even more weird they kept the noises going most of the time."

Following such devastation, it's fitting that the climax of the mole search should give Smiley "a sense of great things dwindling to a small, mean end." Nor does he feel any upsurge of pride or patriotism after arresting Haydon. The opening lines of the chapter following the arrest deny him all satisfaction and sense of achievement: "For the next two days George Smiley lived in limbo. To his neighbors, when they noticed him, he seemed to have lapsed into a wasting grief." His first words to an incarcerated Bill Haydon on the next page reverse what we might expect a triumphant justifier to say to the traitor he apprehended the night before: "Cheer up.... You'll be out of here soon." While recalling Smiley's prison-cell encounter with Karla in Delhi, this meeting also strikes a chord with the rush of thoughts and impressions blitzing Peter Guillam at the moment of Haydon's arrest. Guillam found himself wanting to protect Haydon even as he was seizing him. He manhandled Haydon not because he did wrong but because his wrongdoing smashed Guillam's image of him as "an inspiration, the torch-bearer of a certain kind of antiquated romanticism, a notion of English calling." Like other men in le Carré, the newly "orphaned" Guillam feels both shamed and numbed by his more adventurous, vibrant father figure.

Smiley also blenches in the company of the closely guarded Haydon during their first meeting after Haydon's arrest. Having armed himself with reasons to censure Haydon, he finds himself siding emotionally with his former colleague and regretting that he has lost his chance to know him better. Both he and Haydon have become slaves of policy. The same political necessity that dictated Haydon's being stopped has also made him opaque to Smiley as a person—ironically, despite the hoard of new information amassed about him. As Haydon moved into the public domain, his existence flattened into an operational problem, and he has retreated forever from Smiley with the label of public enemy hiding his face. Smiley's polite silence with him during their last meetings stems from a sense of loss. Stripped of philosophical precepts and political nostra, he's mourning the trivialization of Haydon's rich humanity into so many journalistic and diplomatic phrases.

But Haydon's capture and death do bring benefits, even though they're presented with the grudgingness that always accompanies le Carré's affirmations. The villain's death in traditional melodrama frees his close associates to proceed with new vigor and purpose. Ironically, the shock of Haydon's death stops these others from living, just as his existence, treacherous as it was, had helped them to live. *Tinker, Tailor* ends like the rest of le Carré's novels. Knowledge doesn't bring power, only defeat, and usually to the most sympathetic. The lifting of the burden, i.e., the mask hiding Haydon's guilt, distresses, rather than relieves, Smiley, Guillam, and Prideaux, all three of whom had intuited the guilt but shrunk from scotching it.

The member of this trio of spies who surrenders his illusions most dramatically is the one most deeply stung by Haydon, Jim Prideaux. Revenge was already on Prideaux's mind in the book's first chapter, together with an awareness of the problems besetting him as an avenger. Within seconds of referring to "the unpaid Bill," to Bill Roach, whom he has just met, he says, as has been noted, "Known a lot of Bills. They've all been good'uns." The unsettled accounts vexing him can only be discharged at great personal cost. His killing of Haydon both divides him from and joins him to his victim. This paradox sounds tragic depths. Like the mole who betrayed his country, Prideaux kills a love object in snapping Haydon's neck. This dismemberment of head from body re-enacts the dualism Haydon instigated by pitting political conviction against his steadily lived life and also faraway Moscow against the Circus, where he has worked for decades among intimates. Now le Carré invites the possibility that the common plight shared by Haydon and Prideaux, that of devastating something or someone they love, will carry forward to include Prideaux's early death. The two ex-lovers attain a deathly consummation; also, the pedantic Karla has both the spite and the resources to punish Prideaux for killing his mole. But more important is Prideaux's having suppressed his feelings in favor of objective moral standards. Regardless of how long he'll live, he has given up his schoolboy values both to perceive the truth and to act on it.

Most of the components of *Tinker, Tailor* are so superior that it seems churlish to have any reservations about the book. But I do. Security at Sarratt, the Circus post where Haydon is held under guard till his repatriation to the USSR, is incredibly lax. It's nearly as if le Carré helped Prideaux kill Haydon by weakening the wall of security around him. But this flaw means little alongside the flavor and force, the suppleness and colloquial ease, distinguishing the novel. Sharply observed details lend amplitude and edge throughout, le Carré's astonishingly keen eye recovering with shocking accuracy data which most writers would shun. Note his description of the little storm caused by Smiley's performance of a routine action at the start of Chapter 6: "His hooded eyes had closed behind the thick lenses. His only fidget was to polish his glasses on the silk lining of his tie, and when he did this his eyes had a soaked, naked look that was embarrassing to those who caught him at it." The boldness of le Carré's metaphors also reflects a new assurance and command: "Aleks Polyakov [a Soviet spy] had blown his cover and run up his true colors at last. They were splashed all over the masthead." Other data get their value from their suggestiveness, like the nosebleeds of Bill Haydon during his internment at Sarratt. This image has all the evocative drift of the late-evening dinner of cold chicken and ale consumed by the conspiratorial Tom and Daisy Buchanan in *The Great Gatsby,* a book le Carré alludes to several times in his later work. Besides mentioning Fitzgerald, *Tinker, Tailor* has the same virtuosity, conversational smoothness, and instinct for social class illuminating his gemlike 1925 novel. But the English subject matter, the more extended dramatic irony, and the intellectual muscle power of *Tinker, Tailor, Soldier, Spy* both make the book le Carré's own and get his Karla trilogy off to a flying start.

Chapter Twelve
Beyond the Typhoon Shelters

Extending from mid-1974 to the early spring of 1975, *The Honourable Schoolboy* portrays a depleted, morally ransacked Circus. Smiley has been running the special branch since November 1973, when he masterminded the Bill Haydon snatch, and he has made many important changes in Circus security and policy. But his efforts haven't checked the loss of prestige, purpose, and morale suffered by the Circus. Because Haydon's arrest has smirched the branch's reputation in the intelligence community, insiders call it "the fall." Disgruntled by their notoriety, they also term the Haydon case "a victory of technique. Nothing more" and Smiley's conquest "a fluke." Prospects to recoup lost ground look bleak, with the Circus's camaraderie and assets in such disrepair. Nor does the "special relationship" Britain enjoys with the United States promise hope for recovery. Whereas the Circus needs American money and technology to carry out any major operation, it also runs the risk of being buried by the bigger, better-equipped "cousins" in any joint effort. The reference in Chapter 1 to "the shotgun marriage with the cousins" alludes to the Circus's loss of options. While pressure is building on British Intelligence to regain esteem, hopes keep shrinking. No security outfit can produce intelligence without networks, and the Circus has already shut down its headquarters in Asian capitals like Seoul, Bangkok, and Manila. The first chapter of *Schoolboy*, entitled "How the Circus Left Town," shows it pulling out of Hong Kong, Britain's only remaining colony, as well.

Depletion pervades all. When the action moves from Hong Kong to Laos, Cambodia, and Thailand, it discloses artifacts that are rusting, rotting, and falling apart. One bombed-out town in Cambodia has lost its name together with its farms, houses, and people. The Asians have been weakened and beaten down by a never-ending war. They move like wraiths. Even non-partisans are victims. Nearly everyone in the book is maimed or marred; everyone also feels either on the run or caught in a losing battle. Le Carré's ability to sustain the mood of emotional suffering within the format of adventure fiction makes *Schoolboy* both a thriller and "a substantial novel in its own right," as T. W. Binyon said in the *TLS*.[1] The plot begins with Smiley's discovery of a "gold seam," a channel through which huge sums are being paid regularly from Moscow Center to Hong Kong. To undermine Peking's economy, these clandestine funds are being leaked into mainland China; to wreck the moral fiber of the Chinese, part of them are being used to revive the Chinese traffic in opium. Operation Dolphin starts here. Smiley's first break-through comes in his discovery that funds are going into the acount of a Hong Kong businessman via the Soviet Embassy in Vientiane, capital of Laos, where the businessman operates a small airline. This Asian circuit is important. Illustrating le Carré's ongoing practice of testing new artistic skills in each of his books, his 1977 novel ripples with exotic color, movement, and a new attentiveness to motives. A new awareness of the reader, perhaps to help him/her through the work, le Carré's longest, also distinguishes the book. *Schoolboy* rejects the unity of the action principle, the linear thinking that moves the plot from point to discernible point. But it also explains some of the in-group jargon that might have baffled and disconcerted readers of *Tinker, Tailor*, terms like mothers, sound thieves, and reptile funds. Then it yokes a banking irregularity to a more serious problem, which implicates a wide range of people. Again adapting the aesthetics of the California private-eye story, it unties a complex of interrelated motives for the sake of producing a sudden and startling denouement.

Part of this snap comes from the denouement's dramatic focus. Instead of lamenting England's decline, *Schoolboy* turns to more basic matters. Replacing patriotism is the family. So far has the United Kingdom fallen that patriotism has become passé. Perhaps the sceptered homeland celebrated by Rupert Brooke and symbolized in part by T. E. Lawrence never existed. Such strength and beauty, peace and dedication, couldn't have sunk so quickly. The guilt and loss coursing through *Schoolboy* is subjective and prepolitical. Being deprived of a family member—a brother for Drake Ko, a wife for Smiley, and a daughter for Jerry Westerby—is life's worst setback. The mirroring patterns that join home and work, public choice and private impulse, and also investigators and witnesses or suspects portray a collective nightmare. Everybody is wounded by the loss of an intimate family member. Everybody sees reminders of the wound wherever he/she looks. One place where le Carré directs our sight is the Circus itself. The wealth of hindsight regret portrayed in *Schoolboy* occurs in the shadow of British Intelligence. The book's opening sentence implies that the story about to take place has been told many times; still open to interpretation and dispute, the Dolphin case forms a seminal episode in Circus folklore: "Afterwards, in the dusty little corners where London's secret servants drink together, there was argument about where the Dolphin case history should really begin." What follows treats the Dolphin case as a controversial affair whose leading elements comprise the stuff of legend. Intrusions like "as all later agreed" and "remains to this day," besides giving the case a legendary patina, convey the force of both precedents and first truths. With *Schoolboy*, spy fiction becomes an important investigation of humankind; the book infuses the drama of self-definition with drives and needs that govern many kinds of behavior. More than anything else in the canon, this dovetailing of personal and collective motives confirms le Carré's ability to describe spying as a metaphor of the human estate.

I

Le Carré's injection of dramatic realism into literary espionage raises important questions about the trauma of self-negation. All of the book's leading figures live apart from their closest intimates; all suffer from the rift; some risk their lives trying to heal it. *Schoolboy* doesn't link the shape of history to human intelligence. The years don't bring wisdom to public policy or efficiency to governmental agencies. Time provides no guidelines of morality or logic. Like Smiley himself, two members of the Circus's innermost core are ex-retirees in their sixties; these two, Connie Sachs and Doc Di Salis, also follow Smiley in being sacked at the end. Their dismissal shows that the contemporary world isn't unified or ennobled by the past. Also, the promise held by the future can ring false; Smiley must be pulled out of retirement in both *Tinker, Tailor* and *Smiley's People* to halt the collapse of a Circus allegedly committed to innovation in both leadership and outlook. Such progress rests upon false premises. The driving force behind human behavior in the Karla trilogy is the instinct, and it expresses itself most forcibly through the family; the cultural stream runs fastest and strongest near the homestead.

What is more, the impulse for this dynamism usually comes from an absent family member. "I lost two mothers," says an orphaned Drake Ko after learning of the death of the Englishwoman who helped raise him. The dead woman's husband, a British missionary based at the time near Shanghai, recalls Drake crying for the only time in his presence upon hearing the sad news. Perhaps the news has left its mark. To make good his wartime loss of both a surrogate and a natural mother, Drake may have married an older woman. He also clung to this younger brother, Nelson, after being separated from him by war. But his fanatical love for Nelson undid him. Drake worked for six years on the docks to send Nelson to school. He couldn't have predicted the results of his drudgery. Nelson's Marxist fervor had a separating, rather than a binding, effect, taking him to Leningrad to study marine technology and then installing him in both Shanghai and Peking, cities where Drake, having settled in Hong Kong, couldn't join him. More grief followed. Because of the ideological split between Peking and Moscow, the Ko brothers haven't seen each other for twenty-five years. The separation has gone through several stages. Once an advantage, Nelson's Russian education then put him out of favor with his Chinese chiefs. Years passed before the shock waves of the Sino-Soviet breach of 1959 subsided enough for him to climb back into the upper ranks of the Chinese Communist Party, where he had been spying for Karla. But blood exerts a stronger claim than ideology. Drake only agreed to work for Moscow Center because the Soviet link opened a channel to Nelson. Nelson, in turn, risks the wrath of both Moscow and Peking by coming to Hong Kong (where, ironically, he's captured by western secret service men).

Others share the Kos' plight of leading an everyday existence that bypasses the interior realities ruling them. The novel collapses the distinction between external perception and inward mood, yoking consciousness and dream to the same dark source. The people in *Schoolboy* act from the unknowable, impulsive, and chaotic inner life that inhabits us all and that we know so little about. A Whitehall cabinet officer calls Drake "O. B. E., Steward of the Royal Hong Kong Jockey Club, millionaire, and citizen above suspicion," adding, "it's hard to see how he could be a less suitable object for harassment by a British security service, or recruitment by a Russian one." Smiley's reply, "In my world, we call that good cover," rests on the truth that rebels often act from sources deeper than reason or morality. Though these sources are hidden, their results can be predicted. The discovery of a spy's ruling passion wrecks both his/her peace and effectiveness; the application of pressure to this heretofore unknown element in a complex equation will shake the spy from his place of safety. Several characters in the book forfeit security by following their hearts. Anyone tempted by love both puts him/herself and the beloved at risk. The Ko brothers are struck down when Drake tries to help Nelson come ashore—advisedly, in the same inlet of Causeway Bay where Drake first set down in Hong Kong from a fishing junk twenty years before.

In the past two decades, Drake has earned a fortune, won civic honors, and become a local philanthropist, even though he arrived in the colony "without a cent to his name." But his laurels count less with him than his missing family. He has named his racehorse, his yacht, and his now-dead son after his absent brother, Nelson. His priorities here and elsewhere show that this opium dealer and gang boss has hidden depths of tender, delicate emotion. Still glowing from his horse's victory in a big race, he has his beautiful blond mistress drive him, not to her apartment, but to the cemetery where his son is buried. Looking at the large bouquet of orchids that Drake sets at the foot of little Nelson's statue, Jerry Westerby finds himself touched. The winner has rejected the splash and show of his easy victory in favor of deeper vibrations. Like the law degree Drake worked toward but never finished, "the stone boy" reminds the absentee father and failed husband Westerby of his own isolation. The reminder unleashes force. The tender-hearted crook also stirs in Westerby "such complex and conflicting insights" that he sees Drake "more clearly than he had ever seen himself." This powerful moment continues to resonate. Westerby's falling in love with Drake's mistress and his equating Drake with his father, another millionaire owner of race horses, smudges his ability to deal with Drake as a professional target. A spy posing as a journalist and the book's title figure, Westerby has the job of luring Drake into the open, where he'll unwittingly expose Nelson, with his fund of Communist secrets, to western intelligence officers.

Drake deserves the emotional energy that Westerby directs to him. Smiley's comment in Chapter 14 on Drake's strategy, "He's to wait till the green light," refers to the safety signal Drake must get before joining his brother (the junk that will carry Nelson into Causeway Bay in Chapter 21, intriguingly, is equipped with two green lamps). In case we've overlooked the allusion to Fitzgerald's Gatsby, le Carré has Connie Sachs refer to Drake in Chapter 18 as "a latter-day Jay Gatsby." The reference is apt. Like his American predecessor, Drake, another big-time gangster motivated by love, never smirches his ideals. The end of Chapter 19 shows him gazing out to the sea that will bring Nelson to him. The comparison with Gatsby's yearning for the green light at the end of Daisy Buchanan's dock reminds us that, like Gatsby, Drake lives on the extremes. He's both the best and the worst character in the book. He cheats on his wife. To drive up the odds against his horse and thus to sweeten his take at the pari-mutuels, he hoses and then back-combs the horse to make him look sick. He peddles opium for the Kremlin—to his own people. Without remorse, he has ruined a bunch of lives while clawing his way to a fortune. Part of this claw-work is literal. When he warns Westerby, "if you have played a trick on me . . . your Christian Baptist hell will be a comfortable place by comparison with what my people do to you," he can be believed. Frost, the Hong Kong bank executive, already died horribly for disclosing information about deposits and withdrawals that confirmed Drake as the East Asian end of the gold seam extending from Moscow:

> He had died twice. . . . Once to make him talk and once to shut him up. The things they had done to him first were all over his body, in big and small patches, the way fire hits a carpet, eats holes, then suddenly gives up. Then there was the thing round his neck, a different, faster death altogether. They had done that last, when they didn't want him any more.

Yet the same man who butchers his enemies can act with honor, imagination, and delicacy, as has been seen. He endows hospitals and churches. He keeps faith with those he loves, regardless of barriers erected by miles, years, or even death. He has never broken a promise in his life.

Insight into his moral fastidiousness comes in his treatment of Ric Ricardo, the Mexican-American pilot who stole a large shipment of opium belonging to Drake. Rather than delivering the opium to Drake's customer, as he had agreed to do, Ricardo sold it and kept the money. But Drake didn't kill him or have him jailed, as he could have done. Instead of punishing him, he agreed to let the traitor live in exchange for his common-law wife, whom Drake had fallen in love with; Lizzie Worth promised both to become Drake's mistress and never to see Ricardo again if Drake spared him. In view of the possibility that Ricardo was to have collected Nelson from Drake's opium customer and then flown him to safety, Drake's pardon shows outstanding generosity—even if it restricts Ricardo to a jungle village in Thailand. Drake's forgiveness has moved Lizzie, whose last words, both to Westerby and the reader, are "Tell him [Drake] I kept faith." Drake's own faith has already impressed Westerby, whose several wives, many lovers, and betrayals of the service have shown him the courage and self-denial that faith rests on.

Westerby lacks Drake's integrity, and he knows it. His very presence on the strand at Po Toi defies a direct order from Smiley. But love hurts the spy as well as strengthening him or her. Westerby's birth into a world of loving that transcends officialism lives but briefly. Seeing "no one but each other," the Ko brothers ignore the helicopters preparing to swoop down on them. Their mutual absorption, as total as it is brief, inspires Westerby. He sees that "what linked them" also links him to Lizzie and that life offers no greater boon. But, like one of Shakespeare's tragic heroes, he can't savor his revelation or put it into practice. No sooner does he begin to live fully than he's shot to death by a Circus colleague he had crossed. The system can't tolerate infractions like his. If he has outgrown the retributive morality of his trade, his angry colleague has not. Acting from cruder, more primitive motives than Westerby, the office punishes him. What his colleagues never learn is that he dies for having evolved a more refined morality than theirs.

The person with the most refined morality of all probably suffers the most. Pain links Westerby to Drake during the reunion-abduction scene. His body aching, Westerby hears that he faces a threat worse than "the Christian Baptist hell." Then he's killed. Drake's depression after living at full stretch momentarily, like Westerby, might represent a loss worse than death. Perhaps pain has been welding him to Westerby all along. In their fraught encounter on the beach, the men both address each other as "Mr." The effect of le Carré's technique here is to inject formality between character and incident. This distancing takes the encounter beyond personality and the heat of the moment and pushes it into an archetypal sphere. Le Carré has infused it with drives so basic that it transcends individual psychology. As has been seen, Drake reminds Westerby of his shrewd, powerful father. Like Drake, Sir Samuel Westerby excelled with women, money, and horses, three spheres of activity that count heavily with competitive, conflictive Jerry. Aside from calling attention to his tendency to bend or break rules, Jerry's nickname of Schoolboy pits him against all fathers; he kicks against authority at every opportunity. The horses he can't escape symbolize the stiff resistance his rebelliousness has always met. The book throngs with horses, those radiant symbols of our instinctive lives. Le Carré calls Chapter 3 "Mr. George Smiley's Horse" and Chapter 7 "More about Horses." Beth Sanders, Jerry's English acquaintance in Italy early in the book, owns horses. Jerry and Drake meet at Hong Kong's Happy Valley Racecourse. The interlude at Happy Valley teaches Jerry that Drake named his winning horse after his dead son.

The drumming of horses' hoofs near the homestead means trouble, as it does in Peter Shaffer's *Equus* (1973). Theoretical insight into this conflict lies in Freud's famous case history of Hans and the castrating horse. According to Freud, the son concedes victory to the father in their struggle for the mother because he fears that his vital, powerful father will castrate him in combat. By extension, fear of authority in general prompts the son to develop a conscience, which subdues the pleasure principle but aids survival. This scheme, le Carré knows, is too strictly formalized for a novel. The Oedipal urge to kill the father need not lead the son to the mother's bed. The desired goal can also be fame, money, power, or freedom from authority. Or the son may simply want to outpace the father. Jerry Westerby follows *his* father in changing houses and women often. Even while risking his neck to rejoin Lizzie Worth, he sleeps with prostitutes. He defies the instructions of his Circus chiefs as often as his father broke the law in his shady business dealings. He has followed this same father into newspaper work. And even though he appears with more than one woman in Italy and the Far East, he only sees his father's widow during his time in England. On native grounds, where he's most himself, he acts the respectable, dutiful husband his father had become in his last years. He only needs to play the role of monogamous husband once to surpass Sir Samuel, whom death took from Pet Westerby's side. The lone visit to Pet is all Jerry needs because much of his rebellion is impeded by love. He'd not have emulated Sambo Westerby unless he were a good mentor. Jerry harbors no false sentiment. He takes his father's vintage 1930-odd tennis racket with him to Hong Kong because he had fitted its pommel to hide a tiny camera and matching film. Yet, the tennis racket shows that most of his major choices refer to his father. His not following through on his plan to overthrow Drake is wholly in character. Had he not respected Drake, he'd not have offered to swap his brother for Lizzie. On the other hand, taking the powerful Drake Ko's woman away from him would make Jerry's rebellion perfect.

Lizzie's own search for stability, like Jerry's, sends her to father figures. As with Jerry, too, the father always generates erotic drive. After leaving home because her literal father tried to force her, she chose a father surrogate as a husband, a big, rugged-looking schoolteacher, whom she would call either "my anchor" or "schoolmaster." The marriage fell apart when she had a baby. Needing guidance and ballast herself, she couldn't bear being depended upon; she even forbade her son to call her "Mummy." The need to be sheltered, protected, and fed took her to Drake, a physically large man nineteen years her senior. Intriguingly, the first two times Jerry appears with her in public, she consumes food paid for by someone else. (Just as intriguingly, he greets her for the first time holding a bouquet of orchids, the same love gift he saw Drake put at the grave of little Nelson.) And the first time the Reverend Mr. Hibbert sees the Ko boys, as survivors of the 1936 clash of arms in which their mother died, Drake is performing the parental office of protecting and feeding the injured Nelson. Lizzie's mother speaks truly when she calls Drake "a real father" to Lizzie. Despite being a crook and a Soviet agent, Drake rules his life by the intimate creed of the family. His adult role model has been the church father, Mr. Hibbert, the retired Baptist missionary who helped rear him, converted him to Christianity, and, years later, recommended him to Gray's Inn, where he studied law. When this old China hand discusses Drake with two Circus operatives, he looks as proud as "if it had been his own son he was talking of." He has forgiven Drake his shady business ethics and the rough passes he once made on his daughter. For his part, Drake honored Mr. Hibbert by adopting his North Country English accent, by offering to donate 1000 pounds to his church, and by renaming Lizzie Liese, after Mr. Hibbert's dead wife.

The connections between people in *Schoolboy* are deep and subtle, making us wonder how much freedom the people enjoy. Jerry's stepmother also has a North Country accent, and Smiley refers to Jerry's "obsession with that wretched daughter of his." The half-Chinese Phoebe Wayfarer serves British Intelligence in Hong Kong because it symbolizes her dead father, a Dorking clerk, to her. But the motivation provided by family ties rejects the sharp unity or affirmation implied by the novel's deep structure. Le Carré's pessimism in *The Honourable Schoolboy* is all the darker for the false gleams of hope it imparts. This darkness is carefully prefigured, as the Dolphin case begins with two dissolutions. In what later proves to be a "duck dive," or decoy action, the Circus closes High Haven, its Hong Kong residency. It also takes Jerry from his novel-in-progress and much-younger lover, who gratifies both his sexual needs and his daughter craving (at twenty, "the orphan" is only three years older than his daughter Catherine, or Cat).

Known as "the schoolboy" in the village near the Tuscany farmhouse he has been occupying for months, Jerry has been a Circus spy for twenty years. Almost always seen wearing the same shabby suit and scuffed buckskin boots, grinning, bulky Jerry underplays his role elegantly. His assignment sends him to battlegrounds in the Far East, where he barely escapes death several times. But luck runs out for him. His death at the hands of a Circus colleague typifies le Carré. The complex of motives actuating Jerry at the end dissolves in the gunblasts that kill him. But they're certainly nobler than those of the security agent (or agents?) that does him in. As in *Small Town*, the hero is killed by our side, not theirs, and he dies because he opposes policies most readers would also oppose. The architects of the operation that nets Nelson Ko, an outstanding triumph, are either demoted or discharged, and the Circus, having failed to improve its tarnished image, gets absorbed into the CIA. The novel ends on a bitter note. Although the Brits get their man, while maintaining a gentlemanly style, they find themselves bedeviled by rumors, unanswered questions, and needless death. The relocation of Nelson, Karla's Peking mole, to greater Philadelphia for interrogation, rather than to Britain, robs the Circus of its rightful share of the prize. The pillage spreads. Smiley himself shows, on the book's last page, how spying has lost its old sense of purpose. A career that once promised heroism and honor has become a tangle of treachery spun by nasty, twilit men.

Smiley deserves a reward, not a rebuke, for his part in Operation Dolphin. The Circus directorship he inherited from Bill Haydon's dupe, Percy Alleline, had never fought through so many problems as those caused by the Haydon catch. He launched Operation Dolphin divested of resources. The Circus's effectiveness, reputation, and morale had sunk to an all-time low. Circus staff had been cut back and its budget, frozen. Without influential friends in Washington or Whitehall, Smiley lacks the contacts and materials to produce intelligence. What he doesn't lack is detractors. As has been seen, the corridors of the Circus have been buzzing with the talk that his catching of Haydon was a fluke. He has been making still more enemies by having had the Circus rewired to stop security leaks and by rehiring both Connie Sachs, the Soviet security expert, and scrofulous old Doc Di Salis, her counterpart in Chinese intelligence. Never mind that these two are prodigies or that Smiley has been finding microphones strategically placed during Haydon's incumbency. Granted, the impression Smiley gives of being tired and slow, weak and old, invites personal attacks. These don't daunt him, though. During high-level conferences, he'll withdraw into himself. But just as he's been dismissed as a has-been, he'll execute a brilliant *coup*. What's more, his dismissive colleagues can see that his *coup*, far from being lucky, stemmed from knowledge, timing, and instinct. For instance, he has assessed accurately the delicate balance of power in the Far East. Hong Kong, he reasons, owes its life to Peking, which could invade and occupy it at any time. Peking's discovery of a Kremlin agent in Hong Kong would thus endanger the colony's continuance. Yet, Smiley has inferred, the Kremlin must risk such an upheaval. Having failed to get both the U. S. and Taiwan to league with them against the People's Republic, the Soviets must try Hong Kong. Smiley explains all this at a high-level steering session, his eyelids drooping and his voice growing more indifferent as the urgency of his argument builds. His throwaway brilliance and his wry hint that he knows more than he's telling win the day for him. His reluctant colleagues in the Treasury and Defense Departments empower him to wage intelligence operations in Hong Kong.

His winning of both an important brief and the financial backing to carry it out surprises Peter Guillam, his longterm colleague and closest friend at the steering conference. When Smiley asks for permission to reopen the Circus's Hong Kong residency, Guillam cringes: "Of all the damn-fool ways of overplaying one's hand.... You've thrown it.... Poor old sod: finally past it. The one operation which could put us back in the game. Greed, that's what it is. The greed of an old spy in a hurry." Smiley has read his fellow cabinet members more accurately than Guillam. Ironically, High Haven *will* reopen at the end of the novel. But the same cabinet chiefs who implement Smiley's idea will also fire him. When Smiley introduces the idea of reopening High Haven in Chapter 8, he isn't overplaying his hand at all. He has been controlling both the flow of information and the tone of the steering session all along. Practicing the art of misdirection, he also gives his grudging colleagues something to reject while they hand him the big prize—the charter that does put the Circus back in the game. He has handpicked the victory he's willing to sacrifice in order to win the one he really wants.

A brilliant negotiator, he has both the grip and the foresight to trade any number of small losses for the big gain. He'll stall or hold back information to gain bargaining power. At other times, he'll go for the quick strike. And he won't squander his assets. Having gained the Circus a charter to investigate Drake Ko, he knows how to protect it. He invokes the written agreement giving the British Secret Service exclusive operating rights in the Crown Colony. His need to spell out his mandate shows that spies often face worse threats from their friends than from their enemies. The rise to power of the pro-American Saul Enderby in the Circus hierarchy puts pressure on

Smiley to share his charter to operate in Hong Kong. Perhaps Enderby is feeling some pressure himself. His new wife is an American, as is his best friend, Marty Martello, a high ranker in the CIA. Martello's ambitions assert themselves most boldly when seen in the context of Joyce's *Ulysses*. As in *Ulysses,* islands dominate *Schoolboy;* an important scene occurs on a beach, or strand; an underdog wins a big horse race.

Also, most of the major characters in both books feel threatened and homeless. Just as Joyce's Leopold Bloom had to avoid the home where his wife was meeting her lover, so does Smiley live away from Bywater Street during his time in London. In fact, the one time he avoids Bloom's discreet example and does come home, he sees Ann preparing to embrace her lover. The faceless lover has usurped Smiley's husbandly role. The wresting of Stephen Dedalus's key by his housemate Buck Mulligan in the first chapter of *Ulysses* also prompts Stephen to call Mulligan a usurper. That the house Stephen and Mulligan occupy with another student is called Martello Tower sounds an important pre-echo with *Schoolboy*. By looking to jump into Hong Kong and seize Drake Ko, the CIA chief Martello is also a usurper. Not only does he try to flout his country's written agreement with Britain; his friend and fishing partner Enderby's succession to the Circus's directorship will later rob Smiley of his job and the British government of control over its security service.

This usurpation causes deep regret. The Smiley of *Schoolboy* enjoys more official power than before but also feels more alone and adrift. Recalling his and Ann's visit to Lucca, the Tuscan village where Jerry is living at the start of the book, he says that it rained. The weather is also bad in Cornwall for his visit to Ann in *Smiley's People.* Perhaps he and Ann combine to create bad weather. Their meeting at the end of *Tinker, Tailor* after a long separation occurs on a "bitterly cold" day. This inclemency sorts with Smiley's having failed to define his feelings. After enduring great travail to reconcile with Ann, he leaves her to spend nights at the Circus in *Schoolboy.* Whether his new sleeping arrangement stems from dedication to work or from resentment of Ann for having left *him* so many times can't be known. More clearly ascertainable is Karla's having replaced Ann at the emotional hub of Smiley's life. Hatred, admiration, and bewilderment mark Smiley's complex reaction to both Ann and Karla. But now that Smiley has focused his energies on Karla, Ann hardly exists for him. Besides moving out of Bywater Street, he has also sent her away. The blown-up passport photo of Karla hung behind his Circus desk, meanwhile, makes a couple of colleagues wonder how much emotion he has invested in his Kremlin foil.

Their puzzlement has merit. Perhaps his feelings are safer with Karla. In Chapter 5, he ponders the "hatred toward the man who had set out to destroy the temple of his private faith . . . the service he had loved, his friends, his country, his concept of a reasonable balance in human affairs." Yet these ruminations lead to the moment when he walks into Bywater Street, looks into the window of Number 9, and sees Ann extending her arms to a man. Then the lights in the house go out, and the bolts slide home on the front door. Has Ann forgotten her plans with Smiley? (Did Smiley forget to tell her that he was coming home? For what it's worth, he doesn't speak his intentions to her in our hearing.) Regardless of whose memory is at fault, the apparition he has seen at the window drives Karla from his mind. But he'll resurrect Karla to protect himself. Karla's villainy sustains him. He has already defeated him once by arresting Haydon, his London mole, and now he's closing in on Nelson Ko, his top Peking source, to score another big win.

The pain caused by this win extends beyond office politics. Once the hurt roused in him by Ann has revived, he can't escape it. His interview with Peter Worthington, Lizzie's abandoned husband, had already presented him with a mirror image of himself, another self-pitying, self-deceived discard. The words Worthington uses to describe Lizzie also pertain to Smiley, and his invocation of "basic human behavioral psychology" echoes Smiley's failure to see Ann clearly. To clinch the parallel between the two wounded husbands, le Carré makes Worthington a schoolteacher. Worthington's job reminds readers of *Call for the Dead* that Smiley both worked as an academic and was living with Ann in the scholastic center of Oxford when she first left him. But if Ann's adulteries have saddened Smiley, they haven't crushed him. In the next-to-last chapter of *Schoolboy*, the CIA chief Martello, baffled by the contingencies governing the proposed Nelson Ko catch, growls, "Is this a blackmail thing now, a disruption? I don't see a category here." Smiley, to whom the remark is addressed, sees no category, either. And for a good reason: he's not looking for one; categories mean less to him than people. Though the mission he's conducting is a military one, it's also a human drama involving the feelings of many people. He always rates the human over the operational. In Chapter 3, having looked in vain to German poetry for solace, he weeps over the death of a field agent.

The agent who tries his patience and who puts Martello in a panic about categories at the end is the book's title character, Jerry Westerby. "A large man, pepper and salt hair, athletic, full of energy, an aristocrat, shy," this robust invention steers the plot. He also controls the direction, along with the flow, of Operation Dolphin, forcing Smiley and his security aides to change their plans as they close in on the Ko brothers. A man of impulse and instinct who also values order and restraint, Jerry probably has a sharper human outline than Smiley himself. This claim can be supported. He appears alone for longer stretches; he makes more things happen; he invites more psychological speculation. We find ourselves wondering often about the purpose of his schoolboy's protest and rebellion. H. D. S. Greenway's reading of him, though suggestive, slights the psychological aspects of his conduct in favor of institutional ones; Greenway calls Jerry "Conrad's Lord Jim brought up to date and turned inside out. Whereas Jim tried to atone for having broken faith with a rigid code of conduct, Westerby realizes in the end that the code expected of him has all along been immoral and cruel."[2] He has long since shed his illusions about the purity of the Circus; nobody who has spent twenty years in British security could see it as a force for reason, justice, and the rule of love. Ironically, his clarity of vision both helps and hurts him. Like other schoolboys, he rejects constraints; no orderly suburban routine of a family, desk job, and commuter train for him. Even in the field, he strays from his brief, investigating on his own and substituting his own itinerary for the one given him by the office; at the outset, he dallies before reporting to the Circus, as ordered to do immediately by cable.

His unruliness makes him unpredictable. It also enhances his effectiveness. By trusting his fieldman's instinct, he can investigate beyond his case officers' range of knowledge, and he can profit from new developments. And why shouldn't he? The schoolboy who never acquires self-trust reproaches, rather than rewards, his teachers. But Jerry's self-trust threatens the operation. He disobeys orders to return immediately to London after an unauthorized visit to Thailand. In Hong Kong, he defies orders again. Smiley, whom he meets in Lizzie's apartment, sends him to London and puts two secret service men into an airport-bound staff car to take him to the next departing plane. But Jerry breaks away from his guards. He has challenged the bureau because he wants to reunite with Lizzie. No usurper of political prerogative, he has shifted his loyalties from the operational to the human sphere. He has fallen in love, and joining with his beloved outranks every other claim. He wants to enrich his reality. A seasoned spy, he also knows the dangers of intercepting Drake Ko at Po Toi just before Nelson's arrival. But he has forgotten that his colleagues at the Circus and their "cousins" pose a worse threat than the Hong Kong crime czar. Lizzie has created a need in him. He dies for love, just as hatred recoiled upon and killed Bill Haydon in *Tinker, Tailor*. Honor can't save a life that has gone operational. An honorable schoolboy will die as quickly as a dishonorable one if his aims clash with those of his chiefs.

Jerry's falling in love with Lizzie tallies with both his past and his psychological makeup. A man with several broken marriages behind him might well call "the prize of his survival" a woman with whom he has spent only four hours, which she filled with lies, evasions, and transparent pseudochic; a woman, moreover, so vacuous that, since coming to the Orient, she has been passed from hand to outlaw hand. Jerry only approached her to begin with because, as Drake Ko's mistress, she was an excellent point for British Intelligence to apply pressure. Yet her beauty blinds Jerry to her stupidity. Some weeks after meeting her, he perceives the "animal stupidity" of Ricardo, her ex-common-law husband, within minutes. If her conduct with Jerry has defined her as a suitable mate for Ricardo, Jerry's heart rejects the connection. He never condemns her for loving such a fatuous brute. He never judges her accurately at all. Only her shallow conventionality permitted him to know her to begin with, and he should have known it. He started talking to her in the elevator of her apartment building because he and the Circus colleague who investigated her after learning of her tie with Drake Ko knew that she'd break her weekly date with a local woman to dine with an attractive man. Jerry's addressing her as an old friend in the elevator even fools her into thinking she had met him before. Her sensuality has betrayed her again. She has always relied on her beauty to solve her problems. As a result, she's nearly all surface. The lavish, expensive trappings of her flat seem chosen more for appearance and effect than for comfort. Lacking character, they fit an image, not a person. Jerry would have grown bored with her after a month. Even her kitchen is for show, a place "where nobody cooked or ate." It's no wonder that she's treated like a commodity. She barters herself to Drake in exchange for Ricardo's life. But she had put herself on the trading block months before by rejecting the warmth and continuity of marriage.

Perhaps she perceives her own emptiness. She may have shortened her last name from Worthington to Worth in order to degrade or insult Peter. She seems to resent him inordinately. Before she met him, she had made little headway at school, at work, or in her personal development. Peter's decency, solidness, and dedication represented her last chance for a family. Within weeks of rejecting this chance, she started sleeping with men and got involved in a drug racket. And like most moral cowards, she blamed someone else for her lapse. Jerry's lapses come from him alone, too. So great is his need for her that he appeals to her on a pretext that would make any sensible woman howl. "The Ko thing is getting very grubby," he tells her in Chapter 20. "They're very rough boys you're mixed up with. I thought maybe you'd like a leg out of it all. That's why I came back." His "Galahad act" consists of rescuing her from a life of danger, dirt, and crime. Avoiding all mention of love, he has offered to redeem her. It's plausible that all his marriages have failed. Lizzie's first words to him the next time they meet, "Christ, it's Galahad," register the fear wrought in her by his well-meaning innocence. She already knows about Drake Ko's business ties and ethics. She also knows that she's lucky to have Drake's protection. Jerry can't help her. What his schoolboy romanticism *can* do is inflict havoc. She has survived enough hardship to know that his kind of rescuing knight poses the worst imaginable threat to her safety.

Rescue her he does not. But it's a sign of le Carré's faith in the power of love that her short association with Jerry sensitizes her heart. The bizarre form this growth takes might teach her how to comfort Drake, heretofore *her* comforter-protector. Drake will certainly need comforting after having rejoined Nelson only to lose him seconds later. Such a role reversal would chime with the inversions characterizing the lesson in emotional bonding that Lizzie and Jerry are given. As Leamas did with Liz Gold in *Spy*, Jerry confirms his love for Liz by parting from her when danger threatens; rather than exposing her to risk, he forgoes the joy of her company. This joy gains in intensity for being more imaginative than physical. The little time he and she have had together has been spent mostly in the company of others; Mr. Tiu, Drake's gorilla-like *aide-de-camp*, joined them for dinner the evening Jerry accosted her in the elevator. Nor have they had sex, a highly ironic turn in view of their sexual permissiveness. Lizzie's mother admits, "My little Lizzie went behind the bush with half of Asia before she found her Drake." Jerry's libido also thrives in Asia. But while enjoying women in places like Phnom Penh and

Bangkok, he fantasizes about Lizzie. His fantasies never convert to reality because, during his only time alone with her, other matters claim precedence. How does the precedence assert itself, though? One can argue that Jerry was hacked and kicked so hard by a Circus bully that he probably couldn't have had sex, anyway. Yet his knocks also support the argument that he needs the warmth, closeness, and distraction of sex.

Le Carré sets up the sexless intimacy of his two sexual vagabonds with wryness and control. Lizzie and Jerry go to a house which rents rooms to lovers by the night or the hour. Yet after Jerry lowers his aching body into a chaise lounge, Lizzie goes to the bed. This arrangement surprises them. In one of Hong Kong's most notorious love nests, they communicate depths and nuances that neither would have believed possible, particularly without physical contact. The chastity of their exchange proves more fruitful than sex, the staple activity of both their *louche* setting and their private histories. Rather than weakening their bond, the absence of sex strengthens it by fueling their imaginations. A parody of sex, their chaste encounter shatters vulgar romantic illusions. But it replaces them with candor and clarity. Demonstrating his usual obliqueness, le Carré never says what the encounter yields. Jerry dies before he can benefit from its lesson. Lizzie may lack the imagination to learn anything. The main setback of Drake's life—losing Nelson—has occurred so many times that it might have numbed his potential for growth. On the other hand, the ability of the unlikely Lizzie and Jerry to overturn the expectations generated by their sordid surroundings, their pasts, and the desperation of the moment invites the question of attaining values as only the best fiction can—through characters whose internal struggles and hopes live in our minds after they leave us.

II

A controlling principle of *Schoolboy* is bipolarity or dialectic. The book has two parts. There are two Ko brothers; the South China Sea bisects Hong Kong, the book's main setting; Smiley visits Hong Kong twice, once in each of the book's two sections; two colleagues voice their uneasiness over the blownup passport photo of Karla occupying the wall in back of his desk. Bipolarity also declares itself in bisected Hong Kong, a city that varies splendor with poverty; in the title of Chapter 6, "The Burning of Frost"; and in the structure of the opening chapters. Like *Tinker, Tailor* and *Smiley's People*, its companion works in the Karla trilogy, *Schoolboy* begins by alternating two settings. After describing some local reactions to the closing of High Haven in Hong Kong, le Carré cuts to Italy, where Jerry has gone both to sink his family woes and to write a novel. This alternation gives way to another once the book gets under way. To add variety, to build suspense, and to create opportunities for irony, le Carré moves between Jerry's London controllers and the legwork that takes Jerry to Cambodia, Laos, Vietnam, and Thailand, besides Hong Kong. These numerous pairings create more than a stalemate or deadlock. They emit a singing tension. The titles of the book's two parts, "Winding the Clock" and "Shaking the Tree," though syntactically similar, move from the mechanical to the organic. To shake the tree is to dislodge fruit that can be gathered and eaten. But is this fruit edible? Le Carré's tree might symbolize wholeness, as in W. B. Yeats's "Among School Children." But his symbolism has a different reference. The grenades that lie about "like fruit" among firearms and ammunition clips in a treelike structure, the house on stilts where Ric Ricardo lives, describe warfare as natural and constitutive. Nelson Ko, who has known little else, would agree. The arm that never mended right after it was broken in the crossfire between Chiang and the Japanese reminds him that safety is an illusion. Perhaps the broken-winged Nelson needs no reminders. He finds himself caged in a helicopter as soon as he alights in Hong Kong.

His flight to the United States extends the book's warning. Violence can erupt in the East or the West; both places can feel its shock waves; both can generate shock waves of their own. Le Carré universalizes madness and hate by negating differences between the two worlds. Smiley practices an "Oriental self-effacement" during a conference in which he and other westerners discuss security operations in Hong Kong. Simile can also join East and West. A plane flying from Battambang to Phnom Penh rattles "like a London bus on its last journey home up Clapham Hill." The values of the plane's owner, Drake Ko, come from eastern and western sources—his Chinese heritage and his Bible studies. His teacher, the Baptist minister who introduced him to Christian fundamentalism, Mr. Hibbert, may have lived as long in China as he has in England. Along with his spiritual legacy to the Ko brothers, his remembering them in his daily prayers qualifies him as their spiritual father (their natural father is never mentioned). And sex, the great democratizer, transcends racial and geographical barriers as effectively as does spirit. Lizzie and Drake are lovers, and the bloodlines of East and West meet in the face of Charlie Marshall, which is described as having "sleepy Chinese eyes and a big French mouth."

Such convergences occur when the action needs tightening. In the main, *Schoolboy* favors a flexibility in structure, rating mood over incident and the development of character over linear sequence. The succession of action-filled scenes found in most spy fiction gives way, in the book, to an interest in the people's interior lives and the changes occurring there. Though le Carré shifts settings in the early chapters, he won't rush to join them thematically. Elsewhere, too, he makes us wait before satisfying expectations. For instance, we learn "the forbidden secrets" that Charlie Marshall gabbles out in the "ruin and despair" of opium withdrawal a chapter (and twenty pages in the original hardcover edition [New York: Knopf, 1977]) after they're uttered. Le Carré will also remove characters from the action to justify motives, to dovetail public and private contexts, and to promote the irony of discrepant awareness. Thus the Circus calls Jerry to London in Chapter 2. He leaves Italy at the end of the chapter (p. 39) and doesn't return to view till Chapter 5 (p. 92), when the purpose of the Circus's telegram has been explained. This three-chapter interim also recounts the qualities in Jerry that make him both an asset and a danger in the Dolphin case. Once set forth for the reader, these qualities can exert drama quickly. Thus Jerry leaves the reader again between Chapters 8 and 12 (pp. 165-281), during which time other narrative elements get the attention they need to enrich the theme. Le Carré's treatment of Drake Ko reveals his ability, on a larger scale, to give off-stage characters vitality. Drake enters the action on p. 155 and speaks his last words in our hearing on p. 160 before coming back for his last bow on p. 521. Nelson only comes in for a page at the end, where he's barely seen, owing to the darkness, and unheard.

The deployment of character strengthens the plot. The absent Ko brothers exert increasing magnetism as both Jerry and Smiley get information about them, piece it together, and try to learn what it means. Consulting different sources, the men talk to different intimates of the brothers, so that the reader knows more about the Kos than either investigator. The alternation of Jerry's field work in the East and Smiley's policy meetings in London yields other benefits. Besides testing ideas that Jerry sometimes ignores, Smiley's councils of state feature backstairs intrigues and factional struggles that will impinge on Jerry's freedom. Most of these cabals reach us from the point of view of Peter Guillam. Sympathetic to Smiley and not jaded from years of bureaucratic infighting, the impressionable junior officer

Guillam provides a fresh, intimate outlook on the maneuvering. Le Carré takes special pains to dramatize his perceptions. Recalling the reactions of Agatha Christie's Captain Arthur Hastings to Hercule Poirot, Guillam will lose patience with Smiley. But his impatience vanishes quickly. No sooner does he begin patronizing Smiley than he finds himself awed by the man's negotiating genius.

Most of these energies channel into the plenary session of Smiley's inner circle of advisers that opens Chapter 8, advisedly called "The Eighth Day." To describe the conference, le Carré shifts from the past tense to the present. The shift advises the reader that the important revelations about to occur will usher in the new start alluded to by the chapter's title. And the novel's pace does speed after the conference. The corpse of Frost, the Hong Kong banker who divulges Drake's account to Jerry, materializes shortly. Then, after Jerry barely escapes being killed by Ricardo, he finds the corpse of an American reporter-friend, whom Drake's thugs killed when they mistook him for Jerry. Powered by graphic, evocative writing, this violence moves the action to its suspenseful climax. More dramatic force and flavor stem from the Hong Kong setting of the book's closing chapters. One of the world's most exciting places, Hong Kong challenges the creativity of any writer. Le Carré's feline sensitivity to atmosphere and his sharp observational powers help him meet this test. He moves easily between Hong Kong's teeming streets, with its skyscraper slums, and the bobbing junks, sampans, and shacks housing the colony's fishing village.

Different kinds of imagery lend vividness to this varied portrait. Le Carré reproduces the gongs of temples and shrines along with the chatter of the pajama-clad proprietors of food stands; meanwhile, the fragrance rising from the proprietors' wares mingles with the exhaust fumes of the cars creeping between the press of foot traffic. Informing le Carré's portrayal of exotic modern Hong Kong is the same penchant for dialectic that attracted him to Schiller's doctrine of the naive and the sentimental. Poverty and deprivation have always coexisted in Hong Kong with wealth and splendor. In the book's last minutes of comic relief, Jerry attends a reception given for the colony's nobility. The baroque decadence displayed at the reception, given by a local perfumerie, includes a six-foot-high pyramid of champagne glasses, a "wheelbarrow full of cooked lobsters and a wedding cake of pâté gras." The reception's climax, a writhing dance step executed by two naked black women with shaven heads and oiled, bejewelled limbs, has the drive of "absolute sexuality." Le Carré's brilliant imagery captures the desperation with which Hong Kong's super-rich merchant class seeks thrills. Ironically, the perfumerie hosting the reception is called Maison Flaubert. This ironic name, another product of le Carré's bipolar mentality, rises from the clash between Flaubert's consummate artistry and the wild excess encouraged by his manufacturer-namesake. The aloofness Flaubert deemed essential to artistic creation has degenerated into an assault on the senses.

Curiously, the dancing girls jar the cool poise distinguishing the novel up to their appearance. What follows the lavish reception is a series of sensational effects wholly unexpected in a craftsmanly, delicately adumbrated book like *Schoolboy*—unless le Carré included them to spoof the conventional spy melodrama. The butane cylinders aboard the launch ferrying Lizzie and Jerry across a bucking, pounding sea start leaking. This mishap could doom the couple because the festival taking place on shore has the full attention of the noisy crowds; any explosion that occurs at sea will go unheard. The melodrama intensifies. The fierce sun and the dragonflies filling the air vex Lizzie and Jerry as they head for safety. But safety keeps eluding them, the dry land they craved disclosing threats of its own. After beaching their craft, they climb a mountain where a blast of wind makes them "gasp and reel back." Luckily, they weren't buffeted from behind, because at the moment of impact they're standing at the knife edge of a cliff 200 meters above a creaming sea. Such lurid effects make us wonder if we're reading a film script or a harlequin romance rather than a sophisticated novel by one of England's shrewdest, subtlest literary artists. Our confusion keeps building, as le Carré bounces Lizzie and Jerry from one near disaster to another.

Fortunately, Jerry's climactic meeting with Drake Ko ends the contrivances. But here narrative tempo swings in the opposite direction, le Carré exerting little or no control over his people. What follows the meeting of Drake and Jerry needs more authorial supervision, just as the scenes prior to it suffered from a glut of it. As has been seen, Jerry fled his Circus captors to rejoin Lizzie. His love for her has hampered his effectiveness as a spy. But it has also promoted internal growth. His hearing that Drake has never broken a promise cools the revenge he wants to exact on Drake for killing Luke, an American journalist-friend. A man who has violated nearly every professional and sexual commitment he ever made, Jerry respects Drake's integrity; a person who always keeps his word deserves charity, he admits. Then, too, Jerry may also resist punishing Drake to atone for any guilt he feels toward his father, Drake's older double. Neither of these motives could occur to Drake. While he's waiting on the beach for his brother Nelson to come ashore, Drake keeps calling Jerry political; Jerry has come to negotiate for a commodity. This assessment is correct. In exchange for the safety of Nelson, whose movements are known to western security agents, Jerry wants Drake to give him Lizzie. Drake doesn't hesitate. "If you help me I give you everything," he says; "That is my contract and I never broke a contract in my life." But he can't honor a bargain that circumstances destroy. The western intelligence officers that snatch Nelson also kill Jerry, sending Drake to the only person capable of consoling him, Lizzie, whom he has just peddled to Jerry without blinking.

Or has he? Although he has agreed to give Jerry "everything," he doesn't specify Lizzie as part of the spoils. Nor does Jerry do more than surmise that his assassin is the Circus bodyguard and "silent killer," Fawn. Perhaps this indeterminacy is meant to call our attention to Jerry's inner drama. Like other modern fictional heroes from Hemingway's Francis Macomber to Patrick White's Eddie Twyborn of *The Twyborn Affair* (1979), Jerry dies as soon as he attains full growth. Le Carré has already pointed the moral he has enacted. A person's humanity correlates negatively to his/her effectiveness as a spy. Spies are expected to act with surgical efficiency, even ruthlessness, security work holding no brief with scruples or doubts. Because spying and humanity exist inversely, the spy who achieves human growth must die. A profession that rewards or punishes on the basis of results will disregard all motives. The expediency it has committed itself to denies feelings; a spy distracted by human depth and complexity has lost his edge. He must be disposed of like any other liability. The emergence of Leamas's heart brought about his death in *Spy* because it challenged the purposes of the secret service.

Death also comes to Jerry for following his heart. But *Schoolboy* is a subtler, richer novel than *Spy*. It also attempts more. Curiously, this enlargement of vision can look like carelessness. Le Carré seems to be raising issues he later slights; he kills Jerry before he can test his illumination, and then he relieves Drake of the stress of handing Lizzie over to Jerry. But these omissions aren't faults. Le Carré channels the irresolution they create into the legend that Operation Dolphin is acquiring. By relying upon impressions and fragments rather than facts, he invites the reader to join the debate waged by Circus staffers. His invitation is no evasion of authorial responsibility. *Schoolboy* only appears to be giving the reader work le Carré should have done himself. The impression is a false one. All the work is there. The novel achieves its goals by avoiding conventional narration. It attacks narrative continuity, first of all, by disjointing acts from motives. The question asked by a minor character in Chapter 14, "Who believes in *motive* these days?" reminds us that spying reorders normal expectations. Intelligence agents ignore the guidelines furnished by the cycle of day and night. Smiley's research section toils through the night. Smiley and his London aides hold an important meeting at five o'clock in the morning to synchronize with an operation occurring simultaneously in Hong Kong. The technique of the novel also denies linear sequence. If history is sequential or successive, the drives moving the people in *Schoolboy* defy chronology. The round-the-clock labors of Smiley melt modalities while collapsing both moral and political issues. Points that are scored or arguments, won fade into new urgencies.

These often assert their might by violating paradigms. Differences between pursuers and their quarries and between interrogators and their respondents can vanish immediately. For all Charlie Marshall's talk about killing, his anchor is the family, especially his father, a Kuomintang general whose love Charlie craved but never won: "We all got to hold on to each other tight or we fall off the crazy mountain," he shrills within hours of boasting, "Jesus Christ, I hate mankind so much that if it don't hurry and blow itself to pieces, I'm going to buy some bombs and go out there *myself.*" Then this would-be destroyer asks his tormentor, Jerry, if *he* had a father. Jerry's response, "Yes, sport, I did.... And in his way he was a general, too," probes a common disquiet. As his fraught response to Drake Ko shows, Jerry is as haunted by Samuel Westerby as badgered, cringing Charlie Marshall is by *his* powerful father. Jerry's nicknaming his father "Sambo" blackens the father's image but doesn't blunt his force. Fathers exert drive elsewhere. Interviews in successive chapters with Peter Worthington, the father of Lizzie's son and, as a schoolteacher, a father figure, with Lizzie's natural father, and with the church father, Mr. Hibbert, reveal Lizzie to have spent most of her adult life looking for a father. Drake Ko offers her the same control and nurture that Jerry does to the orphan and that the Kremlin does to Nelson. So prevalent is the father search that it sends people thousands of miles from home, sometimes razing psychic barriers, as Jerry's grilling of Charlie Marshall in the Cambodian mud showed.

Jerry isn't the only investigator nettled by similarities between himself and his quarries. In his talks with witnesses, Smiley, too, keeps bumping into the crises that have broken his peace. He leaves Peter Worthington convinced that he knows Ann no better than Worthington knows Lizzie. When he tells Worthington at the end of their interview, "Yes, I understand," he's speaking more truly than Worthington can know. The uncanniness with which people keep seeing themselves in others also accounts for the interchangeability of winners and losers. The moral and spiritual poverty infecting espionage is so great that it destroys differences between victory and defeat. This fever has spread everywhere. So much subterfuge is going on in Anglo-American security that the reader wonders along with Peter Guillam if the Circus wouldn't serve itself best by dropping the Ko project. The project's success, Guillam foresees, will sink Smiley and convulse the Circus. His forecast proves correct. The dismantling of a big drug operation and the arrest of Moscow's Peking mole benefits British Intelligence no more than it did the Kos. The novel's last chapter, ironically called "Born Again," records a series of defeats to the special branch. Smiley is pushed out of office; his friends are demoted; the Circus falls under the controlling arm of Washington, D.C. Despite its success in the Dolphin case, British Intelligence is worse off at the end of the novel than at the beginning, when it was looking to rebound from the disgrace caused by Bill Haydon's arrest. In an irony consistent with the upsidedown morality that rules spying, the successful are punished, not rewarded.

This bitterness gives the book's other resurrections a jagged edge. In Chapter 1, le Carré speaks of "old [Bill] Craw's near death and resurrection" after the closing of High Haven. Chapter Three contains the news, "Smiley resurrected from retirement one Roy Bland." Smiley wants Bland to help him capture Nelson Ko, who is believed dead. As has been seen, Nelson's resurrection only lasts long enough for him to be snared and flown to the United States for questioning. Ric Ricardo, the pilot ransomed by Lizzie after he stole Drake's opium, also turns up dead on official reports. His resurrection, which Drake brings about just as he will bring about Nelson's, proves as dismal as the others in the book. Chapter Twelve, entitled "The Resurrection of Ricardo," leads to the discovery of Ricardo (by Jerry, whom Ricardo had heard was dead) in a jungle where he's subsisting in a midway state between prisoner and monkey. Smiley's statement in Chapter 14, "This case is littered with people pretending to be dead," needs to be extended to include the half-lifer, Ricardo.

The rhythm of death and birth the statement rests on also informs official policy, and with the same sad results. The novel bristles with evidence that spying kills any hope for progress or improvement in human affairs. Terms used by le Carré like "throne room" and "cupbearer" turn our thoughts to the middle ages. But the medieval soon gives way to the primitive. Many of the energies pulsing through *Schoolboy* are precivilized. Drake Ko's summary of his family background reminds us that if the characters' hopes aren't foiled by the false gleams of resurrection, they founder on the reefs of repetition: "My people are Hakka from Chiu Chow. We breathed the water, farmed the water, slept on the water." The evolutionary drama he's acting out has stalled. Smiley seizes Nelson Ko because he knows that Nelson will enter Causeway Bay the same way Drake did twenty years ago. Even a weary Lizzie, relying only on intuition to back her claim, calls the coming reunion of the Ko brothers a "replay": "It's all to be exactly the way it happened before." Advisedly, the brothers are last seen at the water's edge, as if their evolutionary development hasn't lifted them to dry land. Their predictability is making them repeat the ordeal of being parted. Drake's having named his son, his horse, and his yacht Nelson attests to the pain this parting will cause him. It may also indicate Drake's helplessness. Like many other western writers including Dante and Nietzsche, le Carré describes repetition or recurrence as an affliction of the weak. Were Drake strong enough to break the pattern of repetition, he'd have Nelson by his side, not reminders of him. These reminders, part of the same pattern of regressiveness, stand as tokens of defeat.

III

Is the defeat self-inflicted? In line with the name given a South African journalist, Deathwish the Hun, one of the first characters to appear in the book, a secret love of defeat, perhaps even of annihilation, pervades *Schoolboy*. This destructive impulse accounts for the death of institutions, the slaughter of people, the devastation of land, and even self-destruction. As if marked out by death, the book's cast of characters includes people known only by a nickname, one name, an assumed name, or a double name (like Ric Ricardo and Marty Martello). Other half-lifers in the book include drug addicts, persons denied by a parent or child, and exiles. Family means a great deal to these isolatoes, most of whom live and work far from home. Lizzie Worth's name changes convey the loneliness of the archetypal figure. People who suppress the self-truth conveyed by a name lose touch with their core of being. They miss who they are. It's inevitable that their victories ring hollow and that they can't escape the snares of repetition. They yearn for the solidness and depth represented by the family. The opium wreck Charlie Marshall calls Lizzie his sister, and when Jerry later tells her that he knows both Charlie and Ric Ricardo, she answers, "Great. So now you're family." The nonbelonging vexing le Carré's lonelies takes corporeal form, as well. They wear their pain. One thinks of Ricardo's limp, Nelson Ko's skewed arm, Connie Sach's painful arthritic joints, and the "webbed claw" that has been serving American journalist Max Keller as a hand since he got burned years ago in the Congo.

Repeating an idea from *Lover,* le Carré refers to "the clarity which pain sometimes brings." The pain that doesn't inhibit lends sharpness and drive. After being hit so hard in the groin that he fears internal bleeding, Jerry seems "to run faster under the impetus of the pain." But pain that persists also depletes. The catastrophes that pile up at the end of the book record the depletion. Pain is the body's signal that further stress applied to an afflicted area could cause serious damage. Images of desolation in a Cambodian war zone symbolize the process: an armless corpse whose face is crawling with a "black lava" of flies, an empty barber chair being pelted with rain, an airplane with bullet holes in wings that "wept dew like undressed wounds." These images portend the casualties that pepper the end. Fawn gets his face battered and Guillam sustains a broken shoulder when Jerry fights free of them to return to Lizzie. Jerry is aching "from head to toe," as well, this whole evening. Then there's Luigi Tan, the half-Portuguese Wanchai tradesman who rents Jerry and Lizzie the launch they take to Po Toi. An amputee, Luigi Tan refers to himself as a "big guy with one leg." His description is only half true. He's a tiny man, just as Ricardo, who's sometimes called Tiny, is huge.

The person whose name or self-description belies his reality resembles the one who, like Lizzie (or Smiley), uses several names. They both practice self-denial. Out of joint with the central realities governing their lives, they face the world slantwise instead of head on. They can't even see themselves straight. Although Ricardo limps, he claims to play excellent tennis. He talks constantly about his athletic skill, his physical strength, his good looks, and his virility. He's using this bluster to hide his fears, mostly of Mr. Tiu, Drake Ko's crusher and chief aide. Ric's arsenal of weapons conveys his insecurity. Anyone who keeps a machine gun, a cache of grenades, and several handguns at the ready feels menaced. Ric's fears are justified. He's virtually a prisoner. If he tries to flee his village, Mr. Tiu will find out and have him jailed for his many crimes. The Thailand jungle clearing he lives in is all the space he has. But if he's paranoid about the safety of his little space, he has also assessed it accurately: "I live in the jungle like a monkey," he says in his stilt house, comforted by the heft of the automatic pistol in his hand.

The half-lifer who calls forth animal associations recurs often in the novel. Nearly every character feels threatened; nearly every one clings desperately to the little he/she has. And why not, if the world is run by jungle ethics? The various animal references remind us of the insecurity of every job, relationship, and life in the book. The link between insecurity, animal subsistence, and death snaps into place in Chapter 1 when the South African photo-journalist Deathwish is called an "African ape." In Chapter 12, Lizzie's father calls his wife an "anthropoid ape." Chapter Twelve also yokes animal instinct to resurrection when Lizzie's mother calls Ricardo a *"lamb"* who was restored to life by Lizzie "with the only currency she has." (Jerry will later allude to Ric's "animal stupidity" and to "the slumbering animal in him.") Other animal associations summon up the vulnerability, rapacity, or nastiness of ordinary life. Jerry, who calls himself a newshound, first appears to us sitting "like a locust" on the floor of his Tuscan farmhouse, typing in "the eagle's way." Life languishes in this fertile, fabled region. The postmistress who delivers the telegram ordering Jerry to London hobbles "like a lame beetle." Animal associations dwarf other characters. Jerry's widowed stepmother, Pet Westerby, is "a painted hen-like woman"; his daughter, Catherine, is called Cat; the cabinet chief Oliver Lacon is a capon. Leaving the barnyard, le Carré has Connie Sachs, whose greatest joy in life is her dog, call Peter Guillam a "lecherous young toad." Animal references reach to the Orient, Mr. Tiu being termed a "fat bulldog" and Charlie Marshall describing himself as a spider. Fawn, Smiley's bodyguard, punctures Jerry's stomach and breaks the arms of a Hong Kong street thief who reaches for his watch. Le Carré also varies the naming pattern. Misnamed, this "silent killer" isn't shy or timid, especially when it comes to attacking an enemy. Besides, le Carré never says whether Fawn is his first or last name.

He introduces other name puzzles, too. The first names of Mr. Tiu, Tiu's banker-victim Frost, the minister Mr. Hibbert, and the intelligence officer Doc Di Salis remain unknown throughout the novel. Clive Gerald Westerby is known by his middle name. Two other characters are referred to only as the dwarf and the orphan.

The double names of Ric Ricardo and Marty Martello convey the futility of going around in circles. The more one thinks about *Schoolboy*, the more despairing becomes the book's outlook. The sufferers peopling the novel, trammelled by physical and emotional burdens, must fight the darkness without the help of self-knowledge or external support systems. Sometimes, the fight looks hopeless. Nelson Ko's arrest at Causeway Bay denies all progress, including that inferred by evolution. Other settings also infer a failure to evolve or develop. The orphan has red hair, traditionally the mark of the devil. Le Carré dramatizes the association. The farm where she and Jerry live stands on a prominence known as the devil's hill, and her eyes burn "like the devil's" when she's angered. Would Jerry have fared worse with her than with his colleagues? Both alternatives put forth the idea, propounded elsewhere in le Carré, that people have more to fear from their intimates than from strangers or acquaintances. This plight creates a powerful, if disturbing, unity. Clive James miscued by indicting *Schoolboy* for "myth-mongering."[3] *Schoolboy* is a work of unusual depth, finish, and elegance. If its air of conscious literary performance stops it from being a book to warm our hands by, it's nonetheless a strong and stirring work, beautifully told.

Some of this beauty comes from the sounds it makes. Some of le Carré's most memorable characterizations describe people who only appear once. These people represent lyrical challenges more than they do problems in plotting or narration. They allow le Carré to use his skills as an impersonator. Nicholas Wapshott's reference to his "brilliant skill at mimicry"[4] applies most forcibly to *Schoolboy*. The unity the book gets from motifs like the family, the name-as-disguise, and the animal symbolism lets le Carré exploit the vignette without blurring narrative focus. *Schoolboy* juxtaposes highly contrasting voices for the sake of comedy, variety, and thematic breadth. The vignettes featuring Humphrey Pelling, Lizzie's father, and the church father Mr. Hibbert in Part I and Charlie Marshall and Ric Ricardo, Lizzie's adopted family, in Part II sidestep the twin traps of condescension and caricature. The speech of Bill Craw, the Australian journalist-spy, gains a robust irreverence from its counterpoint of archaism, Shakespearean allusion, and slang. Enriching the novel's texture while extending its subject matter, these triumphs of verbal impersonation also sound troubled depths. But they don't always sound them successfully. For instance, le Carré needs to listen more carefully to Americans. An American wouldn't say, as the CIA chief Martello does in Chapter 14, "See you in ten days, maybe fourteen." Martello's speech is also too colloquial for a top-ranking Pentagon bureaucrat with a Yale degree. A man of his background wouldn't say the vapid, "Guess us worker bees had better get back to our hives" any more than he'd wear suits that were "honest-to-cornball American." Nor would he align subject and verb as he does in Chapter 21 when he says, "Navy int. have seen...." (Curiously, a junior colleague of Martello's says later in the same chapter, "Navy int. has....") Max Keller, the American journalist Jerry meets in Cambodia, also sounds as if he came from somewhere else. Australians, not Americans, call the English "poms," and an American would end the following sentence by saying either "road" or "path": "We should have taken the other lane!"

The style of *Schoolboy* invites other complaints. Le Carré's artistic intent of conveying the phenomenology of spying, rather than writing a neat, consecutive account, creates some confusion. At times, the reader is blitzed by impressions that le Carré hasn't shaped or organized. Density often replaces design in *Schoolboy*, the data of which aren't arranged to build suspense but to convey the time, toil, and frustration of any major spying operation. A word-heavy book, *Schoolboy* slogs along slowly as it describes false starts, red herrings, and bureaucratic maneuvering. But Moynahan is wrong to call the novel "much inferior to its companion volumes" in the Karla trilogy.[5] The sophisticated narrative technique of *Schoolboy*, no highbrow indulgence, regulates the action. The story is exciting. Rockets explode, machine guns chatter, racketeers smuggle drugs, and security nets stretch from London to Hong Kong. But the ambience of the novel is slow, quiet, and meditative. Suppressing the adventure of his adventure yarn, le Carré looks at it critically—pointing ironies, showing how it effects the inner lives of people, and yoking it to some encompassing rhythm or truth. He'll also use dialogue and shift point of view both to vary the class of material he includes and to create outlets for his wit and energy. *Schoolboy* avoids the extremes of strutting and solemnity. A firmly crafted work of solidness, subtlety, and precision, it stands securely as the keystone volume of the Karla trilogy, le Carré's major effort to date. Its urbanity, polish, and thematic breadth also make it le Carré's most ambitious and perhaps best book.

Chapter Thirteen
Drowned Harmonies

The people, time sequence, and main activity of *Smiley's People* (1980) all stem from the book's two predecessors. As the title implies, Smiley defeats his foil from Moscow Center; the last scene of the book shows Karla defecting to the West and thus joining the ranks of Smiley's people. This victory, although Smiley wouldn't term it such, carries forward from those described in le Carré's two previous books, where Smiley captured two of Karla's top aides—his moles in London and Peking. As in *Schoolboy*, le Carré will say things like, "For years afterwards, and probably for all of his life, Peter Guillam would relate ... the story of his homecoming that same evening," to endow the action with a legendary gleam. Such intrusions matter, as they did before. Besides alerting the reader to look closely at what is going to happen, they explain that the event about to unfold has been often pondered and discussed. The reason? The event has helped form both the character and folklore of British Intelligence.

This record continues to drip shame. Whatever gains the Circus has made in solvency it has paid for many times over in both credibility and morale. Classic stratagems of security work, like double agency and the honey trap, till recently "the very meat and drink of counter-intelligence," have been discontinued on the grounds of being obsolete, wasteful, or in conflict with Whitehall's policy of *détente*. But Smiley isn't only bereft of time-honored resources of security work. Although his ex-chiefs pull him out of retirement without qualms to risk his neck in the field, they withhold vital information from him, and they don't let him operate freely till they've first protected themselves from blame in case his operation fails. Judging from their ineptitude, they'll need all the protection they can get. Crucial data can't be retrieved because it won't appear on the Circus's central retrieval system. Lacking the dedication of their predecessors, section heads will take two-hour lunches and then flee the office within minutes of checking back in to start a long weekend. They don't send for the dossiers of agents under their care; they also neglect the procedures governing the handling of these agents. To avoid scandal, one erases the tape carrying the demand of an agent, who has since been murdered, for an emergency meeting.

Still in charge of the Circus, since helping oust Smiley at the end of *Schoolboy*, is Saul Enderby. Little besides his CIA connection has earned him his laurels. Speaking in a "lounging Belgravia cockney [idiom] which is the final vulgarity of the English upper class," he still kowtows to the Americans. His nervous habit of picking his teeth with a matchstick and his constant flow of literary allusions (Chapter 19 finds him referring to Sherlock Holmes, Hercule Poirot, Captain Ahab, and Tennyson's Maud) create a glaring incongruity. Restive, insecure Enderby has cobbled up some ersatz learning to shore up his claim to his high post. His aide-de-camp, Sam Collins, once a maverick field agent, has degenerated into a yes-man in order to protect the pension slated to come his way in a few years. Lauder Strickland, the high ranker who erased the tape bearing Vladimir Miller's demand for a crash meeting, lifts his arm "in a Fascist salute" from a prone position during Smiley's briefing; apparently, the Fascist will to power can't energize its adherents. This same briefing finds Smiley repelled when he sees the veteran Miller's case officer to be an *"uncut boy"* in his twenties. Oliver Lacon, the Cabinet chief who appeared in both *Tinker, Tailor* and *Schoolboy*, has more experience but less humanity. Alluding to his wife's having left him for another man, Panek calls him a eunuch.[1] The epithet is just. Impotence also describes his conduct in the office. Even though Miller's face has been destroyed by a Soviet assassination device, Lacon discounts the incident. He wants to bury it because Miller no longer had any official tie with the special branch. His Circus colleagues, Lacon claims, did well to ignore his pleas for help; the adventurism of a figure from the sanitized past should be ignored.

Obstructionism like Lacon's forces Smiley to investigate on his own. And the field he investigates is as morally ravaged as that of *Schoolboy*. Homelessness still haunts many. The Estonian immigrant Villem, now living in London as William Craven, guards his family closely because he knows the devastation caused by being cut off. Two of his compatriots living in the West, Vladimir Miller and Otto Leipzig, get murdered. Another Soviet exile, Marya Andreyevna Ostrakova, barely escapes a third murder plot. A person needn't be an exile to live under threat. Although neither is cut off from his land or language, Smiley and Lacon both suffer deeply from being deprived of their wives. Smiley sees Ann and reminders of her infidelity wherever he turns. A photograph of a young woman wearing earrings reminds him that women preparing to have sex usually take off their earrings first; "Ann had only to go out of the house without wearing them for his heart to sink." Later, a figurine of a dancer arching her body evokes Ann having sex—naturally, with another man. The woman who causes pangs of alienation needn't be a wife. Karla is divided from a daughter he thinks of constantly. And the daughter's own division from her parents and her native Russia has cut her off from herself. At the time of the novel, she's living in a Swiss mental home, having been diagnosed as a schizophrenic.

The search for wholeness that drives her, her father, and Smiley is full of pitfalls and portents. The book opens on 4 August (probably 1977), anniversary of the start of the Great War. After giving the date in the book's second paragraph, le Carré connects it several pages later to a character's "old sensation of being crippled." This connection suggests another—the death of civilization that the Great War represented to writers like Virginia Woolf and J. B. Priestley, who both believed that human nature itself changed by 1914. This deathliness haunts the action. The background of the case Smiley is investigating is deeper and nastier than he had thought. It goes back many years, invades families, and cuts across both military and public policy. Nearly every step of the case includes a death—of a person, a home, or an agency. Le Carré, whose imagination has grown bloodier with the years, reproduces this gore. (Characters are tortured and killed in his last three novels.) Like the Hong Kong banker Frost in *Schoolboy*, Otto Leipzig is mauled by his inquisitors before being allowed to die. Smiley, who suffers physical injury in both *Schoolboy* and *Smiley's People*, studies this brutality, just as he examines the remnants of Vladimir Miller's face in Hampstead Heath. Such violence tallies with a world as warped and demented as that of *People*. Smiley's ability to look at it without flinching shows him to be in step with reality. Everybody connected with the Circus except for him believes that Miller was either mad or greedy; he was either too old to be trusted or too eager for a quick landfall. His not asking for money for his part in the scheme to stop Karla fails to impress even his controller. This plight has antecedent in modern literature. Like the character Bananas in John Guare's 1971 play, *The House of Blue Leaves*, and also Bobby in David Mamet's *American Buffalo* (1975), the truthsaying Miller gets no hearing from his intimates.

His many rejections both before and after his death describe a disordered, incoherent world. This description holds good elsewhere, too. Time and again, Smiley will have trouble getting his bearings. Some Victorian terraces he passes in London's Paddington district, "painted as white as luxury liners on the outside," have dark, cramped interiors. Connie Sachs's home near Oxford is "a house of day and night at once." Entering Berne's Bellevue Palace later in the book gives Smiley "the feeling of stepping onto an empty liner far out at sea." Smiley also notes in Chapter 23 that the Swiss capital is "out of season and out of time." Guidelines and controls he has always relied on are vanishing everywhere. Walking in a warehouse district south of the Thames, he's struck by the discontinuity created by three adjoining houses: "The first was called Zion, the second had no name at all, the third was called Number Three." Such discordancies carry forward from le Carré's earlier work. Instead of soothing and healing, as it does in works as different as Shakespeare's *Twelfth Night*, Mozart's *Magic Flute*, and Sartre's *Nausea* (1938), music aggravates the harshness of today. Music was playing when Leo Harting was murdered in *Small Town;* Ann was listening to music with Bill Haydon when Smiley found them together in *Tinker, Tailor;* the father of Ostrakova's daughter in *People* is a musician.

This cacophony leads to the loss of life. But other poetic motifs infer that it must be faced. Gardens, no seedbeds of renewal and hope, develop the idea. Several disconcerting scenes in *People* take place in gardens or parks, most notably the murder of Vladimir Miller in London's Hampstead Heath. Key scenes occurring on bodies of water invite us to conclude, as well, that the realm of the Fisher King has become ransacked and sterile: "I have been fishing and I am happy," says Miller to a fellow Balt, mistakenly believing that the Circus will help him restore potency and health to the stricken realm. Only later, from a lake near Hamburg, does Smiley pull up a gym shoe containing, in a hand-stitched pouch, the scrap of paper he'll later present to get the cassettes storing information which will sink Karla. But even while recounting Smiley's big catch, le Carré sustains the negativity he has been associating with flowing water. The gym shoe containing the crucial scrap of paper was submerged by Leipzig, who died protecting its whereabouts from Eastern bloc spies. Then Smiley can't leave the lake site with his find until he sees his rented car vandalized by some young campers. Advisedly, the last ravage performed by the vandals consists of snapping off one of the car's windshield wipers, an aid intended to protect drivers against the visual constraints caused by rain.

Such acts enhance the book's apocalyptic aura. The daughters of both Ostrakova and Karla are hellions. Their wildness stems from both Soviet repressiveness and the fusion of genius and mental imbalance inherited from their parents. Alexandra, who has the weird clarity of a demented savant, can't escape pain. Her mother, we learn, was also difficult. In Chapter 23 of *Tinker, Tailor,* Smiley said that Karla married a girl in Leningrad who killed herself upon learning that Karla had been jailed, most likely for life, in Siberia. *People* tells a different story: Alexandra's mother, who, admittedly, might be a different woman, was killed by Karla's own order for opposing the Marxist-Leninist view of history. But Europe's depletion and malaise takes le Carré's skepticism beyond partisan politics. Soviet agents kill without being detected in England and West Germany; Ostrakova's would-be murderers in Paris also go free. The stain their escape signifies has spread beyond political thuggery. Ann Smiley's belief that there's no loyalty without betrayal touches society everywhere, including the family. William Craven risks losing his English passport by working for his Estonian father's old friend, Vladimir Miller. While she's recovering from her bruises and aches, Ostrakova keeps by her bedside pictures of both her husband and the man she deceived him with. Nor is Ostrakova the book's only cuckold. Elvira, the wife of Mikhel, operator of London's Free Baltic Library, had an affaire with Miller, and Val Lacon and Ann Smiley have both left their husbands for other men. The pattern of adultery varies. Though Anton Grigoriev, Karla's Swiss link to mad Alexandra, has a faithful wife, he beds other women. His rutting recoils on him, too. His need to keep it a secret from his wife compels him both to tell Smiley about his tie to Karla and to let Smiley stand in for him at his next visit to Sasha.

Smiley's demeanor at the Thun sanatorium where Sasha is confined falls short of a conqueror's. Mother Felicity, the worldly, ironical director of the home, notes that he looks pale and that his hand shakes. Although his errand has put him under a strain, he's also feeling the anguish of ordinary existence in our spy-ridden world. He still prefers working over dwelling on his inner life. Yet work can deepen his pain as well as distract him from it. Though innocent of Miller's death, he feels implicated. Miller brought two pieces of evidence to the Heath. Possessing only one of them, Smiley shares Miller's legacy with his murderers. But the line joining Smiley to the death squad runs stronger yet. As Miller's first case officer, he brought the old spy to London. Further dismay comes from his knowledge that he's working for people who have protected themselves against his possible failure. Spies have to watch their friends as closely as their enemies because most operations include provisions to blame others in case the operations miscarry or abort. That these others are usually one's friends makes sense. By teaming with one's friends, one can leave a trail of clues that fit the friends' movements.

The bureau's disdain of Miller smirches Smiley's purpose again. Smiley feels no sense of achievement when he watches Karla cross into West Germany. Only barely does he qualify as a nonhero whose poor self-image has stopped him from seeing that he has made the best deal he can. As always in le Carré, the self is divided, the crafty pro in Smiley struggling against the sentient, bruised human. He and Karla have approached the truth, from Conrad's *Victory* (1915), voiced in Graham Greene's epigraph to *The Human Factor* (1978), from opposite sides, viz., "He who forms a tie is lost. The germ of corruption has entered into his soul." The person who's trapped and betrayed by his virtues recurs often in Greene. Maurice Castle of *The Human Factor* voices the plight of others like him when he says that a man in love walks the world like an anarchist carrying a time bomb. Yet as he, his creator Greene, and le Carré all know, the love that corrupts also humanizes; the germ of corruption germinates. Many of le Carré's people feel torn between sharing the self and withdrawing. Mikhel of *People* conveys the realities of this tension in his statement, "After many years we are married. I resisted. It is not always good for our work. But I owe her this security."

Nobody can silence the clamor of the heart. Nobody should. But the spy who listens to his heart must know two things—that he has made himself blackmailable and that he has blunted the knife edge his work demands. Smiley lost his zeal for the job of corralling Karla long before his frontier meeting with his Moscow foil. The blackmail he used to win Karla's defection has soured his victory. Formerly content to view himself as an angel of light (Alan Angel is one of his worknames), in contrast to his image of Karla as a demon of darkness, his discovery that Karla's fatherly love overrode all his other impulses, including personal safety, redeems Karla. His assuming a human face makes him less of a villain that must be stopped than a fellow sufferer who deserves compassion. Smiley extends compassion by arriving at the crossing point two hours early; Karla deserves this care because, as a defector, he has nobody else to help him.

As le Carré's earlier novels have done, *People* uses narrative structure to mute any glory that may crown his finale. Characteristic of this technique is the use of ambiguity and obliqueness rather than direct statement to achieve an undercutting effect. Chapter Fourteen, the midmost chapter of this twenty-seven chapter novel, takes Smiley to Connie Sachs. The help that Connie gives Smiley equals in import any service she performed during her long heyday as Mother Russia, the Circus's Soviet expert. It's a tribute to her expertise and her humanity, too, that she ignores the insult of being sacked twice by her Circus chiefs to help Smiley trap Karla. It's a further tribute to her mettle, here in the book's central chapter, that she extends wisdom to Smiley along with information and that this wisdom applies more strictly to his person than to his job. On the subject of "the demon Ann," she tells him to take a definite stand: "Gather her up for good is what you should do. Or else put powdered glass in her coffee." Either option will help him fill a void. Having found love late in life herself, she's advising her old colleague and friend to do the same.

How much credibility does this advice deserve? Smiley never refers to it in our presence after hearing it. Perhaps the source of the advice has blunted its force. The love Connie has found is lesbian, implying unreality and negation rather than the fulfillment she claims for it. What's more, decades divide her and Hilary in age, and intergenerational sex in le Carré usually ends in grief. Then there are the daily realities of her life. She and Hilary board pets while living rough, in a hovel with clapboard walls, a wood-shingle roof, and a tin chimney. Both her ramshackle dwelling and her humble job hint at the process by which she has gone to the dogs. Wheezing, arthritic, and alcoholic, she even calls herself "a rotting old hulk." And so advanced is her decrepitude that for one moment during her giddy self-unburdening to Smiley, she fears for her life. This life deserves her fears—and ours, too. Our last sad glimpse of it includes the possibility, enhanced by the dog-god word play, that the withering of her body has ushered in both a freshening and burgeoning of her spirit; her choice of love over ease and convenience is creative.

But her example seems lost on Smiley. And more's the pity because, nearing her age and lacking both a job and an everyday wife, he needs a boost. Paradoxically, his outstanding professional triumph, the reining in of Karla, negates him as a man. Karla's defection has robbed him of purpose. Yes, he can go home and cultivate the joys of the retirement he richly deserves. But the finales of *Tinker, Tailor* and *Schoolboy* and the second chapter of *People* showed that repose brings him more vexation than joy. Karla's defection also challenges le Carré. Now that Karla has been stopped along with his prized lieutenants, Haydon and Nelson Ko, le Carré must write about something new. He has all but exhausted Smiley as subject matter. But the change of venue, approach, and character type disclosed in *The Little Drummer Girl*, an exciting new direction for his inventiveness, infers no tallying growth in Smiley, an older man lacking his author's outlets for self-expression. It's also disturbingly consistent with le Carré's irony that the resurgence grazing both Connie Sachs and the new father-to-be Peter Guillam should bypass Smiley, who, having appeared before us in seven novels, means much more to us.

I

Other people in the canon give insight into Smiley, as well, notably his foil, black grail, and obsession, Karla. In 1982, Anatole Broyard described Moscow's master spy thus: "Thin, merciless, ascetic, and amoral, Karla is a fanatic, the priest of a new inquisition. Nothing matters to him but a purity of doctrine, a passion for certainty."[2] This description of Karla as a son of night who despises all things human and divine needs softening. Granted, his deputy in Berne, Anton Grigoriev, refers to him as a priest, "a great Soviet fighter, and a powerful man." And the Machiavellian wiles he uses to press Grigoriev into service makes him look diabolic. But Grigoriev also calls his tormentor a "man of deep experience . . . a man from the very roots of his country." Anyone capable of exuding his country's folk spirit must possess a humanity that transcends evil; there's more to Karla than his fabled ruthlessness. And his humanity, like anybody else's, is corruptible; speaking of him in *Tinker, Tailor*, Smiley said, "lack of moderation will be his downfall." This excessiveness has already impressed Grigoriev, Jim Prideaux of *Tinker, Tailor*, and Smiley himself. Cool, wrinkled Karla chainsmokes American cigarettes. Even before he lets on that Alexandra has distracted him from his duty, his addiction to the bouquet and flavor of Camels declared his fallibility.

This addiction calls forth still another epigraph from a Graham Greene novel, *The Honorary Consul* (1973). The epigraph, coming from that sour ironist Thomas Hardy, reads, "All things merge into one another—good into evil, generosity into justice, religion into politics." Let's deal with it cautiously. To say that Karla's defection blurs all moral differences between himself and Smiley is to distort le Carré's meaning. We can say, though, that in le Carré's view, spying speeds synthesis; things come to merge, nourish, and constitute their polar opposites more quickly in the shadow of espionage than elsewhere. Le Carré shows why. The expediency ruling the intelligence profession disallows distinctions. Reality has only instrumental or situational value to spies because they judge things and people on the basis of how they can be used to bring about preordained goals. A shift in policy can also turn a saint into a sinner or a valued prize into trash. The spy is thus at the mercy of forces he can't control. This process can jade or twist him. Twenty years before Karla defected, he heard Smiley say:

> We're getting to be old men, and we've spent our lives looking for the weakness in one another's systems. I can see through Eastern values just as you can see through Western ones.... Don't you think it's time to recognize that there is as little worth on your side as there is on mine.... Both of us when we were young subscribed to *great* visions.... But not any more.... In the hands of politicians grand designs achieve nothing but new forms of the old misery.

Acknowledging the reflected shabbiness of their own systems underlies this appeal. Smiley calls it "negative vision." Nor would Karla have denied his formulation. Only blind faith sent him home to be punished, perhaps by death, for a wrong he never did. He snubbed Smiley's offer of asylum and a new start in the West. Twenty years later, he accepts Smiley's less generous offer. The reason for his acceptance is clear: Smiley has improved his bargaining position and thus weakened Karla's. At stake is nothing less than life. Love has smudged Karla's loyalty to Moscow. He loves Sasha so much that he has been misusing the Kremlin's money and facilities to protect her. Smiley only has to remind them that these crimes endanger Sasha as much as they do him. A victim of excessive love himself, Smiley knows exactly where to apply pressure on Karla. The interview in the steaming Delhi prison twenty years before showed Smiley that Karla will face dangers he'd never subject his daughter to.

But the warmth Karla extends to Sasha is matched by the coldbloodedness he metes out to others. He dramatizes the carnage that can result from the Leninist dictum that good ends justify wicked means. Without discrediting his fatherly love, le Carré fends off reader sympathy for him. Karla claims to have infiltrated a young woman into France as his secret spy. To devise a cover story, or legend, for his supposed spy, he fiddles accounts, misallocates materials, and arranges three, possibly four, murders. The one murder plot that miscarries is the one we know the most about. And what we best know from it is his craft and resourcefulness. The first character who appears in the book, Marya Andreyevna Ostrakova, a fat, waddling frump of fifty, wears cracked shoes and carries a shabby bag. Fantastically, this dumpy, obscure checker in a Paris warehouse appears on Karla's hit list. Coincidence has foiled her. Her daughter Alexandra was born around the same time as Karla's Alexandra, i.e., 1955 or '56. What is more, both girls are rebellious, and both have at least one parent who defied the state. Just as Karla's woman died for opposing Marxist-Leninist writ, so did Ostrakova leave her small daughter in Russia to nurse her dying husband, a political defector, in France. Karla wants to profit from her guilt and vulnerability. Taking advantage of a recent trend in the Politburo to reunite broken Soviet families abroad (undertaken to improve Moscow's image in the area of human rights), Karla offers to send Ostrakova's daughter to France. He doesn't plan to make good his offer. He has raised Ostrakova's hopes in order to smash them. By killing her, he can stop her from learning that a young Russian schizophrenic with her daughter's name is living in a Swiss mental hospital. "The killing comes first, the questioning second," Miller said accurately of Karla before Karla ordered his murder. His statement discloses the black heart of Karla's villainy. It's bad enough for him to kill spies, like Miller and Leipzig; spies are supposedly paid very well because they risk their lives. But when he orders the death of a creaking, neglected compatriot to remove the remote chance that she'll start asking questions embarrassing to him, he forfeits all our sympathy.

Treating Smiley more gently than Smiley treats himself, le Carré redirects to his pudgy, worried-looking spy the sympathy he shunts away from Karla. After the book's opening sequences in Paris and Hamburg, where Smiley is mentioned but doesn't appear, he stays in view most of the way. Le Carré keeps him in sharp focus by resisting a growing tendency to break up narrative structures. He knows that undermining the continuity of cause-and-effect will discourage emotional response. Instead of turning our attention to technique, the more conventional, linear approach of *People* makes for a Victorian interest in character. The human factor moves to the fore. Shortly after its publication, he called *People* "in many ways a very sad book. At the end, Smiley must accept as part of his condition Ann ... as well as his own fulfillment."[3] Yet much of Smiley's pain comes from his private guilt, his low self-esteem, and his tendency to pity himself. Consistent with both his personality and his past, this pain feeds upon itself. Le Carré hasn't engineered this defeat. He has no reason to heap misery on a character who has served him well for seven novels spanning nineteen years. In fact, he pays tribute to Smiley in his last bow by modifying his technique to help Smiley face us more fully than ever before.

Smiley answers this challenge by exhilarating rather than exhausting us. A man in his sixties who was twice ousted from the service he loves, he's a fringe figure and a semi-outsider to his ex-colleagues. A junior officer who tells him about one of the Circus's electronic retrieval units draws an immediate rebuke from a superior: "Damn you ... that's a confidential matter ... Mr. Smiley may be a distinguished ex-member, but he's no longer family." His semioutsider status (mirroring his ambiguity as a husband) distances him enough from the Circus's staff to help him perceive their foibles. But it preserves in him the insight to understand and even to sympathize with them. The Smiley of *Smiley's People* extends the office's concept of doing one's job properly. Perhaps more seriously than before, the book questions, through him, the quality of a spy's life—his beliefs, intellectual style, and emotional attitude. Can a spy satisfy the requirements of ambition, security, and idealism at the same time? Can he help his colleagues without forfeiting creativity and self-expression? Although alienated, the Smiley who cries when he learns of an agent's death is neither narcissistic nor emotionally inaccessible. Neither need he worry, as a temporary, about empire building or organizing a winning team. His tradecraft serves his flair for deep experience, spontaneity, and productiveness. Perhaps aware that he's conducting his last mission, he displays a new boldness and command.

This decisiveness shows straightaway. When Lauder Strickland accuses him of praising Vladimir Miller because he, Smiley, recruited him, Smiley answers with force and clarity, marshalling facts to support his advocacy. Later, he has the courage to tell Saul Enderby, chief of British Intelligence, that he mishandled the Karla case; his reproof comes, furthermore, within a minute or so after Enderby indicts him for meekness. He trusts himself enough to follow his impulses elsewhere, too. On the spot, he decides to take a night sleeper to Penzance, in Cornwall, to see Ann, even though he has no toilet articles or pajamas with him. His meeting with Ann (their only present-tense encounter in the canon and Ann's only talking turn) says a great deal about both of them. First, Smiley confirms our impression of him as one of the most put-upon husbands in modern English fiction, along with Ford Madox Ford's Christopher Teitjens *(Parade's End)* and Anthony Powell's Kenneth Widmerpool *(The Music of Time)*.

Pain is all he can expect from his marriage, since Ann can't be faithful to him or any other man. While talking to her, he sees in the sea below no cradling mother but another manifestation of the destructive female: "Below them in the rock's cleft, the sea broke and formed itself furiously in patterns of writhing foam."

Powerful as it is, this apparition doesn't identify Ann as the destructive siren in our minds as quickly as it does in Smiley's. Granted, her sexual vagrancy has strained and perhaps also wrecked her marriage. And rather than backing down, she increases the pressure initiated by his surprise visit. But besides telling him that she loves him, she also blames her wildness on his compliance. She argues that he should have known her better and acted on his knowledge. His failure gave her too much power. *Her* knowledge that he'd always take her back and that he'd never commit adultery himself made him all too tame, stable, and predictable. This steadiness eroded his mystery and sent her outside the home for thrills. To unify his portrayal of hangdog Smiley, le Carré shows his master spy's marital failure clouding his vision of his part in the Karla snatch. He hardly hears the applause his colleagues direct to him as Karla walks into their arms. When Guillam tells him, "George, you've won," he answers, "Did I . . .? Yes, well I suppose I did," and the book ends there. We may never see or hear from him again. Nor has le Carré helped us understand him just prior to this parting glimpse. Such strategy is typical. He'll hold back at times when speaking out would focus our responses. When Smiley and Karla look at each other in a pool of light just beyond the frontier crossing, le Carré offers only the following nibble: "They exchanged one more glance and *perhaps* each for that second did see something of himself" (emphasis added). Moments later, le Carré again refuses to help us interpret Karla's act of dropping, in Smiley's view, the cigarette lighter, inscribed "To George from Ann with all my love," Karla had pinched twenty years before: "He [Smiley] thought of picking it [the lighter] up, but somehow there seemed no point and no one else seemed to notice it."

Both Smiley's impulse to ignore the lighter and his incredible explanation rouse our activity. Le Carré's evasiveness about the incident makes us work out its meaning for ourselves. Why is Smiley so defensive? This question can be answered to his credit. He has succeeded brilliantly in both understanding Karla's life and coming to terms with his own. He has no reason for subterfuge or remorse. The honor and patriotism he had sought to protect exist no more, having been wiped out by compromise, emptiness, and doubt. The most brilliant *coup* of his career won't help the cause of justice. But it will leave him without a purpose or a cause. Automatically, his heart opens to his old foe. He half wishes that Karla will be shot by the East German border guards before crossing into the West. Karla's love of his daughter had already proclaimed his humanity. A man capable of his tenderness and sacrifice deserves to be spared the onus of defecting. But the atrocities he has committed also dictate that he be treated like a prisoner. Smiley's disregard of Ann's lighter keeps his mirror meeting with Karla operational. The lighter is Karla's reminder to him that he, too, stands with the defeated. A week or so before their meeting Smiley had said inwardly, "for the first time in his career, he held the advantage over his old adversary." Clearly, this is nonsense. He has underrated himself. But his wrongheadedness does explain why he robs Karla of the satisfaction of knowing that he has been stung. The quiet, devastating finale of *People* succeeds both logically and dramatically. Had le Carré dwelt on Karla's love for Sasha, the poignancy might have crushed Smiley. Instead, he displays Karla's vindictiveness. At the moment of defeat, Karla puts himself beyond compassion. He tries to score a point off of Smiley. Smiley answers this sneak attack in the best way possible. By ignoring it, he not only robs Karla of his compensatory victory; he also breaks the chain of deceit linking Ann, Karla, and himself.

His efforts justify the splendor he emanates. He hasn't been afraid to ignore or defy authority. As he did in his debut, *Call for the Dead*, he plays a lone hand, following his own lights rather than waiting for official approval. His solo effort includes working twenty straight hours. Chelsea, Cambridge Circus, Charlton, Paddington, the Heath, the Strand, the docks south of the Thames near Vauxhall Bridge, Bloomsbury, Soho, and Bayswater all see him in little more than a day. (Admittedly, he visits these sites by car. Whereas le Carré won't overtax his man's powers of endurance, his allowing Smiley to drive a car in our view for the first time in his career provides a questionable measure of authorial help.) The annoyance with which he's greeted by two women during his London odyssey (and by Connie Sachs's Hilary the next day) shows that he's not afraid to anger people in the execution of his job.

His determination joins hands with his other energies. In turning Karla's handpicked agent, Grigoriev, he practices brilliant tradecraft. Early in the book, he reconstructs a murder around a small, easily overlooked detail. His insider's knowledge that spies carrying messages must also carry the means to discard those messages helps him discover why Vladimir Miller, a smoker, brought matches to the Heath but no cigarettes. Mendel's statement that Smiley was the best field man he ever knew applies here. Mendel might have added that Smiley's expertise included insight into the tradecraft of other spies. Smiley revisits the last moments of Miller's life, when Miller knew that death was near. He then pays his old friend the tribute of assuming that he behaved as Smiley himself would have done in similar straits. His act of imaginative identification helps him both find Miller's message and perceive its importance. Impersonating Miller to get closer to his life situation, he retraces his old friend's actual steps on the Heath. The parallel with Poe's "Purloined Letter" is clear; reproducing Miller's physical movements helps Smiley invoke his man's desperation. His act of depersonalization shows him why Miller moved his walking stick from his right hand to his left when he was running for his life.

Miller's trail leads Smiley to a pack of cigarettes wedged into a tree branch. The negative hidden in the pack takes him by turns to Hamburg. Guided by an impulse less reliable than knowledge but more cogent than intuition, he both assembles the pieces of the puzzle and reads their meaning accurately. His thoroughness and imagination bring him success. But the success comes to us both piecemeal and indirectly. Le Carré's treatment here enlivens his realism. Often, he'll withhold explanations for Smiley's reactions to what he finds because, acting on impulse, Smiley hasn't yet worked out the value of his discoveries. His unformed perceptions reach us at the moment they occur so that we can see the process by which they become information and ideas. Sometimes, le Carré will only report Smiley's physical responses to an event, leaving us the job of interpreting them. Thus Smiley crowns his brilliant stroke of finding Miller's hidden negative with another just as brilliant. By resisting the temptation to remove the negative from its niche, he avoids smudging or tearing this potential treasure. Characteristically, he performs this triumph of restraint when he's alone. We feel his aloneness. Le Carré's decision to block his thought processes from us intensifies them while also reconfirming the truth that he must bypass the bureau to get results. An old pro, he knows both the penalties and the rewards of working alone. He doesn't surprise us when he develops the film strip himself rather than taking it to one of the Circus's many experts, all of whom can do the job more quickly and efficiently than he.

Perhaps his finest moment comes in his tender, affecting interview with Karla's daughter in the Thun hospital, near Berne. Alexandra, he reasons, merits his personal attention simply because her powerful father has been risking so much for her sake. Thus he appears instead of Grigoriev for what becomes the last of the regular visits (just as Alan Turner stood in for Leo Harting at the last weekly meeting with Hazel Bradfield in *Small Town*). Smiley's exchange with Sasha, whom V. S. Pritchett accurately calls "a brain-washed schizophrenic, confused by ideology, a double identity, and ghastly lust,"[4] all but stops him from trapping her father. Achieving delicacy and compassion without straining, Smiley knows that Sasha has intuited the tie joining him, her, and the natural father she believes "a secret prince more powerful than the Czar." Perhaps she welcomes that father's future destroyer because she believes that the father killed her mother and even banished her from the sight of God. She treats Smiley more like an angel than a demon, kissing his hand, trying to leave the hospital with him, and asking him if he's both her father and God. Smiley has stirred in her something more than a passion for revenge.

The depths he has touched in her he can never know. Shrewdly, le Carré invokes the irony of discrepant awareness to alienate Sasha from her kindred spirit, Smiley. What emerges from this rift illuminates barriers the novel has been setting up between sexes, generations, and nations. A beautiful American patient at the hospital had to be taken away for acting worse than a French one who flew into rages and slashed her wrists. Without detailing this wildness, le Carré tells us that, like its American perpetrator, Sasha is also beautiful. The likeness strikes home. Le Carré needn't remind us of the prevailing Soviet-American feud to convey his pessimism; division, subdivision, and the sharp split between appearance and reality bode ill for world peace. The nun in charge of the hospital grazes this portent when she says of Sasha, who sometimes calls herself Tatiana, "Sometimes she lives in the dark. Sometimes she sees too much." What has rattled Sasha is the intimation that the realities governing her life are too grand and paradoxical to be controlled. Referring to herself, she tells Smiley, "Tatiana is the daughter of a man who is too important to exist.... He does not exist but everyone is afraid of him." Harking to Grigoriev's description of Karla as a priest and a monk, Sasha's tormented vision of her father puts him in the religious sphere.

Grigoriev's presence in Thun enforces this idea. Karla is like a god whose inability to love his creatures directly calls for the use of intermediaries. And whose inability to suffer invites pain on those same creatures? Le Carré rewards this interpretation. Karla's lack of first-hand contact with Sasha has distorted his love for her. This distortion of love into brutality and madness invokes another iron legacy. Unable to express love directly any more than her father can, she must wear a mask. "Tatiana does not exist.... There is only Alexandra," she says, alluding to a truth both she and her father know all too well, i.e., that the exceptional person gives up the simple joys that warm and soothe the rest of us. Her purity and intensity push Smiley into the evasiveness of platitude and silence.

Sasha's own failure to cope with her searing vision expresses itself in her schizophrenia; the attempt to make sense of her parental legacy has torn her in half. She shakes Smiley's hand "in a very stylish way" right after telling him with "awesome" clarity and courtesy that he represents "the forgiveness of the authorities." This wisdom is born of great pain. As she speaks it, this soul in chains is forcing her thumb so far back upon itself that it looks as if it's going to snap. Within moments both her hands have joined in, "fighting each other furiously," and she has to be carried away screaming. Her disorientation is that of the schizophrenic. On the one hand, she enjoys fouling herself with gross sexuality. On the other, she lives in the timeless white limbo of infancy or a convent, "where everything was shadowless.... White light bulbs, white walls, and a white iron bed frame. White radiators." The featureless monotony of this world, lacking texture, tone, and shadow, suggests eternity. It also invokes the bleak absolutism of her father, whereas Tatiana, her whorish self, calls forth his darkness. The wide gulf between these two Karlas accounts for the mad, twisted images thronging Sasha's mind; these teeming images have wrecked her sanity.

It's easy to see why she resists waking up in the morning to face the day. Her polarized psyche has put her at odds with reality itself. Defeated and despairing, she finds it easier to revert to the womb and perhaps to inanimacy than to reconcile her warring selves. "God make me four. I am three years old and need my sleep," she murmurs, fighting the onset of the new day. Then she adds, "God make me two, God make me one, God make me nothing and unborn." Le Carré makes us feel the pain behind her will to regress. Some of her thoughts are clear and sharp, and she'll phrase them with wit. Then there are those muddy moments when she can't tell if her thoughts have been spoken. At still other times, she feels her unarticulated thoughts flying "around inside her skull like ... birds," clattering wildly. These times convey both the distance that divides her from sanity and the futility of any efforts she might muster to close the distance.

A character not subject to her tantrums and one of much less import is Smiley's friend and colleague, Peter Guillam. Guillam plays such a small part in *People* that one feels his inclusion stems from his having been one of Smiley's people from the start. This honor recoils upon both him and le Carré. Donnish to the point of being effete in *Call*, he's furious through much of *Tinker, Tailor* and *Schoolboy*. His anger fades in *People*, where he's a dutiful, protective husband and father-to-be. "Close to fifty" and married to a much younger French woman, he will also discuss in fluent French landscape gardening, a subject he knows very well. But perhaps it's churlish to fret about the puzzling changes that have overtaken him since his first appearance. He has also been loyal, skillful, and discreet during these nineteen years. If le Carré makes him Smiley's last interlocutor, we might as well acquiesce in the tribute.

III

People shares an assumption that underlies much of crime and adventure fiction, *viz.*, that a single truth underlies the mystery. As soon as Smiley discovers Karla's susceptibility, he can make Karla his slave or victim. His discovery of a hitherto unknown variable in the complex equation of international espionage changes everything. Although Smiley regrets using blackmail to gain his goal, his longterm obsession with Karla overrides his scruples. Joseph McLellan has described the mentality fueling the scheme to turn Karla: *"Smiley's People* tells us ... that we are now engaged in an intense dialectical process; that the terms on which the process operates have no regard for traditional human values except as points of leverage."[5] The most orthodox in technique of the trio of books comprising the Karla trilogy, *People* exploits many conventions of crime and adventure writing. It describes the methods used by Moscow Center assassination teams. It provides an inside view of detective work, supplying insights that wouldn't occur to an outsider: "Early in the morning is a better time of day to come out of a building than to go into it," and "a soft knock [on a door] is more conspicuous than a loud one," we learn in Chapter 7. Ten chapters later, we're taught the art of approaching witnesses and suspects who may be dangerous. To discourage the impression that he means harm, Smiley moves back from the house whose doorbell he has just rung so that he can be seen from inside. In conspicuous view are his hands, which are both empty and clear of his pockets, and his car, which is parked sideways to the house, "so that anyone indoors could see the car was empty." After entering the cabin of a launch, in the same chapter, he pulls the curtains to give himself more light, but, advisedly, the curtains on the seaward, rather than the landward, side, so that his movements can't be seen from the shore.

Colorful, original phrasing lends such developments conviction. Hamburg, which is near the Schleswig-Holstein lake where Smiley's investigations take him, has been "almost pounded to death by the thunder of its own prosperity." Earlier in the book, le Carré's quick sense of incongruity forms the following image of Ostrakova being hit by a car. Though she fears immediate death, the crazy flight of her legs caused by the car's impact implies parturition, an implication which works dramatically because the daughter she bore some twenty-one years before has put her at peril: "she reeled ... and as the car swerved to knock her down ... her feet ... were straight up in front of her face, and her bare thighs were parted as for childbirth." Le Carré doesn't need violence to stir his rhetorical powers. The next chapter selects and arranges the sounds and smells in a crowded London walk-up to describe urban squalor. The sentence following the description explains quietly but irresistibly the inability of those condemned to live in this squalor to stave it off:

He [Smiley] heard a dog howling and the morning news in German and the flushing of a communal lavatory. He heard a child screaming at its mother, then a slap and the father screaming at the child.... There was a smell of curry and cheap fat frying, and disinfectant. There was a smell of too many people with not enough money jammed into too little air.

The stylistic graces distinguishing *People* include dialogue, le Carré's keen ear for the tones and nuances of speech carrying over from *Schoolboy*. Speech continues to reveal human traits in the trilogy. The following reproduction of Willem, or William, Craven's voice takes hold of Craven himself, a native Estonian defending himself against Smiley's warning that his spending time with Miller a few hours before Miller's death could bring trouble. The reproduction, an amalgam of word choice, inflection, and syntax, no mere copy, carries the added benefit of putting Craven before us in a state of excitement, where the tearing away of his defenses leaves him most manifestly himself:

Vladi is of Beckie the godfather ...! Stella don't like him, so he must come here like
a thief, okay? He bring my Beckie toy, okay? Is a crime already ... ? Is a law, an
old man cannot bring to his godchild toys?

Characters exist vividly to us even when they're silent. Le Carré's
thematic incorporation of the epigraphs from *The Honorary Consul*
and *The Human Factor,* of the Greenean motif, in Chapter 1, of dental
decay, and of the simile in Chapter 8, "Smiley felt the excitement
seize his stomach like a nausea," with its Greene-like ring, all direct
our attention to Greene's influence. Reviewers of *The Human Factor*
said that Greene wrote his 1978 novel to correct the impression allegedly
created by le Carré, spy fiction's best seller, that the genre excludes
the private fears, hopes, and struggles of commonplace people. The
allusions to Greene in *People* show le Carré's sensitivity to this charge.
A commitment to humanity permeates the book. "His very air of
humanity" persuades Ostrakova to open her door to Smiley. "Just
half a boring unposted postcard" jammed into the toe of a gym shoe
leads to the overthrow of the mighty Karla. One person this overthrow
would please is Ostrakova, an obscure warehouse checker who becomes
important because Karla needs her to build a legend for Sasha.

Ostrakova and the bedraggled commonness she stands for have
mattered to Le Carré all along. She opens the novel, she remains
the central figure of the long first chapter (23 pages), and she exerts
imaginative force the rest of the way, even when she's out of view.
This centricity invokes Greene's famous argument (in "Some Notes
on Somerset Maugham") that important novelists write about people
who matter to God. Although le Carré's earlier books avoided religion,
People resonates metaphysically, and his next work, *The Little
Drummer Girl,* focuses on a religious war. Metaphysics infuse *People*
subtly. The book portrays no spiritual struggle, only the confrontation
of strategies. This sad shadow game defeats those who play it without
making the rest of us any richer, happier, or wiser. If the novel's
title implies an image of gloating, the joke is on us. We're all Smiley's
people. Yet Smiley's disregard of the cigarette lighter in the last chapter
assures us that we're not Karla's people. It also implies that we may
belong to God as well as to Smiley; Sasha, we recall, asked Smiley
if *he* was God. In her anguished wisdom, she could also be pointing
to spiritual truths beyond anyone's knowledge when she says that
Smiley stands for the forgiveness of the authorities. Smiley's workname
at the time, Herr Lachmann (from Modern German *lachen,* to laugh),
implies the derisive laughter God directs to the nagging
contentiousness of the superpowers.

And the divine forgiveness behind this laughter? It makes one think of Greene's belief that God forgives those who sin out of love because He knows and values what drives them. Another accent from Greene that recurs in the book has already been noted, that the unfavored and the rundown can suddenly assume importance. Le Carré communicates the importance of the neglected by making them central to the plot. He'll also register the action from their points of view— often at times when they see themselves as victims. Ostrakova becomes the central intelligence when her fears of being abducted chill into the knowledge that she's about to be hurled in the path of a speeding car. The confusion and dismay of Sasha reach us from *her* perspective as she tries vainly to sort out her thoughts. Le Carré takes us inside her madness, describing the religious fantasies, the sexual images, and the piercing ideas jostling each other in her mind. This congestion grips us. The tenderness with which she views people from her past, her shrewd insights into the staff members of the clinic, and the tantrums that seize her without warning portray the overthrow of genius which lacks the control of common sense.

Her weekly visitor, Grigoriev, though less desperate, shows how a decent man who has sinned feels when he finds his freedom slipping away. Maneuvered into a car by words at once reassuring and frightening, he lets himself be taken to the apartment where Smiley blackmails him. The grilling session gains in psychological urgency for reaching us, in part, from his badgered perspective. Initial outrage and hostility melt into resentment against Karla for exposing him to Smiley. Then his anger bursts into wild glee. Not only will he collaborate with his inquisitors; requiring their emotional support, he helps them more than they had hoped. Otto Leipzig, whose Spartan self-control led Smiley to Grigoriev, may be another whom distress ennobles. If Toby Esterhase is telling the truth, Leipzig loves only money. Yet his ability to resist his torturers and killers enables Smiley to find the torn postcard that he later exchanges for the cassettes confirming Karla's guilt. Leipzig is thus redeemed, like the mestizo in Greene's *Power and the Glory* (1940). His courage leads to Karla's capture. Perhaps le Carré is using it to say that every life, no matter how brutish or corrupt, can attain greatness. He may also be implying that the assertion of this greatness confirms the grace of a God, Who, like Greene's, makes pain and punishment the seedbeds of the miracles that sustain our guttering hopes for the triumph of justice, reason, and love.

Le Carré's commitment to the ordinary and the everyday anchors the book's metaphysics. Noteworthy among the book's virtues is its striking unity. *People* develops an important theme through characters whose rich inner lives express themselves in highly inventive concrete images. By showing that emotions in fiction come across best as a function of vivid sensory response, *People* also defines the link between narrative build and thematic unity. In 1982, T. J. Binyon, crime reviewer for *TLS*, referred to "the novel's gradual but irresistible acceleration in pace."[6] His praise wins our assent because of the novel's generosity of spirit, abundant assurance, and energy. Flowing beneath the book's tricky surfaces, these strengths impart bone and sinew. Unfortunately, the flow sometimes breaks. Le Carré will sometimes propel us into the midst of an unfolding drama without supplying the background we need to understand what's happening. The novel's important middle chapter (Chapter 15) drags because its central action, Connie Sachs's long account of Oleg Kirov and Otto Leipzig, concerns near strangers; we can't care about characters we've barely met. The scene frustrates the imaginative participation it invites by blocking access to it. But this fault can be excused. Though not trivial, it doesn't diminish the value of *People*, a work distinguished by the richness of language and vision expected of important serious fiction. H. C. Veit's pronouncement in *Library Journal*, that *Smiley's People* is a "complete winner, exciting, well-paced, and convincing," can't be refuted.[7] Or perhaps improved on; the novel frames its central issue with complexity, intelligence, and feeling, and it sustains a strong life line between that issue and the ordinariness that supplies its heartbeat.

Chapter Fourteen
No Curtain Calls, No Encores

The Little Drummer Girl features some of the staples of international intrigue fiction—surprising plot twists, a variety of settings, identity switches, and plenty of sex. Other influences sharpen this debt. A presence throughout is *As You Like It*. Just as Shakespeare's play leans on the conventions of pastoral, mocks them, and examines them, so does *Drummer Girl* both immerse itself in and reflect upon the spy novel. But whereas *As You Like It* is warm and ingratiating, le Carré's 1983 work finds life mad, miserable, and purposeless. Gelber calls the Middle East, source of the work's main issues, "easily the most tortured and morally ambiguous place in the world."[1] Both the Palestinians and the Israelis have accused each other of violating human rights in the Middle East; both demand that justice be exacted against the alleged savagery of their foes. As in *Smiley's People,* where murders planned in Russia are attempted in France, England, and West Germany, war in *Girl* flouts national boundaries. The novel's second paragraph mentions the destruction of Israeli life and property by Palestinian bombs in West Germany, Belgium, and Switzerland; later a PLO activist explodes in a car mined by Israeli agents near Munich, and his brother, the PLO's leading European operative, gets shot to death in the Black Forest. But even before his murder, the brother, Khalil, had part of a hand and a side of his face blown away by a package bomb sent to him in Beirut. One of his colleagues stationed near Beirut lost a leg fighting the Israelis. Like Smiley and Khalil, he shows that spying produces casualties, not victors. By using the whole world, it also invites chaos. Captain Tayeh's physical mutilation shows the devastation wrought on his psyche. Even the survivors of spying operations have been too broken and twisted by their ordeals to live fully.

In developing this tragedy, *Girl* mingles the familiar with the new. Although the authorial hand steering the action is familiar, it moves along new lines of force. These have been deliberately charted. Soon after the book's publication, le Carré said in *Newsweek* that he intended, in *Girl*, to forsake the snug private world of the Circus in favor of the immediate and the relevant: "I wanted to leave myself without him [i.e., Smiley] as a prop, and give myself the opportunity to write about the new generation, younger people, modern problems."[2] Besides using younger characters than heretofore to develop a contemporary problem, *Girl* also includes more sophisticated surveillance systems and a main character who's a woman. Women stay to the fore throughout. To describe the centricity of women in spying, the book both begins and ends with a pretty young woman delivering a time bomb to an unsuspecting older male victim. (Eric Ambler's *The Care of Time* [1981] also opens with the delivery of a time bomb.) The first bomb is planted in Bad Godesberg, near Bonn, a town of 65,000 "whose principle industry," quipped le Carré in *Small Town*, "having once been bottled water, is now diplomacy." Still a diplomatic enclave in May 1982, when *Girl* begins, Bad Godesberg tests le Carré's artistic skills anew. As Frederick Forsyth did in *The Day of the Jackal* (1971), le Carré moves confidently along the seam where fact and fiction meet. But, outstripping Forsyth, his movements occur in an ever-widening context of meaning that includes adult emotions.

The newness of his raw materials doesn't hamper le Carré. Perhaps he began *Girl* in West Germany, where he once lived and which he wrote about as recently as *People*, his last book, in order to root his new subject matter in friendly, familiar soil. The elegance and assurance of his writing confirms the wisdom of his choice. Another legacy of *People*, to go along with the West German setting, is the fictional technique governing most of *Girl*, especially the opening, where le Carré modifies his usual practice of oblique revelation in favor of explicitness. Meaning in the books from *War* to *Schoolboy* often stems from atmosphere, which comes to life through the accumulation of small, sometimes baffling details. These look like little more than shrewd realistic insights. But for the rich interwovenness of the prose, the documentary details and anecdotal tone of the opening sections of *Girl* offer less insight than they do information. The reference to inconsistency in the first paragraph establishes a human context for the ensuing violence, as le Carré pits "the high quality of the planning, as against the poor quality of the bomb" that will blow up the residence of the Israeli Labor Attache. Then a journalistic precision and respect for facts create a realistic foreground. Referring to "a melancholy Scandinavian Counselor," "a South American chargé," and "an envoy from the Ivory Coast," le Carré surveys different facets of Bad Godesberg's diplomatic set at the time of the big blast. A paragraph of extraordinarily perceptive details recounts the noise made by the blast and the blast's immediate effects on those nearby—how they were knocked down, how their skin stretched, and how the sight of chimney stacks parting company from roofs frightened them so much they couldn't scream.

More details show what those shocked by the blast were doing before their lives changed. Press accounts of the blast are included; in a deadpan, factual tone, le Carré recounts injuries and deaths. Control wavers only slightly in the passage leading up to the investigation of the blast by a team of West German and Israeli security experts. Like the occasional newspaper quotation, references to real-life places and institutions and a thumbnail biography or two enrich both the local panorama and the international ramifications of the plot. This cosmopolitanism also tones down the urgency and panic caused by the explosion, enabling le Carré to endow character and idea with the appropriate foreshadowing. A German investigator with a recent divorce and a "mistress twenty years his junior" betrays in le Carré a vague wish to shock. But little, if anything, is lost. If this rare false note doesn't strengthen the plot, neither does it smudge the lightness of tone the plot needs to avoid peaking too early.

This cool urbanity contrasts with the terror evoked at the start of *People,* where the shock of being questioned in Russian at a Paris bus stop panics Maria Ostrakova. Remember, the le Carré of *Girl* had to lay the groundplan for his plot without the help of his usual items and aids. The chic he displays in the early going serves him well. Besides imparting information, it clashes with the force and concentration of the closing scenes, reminding us of the great psychic distance the plot has covered. To sustain his off-handedness, le Carré will introduce confidences like the following from Chapter 2: "The night flight from Munich to Berlin, for the few who use it, is one of the great nostalgic journeys to be made in Europe." His references to the Orient Express, the Golden Arrow, and the Train Bleu in the next sentence flatter us by assuming our familiarity with between-wars European social history. What's more important, they win confidence for le Carré. Like the step-by-step objectivity conveyed by some of his descriptions, they weave a fabric of conviction that lowers our resistance to the deeper insights generated in the coming action.

While praising le Carré's tenth novel, the *Virginia Quarterly Review* singled out "the fervent and irreconcilable claims of both Israelis and Palestinians to the twice-promised land that means identity, sanctuary, and survival for both."[3] The Jordan's West Bank remains a source of tension and unrest. Rights and wrongs there are so knotted that even the coolest, best-informed observer can't smooth them. As a result, most investigations of the historical and moral aspects of the struggle tend to be highly biased. Pauline Kael has described the Sinai conflict as one "where no justice is possible" and where "decent, intelligent, disciplined people in both camps commit unspeakable barbarous acts."[4] The moral rectitude that condones cruelty motivates most of the partisans in the novel. Le Carré understands the irony of their posture. His fictional account of the struggle between two non-Christian nations throngs with images of Christianity, churches in particular. The Christian belief in the sanctity of individual life can't check the novel's drive toward its bloody climax or the mood of depression that follows. Actuated by patriotism, each side will do whatever it must to help its cause.

Each side will also disown motives of anger or revenge. Though Arab and Israeli activists claim to represent justice in its clash with terrorism, neither side interprets its cause in ethnic or personal terms. Thus one Israeli spy calls the young Arab he plans to abduct "a likeable, popular person," while another describes the Arab as "a fine boy" who would make a fine son-in-law. But the esteem the two Israelis share for the Arab doesn't stop them from capturing, torturing, and then killing him. People who sacrifice themselves to causes won't blink at sacrificing others. The Israeli spy chief who kidnaps Salim sees in him "a lot of good looks, a lot of talent, a lot of unused capacity." His willingness to sacrifice these gifts to an operational necessity describes the defeat of both heart and conscience. Such sacrifices, all the worse for parading as loyalty and patriotism, blunt the humanity of victory. Later, Charlie, the English actress of twenty-six whom the Israelis infiltrate into a Palestinian commando camp, learns that she will find the militants there *"an easy people to love."* The warning she's also served, to stifle any regret for subverting these lovable people, again yokes the Israelis to denial and death. How could helping them enhance Charlie? Defeat awaits any participant in a cause which has forsaken its human core; the policy that excludes people from its balance sheets has taken a giant step toward the void.

This negation also pollutes the Arab cause. The Arabs' insistence that their war against Zionism hasn't made them anti-Semitic is fatuous. Anti-Semitism may well be a Christian invention, as several Arab militants say. But coming from people pledged to destroy Israel, the reminder rings hollow.[5] Neither are we impressed by the remark of an Arab guerrilla, whom le Carré later calls "a kind man," that he can respect and honor the foe he's pledged to destroy. The guerrilla is talking about battle strategy, not personal worth. The respect and honor he extends serves as a warning to himself not to underrate the enemy. The enemy is always a target, not a person. Honoring and respecting him will bring him more readily into the crosshairs of one's gunsights. Both sides in the Sinai clash talk about saving, rather than taking, life. But they'll only put by their weapons if their demands are first met. Anchoring these demands in patriotic slogans, historical precedents, and holy writ, they're deaf to reason.

This madness can only worsen, as James Wolcott's description of the novel as "a ... panoramic view of strife and deprivation" implies.[6] The images of brutality that convey this grief culminate in the shooting death of an Arab militant in Chapter 26. As if death could be embellished or improved upon, rather than being absolute, the militant's killer lunges "straight forward" with "arms at full stretch" while squeezing off round after fatal round into his victim's face. The incongruity created by le Carré's first reporting this attack in an adverbial phrase tallies with the attacker's efforts to shrink the distance between him and his victim. These efforts, so consistent with the rules of armed combat but so remote from everyday life, recall the violence described in the earlier chapters. Some months after the novel's publication, le Carré, writing for the [London] *Observer Review,* called "the systematic devastation inflicted on the camps of South Lebanon" by Israeli troops "a horror story of barely imaginable dimensions."[7] No mere intellectual goad, this outrage shook him deeply. The strong sense of Palestinian family unity, loyalty, and pride described in the next installment of his two-part *Observer Review* article fuels his claim, voiced in the novel's Foreword, that his visit to South Lebanon showed him "the Palestinian heart."[8]

More of the history that has tormented this heart needs to be filled in. Seeing themselves as dispossessed, the Palestinians can cite many injustices they have suffered. They can also tell why they've been singled out for grief. To compensate for the Holocaust, a source of guilt to all non-Jewish Europeans, Great Britain gave Palestine to Israel. This 1948 act, many Arabs have complained, both westernized the East and robbed many Jordanians, Syrians, Palestinians, and Lebanese of their homelands. The Palestine Liberation Organization (the PLO) formed in 1964 when Gaza and the Jordan's West Bank still belonged to the Arabs. Arabian attempts to recover these territories have met severe reprisals—like the bombing of Palestinian camps and the bulldozing of Palestinian homes. More butchery has followed. Since 1968, Arab militants in Europe have hijacked, commandeered, and destroyed over forty airplanes, usually targeting those belonging to Israel's El Al Airlines. Then the branch of the PLO calling itself Black September massacred eleven Israeli athletes at the 1972 Olympics in Munich.[9] The early 1980s saw the PLO taking their grievances to places like Antwerp, Zurich, and Düsseldorf, where they killed prominent Israelis to repay what they saw as Zionist atrocities.

They have never basked in this revenge. The plot of *Girl* creates ironies and shifts in point of view that portray the Palestinians mostly as underdogs. History validates this portrayal. In 1981, Chapman Pincher called Mossad, Israel's intelligence branch (which the novel avoids mentioning by name, as it does the PLO), "arguably the best-informed Secret Service in the Western world."[10] Le Carré wouldn't quarrel with this verdict. Though he shows rivalries and personality clashes subverting Mossad's morale, he also portrays the skill with which Mossad uses its hardware, research facilities, and specialists. Discipline and control govern all operations. Acting on the maxim, "If you want to catch a lion, you must first tether the goat," Israeli spies twice resist capturing Arab activists whose freedom can lure bigger game out into the open. This patience and self-restraint distinguish Marty Kurtz, mastermind of the operation around which the novel is built. Evoking George Smiley's praise of Miss Ailsa Brimley's grip in the face of apparent emergency in *Murder,* Kurtz says, "There is nothing so hard in war ... as the heroic feat of holding back." He and his colleagues also practice great caution and thoroughness when they do move forward. Before abducting Salim, for instance, they select an abduction site, devise fallbacks, and consult his medical record to determine his tolerance to the drugs they have in mind for him. During his confinement, they also use electronic and optical devices, forged photographs, and taped simulations of screams, funeral music, and gunfire to win his cooperation.

The same cost, technical sophistication, and imagination go into the recruiting and the running of Charlie, the English actress who pretends to be Salim/Michel's lover in order to penetrate PLO security. Mossad flies the members of Charlie's acting company to Greece and then gives them an expense-free vacation so that she can meet her would-be recruiter. Mossad has wasted nothing, having handpicked Gadi Becker to recruit her and then briefed him on her personal history. A point Becker may refer to casually in conversation, like Charlie's driving, can pertain to a skill his chiefs have researched, discussed, and planned to profit from. Later, she will drive a car containing 200 pounds of Russian TNT from Thessalonika in Greece through Yugoslavia into Austria, some 800 miles. To protect her during her various assignments, Israeli forgery experts not only write letters that copy both her writing style and her handwriting; they also dent the pencils that allegedly wrote these letters with teethmarks like the ones found in her purse and flat.

II

Until the publication of *The Little Drummer Girl*, most of le Carré's women had less substance than his men. Though beguiling, Connie Sachs, Mother Russia of the Karla books, survives in our minds as a voice and a memory. Our interest in Liese, or Lizzie, Worth of *Schoolboy* stems more from Jerry Westerby's strong emotional response to her than from anything intrinsic. The le Carré of *Girl* changes both his technique of portraying women and his outlook on them. These shifts show in the questions he asks. Is woman a sexual creature or a rational, sensitive human being? Does she exist to serve, divert, or please men? Charlie's heroics in the novel reveal a new awareness in le Carré of woman's capabilities. Yes, Charlie's sexual charms distract the PLO's chief European operative long enough for Mossad to kill him. But her self-presence enchants the PLO chief as much as her body does. And the car full of explosives she drives 800 miles is then driven from its pickup point in Graz by another woman in her twenties, perhaps the planter of the time bomb in Bad Godesberg. These developments show that women aren't ciphers, domestic drudges, or sexual toys to le Carré. He tries in *Girl* to show what women are like, how they act in crises, and how their actions touch others. Modern history, for him, takes shape and color from the energies of women. Women are capable, reliable, and resourceful, not merely decorative. Yet they're also figures of poetry and romance, connected to protectiveness, love, and art. Their heart knowledge actuates the waves of feeling permeating *Girl*. Rating character over plot, the novel focuses on people rather than emblems, archetypes, ideologies, and plot twists. And the primacy of the female principle constitutes its human center.

Charlie (no last name given), the main character and the emotional center of the book, has stirred a variety of critical responses. Binyon described her as "a red-haired English actress, a bundle of psychological hang-ups and inchoate left-wing sympathies." Peter S. Prescott, finding more purpose in her, calls her "a loyal girl looking for a place to invest her loyalties." Wolcott sees any self-investment she will make squandered on unappreciative, exploitative men: "She really serves as . . . a plaything (a pawn, a baited hook) of those virile gods" who direct her activities. Charlie's mercurial, many-sided personality lends credibility to all these views of her. But perhaps none equals in penetration Pauline Kael's look at her, or, rather, Diane Keaton's characterization of her, in George Ray Hill's 1984 film version of the book. Agreeing in spirit with Prescott, Kael calls Charlie "a woman without a clear sense of identity" who is "eager for a cause" that will earn her the "involvement and approval" she needs to feel complete. Kael's *New Yorker* analysis of Charlie continues to sound psychic depths:

Charlie is emotionally hungry. Smart and brazenly attractive, she's so miserably starved there's something wolfish about her. At the same time, she's trying to be tough— she's trying not to let herself be kidded. She's a jangled, poignant mess.[11]

The conflict created by Charlie's bipolar urges to give and to hold back finds a synthesis in her acting. The applause of an audience gives her the approval she longs for but has denied herself. The theater also supplies an outlet for her emotions together with the protective interface of a fictional role. She's not wholly on her own. The emotions she indulges are monitored by her script and her director. Regardless of their supposed frenzy, her revels are both prepackaged and contained. This containment furnishes, as well, a principle of male authority she lacked in the home. Her nostalgia for the horses and ponies she rode as a girl points up her need for fatherly control (since Freud's famous study of Hans, writers of fiction have been using the horse to symbolize the powerful father). So angry has she been at her suburban stockbroker father for denying her this leadership that, for years, she has been saying that he died in prison after being sentenced for embezzlement.

Her anger has found other outlets, too. Though expelled from school for sexual promiscuity, she has been insisting that the headmistress, truckling to parents who'd object to their daughters' living alongside the child of a convicted criminal, sent her home. Her homecoming brought more grief. Instead of being punished, as she deserved, she was forgiven. This denial of justice deepened her anger against her parents. But her anger has recoiled upon her. To reject one's origins is to reject one's self. The role-playing her acting demands has sped this flight from selfhood. The sex and drugs she indulges as protests against suburban respectability have only heightened this desperation. Nor has her immersion in radical politics or her kinship with her fellow actors provided effective family or religion substitutes. Nobody with a positive self-image would defer to a lout like Alastair, her hard-drinking, sadistic lover. Her deference proves that she doesn't cherish much in her life. But it also reminds us slyly that progress usually comes from the have-not; risking less, the have-not will act more recklessly than the have.

But fear of the unknown will also encourage the have-not to settle. A survivor, the deprived person tends to shrink from the challenge posed by extending limits. Charlie can't help Mossad unless she's handled properly. Her impressionability, rebelliousness, and political idealism help her identify with Bernard Shaw's Joan of Arc, the role she's playing when Gadi Becker, her recruiter, trainer, and controller, first sees her. But these qualities haven't silenced the guilt that both accompanies and enforces her self-image as a have-not. Mossad has studied this guilt in order to trade on it. Knowing that she lacks the ballast and nurture connected with an older loving male, Mossad rushes in to fill the void. Encouraging its identification with the strong Hebraic father, it becomes the patriarch which Charlie will try to please to compensate for having rejected her natural father. But it wouldn't have martyred her to male authority if it hadn't first seen merit in her. If she's self-defeating, she's also loyal, dependable, and loving. Gadi Becker trusts her high standards—her professional pride and integrity—to see her through the ordeal of masquerading as a PLO guerrilla.

This ordeal reaches its bloody climax in West Germany's Black Forest, a deliberate contrast to the lovely Forest of Arden, setting of Shakespeare's *As You Like It*, a work Charlie looks forward to playing in and one she discusses in an early conversation with Becker. Becker, who already knows her acting history, says of Rosalind, the play's heroine and the role Charlie plans to act, "She is so many people under one hat.... One has the impression of a person occupied by a whole regiment of conflicting characters. She is good, she is wise, she is forfeit somehow, she sees too much, she has even a sense of social duty." If Charlie knew that she was being auditioned, she might suspect that the part she had been tipped to play for Mossad demands this same spread of attributes. Her role in the theater of the real will also require Rosalind's ability to assess quickly the worth of a situation or a person. Infusing this rare gift is a self-detachment akin to that of a mystic; love can fade ("Was is not is" [III, iv, 32]) and/or bring out the worst in us. Yet the absence of social organization, which rests on a bedrock of trust, if not love, turns life into a jungle. And despite its pitfalls, love remains life's greatest gift. Rosalind acts wisely in marrying unripe Oliver, even though he's not her equal. Passing alone through Jaques's seven ages of man is dreary work. Phoebe does well to marry Silvius, too. Silvius loves her, and, as is noted, her inability to sell in all markets makes him a bargain worthy of her love.

Charlie also learns the value of commitment. But she lacks the rosy prospects awaiting Shakespeare's comic heroines. Along with having embraced a tainted cause, she has learned the uses of secrecy, subterfuge, and that infamous underminer of selfhood, double agency. She asks herself in Chapter 23, "Was the actress in her dead at last? Or was she so reconciled with the theater of the real that the difference between life and art had disappeared?" Her confusion shows that the longer a mask is worn, the harder it is to know the face behind it; also, to remove it. Gadi Becker knows all the Palestinian grievances against Israel, and he can support them with statistics, dates, and names. His recitation of them to Charlie, besides conveying information, reflects insight into Arabian history, rhetoric, and family values. The moral passion with which he disclaims his enemies' brief against Israel also shows how easy it is for a spy to slip into double agency. Correctly applied, the slightest pressure could turn most agents, whose loyalty hinges on a belief in the integrity of their friends' cause.

An imaginative, impulsive person whose identity is as fragile as Charlie's needs close watching; the same traits in her that recommend her as a spy also threaten to make her a liability. In the persona of her supposed Palestinian lover, Becker persuades her to drive the Mercedes containing Russian TNT from Thessalonika to Graz. The speed with which he puts on and takes off his mask, switching loyalties and identities, wears her out. When she calls him Michel, she half believes that he *is* Michel. This reaction is intended. Becker's curriculum in indoctrination and field work includes confusing her. If she wants to survive, let alone carry out her mission, she'll have to adapt to the unforeseen both quickly and wholeheartedly, reacting from sources deep within herself. Thus he speaks to her in two voices and from two selves. He shifts scenarios and settings. Purposes will suddenly merge or clash in the shift. And personal motives may mar the bleak purity of operational ones. As Becker and Charlie spend more time together, the fiction they're living grows more complex; identities fragment and fuse; gesture and nuance both subvert and support what is spoken, written, and prearranged.

In his review for Paris's *Magazine littéraire,* Jean Rosenthal said that *Girl* reminds him of a Charlie Chaplin film.[12] No doubt the name of the novel's heroine clinched the identification for Rosenthal. Known only as Charlie, this underdog heroine follows Chaplin's immortal little tramp in making us laugh and cry at the same time. Her efforts also enact the truth that ordinary people can impress us more than the high and the mighty. Even though she calls herself a traitor and a whore, she gropes toward the decent and the true. She brings both talent and commitment to her acting career. She feels strongly enough about issues like apartheid and nuclear war to go to jail for her beliefs. She shows great loyalty to the members of the acting troupe she has used to replace her rejected family of origin. Mossad asks her to rechannel these commitments. The plot concerns her participation in an undercover military operation shaped to the conventions of the stage. Appropriately, many of the book's key scenes take place in theaters—backstage, in darkened auditoriums, in dressing rooms, or in the wings during production. Her training for her role, consisting of both briefings and rehearsals, prepares her for the acting lesson of her life. Because mistakes in the theater of terror can be fatal, she needs all the training she can get. She sees as never before how timing, gesture, and lighting can change the emotional tone of an encounter. A simple act like reaching for a cigarette becomes a feat of bravery when performed under the pressure that spies and urban guerrillas face each day.

To prepare her, Becker writes, stages, and directs her script, besides acting in it. He also demonstrates the power of staging. After thrilling her with a piece of reality staged as theater—the Parthenon under a red half moon—he voices Brecht's belief that drama must promote political action. His remark will color Charlie's coming performance. She's asked to play "the biggest part you have ever had in your life, the most demanding, the most difficult, surely the most dangerous, and surely the most important." The theater of the real poses such a dire challenge because it interweaves life and art so unpredictably. Dramatic pacing has infused it with a poetic truth so urgent that the heart can't withhold belief. Charlie is not being asked to act a part. She must embody Konstantin Stanislavski's ideal to the point where she's obsessed with the rightness of the Palestinian cause; she must also love her paymasters' enemies. The fiction must overtake reality. And indeed it does. She wears clothes she had never worn before; she changes her hair color and style; the different passports she carries include a change of both name and national identity. These outward changes have stirred inner ones, as was intended by her chiefs. Mossad's insistence that she stay with her script includes condoning any impromptu violence the script calls upon her to perform.

Moral values have disappeared. Not only does one set of activists denounce as terrorism acts their opponents call patriotic. Each side also claims to respect its opponent; each can argue its opponent's case brilliantly. Becker knows the articles of Islam together with Arabic customs and traditions; in his role of Michel, he compares the Arabs of the early 1980s to the European Jews before the Holocaust; one of his descriptions of an Arab massacre recalls the 1941/42 Nazi devastation of Jews at Babi Yar in the Ukraine. This blurring of moral distinctions has complicated Charlie's script. The revels are no longer contained; to switch artistic metaphors, the picture has splintered the frame. Values and meanings Charlie had built her earlier life around no longer apply. She has lost all her defining marks; also, both the safeguards and guidelines she had relied upon have been jerked away.

Standing alone creates new pressures for this former member of the establishment of rebellion. Besides terrifying her, the theater of terror brings her new attention and prominence. She must perform under a spotlight. "You are suddenly like Rome, Charlie. . . . All roads lead to you," says an urban guerrilla, confirming her centricity in a drama that has overtaken life. Here is truly confirmation of Marianne Moore's statement in "Poetry" about "imaginary gardens with real toads in them." Never had her craving for approval won her such a large, rapt audience. But never had she felt so cut off. The close scrutiny of so many people deepens her alienation. During her stay at the Palestinian commando camp, her survival depends on her forgetting that she's playing a role; she must sink herself in the world of the rebels. And she *does* feel real grief and weep real tears when she hears of the death of Michel/Salim, her pretended Arabian lover. She playacts with such genius that one of her Israeli controllers, seeing her after her ordeal at the commando camp, fears that she has gone over to the enemy. His fear attests to her brilliance. Besides performing her role naturally and spontaneously, she has also been plucking up the self-detachment to judge her performance and change it in line with new developments.

Inevitably, the demands of moving in and out of her role in an atmosphere of stress and suffering break her down. "Citizen of Nowheresville, born yesterday," she calls herself near the close. The theater of terror ends her acting career. Knowing grief first hand has exposed the sham and artifice of the emotions purveyed by the commercial stage. Gainsaying tragedy, she can only manage light comic roles. But the irrelevance of comedy soon depresses her. She misses her cues, flubs her lines, and ignores her fellow players. She has lost more, though, than her occupation. The upshot of her participation in the theater of terror is the loss of self. Just before the shooting of Khalil, the Palestinian intelligence chief, by Gadi Becker, she tells the marked-out man that she has been working for the Israelis. Her confession neither absolves nor saves her. The truth doesn't set the spy free. It prints in her memory the face of her lover-confessor ablaze with gunfire. Khalil's gently touching her after hearing her confession, "apparently to make sure that she was real," won't ease her trauma. Her only escape from guilt consists of crawling beneath it, an act that negates all values, including that of selfhood.

Charlie's self-negation had begun before she had suspected it. Part Two of *Girl* opens in London three weeks after her fictional lover, Michel/Salim, the younger brother of Khalil, blows up near Munich in the Mercedes hiding the TNT she had driven into Europe. The time of the year is autumn, le Carré's favorite fictional season, with its associations with inertia and the waning of time, hope, and energy. Affecting the smugness of the insider, Charlie thinks about her feat of walking "through the looking glass" from safety to terror; her privileged glimpse of devastation makes her patronize "the innocents around her." This snobbery is ill judged. She's no shrewd insider at all. Just when she thinks she has reached the end of the line in conspiracy and suffering, she finds new limits. London looks mean, nasty, and corrupt. She ignores her former friends and colleagues. Her failure to boost her sagging spirits with sex shows how much the intense, immoral world of spies has changed her. "I am in shock; I am an obsessive, solitary mourner without a friend to turn to," she says to herself after leaving Alastair.

Then the harassment begins. The clamps keep tightening on her, pressure coming from the British secret service, which has learned of her activities. Her hairdresser and her agent both ask her to stay away; her favorite restaurant closes after a police search and interrogation; the police arrest and beat up Alastair; her flat is ransacked. These threats to her safety force her to seek help from her supposed friends, the PLO. But they only heap on more hardship. Of their commando camp near Beirut, she says, "It was the end of the line. It was the worst place of all her lives this far." Again, she'll be proved wrong. Recalling the heroines of Sean O'Casey's tenement tragedies, her pain sharpens; she's forced to dive deeper into the black hole of misery. Hewing to the metaphor of the stage that unifies the action, le Carré says of her, just before she takes a booby trap to an Israeli dignitary, "It was her most fraught wait ever, and her longest; a first night to end first nights." The phrase used later in the chapter, which refers to an act she performed just hours before, "when she was too young to know any better," spells out her progressive immersion in the moral quagmire of spying. That the immersion has wiped out her identity shows in the offers of citizenship given her by both the Israelis and the Palestinians. Her reward for performing brilliantly in the theater of the real is rebirth into the nullity of the exile. Such a rebirth means death. It also comments on her degradation. She has caved in both morally and emotionally. The daze she wanders around in after Khalil's death proves that she'd never have had the strength to remake herself in a strange land among strangers. In either Israel or one of the Arab states, she'd survive more as a monument than a person, a relic that must be tended to rather than a free, active being.

Her defeat helps make *Girl* le Carré's grimmest book. Smiley couldn't savor his victories because he had lived with defeat for so long that it was the only reality he trusted. Charlie loses everything. Unknowingly, she created herself in order to destroy herself. "I'm English, German, Israeli, and Arab," she notes of her new omniform self in Chapter 13. This growth or fragmentation will continue as more and more roads in the land of conspiracy lead to her. A figure of great cunning and courage, she attains the status of a visionary while in motion. She transcends ordinary finite limits (including the psychological boundaries of self) in order to live more intensely. She also achieves the Brechtian goal of stimulating political action. As has been seen, though, her achievements defeat her while they enhance her. She has gone beyond Pirandello, perhaps modern drama's boldest innovator, to revolutionize the relationship between audience and script and between player and critic. Appropriately, the drama she enacts begins in Greece, the birthplace of western theater. Continuing to reverberate in her psyche after the curtain falls, it follows her to

England; she gets distracted during a performance, loses track of the trite, contrived script, and has to be taken from the stage. Her downfall was carefully foreshadowed. The psychic cramp that has always hobbled her shows in her habit of calling people by their short names: Helga is Helg, Marty, Mart, and Alastair, Al. Yet the Arabian lover she never embraced but came to love after his death always remains Michel.

This love, like most others a product of the imagination and the moral will, keeps her alive. In order to convey its force to others, she has to live it. Michel must be her great love; his cause, her ruling passion; his death, her tragedy. So closely is she watched by her Palestinian controllers, some of whom knew him, that her role is her only protection and support. Love for her, as with most other people, grows out of need. But it carries an indwelling danger. Though sad, her last words in the book, lacking an objective focus, "I'm dead, Jose. You shot me, don't you remember?" don't shock us. She has fed on illusions for so long that she believes herself a corpse. This decline makes the rest of us, whose lives are also ruled by illusions, wonder if we're living at full stretch.

The man she's talking to is Becker, whom she last saw when he murdered her lover of minutes before, Khalil. Like her, this legendary Sabra warrior performs brilliantly throughout; like her, too, he feels whipped and woebegone at mission's end. His depression obeys rigorous dramatic logic. Jose, Charlie's name for him, is short for Joseph, the name she and her colleagues gave him when they discovered him on a Mykonos beach. Though his business card identifies him as Peter Richtoven, Charlie keeps calling him Jose. And Jose, or Joseph, is also what his colleagues call him in her presence. It's as if an intelligence officer uses so many names in his work that new ones fasten onto him unbidden. As has been seen, multinymity signals a weak hold on life in le Carré. The person with many names lacks the focus to cultivate a solid, abiding identity; his many names represent a flight from self.

What's more, Charlie's calling Becker Jose on the book's last page shows that he has never told her his name. But his omission may have helped her more than hurt her. Up to now, he has only known her operationally, and those in charge of the operation have wanted him to remain Joseph to her. His joining her in England has nothing to do with work. He's actuated from within rather than by a brief. The personal element makes itself felt straightaway. When he and Charlie leave the theater together, only his firm grip on her keeps her from falling. His walking with her "awkwardly along the pavement" in the book's last sentence, "though the town was strange to them," constitutes an authorial masterstroke. How well the foundering couple will relate, how long the relation will last, and what effect Becker's withholding his name (and perhaps his true self?) will color their chances are all questions that can't be answered. But le Carré invites them. Becker and Charlie are "locked together," however unsure their steps may be. Happiness may not await them, but neither has the happiness of any other couple ever been guaranteed. We shouldn't despair of their chances. If there's no loyalty without betrayal, as Ann Smiley said, then people like them, having stepped through the looking glass of ordinary morality, can build a future on pain and loss.

Becker feels this need as keenly as Charlie does. He had answered her wild attempts to corner him with immaculate poise and capework. Now he feels deprived. His chief, Marty Kurtz, has denied him the credit he deserves in the Khalil operation. His business prospects are so bad that he faces bankruptcy. His marriage has cracked. The novel he starts to write goes unfinished (like that of another loser, Aldo Cassidy, in *Lover*). His finding happiness with Charlie would relieve the sting caused by these setbacks. Before meeting her in Mykonos, he made sure that she saw him in the auditoriums of the Nottingham and York theaters where she performed Shaw's Joan of Arc. His having followed her to Mykonos persuades her to go with him to Thessalonika. This offer was carefully timed. While Michel, or Salim (or Yanuka), is being held prisoner by Israeli Intelligence, Becker is fabricating a blazing love affair for him and Charlie. He makes the most of his opportunity. Besides briefing Charlie, he's both impersonating Michel and leaving footprints of Michel's supposed visit with her to Athens and Thessalonika. He directs the scenario as he creates it; he tells her to act out the scene rather than narrating it; he makes her call him Michel. He plays his own role so well that for one moment in Chapter 8 he makes her wonder if he's not envying Michel the time and intimacy hotel records say that Michel enjoyed with her. In Chapter 19, he has sex with her, setting aside the script—but with the result of helping the operation. Perhaps his motives here are operational, as well. Casualties in the theater of terror don't always get another chance.

Some casualties are inflicted by one's own people. Kurtz, for instance, tells British security that Charlie, a British subject, was implicated in the Munich car bombing that killed two Arab militants.

His reason? He knows that British security will investigate his story. As has been seen, such investigations move forward quickly and mercilessly; Charlie's friends, neighbors, and business associates are threatened, and her flat is turned inside out. The incriminating letters found there were written by Mossad and planted with the help of Becker. By sending the special branch to their hiding place, Kurtz isn't betraying her so much as heightening the drama she's performing in. This added fillip tests her grip along with her acting skills. Mossad would prefer that she crack in London rather than in Beirut or Sidon, where she'll be facing much heavier pressure.

Pressure badgers everybody connected with spying, even Marty Kurtz, "a kind of human ultimatum" who knows how to apply and withstand it. As soon as he shows up in Bad Godesberg to investigate the suitcase bombing, he takes charge, his sheer presence magnetizing the others. His magnetism holds. Acting decisively and boldly, he explores possibilities beyond the investigative skills of the West Germans. He uses different worknames and speaks different languages as he moves about Europe and the Near East. And he never moves without a reason—or a plan. He will be abrupt or conciliatory. Barrelchested and jovial, he will play the soothing, authoritative father with Charlie, calling her "dear" and hugging her. Yet this "broadheaded, bustling veteran of every battle since Thermopylae" also faces deadlines; he, too, is a functionary. Working for a man who has accused him of spending too much money, flouting too many orders, and getting too few results, he fears for his job. He's also frightened that his angry chief will give in to demands from above that Israel's quarrels with the PLO be resolved in open war. Though war is never declared, it might have been, judging from the effects of the Khalil operation upon Kurtz. He appears a loser, not a winner, when he returns to Israel. His depression is inevitable; spying is as destructive in *Girl* as it was in the Karla trilogy. Intelligence missions bring grief. Charlie is disoriented. Becker can't find his bearings in Jerusalem or Berlin. Recalling the lieutenant at the end of Greene's *The Power and the Glory* (1940), Kurtz's success has drained and wrung him: "His body seemed to shrink to half its size, his Slav eyes lost all their sparkle, he looked his age, whatever that was, at last." He has little incentive to lift his drooping spirits. Any pep and vim he recovers he'll direct to his ongoing quarrel with his chief.

III

Critics have taken the hint supplied by Kurtz's name to look for Conradian elements in *Girl*. Wolcott calls the work "a meditative adventure saga in the tradition of Joseph Conrad.... A concealed bomb is the book's heart of darkness."[13] Like Conrad, the le Carré of *The Little Drummer Girl* presents heroic characters ironically; their heroism recoils upon them. Le Carré also conveys their defeat in a narrative mode that is emotionally fragmented, obliquely rich, and subtle in the manner of Conrad. The legacy of Graham Greene, another intrigue writer strongly influenced by Conrad, expresses itself more quietly than in *People* but in a way consistent with Greene's sense of humor. An inn in Graz is called The Carpenter's Arms, after a joke in Greene's *Confidential Agent* (1939); several weeks later, Charlie's Alastair gets pounded by some policemen as "hard as bloody Brighton rock." Perhaps more conspicuous in the novel than Greene is Alfred Hitchcock. *North by Northwest*, Hitchcock's 1959 movie starring Gary Grant and Eva-Marie Saint, asks whether government security agencies can press into service innocent nationals; in democracies in particular, we're reminded, everybody takes responsibility for the commonwealth. *Girl* carries the question a step further. Nations have become so intertwined by alliances and treaties that partisanship transcends frontiers. The security network that enlists Charlie belongs to a nation whose ties to her own are moral and historical as well as political and economic.

Le Carré's irony doesn't sentimentalize or mock her; rather, it shows how she copes, owning up to pain without losing her humanity. Some of the others she meets during her trail sharpen the issues she's trying to muddle through. Astrid Berger, the Palestinian guerrilla from Germany who calls herself Helga, shows how spying dwindles souls. When she's not ogling and touching Charlie, she's threatening to kill her. This enemy of civilized process also enjoys cultural artifacts, particularly cathedrals and religious statues. Later, she plots the death of an Israeli dignitary friendly to the Palestinians. Another menace to Charlie who grips our imaginations is Deputy Commander Picton, the English security officer who unleashes his aides on her after learning of her part in the Munich car bombing. Picton has a Dickensian gusto that le Carré will sometimes attempt with minor characters. He comes before us with little authorial intervention. Italicized by mannerisms and crotchets natural to someone of his rank, his speech is a piece of brilliant mimicry.

Khalil, too, has the personal force to justify the great lengths Mossad goes to stop him. A distinguishing mark is his elusiveness. It has been said that he never sleeps in the same bed two nights running, and Mossad doesn't know what he looks like, having no picture of him in their files. But he's a man as well as an ace in self-protection. Though he loves his martyr-brother Michel, he also views him as a sexual rival. Thus he's peeved by Charlie's love for him. He calls him "a silly little boy, too much with women and ideas and cars," and one of the reasons he takes Charlie to bed is to show her that he's a better lover. The intended victim of the homemade bomb he builds, Professor Minkel of the Hebrew University in Jerusalem, also knows self-division. The topic of his University of Freiburg lecture is the integrity of Palestinian rights. He believes that Jewish self-realization hinges on the Israelis giving the Palestinians more power in Gaza and the West Bank.

Such riveting characters create excellent scenes, one of which occurs when Kurtz and his chief aide, Shimon Litvak, visit the London office of Ned Quilley, a theatrical agent. Litvak and Kurtz are masquerading as American producers who want Charlie for the touring repertory group they're forming in the United States. Their impeccable timing and teamwork control the interview perfectly. So fooled by them is Quilley that he never imagines that their visit to him was carefully scripted and rehearsed. Le Carré also defines the theater of the real broadly enough to include in it passages resembling ethnic vaudeville turns. For instance, one side of an important phone conversation between Mossad high-rankers begins, "Nathan, here is Harry. Hi. How is your wife? Great, and give her mine." The same disguised sense of purpose governs the interview with Ned Quilley. Claiming that the conservative midwestern backers of their theater group might balk at Charlie's political radicalism, Kurtz and Litvak press Quilley for information about the marches, rallies, and demonstrations she has taken part in. They're asking him to supply information they already have on record for two reasons. First, the snag they create will make the transaction look more natural to Quilley. Were it to go too smoothly, he might grow suspicious; any prize won too easily invites contempt. Next, having heard of Quilley's fondness for drink, his visitors know that he'll reach for the bottle if upset. The drinks he downs at lunch do quiet his nerves. They also make him drowsy. Once back in the office, he falls asleep. Kurtz and Litvak then ransack his records for Charlie's file. The file they never have to return; they're not theatrical producers and thus can't be traced through trade publications. Nor can Quilley moan about being robbed, lest his hearers infer that alcohol has done him in again.

The scene involving him and the two Israeli spies takes its place in a careful orchestration. For the sake of symmetry, Part One begins and ends with an explosion. The two-part structure and the plot that centers on the apprehension of two dangerous brothers who live apart both carry forward from *Schoolboy*. But little in Part One, prosaically called "The Preparation," identifies the goal referred to in the title of Part Two, "The Prize." Although Kurtz's refusal to capture Michel/ Salim in Munich shows that his freedom can help the Israelis snare bigger game, purposes remain dark. Light comes in the book's middle chapter. Chapter Fourteen takes place in Munich, where Michel first appeared and where, we recall, Arabian militants slew eleven Israeli athletes during the 1972 Olympics. Munich is also where Charlie gets her only glimpse of the real-life Michel, her supposed lover whose cause she has already been making her own. Mossad knows that her training isn't complete till she loves Michel. Thus they show her his naked beauty, which wrenches her heart all the more for being broken, bent, and violated by drugs. Ironically, she's in the company of others while looking for the only time at the man with whom she allegedly shared the utmost of intimacies. The moment enlarges her understanding of theater. Having already fallen in love with Becker, she now sees the man he has been impersonating while winning her heart. The slap in the face with which Becker answers her insult, an expression of her confusion over the art-life interplay, signals the start of her new life. Moments later, she perceives herself as "a proven soldier now, a veteran." The replica of Michel has produced the original. Art threatens to outpace reality. She also sees herself recreated in the letters she allegedly wrote to Michel during the blazing early weeks of their romance.

So convincing are these simulations that the fiction they help create seems more solid to her than her previous flesh-and-blood reality. She takes her new self to England at chapter's end. Yet, following his penchant for discontinuity, le Carré cuts away from her, omitting her from the important next chapter. He doesn't only leave her out of Chapter 15. Refraining from mentioning her, he turns his attention to another female spy, the Dutch driver of the explosives-laden car slated for delivery to the PLO. This denial of narrative closure bodes ill for Charlie. The Dutch woman drives the same Mercedes brought up to Austria from Greece; she's about Charlie's age; again like Charlie, she's not a citizen of either of the warring nations. Has she replaced

Charlie in the plot? we wonder. The "stage of half-reality" in which Charlie returns to view in Chapter 16 only deepens our fears for her.

These fears show that le Carré deserves—and repays—the close attention given to serious mainstream novelists. His people lead complex lives in complex, dangerous settings. He'll downgrade a climax he has been preparing for to create the flow of new life. He'll also shift emphasis, use repetition to give phrases or gestures new weight in new contexts, or create unexpected significance by including a crucial insight at just the right spot. His insights have offended some. Paul Gray said of *Girl*, "It is ... controversial in a way that his earlier novels did not have to be..... Zionists and Palestinian sympathizers will find much to dislike here." The columnist who writes as M. P. in the *New Republic* decried the book in broader terms, censuring le Carré for inciting generations of Arabs to violence that will fly past his "never imperiled head."[14] These judgments can be debated. The skill with which tenderness and loyalty temper the brutality pulsating through the book shows that le Carré's new material hasn't clouded his eye for deep meanings. He brings highly controversial emotional issues into sharp focus without feeling obliged to resolve them.

But he has also let on indirectly that these issues have touched his heart. The hint lies in his personal and artistic past. In his 1967 *Saturday Evening Post* story, "Dare I Weep, Dare I Mourn?" a Mercedes car symbolized destructive arrogance. The Foreword of *Girl* ends with a reference to his own "red Mercedes car." Michel is also driving a red Mercedes when he's captured by Israeli agents, and he later dies in the same car. Perhaps le Carré identifies with him because, in writing about his entrapment, he's also setting a trap for himself so cunning that he can't escape it. Like Michel/Salim, he has assumed a French name. And like him and Charlie, perhaps the book's two main victims, he drives a red Mercedes. To write about spying can be as dangerous as performing it to an author who visits battle areas and interviews armed militants. His writing about the Arab-Israeli conflict is a tribute. The passions engendered by the conflict have inspired him artistically. By trying to recreate the conflict's phenomenology, he's responding to it viscerally. His use of Charlie as his main figure, with her reformer's social conscience and fraught emotions, keeps his response lively.

But it also creates the need for distancing. The objectivity that has made him such a shrewd observer has also kept him, over the years, from identifying with any faction or party, left-wing or right-, Eastern or Western, that promises new panaceas. In *Girl*, his viewpoint is humane without being partisan. The book has the complexity and scope of his best work. Nearly every reviewer has praised its elegance of language and intellectual drive. Gelber singled out its levelheadedness: "Without condoning terrorism, the book makes the reasons for it understandable—perhaps the first popular novel to do so." Gray called it "both a daring departure . . . and a triumph of narrative control." Referring to le Carré's exploration of the moral and tragic dimensions of spying, William F. Buckley, Jr., sees the novel as "the most mature, inventive, and powerful book about terrorists-come-to-life" he has read.[15]

This praise is well judged. Even for a writer of le Carré's consistently high ambition and performance, *Girl* marks a big step forward. Written in urbane, expressive prose, it absorbs all our sympathy while holding our interest. Few novels of the 1980s have combined so much daring and excitement with style and entertainment. Few have attained such high intelligence. Precise, evocative, and far reaching in its range of reference, it also confirms le Carré's belief in the act of reading as an active, collaborative process. *Girl* will omit information or misdirect our attention to shift to us the creative burden of working out meaning. But the artistic cooperation it invites goes beyond the formal cleverness of puzzle-solving. Its inventiveness impinges upon the larger humanity in the form of deep expressiveness, sensitivity, and emotion. This breadth of sensibility has occasioned striking advances both within le Carré's art and in the field of spy and intrigue fiction itself.

Notes

Chapter One

[1]Nicholas Wapshott, "Tinker, Tailor, Soldier, Novelist," *The Times* 6 September 1982: 7; Melvin Bragg, "A Talk with John le Carré," *New York Times Book Review* 13 March 1983: 22.

[2]Evan Hunter, "Spies and Moles and Other Entertainers," *New York Times Book Review* 24 January 1982: 12.

[3]John le Carré, "An American Spy Story," *New York Times Book Review* 14 October 1979: 48.

[4]Alexander Orlov, *Handbook of Intelligence and Guerrilla Warfare* (Ann Arbor: U of Michigan P, 1963) 1.

[5]John le Carré, Introduction, *Philby, The Spy Who Betrayed a Generation,* by Bruce Page, David Leitch, and Phillip Knightley (London: Andre Deutsch, 1968) 16-17.

[6]Abraham Rothberg, "The Decline & Fall of George Smiley: John le Carré and English Decency," *Southwest Review* 66 (Autumn 1981): 383.

[7]Nigel West, *MI5: British Security Service Operations 1909-1945* (London: The Bodley Head, 1981) 16,49.

[8]Le Roy L. Panek, *The Special Branch: The British Spy Novel, 1890-1980* (Bowling Green, OH: Bowling Green U Popular P, 1981) 236.

[9]See Rebecca West, *The New Meaning of Treason* (New York: Viking, 1964) 212.

[10]Chapman Pincher, *Their Trade Is Treachery* (London: Sidgwick and Jackson, 1981) 56.

[11]Le Carré, "An American Spy Story" 46.

[12]Michiko Kakutani, "Mysteries Join the Mainstream," *New York Times Book Review* 15 January 1984: 37.

[13]Alex Gelber with Edward Behr, "The Spymaster Returns," *Newsweek* 7 March 1983: 70; Stefan Kanfer, "The Spy Who Came in for the Gold," *Time* 30 October 1977: 58; William F. Buckley, Jr., "Terror and a Woman," *New York Times Book Review* 13 March 1983: 1; Steven Marcus, "Grand Illusions," *New York Review of Books* 5 August 1965: 20; Clive James, "Go Back to the Cold!" *New York Review of Books* 27 October 1977: 30; Richard Locke, "The Spy Who Spied on Spies," *New York Times Book Review* 30 June 1974: 2; Robert Lekachman, "Good Boys, Bad Boys, Old Boys," *Nation* 26 April 1980: 505; Timothy Foote, "Playing Tigers," *Time* 24 June 1974: E7; Hugh Kenner, "The Spy Who Came into the Drugstore," *National Review* 27 July 1965: 656.

[14]Bruce Merry, *Anatomy of the Spy Thriller* (Montreal: McGill-Queen's UP, 1977) 1; the quotation continues, "The narrative image [in thrillers] rarely corresponds to the known and ascertainable facts about real-life networks and intelligence operations."

[15]Rothberg 377.

271

[16]Rothberg 383.

[17]David Monaghan, "John le Carré and England: A Spy's Eye View," *Modern Fiction Studies* 29 (Autumn 1983): 570.

[18]John R. Coyne, Jr., "Twentieth Century Heroes," *National Review* 2 August 1974: 880.

[19]For the meaning of these esoteric terms and others used widely in le Carré's fiction, see "Le Carré's Code," *Time* 3 October 1977: 67.

[20]Merry 212.

[21]Merry 100.

[22]T. J. Binyon, "Your Whole Range of Faces," *TLS* 5 November 1982: 1218.

Chapter Two

[1]Panek 229.

[2]Monaghan 573.

[3]Nigel West 118.

[4]Nigel West, *The Circus: MI5 Operations, 1945-1972* (New York: Stein and Day, 1983) 25.

[5]Merry 114.

[6]See Chapter One, n. 5.

[7]Merry 142.

[8]John le Carré, "Wrong Man on Crete," *Holiday* December 1965: 75.

[9]Celia Hughes, "Serious Reflections on Light Reading: The World of John le Carré," *Theology* 84 (July 1981): 277.

[10]In Granville Hicks, "Spies without a Sense of Mission," *Saturday Review* 24 July 1965: 40.

[11]John le Carré, "In England Now," *New York Times Magazine* 23 October 1977: 34, 35, 86, 87.

[12]Gelber, with Behr 71.

[13]Hughes 276.

[14]T. J. Binyon, "Theater of Terror," *TLS* 25 March 1983: 29.

Chapter Three

[1]John le Carré, "What Every Writer Wants," *Harpers* November 1965: 145.

[2]See Chapter One, n. 13.

[3]Richard Condon, "Buried Treasure: 'Smiley's People,'" *New York Magazine* 24 December 1979: 66; Carl Ericson, "Judas and Other Spies," *Christian Century* 25 March 1981: 319; Nick B. Williams, "Curtain Call for the Smiley Spy," *Los Angeles Times Book Review* 9 December 1979: 27; James 29,30.

[4]See above, n. 1.

Chapter Four

[1]Julian Moynahan, "Smiley's People by John le Carré," *New Republic* 19 January 1980: 31.

[2]Rothberg 378, 377.

Chapter Five

[1]John Kirk, Introduction, *The Incongruous Spy: Two Novels of Suspense by John le Carré* (New York: Walker, 1963) n.p. [3].

[2]John Vincent, "The Hollis Launch," *London Review of Books* 7-20 May 1981: 8.

Chapter Six

[1]Anthony Boucher, "Criminals at Large," *New York Times Book Review* 8 September 1963: 45.

[2]John le Carré, "A Writer and a Gentleman," *Saturday Review* 30 November 1968: 4.

Chapter Seven

[1]Anthony Boucher, "Temptations of a Man Isolated in Deceit," *New York Times Book Review* 12 January 1964: 5.

[2]John Gardner, "The Espionage Novel," in *Whodunit? A Guide to Crime, Suspense and Spy Fiction*, ed. H. R. F. Keating (New York: Van Nostrand Reinhold, 1982) 77.

[3]Monaghan 580.

[4]Merry 49.

[5]In James Cameron, "The Case of The Hot Writer," *New York Times Magazine* 8 September 1974: 55.

[6]Orlov 79.

[7]"Limits of Control," *TLS* 13 September 1963: 693.

[8]George Grella, "Murder and Loyalty," *New Republic* 31 July 1976: 24.

[9]Andrew Rutherford, *The Literature of War: Five Studies in Heroic Virtue* (London: Macmillan, 1978) 146.

[10]Kenner 665.

Chapter Eight

[1]"More Le Carré Capers," *Time* 29 May 1965: E4.

[2]Nigel West, *The Circus* 183-84.

[3]In Marie Francoise Allain, *The Other Man: Conversations with Graham Greene*, trans. Guido Waldman (New York: Simon and Schuster, 1983) 173.

[4]Rutherford 148.

[5]William Barrett, "Tradition of the Spy," *Atlantic* August 1965: 125.

[6]Hicks 39.

[7]George P. Elliott, "It's the Spy Who Counts," *New York Times Book Review* 25 July 1965: 5.

[8]Eric Ambler, "John le Carré Escapes the Follow-up Jinx," *Life* 30 July 1965: 8.

[9]Grella 23.

Chapter Nine

[1]Gardner 77.

[2]In Cameron 64.

[3]Merry 164.

[4]John le Carré, "Dare I Weep, Dare I Mourn?" *Saturday Evening Post* 28 January 1967: 54-56, 60.

[5]See, for instance, Ales Adamovich and Daniil Granin, *A Book of the Blockade*, trans. Hilda Perham (Moscow: Raduga Publishers, 1983).

Chapter Ten

[1]Kirk 3.
[2]Kanfer 68.
[3]Geoffrey Stokes, "The Reluctant Cowboy," *Village Voice* 14 January 1980: 3.
[4]Geoffrey Wolff, "All Naked into the World of Art," *New York Times Book Review* 9 January 1972: 7.

Chapter Eleven

[1]H. R. F. Keating, in Keating, ed. 194.
[2]Le Carré, Introduction, *Philby* 22.
[3]Orlov 107.
[4]Merry 213.
[5]In Cameron 57.
[6]John le Carré, "What Ritual Is Being Observed Tonight?" *Saturday Evening Post* 2 November 1968: 60, 62, 64, 65.
[7]Karl Miller, "Gothic Guesswork," *New York Review of Books* 18 July 1974: 25; le Carré, Introduction, *Philby* 9.
[8]Le Carré, Introduction, *Philby* 15.
[9]Rutherford 153.
[10]Rutherford 150.
[11]Wood 17.

Chapter Twelve

[1]T. J. Binyon, "A Gentleman Among Players," *TLS* 9 September 1977: 1069.
[2]H. D. S. Greenway, "Travels with le Carré," *Newsweek* 10 October 1977: 102.
[3]James 29.
[4]Wapshott 7.
[5]Moynahan 32.

Chapter Thirteen

[1]Panek 250.
[2]Anatole Broyard, "Reading and Writing: Le Carré's People," *New York Times Book Review* 29 August 1982: 23.
[3]In Tony Chiu, "Behind the Best Sellers," *New York Times Book Review* 6 January 1980: 30.
[4]V. S. Pritchett, "A Spy Romance," *New York Review of Books* 7 February 1980: 24.
[5]Joseph McLellan, "George Smiley's Revenge," *Book World—The Washington Post* 23 December 1979: 1.
[6]Binyon, "Your Whole Range of Faces." 1218.
[7]H. C. Veit, *Library Journal* 104 (1 December 1979): 2590.

Chapter Fourteen

[1]Gelber, with Behr 70.
[2]Gelber, with Behr 74.
[3]"Notes on Current Books," *Virginia Quarterly Review* (Summer 1983): 92.
[4]Pauline Kael, "The Current Cinema: Faked Out, Cooled Out, Bummed Out," *New Yorker* 12 November 1984: 179.
[5]See Dov Bing, *Israel and the Palestinian Arabs*, Ocean Monograph No. 6 (Hamilton, New Zealand: Outrigger Publishers, 1982) 13.

⁶James Wolcott, "The Secret Sharers," *New York Review of Books* 14 April 1983: 20.

⁷John le Carré, "Exiles in the White Hotel," *Observer Review* 26 June 1983: 25, 26.

⁸John le Carré, "The Betrayal," *Observer Review* 3 July 1983: 23-24.

⁹Bing 13.

¹⁰Pincher 186.

¹¹Binyon, "Theatre of Terror" 289; Peter S. Prescottt, "In the Theater of the Real," *Newsweek* 7 March 1983: 72; Wolcott 19; Kael 180, 179.

¹²Jean Rosenthal, "Le Carré Au Proche-Orient," *Magazine litteraire* (Juin 1983): 35.

¹³Wolcott 19.

¹⁴Paul Gray, "In the Theater of Deeds," *Time* 14 March 1983: 88; M. P., "Washington Diarist: It Almost Doesn't Matter," *New Republic* 29 August 1983: 43.

¹⁵Gelber, with Behr 71; Gray 87; Buckley 23.